Adult Development
and Aging

Editor: Christine Cardone
Production Supervisor: Patricia F. French
Production Manager: Paul Smolenski
Text Designer: Susan Bierlein
Cover Designer: Russ Maselli
Photo Researcher: Diane Kraut
Illustrations: Jane Lopez

Cover Art: Robert Delaunay, *Windows Open Simultaneously*, 1912. London, Tate Gallery/Art Resources, New York.

This book was set in Palatino and Helvetica by V & M Graphics, Inc., and was printed and bound by Arcata Graphics/Halliday. The cover was printed by Lehigh Press Lithographers.

Macmillan Publishing Company
866 Third Avenue, New York, New York 10022

Macmillan Publishing Company is
part of the Maxwell Communication
Group of Companies.

Maxwell Macmillan Canada, Inc.
1200 Eglinton Avenue East
Suite 200
Don Mills, Ontario M3C 3N1

LIBRARY OF CONGRESS CATALOGING-IN-PUBLICATION DATA

Schulz, Richard, 1947–
    Adult development and aging : myths and emerging realities /
  Richard Schulz, Robert B. Ewen.—2nd ed.
       p.   cm.
    Includes bibliographical references (p. 439) and index.
    ISBN 0–02–407781–X
    1. Adulthood—Psychological aspects.   2. Aging—Psychological
  aspects.   I. Ewen, Robert B., 1940–   II. Title.
  BF724.5.S38   1993
  155.6—dc20   91–35030
                    CIP

Printing: 2 3 4 5 6 7   Year: 3 4 5 6 7 8

To my grandmother Jullianna Voth
and to my father Adolf—*R.S.*

To Judy and Meredith—*R.B.E.*

Preface

The study of adult development and aging is a young but rapidly growing science. Although we know much more about this area today than we did a decade ago, many of us still subscribe to unfounded myths about adult development and aging. Therefore, one of the major goals of this book is to contrast existing myths about adult development with the best available empirical data (wherever possible), in order to separate fiction from fact. To this end, we have attempted to summarize and synthesize the most current research literature available at the time of the writing of this second edition.

Much of what we know about adult development is emergent: We have some understanding of this complex process, but definitive answers are not always available. Indeed, we may never have definitive answers to some questions, because the answers change along with changes in the social and technological environments within which individuals develop. Therefore, throughout this book, we identify many important questions for which the existing empirical data are still speculative. New information may quickly alter existing conceptions of the field.

Writing a book on adult development and aging inevitably raises the question: Should individual chapters be organized by chronological age or by topic? We have opted for the latter strategy because age *per se* is not necessarily a good marker of adult development, and because we believe that the complexity and diversity of this material is easier to understand when organized by topic. Although our choice of topics is heavily influenced by our backgrounds in psychology and gerontology, we have not ignored important biological, sociological, and medical contributions to our understanding of adult development and aging. This book covers traditional psychological topics, such as sensation and perception, memory and learning, intelligence and creativity, and psychopathology; but it also includes separate chapters on such topics as stress and coping, social relationships, and work and retirement.

Our approach differs from existing topical treatments of adult development in that we place a strong emphasis on providing the reader with a fundamental understanding of a particular topic and the most current age-related data. For example, in discussing memory and cognition, we provide sufficient background information on relevant theories and research methods to enable the reader to appreciate how research on age-related changes has evolved, and to understand the significance of the most current findings on this topic.

For this second edition, the chapter on adult psychopathology has been completely rewritten. All other chapters have been revised, updated, and thoroughly reviewed for readability. Many of these chapters have changed significantly: Some questions have been resolved since the previous edition was published, and new issues have been raised by recent findings. Among the topics added in this edition are

- Aging: Geographic trends
- Aging: International trends
- Practical intelligence
- Wisdom
- The "empty nest"
- The economic future of the elderly
- The right to die
- Bereavement and health outcomes

Numerous other topics that appeared in the first edition have been extensively revised and/or expanded, including

- The brain and aging
- Cardiovascular disease, cancer, and stroke
- Adult friendships
- Type A and Type B individuals
- The diagnosis and assessment of adult psychopathology
- Alzheimer's disease
- Anxiety disorders
- The treatment of adult psychopathology
- Understanding the dying patient

This book also includes several valuable aids designed to make this complex, interdisciplinary body of knowledge more accessible to the reader. Each chapter contains a section called "Myths About Aging" that highlights key issues and contrasts old beliefs with current views. At the end of each chapter is a summary of major concepts and a list of terms to remember, which are clearly defined in the Glossary at the end of this book. This edition also features study questions at the end of each chapter, which are designed to promote critical thinking about the material presented therein. An extensive reference list will enable students and instructors to pursue in depth topics of special interest. Finally, an *Instructor's Manual* is available to all instructors who adopt the text. It includes an extensive list of multiple-choice and discussion questions for each chapter, cumulative exams, learning objectives, and suggested readings rated by level of difficulty.

In sum, this book is designed for those who value textbooks based on the best available current data and who appreciate that knowledge about adult development is in a state of flux, with new data becoming available almost daily. This book will especially appeal to instructors who want to encourage their students' critical thinking skills and ability to understand and use research-based knowledge, along with conventional wisdom, as the basis for thought and action.

Acknowledgments

We would like to thank Lynn Reder, Joan Rogers, William Sauer, Jim Staszewski, Connie Tompkins, and Ann Yurick for their comments and suggestions. We would also like to thank the following reviewers for their valuable comments: Marc D. Baranowski, University of Maine; Jeffrey I. Flatt, Westfield State College; William E. Haley, University of Alabama–Birmingham; Virginia Nilsson, Athabasca University; Richard L. Port, Slippery Rock University; Frank J. Prerost, Western Illinois University; Matthew J. Sharps, California State University–Fresno; and Diana L. Veith, Richard Hutchings Psychiatric Center.

R.S.
R.B.E.

Contents

Part II   *Physiological and Cognitive Development*

Part IV   *Crises and Problems*

Chapter 10

Stress and Coping   *317*

Chapter 11

Adult Psychopathology   *347*

Chapter 12

Death and Dying   *383*

Adult Development
and Aging

Part I

Introduction

Chapter 1

Introduction

Susie Fitzhugh/Stock, Boston

This book is about adult development and aging. Let us consider each of these terms separately.

Adult implies that we will not be concerned with such periods of life as infancy, childhood, and the early teens. Although the law specifies minimum ages for certain behaviors (driving an automobile, military service), there is no clearly identifiable age at which human beings leave adolescence and enter adulthood. As a general guideline, we will be dealing with events that occur after about age 20.

Development means that we will be studying changes that occur over time. Adult humans are not static entities; they change as they grow older, often substantially. However, it is also important not to exaggerate the magnitude of these changes. Many common beliefs about the negative effects of aging have proved to be mere myths when investigated scientifically. In this book, therefore, we will (1) *describe* important differences and similarities between younger and older adults, basing our observations on data derived from empirical research; (2) suggest likely *explanations* for those age-related differences that we discover; and (3) indicate how this information might help us to improve adult life. In addition to describing various phenomena and identifying the underlying causes, behavioral scientists also strive to apply their findings in ways that will *modify* our environment for the better.

The developmental approach focuses on changes within the individual throughout adulthood **(intra-individual changes)**, the extent to which such changes occur at different rates among different adults **(interindividual differences)**, and how individuals adapt to those changes. (See Baltes & Baltes, 1990; Baltes, Reese, & Nesselroade, 1977.) If the typical adult shows a moderate loss of hearing between ages 40 and 70, this is a significant *intra*-individual change. Having described this phenomenon, we next face the task of explaining why such auditory declines occur. For example, a specific part of the auditory system might degenerate with increasing age. If we correctly identify the cause, we may then be in a position to devise appropriate corrective methods (e.g., a mechanical device that takes over the function of the impaired organ).

Alternatively, we might find significant *inter*individual differences in the amount of intra-individual change. That is, some adults may experience much greater auditory declines than do others. Further investigation might then reveal that these hearing losses are caused primarily by frequent exposure to extremely loud noise. This would suggest such corrective measures as protective earmuffs for those who work with loud machinery, and greater caution by those who enjoy listening to rock music on personal headphones.

Some theorists define adult development in terms of a series of distinct stages, ones that are presumably experienced by most or all adults. According to one such model (Levinson, 1986), the period from age 17 to 22 is a bridge between pre-adulthood and early adulthood; the period from age 22 to 28 is a time for building and maintaining an adult mode of living; the period from age 40 to 45 is the time of midlife transition or "crisis," and so forth. If this model were supported by substantial research evidence, it would provide an appealing framework for discussing adult development. In our opinion, however, the available data do *not* support the concept of universally applicable stages of adult development. (We will have more to say about this issue in Chapter 7.) Therefore, the chapters that follow are organized instead by substantive area: physiological aspects of aging, sensation and perception, learning and memory, personality, and so on.

Last, *aging* indicates that we will be paying considerable attention to the behavior of older adults. This is currently an extremely popular research area, for reasons that will be discussed in the following section.

Human Aging and Life Expectancy

Journey back for a moment to the dawn of civilization. During this chaotic era, primitive humanity tried desperately to survive with rudimentary knowledge and few tools. Not surprisingly, very few achieved the age of 40; in fact, the average life span during these prehistoric times was in all probability a mere 18 years! Those who did succeed in reaching their mid-twenties or early thirties were regarded as unusually wise and capable because of this great accomplishment (Dublin, 1951; Lerner, 1976; Schulz, 1978).

As civilizations grew and living conditions improved, however, longevity increased. There are now more than 23,000,000 people in this country age 65 and older, including more than 100,000 over 100 years of age—a phenomenon that has been referred to as "the graying of America."

DEFINITIONS

Aging. Human **aging** consists of changes that are caused by processes within the individual and which significantly decrease the probability of survival. These changes are universal and inevitable. They cannot be avoided or reversed; no one can escape growing old, nor can a middle-aged or elderly person become young again (although some have tried, as we will see in Chapter 3). Thus aging differs from illnesses and diseases, which are evitable, may have external causes, and may be cured or alleviated.

The distinction between aging and illness is very important. (See, for example, Schaie, 1988.) Suppose a researcher finds that 70-year-olds have significantly poorer hearing than 40-year-olds. The researcher might be tempted to conclude that this difference in hearing is caused by aging. If so, nothing can be done about it. Growing older is inevitable, so you would simply have to expect some noticeable (and annoying) hearing losses by about age 70.

However, let us now suppose that the researcher properly decides to investigate this issue more carefully. She finds that the hearing losses among the 70-year-olds are actually caused by a disease that attacks part of the inner ear. This changes the conclusion dramatically! The real problem is that 70-year-olds are more susceptible to this disease than are 40-year-olds. Therefore, these hearing losses can be prevented by finding a cure for this disease (which is certainly more likely than finding a cure for growing older). Or, if you are fortunate enough not to contract this disease, you will avoid the associated decline in your hearing. By correctly attributing the research results to illness, and *not* to aging, a more optimistic conclusion is reached. We will encounter numerous examples of this crucial distinction throughout this book.

Life Expectancy.   **Life expectancy at birth** refers to the number of years that will probably be lived by the average person born in a particular year. In 1970, for example, the life expectancy at birth for women in the United States was 74.9 years. This means that if you are an American woman who was born in 1970, and if the course of your development should prove to be neither more nor less favorable than the average for everyone born in that year, you will live approximately 75 years. You might instead be more fortunate than the average woman born in 1970, and live to 80 or even 90. Or you might be less fortunate, and be struck down by an accident or illness at an early age. The life expectancy figure is an average: it represents the best guess as to your life span, but it could easily be wrong in any one instance.

Alternatively, we may ascertain an individual's **life expectancy at a specific age.** In 1970, the life expectancy for American women age 65 was 17.1 years. That is, the average American woman who reached age 65 during 1970 could reasonably expect to live to about age 82. The *at birth* life expectancy figure (which was only 51 years) no longer applies to these women,

In the United States, women live significantly longer than men. Among adults age 80 and older, women outnumber men by more than 2 to 1.   (Day Williams/ Photo Researchers, Inc.)

because they have demonstrated a favorable course of development: They avoided fatal illnesses or accidents during infancy, childhood, adolescence, and early adulthood.

Maximum Life Span.   The extreme upper limit of human life is known as the **maximum life span**. This figure is typically inferred from the greatest authenticated human age on record: a Japanese man, Shigechiyo Izumi, died of pneumonia at age 120 on February 21, 1986 (*Newsweek*, March 3, 1986, p. 71). Some individuals claim to have lived considerably longer, but this has proved to be one of the many myths that pervade the field of adult development and aging.[1] (See, for example, Schulz, 1978.)

LIFE EXPECTANCY, PAST AND PRESENT

Historical Trends.   It has been estimated that the average ancient Roman lived for only about 22 years, settlers in the 1620 Massachusetts Bay Colony survived for approximately 35 years, and the average resident of the United States born in 1900 lived for some 47 years. By 1990, however, the life expectancy at birth in this country reached a new high of 75.4 years. (See Table 1.1.)

Table 1.1

Human life expectancy at birth from prehistoric to contemporary times.

Time Period	Average Life Span (in Years)
Prehistoric Times	18
Ancient Greece	20
Ancient Rome	22
Middle Ages, England	33
1620 (Massachusetts Bay Colony)	35
19th Century England, Wales	41
1900, USA	47.3
1915, USA	54.5
1954, USA	69.6
1967, USA	70.2
1971, USA	71.0
1983, USA	74.7
1990, USA (projected)	75.4

Source: Lerner (1976, p. 140); United States Senate Special Committee on Aging (1987–1988).

---

[1] Throughout this book, we will highlight common myths and the corresponding empirical evidence in chapter boxes for ready reference.

Table 1.2

Life expectancy at birth and at age 65 as a function of sex and calendar year (United States).

Year	Life Expectancy at Birth			Life Expectancy at Age 65	
	Male	Female		Male	Female
1900	46.4	49.0		11.3	12.0
1910	50.1	53.6		12.1	12.1
1920	54.5	56.3		12.3	12.3
1930	58.0	61.3		12.9	12.9
1940	61.4	65.7		11.9	13.4
1950	65.6	71.1		12.8	15.1
1960	66.7	73.2		12.9	15.9
1970	67.1	74.9		13.1	17.1
1980	69.9	77.5		14.0	18.4
1990 (projected)	71.6	79.2		15.0	19.5
Net Gain					
1900–1990	25.2	30.2		3.7	7.5

Source: United States Senate Special Committee on Aging (1987–1988, p. 25).

Since 1900, the largest gains in life expectancy have been demonstrated by females of all ages, infants, children, and young adults. Conversely, life expectancy at birth tends to be somewhat lower for males. For example, a male born in 1970 had a life expectancy of 67.1 years, which is almost eight years less than the corresponding value for females. (See Table 1.2.)

Life expectancy at birth is also lower for minority ethnic groups than for whites. For example, a black male born in the United States in 1986 had a life expectancy of 65.2 years, as compared to 72.0 years for a white male. (See Table 1.3.) Life expectancy has increased for minorities since 1900, but at a slower rate than for whites (U.S. Senate Special Committee on Aging, 1985).

Table 1.3

Life expectancy at birth as a function of sex and ethnic group for the United States in 1986.

	Males	Females
Whites	72.0	78.8
Blacks	65.2	73.5

Source: U.S. Bureau of the Census (1989).

Interpreting Increases in Life Expectancy.   The data in Tables 1.1 and 1.2 appear to reflect an amazing increase in human longevity. But as we will see throughout this book, appearances are often deceiving. Because of improved medical procedures (e.g., vaccinations that prevent infectious diseases) and better standards of public health (living conditions, nutrition, sanitation), the mortality rates for American infants and children have dropped sharply since 1900. More people are living into their 60s and 70s, so the average life expectancy at birth has increased accordingly.

To clarify this point, suppose that we obtain one small sample of people born in 1900 and a second small sample of people born in 1915. We then ascertain the life span of each of these individuals:

Group 1—Born 1900 (1900 Cohort)		Group 2—Born 1915 (1915 Cohort)	
Person	Years Lived	Person	Years Lived
James	2	Robert	50
Mary	58	Jane	47
Ellen	60	Jeffrey	62
Steven	56	Alma	60
Thomas	61	Louise	64
Mean:	47.4	*Mean:*	56.6

(A sample of only five cases is far too small for any valid scientific conclusions to be drawn, but will serve for purposes of illustration. Also, for convenience, we have rounded off years lived to whole numbers.) All members of Group 1 were born in 1900; this group is therefore referred to as the 1900 **cohort.** Notice that James succumbed to an illness early in childhood, and lived for only two years. The members of the 1915 cohort had the good fortune to be born at a time when a method for preventing this illness had been discovered, resulting in a decrease in childhood mortality rates.

If we look only at the means for each cohort, we might incorrectly conclude that between 1900 and 1915, a way was found to increase everyone's life span by about nine years. In actuality, however, those born in 1915 *who reached old age* did not survive a great deal longer than did members of the 1900 cohort *who reached old age*. Much of the difference between the group means is due to the fact that more people born in 1915 survived the perils of infant and childhood diseases, and reached old age. That is, the life expectancy *at birth* increased substantially.

To be sure, life expectancies at older ages have also increased significantly during the past century. To illustrate, consider the life expectancies at age 65 shown in Table 1.2. In 1900, the average 65-year-old man lived for an additional 11.3 years. A man who reached age 65 in 1990 had a further life expectancy of 15.0 years, or 3.7 years longer. Although this increase is smaller than the corresponding gain in the life expectancy at birth (25.2 years), it is important; many people would willingly spend a considerable amount of money to add almost four years to their lives. The data for women reflect an even greater increase: The life expectancy at age 65 rose by 7.5 years between 1900 and 1990, and the life expectancy at birth gained 30.2 years. (The differences in life expectancy between men and women may be leveling off, however. Notice that between 1980 and 1990, the gains in life expectancy at birth and at age 65 were about the same for both sexes.)

Adults past age 70 are also living longer. The life expectancy at age 85 has increased by 24 percent since 1960, and an additional 44 percent increase is projected by the year 2040 (U.S. Senate Special Committee on Aging, 1985). On the popular morning television show *Today*, the names of persons who have reached their 100th birthday are often announced. If this were done for everyone in this country, rather than just for those who elect to write in, some 42 names would be announced every morning!

In sum: Much of the apparent increase in human longevity is due to substantially greater life expectancies at birth, and to the impact of public health measures adopted in the early part of this century. As a result, many more Americans are reaching old age than ever before. (See Figure 1.1.) There have also been smaller but significant increases in life expectancies at older ages, indicating that those of us who do survive until old age are likely to live a few years longer than did our counterparts of a century ago.

Figure 1.1

Percent surviving as a function of age, 1840–1980 (United States).   Source: U.S. Senate Special Committee on Aging (1983, p. 57).

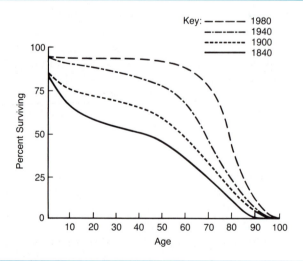

*Because of increased life expectancies worldwide, three-
and even four-generation families are much more common.*
(Arvind Garg/Photo Researchers, Inc.)

Geographical Trends. A common misconception is that most elderly
Americans live in the southern sunbelt states. In fact, as of 1986, California
and New York had the largest number of persons age 65 and older (U.S.
Bureau of the Census, 1987). The use of simple head counts is somewhat misleading, however: These large states have more people of all ages, and therefore more of the elderly.

A better measure can be obtained by dividing the number of elderly in a
given state by the total number of people in that state. Using this index,
Florida does have the highest concentration of the elderly; as of 1986, 17.7%
of Floridians were 65 or older. But the 19 states with the next highest concentration of the elderly are all in the north and midwest, led by Pennsylvania,
Rhode Island, Iowa, and Arkansas. (See Figure 1.2.)

Implications for Our Present Society. Currently, the population of the United
States is approximately 242 million. The distribution by age is shown in
Figure 1.3. Two important facts can be gleaned from this figure. The genera-

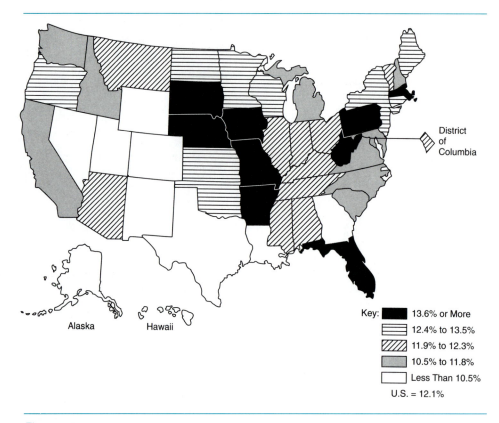

District
of
Columbia

Key:

■	13.6% or More
☰	12.4% to 13.5%
▨	11.9% to 12.3%
▧ (gray)	10.5% to 11.8%
☐	Less Than 10.5%

U.S. = 12.1%

Figure 1.2
Persons age 65 and older as a percentage of total state population, 1986.   Source: U.S. Bureau
of the Census (1987).

tion of baby boomers, those born between 1946 and 1964, will dominate the
age distribution in this country well into the next century. And the "old-old,"
those age 85 or more, currently represent a relatively small proportion of the
over-60 age group and of the population as a whole.

Since 1940, however, the percentage of elderly Americans has increased
markedly. This is due only in part to the aforementioned gains in life expectancy. The annual birth rate in this country rose significantly just prior
to 1920, rose again after World War II, and declined dramatically after the
mid-1960s. As a result, the proportion of Americans age 65 and older is now
larger, and it will increase even more as the baby boom generation ages.

Barring some highly unexpected development, the number of elderly
Americans will continue to increase for the next half century. (See Figure 1.4.)
The gains will be greatest among those over 85, who constitute the most
rapidly growing segment of the American population (Brody et al., 1983). By
the year 2050, it is estimated that the proportion of Americans age 85 and
older will jump from about 1 percent to over 5 percent of the total popula-

tion, and that approximately one of every four Americans over age 65 will be 85 or older.

Dramatic increases are also projected for the over-65 age group as a whole. During the past two decades, mortality rates have declined by 1 to 2 percent per year. If these declines continue, almost two-fifths of the American population will be above age 65 by the year 2080, with the number of centenarians approaching 19,000,000 (Vaupel & Gowan, 1986). These demographic changes may portend major social changes as well:

> Will increased life expectancy be accompanied by increased healthy, productive life expectancy? . . . Who would wish to live to age 120 in, as Shakespeare wrote, 'mere oblivion, sans teeth, sans eyes, sans taste, sans everything'? The evidence [pertaining to this issue] is weak. . . . In any case . . . it would seem to be prudent to place a very high priority on the development of ways of delaying or alleviating debilitating conditions [in the elderly].

As the proportion of the population over age 65 begins to approach the proportion between ages 20 and 64, delayed retirement will almost certainly be required to save Social Security from bankruptcy. If more of the elderly hang on to their jobs, however, promotional opportunities will diminish for the young, and whatever gain there may be in wisdom and experience in an organization may be offset by a lack of fresh thinking and new blood. In addition, the increase in the proportion of the elderly might

Figure 1.3

U.S. population by age and sex (1986).   Source: U.S. Senate Special Committee on Aging (1987–1988, p. 10).

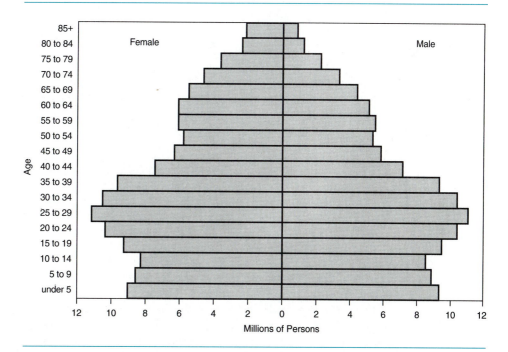

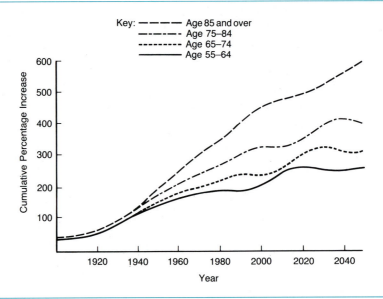

Key: —————— Age 85 and over
     — · — · — · Age 75–84
     - - - - - - - Age 65–74
     —————— Age 55–64

Figure 1.4
Percentage increase of older adults by decade (United States).   Source: U.S. Senate Special
Committee on Aging (1985, p. 14).

result in a further shift of political power, and even greater governmental focus on the
needs of the elderly and inattention to the needs of the young. A major challenge to
society will be to develop career patterns and societal norms that enable the elderly
to contribute while simultaneously giving the young a chance.

When lifespans reach or even exceed a century, the division of life into three successive stages of education, employment, and retirement will undoubtedly have to be
rethought. Not only to contribute productively to society but simply to understand society, octogenarians will have to have learned about the advances and changes that
have occurred since they finished high school or college. Delaying the age of retirement to age 80 or 85 might permit periodic leaves from work—a year, say, every
decade, for ongoing education.

In addition, a reduction in the hours worked per week and an increase in the number of weeks of vacation per year might facilitate part-time education on a more or less
continuous basis. The 64,000 hours or so of lifetime work under the emerging system
of 35 hours per week . . . from age 22 to 62, could alternatively be arranged so that a
person works 28 hours a week, with two months' vacation per year and a year's leave
every decade, from age 22 to 82. If [the] median lifespan approaches a century, that
would still leave 18 years of retirement. (Vaupel & Gowan, 1986, p. 433.)

International Trends.   The dramatic increase in the number of elderly adults
is not unique to the United States. It is occurring throughout the world.

In terms of simple head counts, the United States has the world's third
largest population of adults age 65 and older and the largest "old-old" population (age 85 and older). As of 1985, however, the highest *concentration* of

adults age 65 and older was found in Sweden. The United Kingdom, what was formerly West Germany, Italy, and France also had a higher concentration of the elderly than did the United States. (See Figure 1.5.)

In 1985, the greatest life expectancy at birth occurred in Japan; it was approximately 2.5 years greater than that in the United States. This was due primarily to reductions in infant mortality. Life expectancy at age 65 was about the same in both countries, but the infant mortality rate in Japan was only one-half that of the United States (Population Reference Bureau, 1987). As in this country, females worldwide live longer than males; India is perhaps the only exception.

Of greater importance, however, are projected future developments. Because of worldwide advances in medical care and birth control, many nations face the prospect of an increasingly older population. Among developed countries, Japan, China, and the United States are expected to experience the greatest increases in the concentration of elderly adults. In countries that are still developing, such as China, India, and Mexico, the elderly population will also increase substantially, and at a much faster rate. By the year 2025, the percentage of elderly adults in these countries will begin to approximate today's concentration in the developed countries.

This trend has potentially serious consequences. In many ways, the changes that are expected to occur in the United States will be mild by comparison to those that take place in developing nations. How can the world as

Figure 1.5

Percent of population 65 and older in selected countries: 1985 (estimated) and 2025 (projected). Source: U.S. Bureau of the Census (in press).

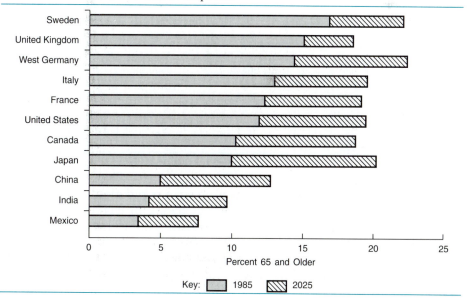

Myths About Aging

Life Expectancy

Myth	*Best Available Evidence*
Some human beings have lived to be 130, 140, or even 170 years old.	Empirical evidence has failed to support these claims. A man from the Ukraine who supposedly was 130 years old had falsified his date of birth in order to escape military service during World War I; he actually was only 78 years old (Medvedev, 1974). A convenient fire destroyed the records of an Ecuadorian man who claimed to be 130 years old. Further investigation revealed that he died at age 93. And an American man who allegedly died in 1979 at age 137, and who was at one time noted in the *Guinness Book of World Records* for this reason, was later found to have died at age 104 (Meister, 1984). Apparently, the notoriety that comes with extreme old age offers a strong temptation to exaggerate the truth. The greatest authenticated human ages are 120 years (a Japanese man), 113 years and 273 days (a California woman), and 113 years and 124 days (a Canadian man).
Most elderly Americans live in the southern sunbelt states.	Florida does have the highest concentration of the elderly, but the states that rank second through twentieth are all in the north and midwest.
The dramatic increase in the number of elderly persons is occurring only in a few developed countries, such as the United States.	Because of worldwide advances in medical care and birth control, many nations face the prospect of an increasingly older population. This includes both developed countries (Japan, Canada, the United States) and developing countries (China, India, Mexico).

a whole provide for the needs of a population that lives longer in retirement? How will countries that are lacking in technology cope with large elderly populations? How can developed countries best assist their less developed neighbors in caring for the elderly? If older adults throughout the world are to avoid deprivation and suffering, these important questions will have to be answered in the days to come.

THE SCIENTIFIC STUDY OF AGING

Because so many more of us are living longer than ever before, the past few decades have seen a considerable growth of interest in the study of adult development and aging. Researchers, policy makers, educators, and lay persons alike have become increasingly concerned with the scientific study of aging and the special problems of the aged (**gerontology**), and with the medical study of the diseases, debilities, and care of aged persons (**geriatrics**). The following are among the problems and issues of current importance.

- Will our physiological, sensory, and cognitive processes sustain us as we grow toward old age? Or should we expect serious deterioration in our physical abilities, vision, audition, memory, and intellectual capacities?
- Are most elderly adults so ill and helpless as to require extensive medical care or institutionalization, or do most remain self-sufficient and independent?
- Should we expect to undergo significant changes in personality during the lengthy course of adulthood? Or is personality most likely to remain relatively stable?
- Are social relationships typically satisfying after middle age? Or are most older adults ignored by their families and peers?
- Because life expectancies are greater for women than for men, the American population includes significantly more older women than older men. This discrepancy is particularly large in the upper age ranges. (See Figure 1.6.) What problems does this cause for older

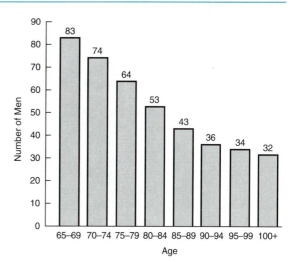

Figure 1.6
Number of men per 100 women by age group (1986).
Source: U.S. Senate Special Committee on Aging (1987–1988, p. 20).

women who become divorced or widowed, and what can be done to improve matters?

- Should we expect retirement to be a rewarding or a traumatic experience? What, if anything, can be done to make the former outcome more likely?
- Will we have considerably more difficulty dealing with our stressful environment in middle and old age? Or will our greater experience in living make us more adept at coping with such problems?
- Are certain kinds of psychopathology more likely to afflict older adults? If so, what can be done to treat these disorders?
- Although some theorists would disagree (Fries, 1983; Fries & Crapo, 1981), the preponderance of data indicates that older adults now live longer after the onset of a terminal illness than ever before (Myers & Manton, 1984a; 1984b; see also Chapter 12). That is, dying is often a lengthy process. How may terminally ill patients and their loved ones be helped to cope with these traumatic months, or even years?

The purpose of this book is to present, discuss, and evaluate the empirical research evidence dealing with such issues.

Summary

Adult development and aging deals with the description, explanation, and modification of changes that occur during the adult life course. The developmental approach focuses on changes within the individual over time (intraindividual changes), and on the extent to which such changes occur at different rates among different individuals (interindividual differences). It is also important to identify major similarities between younger and older adults, so as not to exaggerate the negative effects of aging.

HUMAN AGING AND LIFE EXPECTANCY

Human aging is caused by processes within the individual that significantly decrease the probability of survival. Unlike illnesses and diseases, these changes are universal, inevitable, and irreversible. We all grow old, and none of us can become young again.

Life expectancy at birth has increased dramatically during the past century. In 1900, the average man and woman could expect to live about 46 and 49 years; today, the corresponding figures are approximately 71.6 and 79.2 years. Much of these gains are due to sharp reductions in the number of premature deaths, such as accidents and illnesses during infancy and childhood. That is, many more Americans are reaching old age than ever before. There have also been smaller but important increases in life expectancies at older ages, indicating that those who do survive until old age are likely to live a few years longer than did their counterparts of a century ago.

The percent of elderly Americans has increased markedly since 1940, a trend that is expected to continue for the next half century. In fact, the most rapidly growing segment of the American population is the "old-old." The dramatic increase in the number of elderly adults is not unique to the United States; it is occurring throughout the world. Such demographic changes have focused attention on many important problems and issues, and have caused a considerable growth of interest in the scientific study of adult development and aging.

Study Questions

1. When drawing conclusions about adult development, why is it important to distinguish between changes that are related to *aging* and changes that are caused by *illness*?
2. The life expectancy at birth in the United States has increased by 28 years since 1900, but the life expectancy at age 65 has increased by less than 8 years. Why is the increase in life expectancy at birth so much greater? What does this imply about the likelihood of your living to age 90 or older?
3. The "old-old" is the fastest growing age group in the United States. Ten years from now, what changes are likely to result with regard to (a) health care and costs? (b) Social Security? (c) the responsibilities of young and middle-aged adults to their parents? (d) voting and political power? (e) adult education?
4. Why might the increasing number of older adults be an even greater problem in some foreign countries than in the United States?

Terms to Remember

Note: Important terms (emphasized in boldface type within each chapter) are defined in the Glossary at the end of this book.

Aging	*Intra-individual changes*
Cohort	*Life expectancy at birth*
Geriatrics	*Life expectancy at a specific age*
Gerontology	*Maximum life span*
Interindividual differences	

Chapter 2

Research Methods and Issues

Stock, Boston

Many things that people once "knew" to be true have proved to be wholly incorrect. To cite just two famous examples, we are now well aware that the earth is not flat and that it is not at the center of our universe. This enlightenment was made possible by scientific research, which is superior to subjective opinion in one important respect: it relies on hard data that can be verified and reproduced. When research study after study points to a particular conclusion, only an unusually stubborn individual would continue to argue otherwise.

During the past few decades, gerontologists and geriatricians have taken a closer look at some popular beliefs about aging—for example, that the majority of adults age 65 and older are physically and psychologically incapacitated, lonely, and poverty stricken. Researchers in various disciplines, including psychology, sociology, biology, and economics, have investigated such important issues by obtaining appropriate empirical data. Not infrequently, this research has shown that prevailing stereotypes about aging and the elderly have about as much validity as the flat-earth theory.

Although specific research methods vary from one discipline to another, there is a common underlying logic that binds them together. There are also common problems: Tracing the course of important variables during adulthood, such as intelligence and personality, has proved to be far from an easy task. In this chapter, therefore, we will discuss some of the ways in which researchers gather and interpret information about adult development and aging. We will also examine some of the major methodological difficulties that pervade research in this area.

We realize that your interest in this subject may be more practical than theoretical, and that you may have no plans ever to design and conduct a research study. Even so, there is good reason to be concerned with methodological issues. In your studies, you will surely be a consumer of research results. The behavioral sciences are relatively young, and can boast of few (if any) flawless research methods. Therefore, the procedures selected by an investigator may to some extent bias the results in a particular direction. *What* we know about adult development and aging is often inextricably linked with *how* this information has been obtained, and we must consider both of these aspects in order to avoid serious misinterpretations.

Basic Principles

STATISTICAL INFERENCE

Variables.   Scientific research deals with relationships among **variables,** or characteristics that can take on different values. For example, an economist may be interested in the relationship between aging and level of income: Does the financial state of most adults improve, decline, or remain about the same as they grow toward old age? Or a cognitive psychologist may hypothesize that aging is related to significant declines in intelligence, memory, or the ability to learn.

In the preceding examples, age, income, learning, memory, and intelligence are variables; there are at least some people who score at different levels. If, instead, every adult had precisely the same degree of intelligence or ability to remember, these phenomena would *not* be variables. They would be constants, and researchers would find them to be of much less interest—albeit considerably easier to describe, because knowing the score of one individual would tell you everyone else's score as well. Thus, variation is the *raison d'être* of the research scientist.

Populations and Samples. Researchers in the behavioral sciences must contend with an extremely troublesome problem: They can never measure *all* of the cases in which they are interested. For example, a gerontologist cannot obtain data from all 30-year-olds and all 60-year-olds in the United States; a physiological psychologist cannot study the heart and lungs of all adults in the world; an experimental psychologist cannot observe the maze behavior of all rats. The behavioral scientist wants to know what is happening in a given **population**—a large group of people, animals, objects, or responses that are alike in at least one respect. Yet it would be much too time-consuming and expensive to measure such populations in their entirety. In fact, because the population of interest may well consist of millions of people (e.g., Americans over age 65, women, men, blacks, whites), even measuring a substantial proportion of cases is out of the question. What to do?

One reasonable procedure is to measure a relatively small number of cases drawn from the population (that is, a **sample**). A sample of, say, 100 people can readily be interviewed, given a written questionnaire, or used as subjects in a laboratory experiment. However, conclusions that apply only to the 100 people who happen to be included in the sample are unlikely to be of much interest. To advance our knowledge to any significant degree, a researcher must be able to draw much more general conclusions, such as: "The friendships and social relationships of 60-year-olds in the United States tend to be no less satisfying than those of 30-year-olds." A finding like this is typically obtained from a research study that included 100 or 200 subjects, yet it is stated in terms of the entire populations from which the samples were drawn—that is, all 60-year-olds and all 30-year-olds in the United States.

How is this possible? There are various mathematical procedures for drawing inferences about what is happening in a population, based on what is observed in a sample from that population (**inferential statistics**). (See Figure 2.1.) We will not discuss such procedures here, because they are dealt with extensively in other texts (e.g., Welkowitz, Ewen, & Cohen, 1991). For our purposes, the important point is that there is *no* way to ensure that a

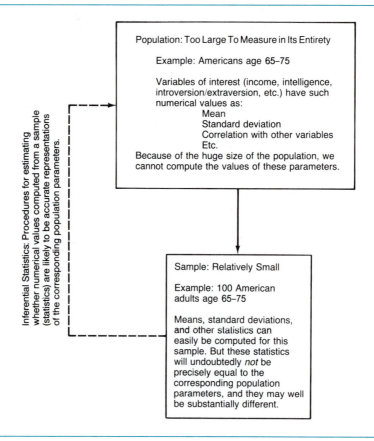

Figure 2.1
Populations and samples.

sample is in fact representative of the population from which it came. To be sure, a larger sample is more likely to be representative of the corresponding population, and larger samples are being used more often in current research. But no matter how carefully a researcher draws a sample, it is still possible that statistics computed from this sample (e.g., means, standard deviations, correlation coefficients) will differ to a substantial extent from the corresponding population values (parameters). The use of appropriate inferential statistics does make correct inferences about the population more likely, but not certain.

Therefore, no single study ever proves or disproves a theory or hypothesis; more substantial evidence must be collected before definitive conclusions can be attempted. For this reason, we must expect to meet with some ambiguity and controversy when we review the findings of research on adult development and aging.

COMMON RESEARCH DESIGNS

Experimental Designs.   In **experimental designs**, the experimenter directly manipulates one or more variables (**independent variables**) and observes the results to various other variables (**dependent variables**). For example, suppose that a gerontologist wishes to ascertain whether a certain training program will enable middle-aged Americans to learn difficult verbal material more quickly. One way to test this hypothesis is by obtaining two groups of Americans age 45–60, one of which receives the new training program (the **experimental group**). The second group does *not* undergo training; this **control group** is used as a baseline for evaluating the performance of the experimental group. To control for the effects of irrelevant variables (such as intelligence), the decision as to which subjects receive the training program is made **randomly** (e.g., by flipping a coin), so that each subject has an equal chance of winding up in the experimental group or the control group. Learning may be indexed by testing the ability of subjects to recognize or recall the material after a specified period of time. (See Figure 2.2.)

In this experiment, receiving or not receiving training is the independent variable, and amount learned is the dependent variable. If the experimental group performs significantly better on the tests of recognition and recall than does the control group, this would support the hypothesis that the training program is beneficial. Because subjects were assigned randomly to

Figure 2.2
A simple experimental design.

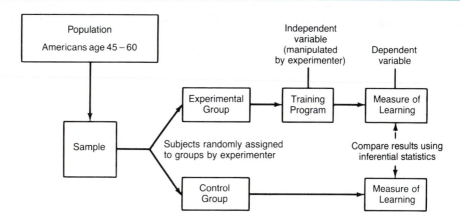

Note. Although the control group does *not* receive the training program, it would normally be given some unrelated activity that would take about the same amount of time. Otherwise the experimental group might perform better on the measure of learning solely because the experimenters spent more time with that group, causing a significant increase in motivation.

treatments, it is unlikely that the observed differences between the two groups were due to some other reason—such as a disproportionate number of more intelligent people in the experimental group, or an unusually large number of adults with poor memories in the control group. Thus experimental designs typically permit cause-and-effect statements to be made, such as, "This training program caused improved performance on a verbal learning task."

One important advantage of the experimental design is that it puts the researcher in control; he or she can test hypotheses by stipulating precisely what the different experimental conditions will be. But this is also a disadvantage, because the resulting experiment may well be artificial and unrealistic (Harre & Lamb, 1984, p. 154). For example, some subjects in the learning experiment previously described may not be motivated to perform well because they regard the task as irrelevant to their everyday lives. This issue will be discussed further in Chapter 5.

Quasiexperimental Designs.   Although **quasiexperimental designs** also utilize independent and dependent variables, subjects are *not* assigned randomly to treatments. Suppose that a gerontologist wishes to test the hypothesis that repeated exposure to loud noise causes significant hearing losses. In theory, it might be desirable to assign subjects randomly to one of two groups: an experimental group that is subjected to very loud noise, and a control group that does not receive this treatment. If the experimental group suffers significantly greater auditory declines than does the control group, the hypothesis would be supported. In practice, however, we obviously cannot risk inflicting significant auditory damage on subjects in order to obtain information.

One alternative is to use a quasiexperimental design. Exposure to loud noise would remain the independent variable, and amount of hearing loss would be the dependent variable. However, preexisting groups would be used instead of randomization. That is, we might compare the auditory ability of adults from three different backgrounds: relatively noisy American cities, less noisy rural American environments, and even less noisy primitive cultures that have no access to radio or television. If those who live in quieter environments demonstrate significantly less hearing loss than those in noisier environments, this would provide some support for the hypothesis. (See Figure 2.3.)

Quasiexperimental designs have more drawbacks than experimental designs, because the failure to assign subjects randomly to groups makes it harder to rule out alternative explanations. Primitive cultures and large American cities differ in many ways other than noise level, and some of these differences could conceivably be responsible for any observed differences in hearing loss. However, when interpreted cautiously, quasiexperimental designs do enable researchers to gain useful information in situations where experimental designs are not feasible.

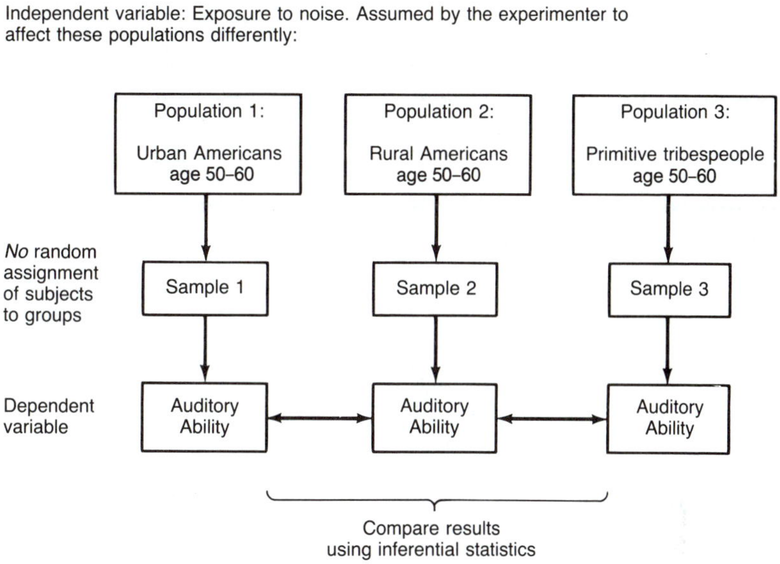

Independent variable: Exposure to noise. Assumed by the experimenter to affect these populations differently:

Figure 2.3
A quasiexperimental design.

Correlational Designs.　In **correlational designs**, subjects are not assigned to groups by the experimenter, nor are there specific independent and dependent variables. Instead, two or more variables are measured in order to ascertain the co-relationship between them.

To illustrate, suppose that a gerontologist wishes to determine the relationship between intelligence and age. One possible approach is to obtain a sample of adults of various ages, measure the age and intelligence of each subject, and compute the correlation coefficient between these two variables. (See Figure 2.4.) If the older subjects are much lower in intelligence than are the younger adults, a substantial negative correlation will be obtained. If the older subjects are considerably higher in intelligence, a large positive correlation will be obtained. And if there is no consistent relationship, with some older subjects demonstrating higher intelligence and some having lower intelligence, the correlation will tend toward zero.

Correlational designs typically do *not* permit cause-and-effect statements to be made. There are three possible reasons for a high correlation between two variables (X and Y): X causes Y, Y causes X, or the co-relationship between X and Y is caused by some third variable. For example, a high positive correlation was once obtained between the number of storks in various European cities and the number of births in each city. That is, cities with more storks had more births, while cities with fewer storks had fewer births.

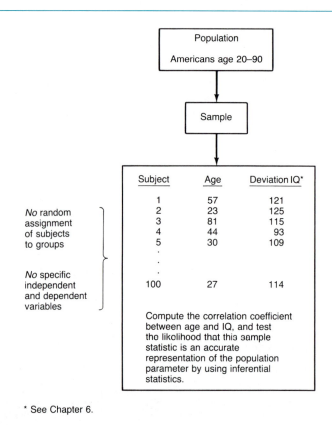

* See Chapter 6.

Figure 2.4
A correlational design.

Taken at face value, these data might seem to support the fable that babies are brought by storks. In actuality, this correlation was caused by a third variable: size of city. Storks like to nest in chimneys. Larger cities have more houses and thus more chimneys, providing more nesting places for storks. And larger cities also have more births, because there are more people. Conversely, smaller cities have fewer people, births, houses, chimneys, and storks. Although this example may well be apocryphal, it does illustrate the difficulty of ascertaining cause and effect when the correlational design is used.

Although correlational and experimental designs differ in many important respects, they are by no means wholly unrelated. In fact, it is desirable to convert significant results obtained from experimental designs into correlation coefficients. A discussion of such issues is beyond the scope of this book, however. (See Cohen, 1965; Welkowitz, Ewen, & Cohen, 1991, pp. 215–218.)

Afterword: Gerontological Research and the Measurement of Change. As we observed in Chapter 1, the study of adult development and aging involves the study of change over time. This poses another important methodological problem: how best to study change? Should we obtain a sample of, say, 20-year-olds, and continue to study them for many years? Or might we save considerable time and effort by obtaining samples of adults of various ages, and comparing their performance on various tasks? Issues like these are vital to research on adult development and aging; yet they are by no means easy to resolve, as we will see in the following section.

Developmental Research Methods

Researchers have devised various strategies for studying adult development and aging, each of which has its own distinct advantages and disadvantages.

LONGITUDINAL RESEARCH

Definition. In a **longitudinal** study, the same subjects are observed over a period of time, often many years. (See Figure 2.5.) In 1955, for example, gerontologists at Duke University obtained a sample of 270 subjects whose ages varied from 59 to 94. On 11 different occasions during the next 21 years, the researchers administered measures of physiological functioning, intelligence, personality, reaction time, vision, audition, and attitudes toward retirement and other issues to those who remained in the study (Siegler, 1983).

In a longitudinal study, measurements are obtained from the same subjects over a period of time, often years. (Courtesy Marilyn McClenahan)

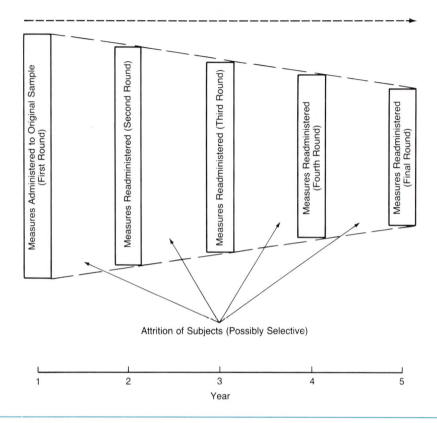

Figure 2.5
Longitudinal research: A five-year study with measurements obtained annually.

Advantages.   The great advantage of longitudinal research is the fact that it provides direct information about intra-individual change. If we wish to test the hypothesis that intelligence, memory, or any other variable declines or increases during adulthood, the most obvious (and theoretically best) procedure is to study a sample of adults for a number of years and trace the course taken by this variable.

   To illustrate, suppose that a sample of 100 30-year-olds is given a test of memory and obtains a mean score of 27.0. Thirty years later, all 100 subjects are rounded up and given the same test once more, and their mean score at age 60 is 18.0. If the difference between 27 and 18 is statistically significant (i.e., likely to be an accurate indication of what is happening in the corresponding populations), this finding would support the hypothesis that memory declines with increasing age. Because the same 100 subjects were studied over a period of 30 years, no critic could argue that the results were biased because the researcher inadvertently obtained a group of 60-year-olds with unusually poor memories (or an overly capable group of 30-year-olds).

Disadvantages.   Considerable amounts of money and effort are required to study a sample of people for many years. Unfortunately, the resources of many researchers are so limited that longitudinal studies are simply out of the question.

Even when the longitudinal approach is feasible, the researcher will usually find that some subjects drop out before the study is completed. Some may move to far-away locations; others may die; still others may not be sufficiently motivated to continue participating. In the Duke study previously cited, only 44 of the original 270 subjects remained at the conclusion despite efforts like these:

> The issue of sample maintenance is important in any longitudinal study. In the . . . Duke study, tremendous care and attention were given to developing relationships with the study participants so that their cooperation over the length of the study would be maximized. As an inducement to participation, the results of the physical examination were communicated to study participants and to their personal physicians shortly after completion of a given round of the study. . . . Special attention was paid to keeping in contact with subjects by sending birthday and Christmas cards and to continuing to stay in touch by mail, even if the subjects had moved away from the Durham area. (Siegler, 1983, pp. 141–142.)

The problem here is not simply that the number of subjects is reduced. If that were the only concern, longitudinal researchers would only have to oversample at the outset of the study in order to ensure that a sufficient number of participants remained at the end. However, a major problem arises if those who drop out are significantly different from those who remain, for this **selective attrition** may well produce misleading results. That is, instead of being representative of the population from which the sample was drawn, the subjects who complete the study will be atypical in some important respects.

This selective attrition is by no means unlikely. For example, subjects with relatively little education may see less value in scientific research and be more likely to drop out. So too may those who are low in ability and find the experimental task unpleasantly difficult. If so, measurements obtained toward the end of the longitudinal study will be based on a sample that is now unusually high in ability and educational level. If the variable being studied does decline with increasing age (e.g., intelligence during late adulthood), and if the sample becomes more and more capable as the study proceeds, these two effects will tend to cancel each other out. Thus the longitudinal study will *underestimate* the amount of intra-individual change over time. That is, the study will show *less* change (and perhaps considerably less) than is actually the case.

Alternatively, a longitudinal study may *overestimate* the amount of intra-individual change over time. If the experimental task is an easy one, subjects who are high in ability may become bored and be more likely to drop out. If the variable being studied does decline with increasing age, and if the sample becomes less and less capable as the study proceeds, the study will show *more* change (and perhaps considerably more) than is actually the case. However, this form of selective attrition is not as common.

In addition to selective attrition, measurement problems may bias the results of a longitudinal study. What seems to be true change over time might actually represent nothing more than measurement error: Psychological research instruments are far from perfect, and we cannot expect subjects to obtain precisely the same scores on two different occasions even if they have not changed at all. (See, for example, Shanan & Jacobowitz, 1982.)

As a second possibility, one measurement period might influence the following one. If subjects remember their previous answers to a psychological questionnaire, and repeat those answers because they erroneously believe that it is desirable to be consistent, they will appear to have undergone less change than is actually the case.

A third measurement problem concerns longitudinal studies that continue for many years: Their procedures may become outmoded. Gerontologists are not solely concerned with questions about aging; they also try to improve their research methods. Thus, a researcher who begins a 20-year study in 1975 may find that substantially improved designs or instruments are available in 1985. There is no way for this researcher to go back in time, change the research design, and replace the data obtained between 1975 and 1985. Yet by current standards, the data obtained with the old and inferior methods may be too flawed to be useful. This problem is particularly important in medical research, in which technological advances in the measurement of physiological functions occur fairly often. For example, we now have much more sophisticated and accurate methods for measuring heart and lung functions than were available 10 to 20 years ago.

There may also be a fair amount of personnel turnover during the life of a longitudinal study, and this may introduce another source of measurement error. Newer staff members may administer or score subjective measures (e.g., the Rorschach) somewhat differently than did the original researchers, thereby producing score changes that have nothing to do with true intra-individual changes.

Some critics argue that even when the longitudinal method does detect significant intra-individual changes, it cannot guarantee that these changes are due to aging. Suppose that the political attitudes of a sample of 20-year-olds are measured in 1955 and again when they reach middle age in 1985, and that the latter measurement reveals a pronounced increase in liberalism. Taken at face value, these data might seem to indicate that young adults will become more liberal as they grow toward middle age. However, a more likely explanation is that the results were due primarily to cultural influences. There were many changes in American society between 1955 and 1985, such as the increasing emphasis on the rights of women and various minorities. Thus it may well be these trends, rather than aging, that caused the increase in liberalism. If so, and if there are no similar societal changes during the next 30 years, then we should *not* expect today's young adults to become markedly more liberal by the time they reach middle age. (One way to deal with this problem would be to measure the political attitudes of a sample of young adults in 1985. If this group proved to be about as liberal as the middle-aged group in the longitudinal study, this would suggest that the results were indeed due to cultural influences rather than to aging.)

Finally, longitudinal studies require considerable patience. It can be quite frustrating to have to wait 10 or 20 years before the results can be published, nor does it do a researcher's career much good to have a lengthy period without any new publications.

Afterword. In theory, longitudinal research is the most desirable way to study adult development and aging. This method enables the researcher to observe intra-individual change directly, and intra-individual change is what adult development is all about. (See, for example, Schaie, 1983.) Research practice, however, is another story. Of the disadvantages discussed previously, the most troublesome is the question of time and effort. A longitudinal study is a major undertaking, one that exceeds the resources of many researchers.

Are there any feasible alternatives? Some theorists contend that not all questions about adult development and aging require the longitudinal approach, or are important enough to justify it. According to this argument, valuable information can be obtained in some instances by using a more convenient research design—the cross-sectional study.

CROSS-SECTIONAL RESEARCH

Definition. In a **cross-sectional** study, all measurements are performed at about the same time. (See Figure 2.6.) For example, a researcher may draw one sample of 20-year-olds and another sample of 60-year-olds and compare them on one or more variables, using any of the research designs discussed previously in this chapter (experimental, quasiexperimental, correlational).

Advantages. Cross-sectional studies are much easier and less costly to carry out than longitudinal studies. The process of gathering and analyzing the data typically takes a few months at most; years of observation are not required. There is no long wait for results to analyze and publish, nor is it likely that the research procedures will become outmoded during the course of the study.

It has been argued that cross-sectional research is appropriate when our objectives are limited to description. If we wish only to describe how today's

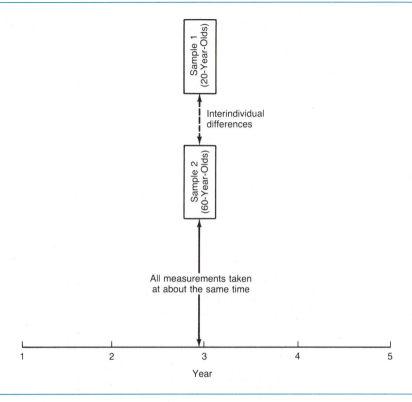

Figure 2.6
Cross-sectional research: A comparison of 20-year-olds and 60-year-olds.

60-year-olds and 20-year-olds differ on certain variables, it is not unreasonable to draw a sample from each population and compare the resulting statistics.

Disadvantages.   Although the cross-sectional approach has achieved widespread popularity, it suffers from major methodological weaknesses. This method is not well suited for *explaining* age-related differences, primarily because it confounds the effects of aging and culture.

To illustrate, suppose that in 1980 a researcher who is interested in the area of personality draws one sample of 20-year-old U.S. citizens and one sample of 60-year-old U.S. citizens. The researcher administers appropriate measures of personality to each group and finds some statistically significant differences between the two samples. These results may have nothing at all to do with aging! The environmental and social influences during the 1920s and 1930s (when the 60-year-olds were children and adolescents) differed markedly from those in the 1960s and 1970s (when the 20-year-olds were children and adolescents). For example, each group experienced different educational practices and expectations: A college education was much less common 50 years ago. Each group encountered different levels of technology: Television and jet planes did not exist 50 years ago. Social standards

Just as these pictures illustrate the difference in dance styles between young and old persons, cross-sectional studies tend to exaggerate differences between generations on many dimensions. (*top:* Spencer Grant/Monkmeyer Press Photo Service; *bottom:* Toni Michaels)

differed considerably, with the attitudes of the majority being considerably more conservative 50 years ago. And each group experienced different national and world events, such as the Depression and Prohibition versus the Vietnam War. Consequently, the personality differences discovered by this researcher might *not* be caused by growing from age 20 to age 60. They could easily result from the different influences on a child in the 1920s as opposed to a child in the 1960s (**cohort effects**). That is, two different possibilities have been confounded in this study:

1. Personality may change as a result of growing from age 20 to age 60.
2. The personality of adults born in 1920 (the 1920 cohort) may differ from the personality of adults born in 1960 (the 1960 cohort) because they experienced different social and historical influences during childhood and adolescence.

More specifically, suppose the researcher finds that the 60-year-olds have more conservative attitudes about politics and sex than do the 20-year-olds. This does *not* necessarily mean that people typically become more conservative about these matters as they grow older. Because the 1920s were more conservative than the 1960s, it is much more likely that the 60-year-olds were also quite conservative as young adults, and stayed much the same thereafter.

Thus a result that appears to be due to aging in a cross-sectional study may be due instead to cohort effects. That is, we cannot determine whether any observed interindividual differences are due to intra-individual changes or to some wholly different reason. Because one primary goal of the developmental researcher is to study and explain intra-individual change, this is a serious disadvantage.

Afterword.   Because cross-sectional studies are relatively easy to carry out, we will find numerous examples in the chapters that follow. But because such research confounds aging effects and cohort effects, the results must be interpreted with extreme caution. Admittedly, longitudinal studies are not exempt from cultural influences. But longitudinal research at least allows us to observe whether or not intra-individual change has occurred, whereas cross-sectional research does not. We must therefore conclude that in areas where appropriate longitudinal studies have been conducted, such research is more likely to provide us with accurate information about adult development and aging.

SEQUENTIAL RESEARCH

Rationale.   As we have seen in the preceding pages, the scientific study of variables is seriously hindered when two or more sources of variation are confounded. The confounding of aging effects and cohort effects in cross-sectional research makes it extremely difficult to explain any differences that are obtained, however valuable the results may be for descriptive purposes.

There is a third source of confounded variation that we have not yet discussed: **time of measurement**. According to one famous (and possibly apocryphal) story, a social psychologist once hypothesized that the attitudes of young American adults toward foreigners become more tolerant with increasing age. This researcher obtained a sample of 20-year-old U.S. citizens, measured their attitudes toward citizens of various other countries, and repeated these measurements annually during the following ten years. In the last round of the study, a surprising development occurred: The subjects' attitudes toward the Japanese *declined* sharply. Before concluding that this change was due to aging, and that young adults in general become markedly more anti-Japanese on reaching age 30, we should note that this study began in the summer of 1933. The final measurements were obtained a few months after December 7, 1941, when the Japanese attacked Pearl Harbor. It was this event, rather than aging, that produced the dramatic change in attitudes. Had the study ended just one year earlier, no such change would have been detected.

Thus there are three important sources of variation in studies of adult development and aging: aging, cohort, and time of measurement. To determine whether or not aging causes certain changes, researchers must somehow control for the effects of cohort and time of measurement. This is far from an easy task. Whereas cross-sectional studies confound aging effects and cohort effects, longitudinal studies confound aging effects and time of measurement effects. That is, because longitudinal research requires that subjects be measured at different times, any significant changes could be due either to aging or to the times at which the measurements were obtained. Even cross-sectional studies may be influenced to some extent by time of measurement effects, because the different samples may well be observed on different days.

In an attempt to resolve these problems, some theorists have created research designs that combine the cross-sectional and longitudinal methods. This approach, which strives to retain the advantages of each method while minimizing the disadvantages, is known as the **sequential research** strategy. (See, for example, Schaie, 1965, 1973, 1977; Schaie & Baltes, 1975.) We hinted at just such a possibility in a previous example: When we studied the political attitudes of a sample of young adults as they grew to middle age between 1955 and 1985, obtaining a second sample of 20-year-olds in 1985 helped us to determine whether the observed increase in liberalism was due to aging or to cultural influences.

Types of Sequential Research.   There are three major sequential research designs. In any one type, two of the possible sources of variation (aging, cohort, time of measurement) are treated as independent variables, and the third source remains uncontrolled. Although it would be preferable to treat

Delegates to a political convention, although not randomly selected, are thought to be representative of their state membership. (Sam C. Pierson, Jr./Photo Researchers, Inc.)

all three sources of variation as independent variables, this is impossible because they are *not* independent of one another: Once the values of two of these sources are specified, the value of the remaining source is automatically determined.

To illustrate, suppose that we wish to study adults age 50 who are members of the 1910 cohort. The only possible way to do this would be to obtain the measurements in 1960. If we collect our measures at any other time, we will have subjects who are either the wrong age or members of the wrong cohort. In 1985, for example, the members of the 1910 cohort were 75 (not 50), and 50-year-olds were members of the 1935 cohort (not 1910).

The researchers must therefore decide which source of variation is least likely to bias the results of the study in question, and choose the sequential design which treats this source as the uncontrolled variable. If, say, time of measurement is regarded as the least likely source of bias, the researcher would select the sequential design that leaves this source uncontrolled and treats aging and cohort as independent variables. (The dependent variable is the one whose relationship to aging the researcher is trying to ascertain, such as attitudes, intelligence, or memory.) Thus the three types of sequential research are the following:

1. Treat age and cohort as independent variables; assume that time of measurement has no effect *(cohort-sequential strategy)*.
2. Treat age and time of measurement as independent variables; assume that cohort has no effect *(time-sequential strategy)*.

3. Treat cohort and time of measurement as independent variables; assume that aging has no effect (*cross-sequential strategy*).

An example of a *cohort-sequential* study is shown in Figure 2.7. The researcher has chosen to study the 1920 and 1930 cohorts, and to compare adults who are 40 and 50 years old. Thus age and cohort are the independent variables, because they are manipulated by the experimenter. Having made these decisions, there is no choice as to the time at which the measurements are taken. To study the 1920 cohort at age 40 and 50, the measurements must be made in 1960 and 1970; to study the 1930 cohort at age 40 and 50, the measurements must be made in 1970 and 1980. In this design, therefore, time of measurement is the uncontrolled variable.

A comparison of groups B and C alone (or groups D and E alone) would be a longitudinal study, because the same subjects are observed over time. Here, aging effects and time of measurement effects are confounded. A com-

Figure 2.7

A cohort-sequential study.

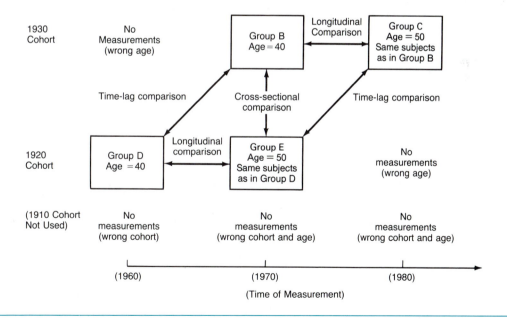

parison of groups B and E alone would be a cross-sectional study (aging effects and cohort effects are confounded), because two different samples are compared at about the same time. And a comparison of groups B and D alone (or groups C and E alone) would involve the confounding of cohort effects and time of measurement effects, because different cohorts of the same age are measured at different times. (This is referred to as a time-lag comparison.) The cohort-sequential strategy strives for broader conclusions by including all of these groups in the statistical analysis. *If* it is correct to assume that time of measurement is not important, then this design makes it possible to compare the relative magnitude of aging effects and cohort effects. A good example of the application of this technique is the Seattle Longitudinal Study (Schaie & Hertzog, 1983).

An example of a *cross-sequential* study is shown in Figure 2.8. The 1920 and 1930 cohorts have been selected for inclusion by the researcher, and the times of measurement have been designated as 1960 and 1970. Thus, cohort and time of measurement are the independent variables. Having made these

Figure 2.8
A cross-sequential study.

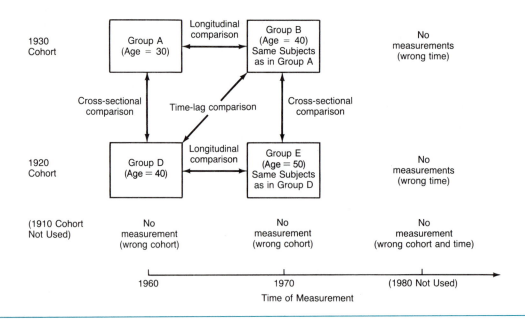

decisions, there is no choice as to the ages of the subjects in this study. When the 1920 cohort is measured in 1960, the members must be 40 years old; the 1930 cohort will be 30 years old in 1960; and so on. In this design, therefore, age is the uncontrolled variable.

Here, a comparison of groups A and D alone (or groups B and E alone) would be a cross-sectional study; a comparison of groups A and B alone (or groups D and E alone) would be a longitudinal study; and a comparison of groups B and D alone would be a time-lag study. In contrast, the cross-sequential strategy includes all of these groups in the statistical analysis. *If* it is correct to assume that aging effects are unimportant, then this design makes it possible to compare the relative magnitude of cohort effects and time of measurement effects. An example of a time-sequential study is provided by Bee (1987, p. 18).

The third type of sequential design, the *time-sequential* strategy, can be represented in a similar fashion. (See Figure 2.9.) The Duke Longitudinal Study serves as a good example of this method (Palmore, 1981; Siegler, 1983). Because the preceding discussion should serve as a sufficient introduction to sequential research, we will leave the details to the interested reader as an exercise.

Evaluation.   Sequential research designs were devised because of dissatisfaction with the longitudinal and cross-sectional methods. When the underlying assumptions are justified, these strategies provide important information that cannot be obtained from the traditional methods. However, sequential designs also have serious drawbacks.

First of all, sequential designs cannot control for selective attrition. Such attrition is just as likely to occur in sequential research as in longitudinal research, and it is just as likely to create the kinds of problems discussed previously in this chapter.

Second, the assumptions that underlie sequential research may well be questionable in many instances. Aging, cohort, and time of measurement are all potentially significant influences, yet we are required to assume that one of these sources is not a problem in each sequential design. This is particularly troublesome in the case of the cross-sequential strategy, in which we must assume that aging itself is unimportant! Nor are matters much better with the time-sequential strategy, which assumes that cohort has little effect on the data. This may be a viable assumption in some instances; for example, declines in visual acuity are more likely to be caused by age-related physiological changes than by cultural influences. But it is highly questionable in many other cases, as we have seen throughout this chapter. Perhaps the assumption of the cohort-sequential strategy is most plausible, namely that time of measurement is relatively unimportant. Yet this source of bias can also be significant.

Finally, sequential designs can be extremely time consuming. The cohort-sequential study illustrated in Figure 2.7 requires some 20 years to complete

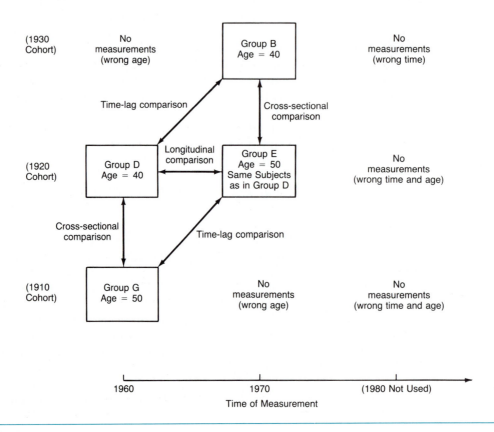

Independent Variables: Age (40; 50)
Time of Measurement (1960; 1970)

Uncontrolled Variable: Cohort

Duration of Study: 10 Years (1960–1970)

Figure 2.9
A time-sequential study.

(from 1960 to 1980). If we broaden the scope somewhat and include the 1940 cohort as well, the duration of the study increases to 30 years, because this cohort will not reach age 50 until 1990. Obviously, sequential research can be just as major an undertaking as longitudinal research—especially because one suggested solution to the problem of questionable assumptions is to carry out all three sequential strategies at once! As one critic has observed:

> Collectively, sequential designs appear to offer ingenious solutions to methodological problems in research on aging. . . . However, completing an experimental aging study that adheres fully to the requirements of any one of these designs is not easy to

accomplish. It requires the wisdom of a Solomon, the longevity of a Methuselah, the patience of a Job, and the backing of a Rockefeller. Moreover . . . the solutions arrived at through the use of a sequential design may be more illusory than real. (Kausler, 1982, p. 134.)

Afterword. Sequential research is designed to separate sources of variation that are confounded in longitudinal and cross-sectional research. In theory, this approach should enable us to determine the extent to which any significant changes in the dependent variable are caused by aging effects, cohort effects, and/or time of measurement effects. In practice, sequential research is better suited to providing an accurate and thorough *description* about changes over time (as opposed to an explanation of why these changes occur). Nevertheless, the simultaneous study of cross-sectional and longitudinal sequences is always desirable, because it affords the opportunity to cross-check results using different methodologies.

As investigators become more familiar with these methods, and as further improvements are made, the quantity of sequential research may well increase. For the present, however, the considerable time and effort required by sequential designs have limited their use in developmental research.

The empirical evidence discussed in the following chapters is therefore based primarily on cross-sectional and longitudinal research, with emphasis on the former. To interpret the results of this research correctly, you must ask yourself the following question: Could the findings be biased by confounded sources of variation? That is, in a cross-sectional study, are results attributed to aging more likely to be caused by cohort effects? In a longitudinal study, might results attributed to aging be biased by the times at which the measurements were taken? Until researchers develop more effective methods for answering such questions, common sense as well as statistical analyses must be used to interpret research results in adult development and aging.

Other Methodological Issues

Much more could be said about the methodological problems that confront developmental researchers. We conclude our discussion by examining some of the factors that threaten the internal and external validity of a research study, and by taking a closer look at the meaning of chronological age.

INTERNAL AND EXTERNAL VALIDITY

Threats to Internal Validity. The preceding pages illustrated the fact that scientific research deals with the relationships among variables. These relationships may involve cause and effect, as when a gerontologist wishes to ascertain whether aging causes declines in intelligence or memory, or they may be correlational. The extent to which a research study correctly identifies such relationships is referred to as **internal validity**.

Among the most serious threats to the internal validity of a research study are confounding, selective attrition, and the effects of practice. If, say, aging effects and cohort effects are confounded, we cannot tell whether any observed changes in the dependent variable are caused by aging or by cultural influences. If the subjects who drop out during the course of a longitudinal study tend to be low in ability, leaving us with an unusually capable group during the later rounds of measurements, we may erroneously conclude that aging does not cause declines in the dependent variable. Or the earlier testings in a longitudinal study might bias subsequent ones: Age-related declines in the dependent variable might be concealed because subjects benefit from the practice provided by the previous sessions, or because the procedures have become more familiar and less anxiety provoking. In each of these cases, the study is low in internal validity; it will *not* correctly identify cause-and-effect relationships among the variables of interest.

Various procedural factors may threaten the internal validity of a research study. Mechanical instruments may wear out over time, making it more (or less) difficult to obtain high scores during the latter part of a longitudinal study. Thus the researcher may attribute declining scores to aging when these changes are actually caused by switches that are harder to operate. Alternatively, if there is a significant amount of personnel turnover during the study, score changes that seem to be age-related may occur because inexperienced staff members administer and evaluate the measures differently.

Comparing behaviors at different ages can also be a source of problems. Suppose that we accept "aggressiveness" as an important aspect of human behavior, and that we wish to determine if this variable changes in any significant way during adulthood. We might find that a young adult is more likely to abuse someone physically, or to deliver a stinging insult. An older adult may, instead, prefer to spread unflattering rumors, or to engage in devious and subtle plots against another person. Should all of these behaviors be regarded as various forms of aggressiveness, or as something quite different? This is by no means an easy question to answer, but unless we can do so, we may well reach incorrect conclusions about the relationship between aging and aggressiveness.

Threats to External Validity.   Earlier in this chapter, we observed that research scientists usually cannot study all of the cases in which they are interested. Instead, they must deal with relatively small samples from the specified populations. **External validity** involves the extent to which the research findings can be generalized from the specific samples included in the study to the large populations in which the researcher is interested.

One particularly important threat to the external validity of a research study is the way in which the sample is obtained. To illustrate, let us suppose once again that we wish to measure the political attitudes of young adults as

Part II

Physiological and Cognitive Development

Chapter 3
Physiological Aspects of Aging

Susan Lapides/Design Conceptions

Most of our physiological functions reach their maximum capacity either before or during early adulthood, and then begin to wane. However, we tend not to notice the declines that occur during our twenties, thirties, and forties. These changes are very gradual, and they are likely to be compensated for by our increased experience and knowledge. Thus, we may be more competent behind the wheel of an automobile at age 35 than at age 20, even though our manual dexterity and perceptual response speed have declined slightly, because we have learned to anticipate potential danger and to drive defensively.

Eventually, however, the physiological effects of aging become more pronounced. Are such declines likely to hinder us substantially later in life? Or do most adults find that their bodily processes sustain them fairly well as they grow toward old age?

In this chapter, we will begin to examine the empirical evidence dealing with this issue. First we will investigate the kinds of physiological changes that occur as we grow from young to old adulthood, or *how* we age. (This topic is too extensive to be treated in a single chapter, so discussions of sensation and perception, sexuality, and stress will be deferred until later in this book.) These changes do not occur according to a strict timetable. Some individuals may become prematurely gray haired during their late twenties or early thirties, but some may retain a youthful physique well past middle age. Adults age at different rates, and such groupings as "the middle-aged"and "the elderly" are actually rather heterogeneous with regard to their physical capacities, amount of energy, and degree of mobility and independence. (Recall our previous discussion of the limitations of chronological age as an index of adulthood.) We will therefore discuss general age-related trends, with the understanding that any specific adult may well differ significantly from this average picture.

A second important issue concerns *why* we age. Scientists have proposed various explanations for the unfailing tendency of human beings to grow older, and we will review the evidence regarding these theories of aging.

Although we characterized aging in Chapter 1 as universal and inevitable, not all adults are willing, in the words of Dylan Thomas, to "go gentle into that good night." Some prefer to "rage against the dying of the light" by seeking ways to ward off the specter of death, and to inhibit or even to reverse the physiological declines associated with aging. We therefore conclude this chapter by reviewing such quests for the fountain of youth, which are as old as humanity itself. Included in our discussion will be a method for estimating, *very approximately*, your own probable life span.

Age-Related Physiological Changes

Prior to 1950, the only available data concerning aging and physiology were derived from cross-sectional comparisons between healthy young college students and ill, institutionalized elderly patients (Weg, 1983). Because these comparisons failed to control for health, they grossly exaggerated the negative effects of aging.

More recent longitudinal studies, as well as experimental studies with animals, have provided more accurate data about normal physiological changes during adulthood—that is, those changes *not* associated with illness and injury. These researchers have found that our bodies possess an enormous reserve capacity: We can survive the loss of one lung, one kidney, more than one-half of the liver, and large amounts of the stomach and intestines if we are not subjected to severe emotional or physiological stressors.

Because of this redundancy, many of our bodily processes decline very gradually even after middle age. To be sure, growing old does have disadvantages. But we can afford much of what we lose, and the age-related physiological declines that occur among healthy adults are not nearly as severe as is commonly believed.

OBSERVABLE CHARACTERISTICS

The process of aging leaves clearly visible traces. Although individual differences prevail, elderly adults do tend to look significantly different from the middle-aged, who typically appear different from young adults.

Skin and Face.   The first facial indication of adult aging is the appearance of lines in the forehead, which usually occurs by age 30. Between ages 30 and 50, additional lines become evident elsewhere in the face. These include

Typical effects of aging of the skin include wrinkling, sagging, and leathery appearance of sun-exposed areas. However, for some individuals such as the woman in these pictures, changes in appearance are minor, even over several decades.   (Toni Michaels)

"crow's feet," lines caused by squinting; lines that link the nostrils to the sides of the mouth, which result from smiling; and furrowed brows, caused by frowning. Thus, during the first half of adulthood, repeated facial expressions produce some of the lines and wrinkles associated with aging. This implies that adults who frown less often, and those who avoid squinting by obtaining needed corrective lenses, will enjoy a smoother countenance.

After age 50, however, more extensive facial wrinkling is likely to occur. There is a significant decrease in collagen, the fiber that makes the skin more resilient, and in the amount of water on the inside of the skin. This makes the skin stiffer and less elastic, resulting in more pronounced facial lines. These changes are hastened by frequent exposure to strong sunlight. The skin also becomes thinner and more spread out, somewhat like a piece of dough that has been stretched too far. This is evidenced in such ways as bags under the eyes and sagging skin on the cheeks. Because of these changes, and because of an increase in capillary fragility, the skin of older adults is more vulnerable to bruising. By age 70, the skin has become rougher and has lost its uniformity of color, with a variety of shades clearly evident (Kligman, Grove, & Balin, 1985).

Our facial features also undergo changes during adulthood. By the time you reach old age, accumulations of cartilage will make your nose a half-inch wider and another half-inch longer. Your earlobes will become somewhat fatter, and your ears will grow about a quarter of an inch longer. The circumference of the head increases by a quarter of an inch every ten years, presumably because the skull thickens with increasing age. However, these changes are usually far less noticeable than are the age-related changes in the skin.

Because these trends are only average tendencies, how might you predict the rate at which your own skin and face will age? The aging of the skin is determined by hereditary influences, so you can obtain some valuable clues simply by observing your parents' features. In fact, except for such remedial actions as cosmetic surgery, about all you can do to preserve a more youthful skin is to avoid excessive exposure to the sun's ultraviolet rays. Furthermore, if you are female, the aging of your skin during the second half of adulthood will probably be more noticeable than if you are male (although dryness can be inhibited by using lotions and protective creams). One reason is that the production of skin oil (sebum) declines significantly after menopause in women, but it remains virtually unchanged for men throughout adulthood.

Hair.   Currently, scientific knowledge about age-related changes in the hair is not much greater than that possessed by the average hairdresser (Kligman, Grove, & Balin, 1985). Most adults over 40 experience some graying of scalp hair, which is caused by hereditary influences. Scalp hair also becomes thinner over the course of adulthood, especially after age 65. This thinning occurs in two ways: The rate of growth decreases, and individual strands of hair gradually decline in diameter. For example, in the case of 20-year-old men, the diameter of a single hair is 101 microns (millionths of a meter). For

70-year-old men, this diameter is only 80 microns. The density of scalp hair varies greatly from one adult to another, however, although blondes generally have more hairs than do brunettes.

Some men experience a loss of hair that begins at the temples, proceeds to the circle on the back of the head (the "monk's spot"), and continues until the entire top of the head is bare (**male pattern baldness**). This form of hair loss is due solely to hereditary influences, and it cannot at present be prevented by scalp massages or other treatments. Other men retain most of their cranial hair throughout adulthood. Even in these cases, some hair loss usually occurs around the temples; but there are exceptions, as the case history of one noted American indicates:

A President's Unusual Hairline

"It's a hairline you normally see only on a child or a eunuch," says Dr. Norman Orentreich, the inventor of the hair transplant. He is referring to [former] president Ronald Reagan, who retained a straight line of hair above his forehead into his 70s. "He's not wearing a hairpiece," Orentreich says, "and he hasn't been castrated, so I'd have to assume that he happens to have some sort of rare hereditary variation [to account for the lack of hair loss around the temples]." Thus [Mr.] Reagan's scalp is further proof of what gerontologists have come to realize during the past few decades, namely that individual variations in aging are enormous at every age and in every part of the body. (*Esquire*, May 1982, p. 45.)

Hair loss among men is a common feature of aging. Most people face this loss with equanimity. (Virginia Blaisdell/Stock, Boston)

Male pattern baldness also affects some 75 percent of all women, though rarely to the extent of becoming totally hairless. This pattern involves a thinning of the hair on the top and sides of the head, and it can become so pronounced that some women in their seventies and eighties opt to wear wigs. Contrary to a common belief, however, childbirth does *not* cause scalp hair loss in women.

In other areas of the body, an opposite trend is observed. As men grow older, hair becomes longer and more profuse in the ears, the nostrils, the eyebrows, and sometimes on the back. Most women past 65, especially those of Mediterranean origin, have an excessive growth of long, dark, and thick hair over the lip and chin. The reasons for such localized hirsutism are not yet known (Kligman et al., 1985).

Height. A man's height decreases by about half an inch between ages 30 and 50, and by another three-quarters of an inch between ages 50 and 70. This is due to the effects of gravity, which causes the muscles to weaken and the bones of the spine to deteriorate and become compressed.

The height loss for women is slightly greater, and may total as much as two inches between ages 25 and 75. One reason is a higher incidence of metabolic bone disease among women following menopause. Another important cause is a loss of bone calcium with increasing age, a decline that can be slowed by regular exercise and an appropriate diet.

Weight. As we grow from young adulthood to middle age, our weight tends to increase. (See Table 3.1.) Many of us become less active during this period, and there is a decrease in the rate at which the resting body converts food into energy (our **basal metabolism,** which slows down by about 3 percent every ten years). Because less metabolizing tissue is available after age 20, the number of calories required each day to maintain our present weight declines by about 10 percent every ten years (Ausman & Russell, 1990).

If we were to reduce our food intake accordingly, our weight would remain about the same. But the typical pattern is to eat much the same amounts, or perhaps even more, as we grow from young adulthood to middle age. The result is an inability to burn up enough food; an accumulation of fat throughout the body; skin that becomes flabby in the waist and chest areas, which may increase in size by as much as five to six inches; and a gain in weight that may total 10 to 15 percent between age 20 and 50. For obvious reasons, these changes are commonly referred to as "middle-age spread."

After middle age, however, our weight is likely to level off and begin a slow decline. During this period, we tend to lose more weight due to tissue and muscle deterioration than we gain in fat.

Breasts. Women's breasts sag with increasing age. The glandular tissues that produce firmness deteriorate over time, and the tissues that support the

Table 3.1

*Average weight as a function of age, sex, height, and frame size.**

	Men					
	Age 25–54			Age 55–74		
Height	Small Frame	Medium Frame	Large Frame	Small Frame	Medium Frame	Large Frame
5'2"	141	150	180	134	150	169
5'3"	134	156	183	136	154	176
5'4"	145	156	185	139	156	169
5'5"	145	163	174	154	158	174
5'6"	147	165	185	150	163	176
5'7"	156	169	185	152	172	187
5'8"	156	172	189	154	172	183
5'9"	163	172	196	165	169	185
5'10"	165	178	191	167	176	191
5'11"	167	178	200	152	185	185
6'0"	163	185	200	167	178	198
6'1"	174	187	205	172	194	194
6'2"	176	194	202	169	209	196

	Women					
	Age 25–54			Age 55–74		
Height	Small Frame	Medium Frame	Large Frame	Small Frame	Medium Frame	Large Frame
4'10"	114	138	189	118	125	202
4'11"	116	145	171	121	136	171
5'0"	116	132	191	118	143	171
5'1"	118	134	178	123	140	173
5'2"	121	134	178	127	140	180
5'3"	121	136	182	127	143	176
5'4"	125	136	173	132	145	169
5'5"	132	138	178	132	147	176
5'6"	127	138	165	149	145	180
5'7"	129	143	176	134	158	176
5'8"	136	147	167	134	154	173
5'9"	138	149	173	136	158	187
5'10"	140	154	167	138	160	187

Note. Frame size is measured by the breadth of the elbow joint (arm extended). For men, small is less than or equal to 2.64"; medium is 2.65" to 3.19"; large is greater than or equal to 3.2". For women, small is less than or equal to 2.24"; medium is 2.25" to 2.81"; and large is greater than or equal to 2.82".

*These data do not reflect ideal weight but rather *actual* measurements of individuals of a given height and frame size.

Source: Based on Frisancho (1984), *American Journal of Clinical Nutrition, 84,* pp. 808–819.

breast by connecting it with the underlying muscles become stretched. In general, small and broad-based breasts sag less than those that are large or narrow based.

These changes are determined partly by heredity and partly by the woman's behavior. Chest muscle exercises are unlikely to lift a breast that is already sagging, but preventive measures can be helpful. These include wearing supportive brassieres before sagging becomes apparent, especially during pregnancy, breast-feeding, and vigorous exercise.

Voice.   As we grow older, the vocal cords stiffen and vibrate at a higher frequency. By old age, therefore, the speaking voice increases in pitch by about two or three notes on the musical scale. The voice may also begin to quaver, presumably because there is some loss of control over the vocal cords.

Afterword.   Most of the changes previously discussed are so well known that they have become hallmarks of the aging process. These changes are primarily cosmetic; they have no direct effect on our vigor, daily functioning, or health. Nevertheless, their psychological effects can be considerable. Millions of middle-aged and elderly women (and some older men) suffer considerable damage to their self-esteem because of these changes, so much so that they spend substantial amounts of money on cosmetic products and/or surgery in an effort to appear younger. As Weg (1983, p. 251) observes, "Societal adoration of youth has placed a premium on looking young; . . .The young, unlined, and gently curvaceous body of the woman and the lithe but macho and powerful body of the man cannot be preserved forever. [Yet] . . . societal attitudes toward aging and the aged have helped to create the fearsome image of old age that can be likened to a punishment."

The desire to look young is understandable. Increasing age brings us closer to the specter of death (see Chapter 12), whereas youth is associated with vitality and the prospect of many years yet to live. Nevertheless, the preoccupation of our society with a young appearance seems excessive. Looking old is not an illness, nor is it necessarily indicative of any serious impairments in functioning. Rather, it is a normal consequence of the aging process.

INTERNAL CHANGES

Musculature.   With increasing age, our muscle tissue slowly declines in strength, tone, and flexibility. Fiber is replaced by connective tissue, which causes the muscles to become stiffer and to heal more slowly after an injury. And muscle is gradually replaced by fat, leading to an overall softening of the body. Thus the typical 175-pound man possesses 70 pounds of muscle at age 30, but he retains only about 60 pounds of muscle by old age.

One consequence of these changes is that strength decreases with increasing age. Strength reaches its maximum during the twenties and declines thereafter, particularly after age 50. This has been observed in such areas as handgrip strength and knee extension strength, among others. In fact, there is a 20 percent reduction in muscle power at age 70 as compared with age 20. To some extent, however, muscular decrements can be slowed by appropriate exercise. (See Frontera et al., 1988; Horvath & Davis, 1990; Schulz & Curnow, 1988; Smith, Bierman, & Robinson, 1978.)

The Heart and Cardiovascular System.   The muscles of the heart also deteriorate as we grow older, so less blood is pumped with each heartbeat. In addition, the arteries become narrower and less flexible; accumulations of cholesterol collect on the artery walls, which are themselves growing thicker. The net effect is to clog the arteries, increasing the amount of resistance to the flow of blood from the heart. Thus, the cardiovascular system of older adults operates less efficiently; the heart must work harder to accomplish less. (See Figure 3.1; Lakatta, 1990.)

Figure 3.1
Average declines in bodily processes with increasing age.   Source: Modified from Weg (1983, p. 253).

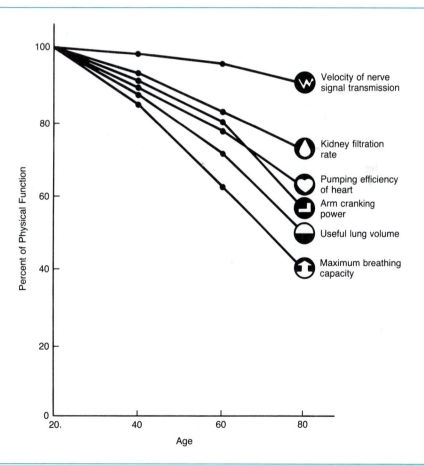

The rate of the heartbeat at rest remains about the same throughout adulthood, but there is a significant decline in the maximum heartbeat during exercise. At age 30, for example, there may be as many as 200 heartbeats per minute of intense activity. This maximum declines to about 170 heartbeats at age 50 and to 150 heartbeats at age 70. It also takes longer for the older heart to return to the resting rate.

Regular and appropriate exercise, as prescribed by one's personal physician, is generally regarded as an effective way to improve cardiovascular health. Exercise lowers the rate of the heart at rest, increases the efficiency of the heart and blood vessels, lowers hypertension (high blood pressure), and reduces the amount of cholesterol in the blood. There is no evidence that exercise will prevent a heart attack, but it can make a satisfactory recovery more likely (Lakatta, 1990; Weg, 1983).

The Brain.   At birth, the human brain consists of approximately *one trillion* neurons. These neurons are the basic building blocks of the brain.

Over the entire life span, the weight of the brain decreases by 5 to 10 percent, indicating that some neurons have been lost. The decline in weight occurs more quickly after age 50, amounting to approximately 2 percent per decade. Ultimately, this weight loss results in smoothed-out ridges and enlarged fissures (Horvath & Davis, 1990).

Other significant changes that occur in the aging brain may have serious consequences. First of all, damaged and dying neurons may collect around a core of protein substances in the brain. The number of these **neuritic plaques** increases with age, and is particularly large among adults age 90 and older. High concentrations of these plaques have been found in individuals suffering from Alzheimer's disease, one of the most destructive of all illnesses that afflict the elderly. (See Chapter 11.) This suggests that neuritic plaques may well interfere with the normal functioning of healthy neurons.

A second important change concerns threadlike structures found within the neurons of the brain. The number of these **neurofibrillary tangles** increases with age in selected areas of the brain, and their presence has also been associated with Alzheimer's disease and other serious disorders.

A less ominous change in the aging brain has to do with **lipofuscin**, a yellow pigment deposited in the neurons as we grow older. The amount of lipofuscin increases linearly with increasing age, but this does *not* appear to be related to serious brain disorders. (See Horvath & Davis, 1990.)

A fourth change involves important chemical substances, called **neurotransmitters**, which facilitate both communication among the neurons in the brain and the normal functioning of the body. One such neurotransmitter, *dopamine*, is responsible for controlling the motor movements of the body. *Acetylcholine* is involved in memory processes, and *norepinephrine* is linked to memory and learning as well as to the body's response to stress. All of these substances show a decline with increasing age. (See Morgan & May, 1990.) Although these declines are usually not substantial enough to affect normal functioning, large reductions in the neurotransmitters are clearly related to pathology. For example, the severe movement disorders of those who suffer from Parkinsonism is due to insufficient levels of dopamine in the brain. Furthermore, modest decreases in these neurotransmitters may be related to other illnesses.

The news about the aging brain is by no means all bad, however, because recent research suggests that the brain may be more flexible and adaptive than was previously believed (Cotman, 1990). Research carried out during the last decade has shown that the brain is capable of preserving, and even repairing, its own circuitry. For example, healthy neurons may grow new neuronal connections to replace ones that are defective or have been lost. At present, there is considerable research interest in identifying those factors that maintain the health of brain cells, stimulate their growth, and protect them against various metabolic insults (Cotman, 1990).

Lungs.   Aging typically brings a measurable decline in the efficiency of the pulmonary system. The muscles that operate the lungs weaken, and the tissues in the chest cage stiffen, reducing the ability of the lungs to expand. At age 30, for example, we can take a maximum of six quarts of air into the lungs. By age 50, this figure may well decline to about 4.5 quarts. And by age 70, the maximum possible air intake for many people is only three quarts.

These declines are not inevitable, however. Adults who maintain a high level of physical activity lose much less of their pulmonary efficiency than do sedentary persons. In fact, many elderly adults who are in excellent physical condition have a maximum oxygen consumption that equals or even exceeds that of younger, sedentary individuals (Fleg & Lakatta, 1988).

Stamina.   Because of the aforementioned changes in the heart, lungs, and muscles, our stamina declines as we grow older. There is less oxygen available to us, and the heart disperses it more slowly through the bloodstream to the muscles. A healthy 70-year-old can still run a marathon with proper training, but it will take him or her at least an hour longer than it would at age 30.

One index of stamina is to determine how many pounds can be turned with a weighted crank in one minute, yet still have the heartbeat return to normal after two minutes of rest. Using this measure, our stamina decreases by about 15 percent between ages 30 and 50 and by another 15 percent between ages 50 and 70. (See, for example, Shock & Norris, 1970.)

The age at which our athletic abilities reach their peak depends not only on physiological factors, but also on the type of activity. For athletic events that require strength, speed, and explosive power, such as swimming and running short distances, peak performance is typically achieved during the early twenties. For tasks that involve endurance, acquired skills, and knowledge (long-distance running, golf), peak performance is usually reached during the late twenties and early thirties. (See Table 3.2.)

Table 3.2
Age of peak performance by type of event.

Age	Men	Women
17		swimming
18		
19	swimming	
20		
21		
22		running short distance
23	running short distance	jumping
24	jumping running medium distance tennis	running medium distance tennis
25		
26		
27	running long distance	running long distance
28	baseball	
29		
30		
31	golf	golf
32		
33		
34		

Source: Schulz & Curnow (1988).

Bones and Joints.   As we grow through adulthood, years of flexing wear down and loosen the cartilage around the joints. Thus our movements tend to be stiffer and slower after age 50, and we are more likely to experience some degree of pain in the joints (Hazzard & Bierman, 1978).

Among middle-aged and older adults, particularly women, calcium losses may cause the bones to become more brittle and less flexible. Severe bone degeneration can lead to a disease called **osteoporosis**, which most often afflicts women after menopause. Osteoporosis is characterized by a loss of bone mass and increased porosity, which significantly increases the probability of bone fractures and makes recovery slower and more difficult. Although osteoporosis is an illness, rather than a normal consequence of aging, it bears mentioning here because it is so common; more than 20 million Americans are affected by this condition (Meier, 1988).

Diet and exercise may help to prevent osteoporosis. Increasing the daily intake of calcium has proved beneficial before menopause, but not afterwards. Adequate amounts of vitamin D are also important. For some women, an estrogen supplement may be advisable at the time of menopause. (See Meier, 1988.)

Reflexes and Reaction Time.   The speed of some simple reflexes, such as the knee-jerk reflex, remains relatively constant during adulthood (Hugin, Norris, & Shock, 1960). However, other reflexes deteriorate with increasing age. Deep tendon reflexes undergo a severe decline, so much so that ankle jerks are absent in approximately one-half of the elderly (Horvath & Davis, 1990).

Aging produces a significant decrease in our ability to react quickly to stimuli (such as a novel sound), especially after age 70 (Shock, 1974; 1985). This is due primarily to changes in the brain, which takes longer to process the information and to respond appropriately. Older adults therefore tend to perform more poorly on tasks that are highly speeded or more complex, an issue we discuss further in Chapter 5.

Digestion.   Digestion involves many body organs, including the esophagus, stomach, pancreas, gall bladder, liver, small intestine, and colon. As we grow older, the muscles of the digestive system act more slowly, and the production of acid is reduced. The ability to digest fat, protein, and carbohydrates may therefore decrease slightly among the elderly, but this usually does not lead to significant problems (Ausman & Russell, 1990). In fact, when digestive problems do occur, they are usually attributable to other causes. Older adults are more likely to require laxatives and sedatives, and these drugs tend to reduce the efficiency of the digestive system. A loss of appetite may also be caused by depression, a common form of adult psychopathology. (See Chapter 11.)

Excretion.   During the course of adulthood, each kidney loses approximately one-half of its nephrons (tubules). Because of this reduced reserve, the kidneys filter waste out of blood only one-half as fast at age 70 as at age 30. Another consequence is that stress is more likely to precipitate kidney failure in older adults.

The bladder loses some 50 percent of its capacity by old age, and it becomes less elastic. As a result, urinary elimination is more frequent, more urgent, and less complete among older adults. Constipation is more likely, however, due to slower peristalsis and increased absorption of water from the large intestine.

Afterword: Aging and Vulnerability to Disease.   The aforementioned physiological changes are part of the normal process of aging. Most of these changes are not troublesome in any practical sense. Some involve a certain amount of inconvenience or discomfort but are not incapacitating or fatal, such as stiffness in the joints or declines in muscle strength. Thus most older people deal quite well with these changes: Of the approximately 95 percent of adults over age 65 who are able to remain in their communities, the large majority (77 percent) suffer no significant limitations in their mobility and cope more than adequately with the challenges of everyday living (Brotman, 1980; Dawson, Hendershot, & Fulton, 1987; Weg, 1981). Insofar as normal aging is concerned, then, there is no empirical support for the stereotype of the physiologically incapacitated and helpless older adult. (See Figure 3.2.)

However, aging does have one ominous physiological aspect. Because of the reduced efficiency of most bodily systems, older adults are more vulnerable to disease than are young adults, and they are twice as likely to be physically disabled and to require hospitalization. Some age-related ailments can cause severe pain, such as arthritis. Others are fatal. Cardiovascular disease, cancer, and cerebrovascular accidents (strokes), the three leading causes of death in this country, have their greatest incidence among older persons. Therefore, to understand more fully the nature of age-related physiological changes, we must now consider the relationship between aging and pathology.

AGING AND PATHOLOGY

Major Causes of Death.   The probability of dying from cardiovascular disease, cancer, or a stroke increases dramatically as we grow past middle age. Among adults age 25 to 44, only about 1 of every 4,000 suffers a fatal heart attack. This figure increases to approximately 1 in 300 for those age 45 to 64,

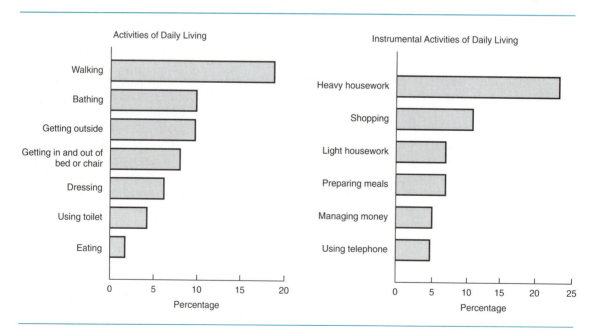

Figure 3.2
Percentage of noninstitutionalized adults age 65 and older who have difficulty with various daily activities.   Source: Brock, Guralnik, & Brody (1990).

Table 3.3
Leading causes of death in the United States as a function of age group (1978).

Cause	Death Rate at Age			
	25–44	45–64	65–74	75+
Heart disease	1 in 4,000	1 in 300	1 in 80	1 in 25
Cancer	1 in 3,500	1 in 325	1 in 125	1 in 75
Cerebrovascular disease (strokes)	negligible	1 in 2,000	1 in 400	1 in 80
Accidents	1 in 2,300	1 in 2,300	1 in 1,600	1 in 600

Note: Rates are based on the total number of adults in each age group. For example, 1 of every 25 adults age 75 and older dies from heart disease.
Source: Based on Sterns, Barrett, & Alexander (1985, pp. 706–707).

whereas about 1 of every 25 adults past age 75 dies from heart disease. Similar age-related increases are found in the mortality rates for cancer and strokes. (See Table 3.3.)

Cardiovascular disease, the leading cause of death in the United States, is defined as any problem of the heart or blood circulation. It is most often caused by a thickening and hardening of the arteries (atherosclerosis). As we grow older, some atherosclerosis is inevitable; it leads to cardiovascular disease only when it becomes so severe that the heart cannot get enough blood and oxygen to function normally. For example, a heart attack (myocardial infarction) occurs when part of the heart muscle dies because of an inadequate flow of blood. Chest pains (angina) are caused by an inadequate supply of blood and oxygen to the muscles of the heart. A stroke occurs when a blockage in the flow of blood and oxygen causes brain tissue to be destroyed (Kerson, 1985).

Each year, cardiovascular disease causes approximately one million deaths in the United States, or roughly one-half of all the deaths in this country. The next most frequent cause, cancer, is responsible for only about one-half as many deaths as cardiovascular disease. Thus, even if someone were to find a cure for cancer, the average life span would be extended by less than two years because heart disease is so prevalent. To be sure, there has been a substantial decline in the death rate from heart attacks since 1950, especially among older adults. (See Figure 3.3.) But the United States still has the greatest number of fatal heart attacks in the world; Japan has the fewest. (See Kerson, 1985; National Center for Health Statistics, 1986; Passamani, Frommer, & Levy, 1984.)

One reason why the frequency of fatal heart attacks has declined during the past two decades is the fact that we have become more knowledgeable. Research has shown that some of the most important causes are within our control, at least to some extent. These include cigarette smoking (which doubles the risk of a heart attack), high blood pressure, a high level of blood

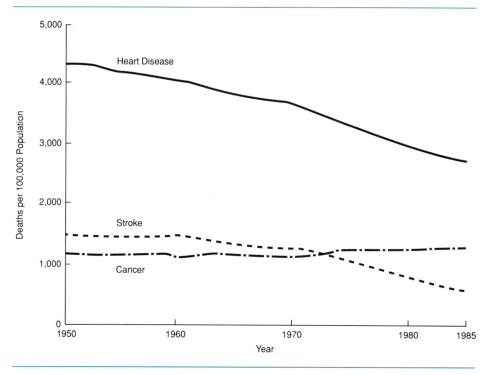

Figure 3.3
Leading causes of death for people age 75 to 84, 1950–1985. Sources: National Center for Health Statistics, *Health, United States, 1986.* Washington: Department of Health and Human Services (December 1986). National Center for Health Statistics, "Annual Summary of Births, Marriages, Divorces, and Deaths: United States, 1985," *Monthly Vital Statistics Report,* Vol. 34, No. 13 (September 1986).

cholesterol,[1] obesity, physical inactivity, and stress (American Heart Association, 1988). Some personality characteristics may also be related to heart disease, although this is more controversial. (See Chapter 7.)

Various demographic characteristics are also associated with a greater likelihood of cardiovascular disease. You are much more likely to suffer a heart attack if you are age 65 or older and if you are male. Heart disease is the leading cause of death among men age 40 and older, and one of every five men will develop coronary heart disease before reaching age 60. Conversely, it is only after age 60 that heart disease becomes the leading cause of death for women. Heart attacks are also more common among whites than among blacks. (See American Heart Association, 1988; Kerson, 1985.)

---

[1] More specifically, low-density lipoprotein cholesterol. The distinction between LDL cholesterol and HDL cholesterol is discussed later in this chapter.

All **cancers** share a common definition: They are an uncontrolled growth of abnormal cells, which spread to other parts of the body through the blood or lymphatic systems. There are five common types of cancer cells, each of which tends to form in a different part of the body and grow at a different rate. *Carcinoma* arises in the surface layer of the skin, glands, or linings of body organs. *Melanoma* is a specific form of carcinoma that lodges in the cells that produce our skin pigment. *Sarcoma* emerges in connective or supporting tissues, such as bones, cartilage, and fat. *Lymphoma* originates in the lymph nodes, and *leukemia* results in transformations of white blood cells.

Cancer is the second greatest cause of death in this country, accounting for approximately 3.5 million fatalities during the 1980s. One of every five Americans will experience cancer directly, and 75 percent will have a family member who contracts this illness (American Cancer Society, 1987; Forbair & Cordoba, 1982; Northouse, 1984). Although the number of cancer cases and resulting deaths has increased steadily during the past few decades, there is some good news: Today's cancer patients are more likely to survive for several years after the initial diagnosis than patients of 50 years ago. Mortality rates are declining for younger people and for certain types of cancer that were formerly considered incurable (Hodgkin's disease, childhood leukemia, ovarian and testicular tumors). Nevertheless, 60 percent of all cancer patients die within five years of diagnosis. (See American Cancer Society, 1987; Burish & Lyles, 1983; Kerson, 1985; Martin, 1982.)

Most cancer is detected in middle age or later; approximately two-thirds of those suffering from this disease are age 55 or older (Morra & Potts, 1980). Cancer is equally likely to strike men and women, although some types occur more often among members of one sex. There are, however, pronounced ethnic differences. During the past 30 years, the occurrence of cancer increased by 27 percent for blacks but only 12 percent for whites, whereas deaths from cancer increased by almost 50 percent for blacks but only 10 percent for whites (American Cancer Society, 1987).

Cancer is most often found in the lungs, colon or rectum, breast, and prostate. Lung cancer is the most common form, for women as well as men, and is the most frequent cause of death among the cancers. In theory, this variety should be the most easily preventable; cigarette smoking is linked to 83 percent of all lung cancer and to 30 percent of all deaths from cancer. One reason for the frequency of lung cancer fatalities is the fact that it stalks its victims silently: The symptoms typically become apparent only when the disease is in its advanced stages, making successful treatment less likely (American Cancer Society, 1987; Kerson, 1985).

Strokes are characterized by brain damage, and by the often severe disabilities that result. Strokes most often occur when a cerebral artery becomes occluded, blocking the flow of blood to the cerebral hemispheres; or when a blood vessel ruptures, producing a brain hemorrhage. The likelihood of a stroke increases sharply with increasing age, making this one of the most common illnesses afflicting older adults. Eighty percent of first-time stroke patients are age 65 and older, and the median age for a first stroke is 71 years for men and 74 years for women. Blacks are much more likely than whites to die of strokes, in part because they more often suffer from high blood pressure. In all, the annual number of strokes in this country ranges from 600,000 to 750,000. (See American Heart Association, 1988; Freese, 1980; Kerson, 1985; Robins & Baum, 1981; Rubenstein & Feldman, 1982; Weinfeld, 1981.)

The frequency of strokes in this country has declined steadily in recent years, and survival rates have increased. Although approximately 30 percent of stroke sufferers do not survive the first 30 days, many live for years. Survival, however, carries a price. Because strokes often cause severe physical, cognitive, and social disabilities, they are the third leading cause not only of death in older persons but also of chronic long-term disability. (See Baum & Robins, 1981; Biegel, Sales, & Schulz, 1991; Garraway, Whisnant, & Drury, 1983; Garraway et al., 1979; Soltero et al., 1978.)

Accidents.   From birth to age 44, you are more likely to die from an accident than from any other single cause. However, the odds against such an event are decidedly in your favor; the death rate due to accidents for this age group is only about 1 in 2,300.

Older adults have relatively low accident *rates*. For example, adults over age 65 suffer only about one-half as many accidents as do children age 6 to 16. But since the middle-aged and elderly have more brittle bones and less efficient bodily systems, the *consequences* of their accidents are more severe; healing is significantly slower, hospitalization is more often necessary, and death is more likely. Thus, for adults past age 75, the death rate due to accidents is approximately 1 in 600. Among adults age 65 to 74, motor vehicle accidents are the most common cause of accidental death (National Institute on Aging, 1989a; Sterns, Barrett, & Alexander, 1985).

Chronic Conditions.   **Chronic** conditions are characterized by a slow onset and a long duration. Although these disorders are rarely found among young adults, they account for the majority of disabilities after middle age. The most common are arthritis and hypertension.

Arthritis may take various forms: an inflammation of the joints (rheumatoid arthritis), degenerative joint disease (osteoarthritis), gout, connective tissue disease, and others. The primary symptom, pain in the joints, can be intense—so much so that arthritis is currently the major cause of limited activity among older adults. However, the severity of this disease varies greatly from person to person; one adult with arthritis may suffer only from occasional flare-ups, whereas another may be housebound. As many as 80 percent of all recently retired persons experience some degree of arthritis (Brock, Guralnik, & Brody, 1990; Kolodny & Klipper, 1978), whereas approximately 25 percent of adults age 45 to 64 and almost one-half of those 65 and older require treatment for this disorder. (See Figure 3.4.)

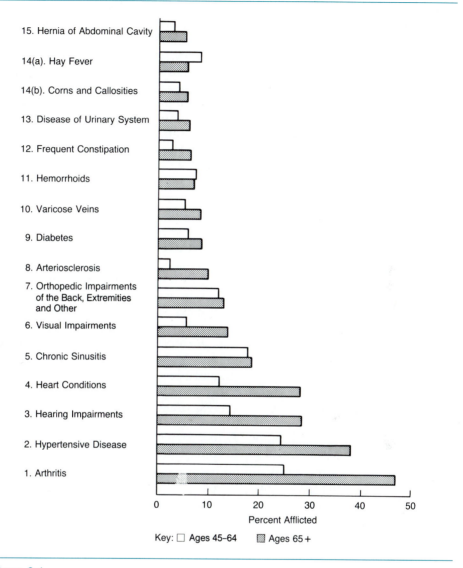

Figure 3.4
Most prevalent chronic conditions as a function of age. Source: U.S. Senate Special Committee on Aging (1987–1988).

The etiology of arthritis is still unclear, nor are there any known cures. Various forms of treatment may help to alleviate pain and to maintain the mobility and strength of the afflicted joints, including anti-inflammatory drugs (e.g., aspirin; cortisone derivatives), mild exercise, heat, and cold. (See Howell et al., 1976; Smythe, 1975.)

Hypertension involves a consistent pattern of elevated blood pressure. Among the probable causes are excessive weight, stress, and perhaps a high salt intake. In contrast to arthritis, hypertension does not produce noticeable pain. Yet it can have even more serious consequences because it increases the likelihood of strokes and coronary heart disease (Castelli, 1978; Robbins, 1978).

Hypertension is significantly higher in blacks than in whites, especially for women. According to one estimate, hypertension afflicts 39 percent of black women, 25 percent of white women, 38 percent of black men, and 33 percent of white men. As a result, blacks are much more likely than whites to die of strokes. (See American Heart Association, 1988; Kerson, 1985; National Institute on Aging, 1989f.)

Various prescription drugs are commonly used to control high blood pressure. Losing weight, eating less salt, and increasing relaxation may also be helpful (Harvard Medical School Newsletter, 1979; National Institute on Aging, 1989f).

The adverse effects of arthritis, hypertension, and other chronic conditions are more widespread than may be apparent. Family members who help to care for their loved one may experience considerable emotional pain (Biegel, Sales, & Schulz, 1991), and society must find ways to provide the professional care that these patients need. (We will have more to say about these issues in Chapter 9.) Furthermore, most chronic conditions affect the patient's sense of well-being, as well as the ability to function. For example, arthritis is not only extremely painful and often debilitating; it also causes a decline in the patient's mental health and perceived physical health. (See Table 3.4.) Thus, even though most chronic conditions are not life threatening, their consequences can be extremely serious.

Afterword: Aging, Actual Health, and Self-Perceived Health. Although physical helplessness and dependency are *not* characteristic of old age, certain painful chronic disorders are more likely (e.g., arthritis). As a result, adults past age 75 experience about twice as many days per year of restricted activity and bed disability as do those age 45 to 54. Also, the probability of suffering a fatal illness or accident is much greater after middle age.

Nevertheless, the majority of older Americans assess their health favorably. As of 1986, some 75 percent of adults age 55 to 64 and 70 percent of those over 65 described their health as good or excellent in comparison to others of their own age. These percentages are only somewhat smaller than the corresponding figures for younger adults: Approximately 82 percent of the middle-aged (age 45–54) and 92 percent of young adults (age 25–34) rate their health as good or excellent (United States Senate Special Committee on Aging, 1983; 1987).

Personal health status is a function of both actual and self-perceived health. Adults who believe themselves to be physically healthy are more

Table 3.4

Effects of chronic conditions on functional status and well-being.

Chronic Condition	Functioning			Mental Health	Perceived Health	Bodily Pain
	Physical	Role	Social			
Angina	X	X	X	X	X	X
Arthritis	X	X	X	X	X	X
Back problems	X	X	0	0	X	X
Diabetes	X	X	X	0	X	0
Gastrointestinal disorders	X	X	X	X	X	X
Hypertension	0	0	0	0	X	X
Myocardial infarction	X	X	X	0	X	0

Key: 0: No significant difference between patients with chronic condition and adults with no chronic conditions.
X: Patients suffering from chronic condition report significant negative effects compared with adults with no chronic conditions.
Source: Adapted from Stewart et al. (1989), *JAMA; 262* (7): 907–913. © 1989, American Medical Association.

likely to be active and independent, whereas those who regard their health as poor tend to behave accordingly and even die sooner (Idler, Kasl, & Lemke, 1990; Idler & Angel, 1990). To be sure, the generally positive self-perceptions of older adults may well be due in part to more pessimistic expectations. It is well known that illness and disability are more common after middle age, so older adults may regard some degree of pain and inconvenience as normal for their age. Even so, we may conclude our discussion of aging and pathology on an optimistic note: Despite the greater likelihood of certain chronic disorders and potentially fatal illnesses, the substantial majority of older adults do *not* regard themselves as in poor health or as seriously disabled.

Theories of Aging

The physiological changes discussed in the preceding pages have been affecting humankind for thousands of years. Nevertheless, the underlying reasons for these changes remain a source of controversy; scientists still do not know *why* we age. Various biological theories of aging have been proposed, some of which appear to be quite promising. However, no one theory has as yet achieved general acceptance.

GENETIC CELLULAR THEORIES

The maximum life span varies greatly among different species. As we observed in Chapter 1, the greatest recorded human age is 120 years. In contrast, the maximum life span for horses is 46 years; cats, 28 years; dogs, 20 years; black rats, 5 years; and the mayfly, only one day. (See Table 3.5; Comfort, 1964; Kirkwood, 1985.) Furthermore, humans with long-lived parents and grandparents live an average of six years longer than those whose parents die before the age of 50 (Dublin, Lotka, & Spiegelman, 1949). It has also been observed that human body cells grown in tissue cultures (in vitro) are able to divide only about 50 times, after which they age and die

Table 3.5
Maximum recorded life spans for various species.

Common Name	Maximum Life Span (Years)
Human	120
Galapagos tortoise	100+
Indian elephant	70
Eagle owl	68
Snapping turtle	58+
Chinese alligator	52
Horse	46
Golden eagle	46
Chimpanzee	44
Gorilla	39
Brown bear	36
Common toad	36
Domestic dove	30
Anaconda	29
Domestic cat	28
Swine	27
Porcupine	27
Domestic dog	20
Sheep	20
Gray squirrel	15
Vampire bat	13
Black rat	5
House mouse	3

Source: Modified from Kirkwood (1985, p. 34).

(Hayflick, 1965; 1973; 1980; 1986). The reproductive capacity of cells taken from old animals is even more limited; these cells can undergo only about one-half as many divisions as those obtained from young animals.

Findings such as these imply that cellular aging is caused by some process within the cell itself, rather than by the lack of environmental requirements. That is, some kind of clock mechanism exists in normal cells, and this mechanism controls the capacity of the cells to function and to replicate (Hayflick, 1986). Since there is a direct relationship between the life span of a species and the capacity of its cells to divide, this suggests in turn that age-related changes are programmed into the genes of each species. Thus, **genetic cellular theories** attribute aging to changes in two complicated kinds of molecules: **deoxyribonucleic acid (DNA)**, which controls the formation of proteins required by the cell to maintain life (Watson, 1969); and **ribonucleic acid (RNA)**, which transfers information from the DNA molecules to another location in the cell where the proteins are assembled.

DNA Damage Theories. Some genetic cellular theories posit that damage to the DNA molecules is responsible for human aging. This damage may be caused by exposure to radiation, or it may consist of harmful cellular mutations (e.g., Curtis, 1966; Szilard, 1959).

Although some early studies appeared to support DNA damage theory, more recent research has unearthed some important contradictions. Mutations and radiation affect dividing cells, whereas the physiological effects of aging are due primarily to cells that are no longer able to divide. Mutations occur too slowly to account for the pronounced physiological changes that occur with increasing age. Furthermore, in marked contrast to aging, damage to the DNA molecules is usually reversible because most cells contain appropriate repair mechanisms. (See Martin, 1977; Tice & Setlow, 1985; Wheeler & Lett, 1974.) For these reasons, it is extremely doubtful that damage to the DNA molecule itself plays much of a role in aging (Shock, 1977).

Error Theories. An alternative model focuses on the transmission of genetic information from the DNA molecules to the place where proteins are assembled (ribosome). This transfer is accomplished with the aid of the RNA molecules. Errors are more likely insofar as the RNA molecules are concerned because these molecules are relatively unstable and are formed continuously, whereas DNA molecules are highly stable and are maintained throughout the life span of a cell. According to this model, errors in transmission produce a protein or enzyme that is *not* an exact copy of the original and which therefore cannot carry out its function of maintaining life. As a result, the cells grow older and die, and so do we. (See Martin, 1977; Medvedev, 1964; Reff, 1985.)

To date, error theorists have not been able to specify the precise nature of the hypothesized errors in transmission. In fact, the details of the transfer process itself have not yet been clearly identified. Although the error hypothesis is a promising one, it remains a source of active controversy and research (Meier, 1984).

NONGENETIC CELLULAR THEORIES

Some researchers argue that in vitro experiments with culture tissue are not applicable to aging as it occurs in living tissue (in vivo) and that the concept of an innate biological clock is therefore incorrect. Instead, these theorists contend that aging involves a gradual deterioration of bodily cells that is *not* internally programmed. Consider an automobile that ages over a period of years: The engine becomes less efficient, the battery dies, rust invades the exterior, and so on. These changes are more or less predictable but do not follow any specific timetable, internal or otherwise. Rather, wear and tear plays a major role: A car sheltered in a garage and rarely driven will last far longer than one driven 20,000 miles per year and parked in the street.

Unlike machines, the human body has mechanisms for self-repair. New cells are continually formed to replace old ones, and molecules may undergo replacement within a single cell. Nevertheless, various factors might conceivably cause cells to wear out faster than the repairs can take place. Thus, **nongenetic cellular theories** assume that with the passage of time, changes occur in the cells that impair their effectiveness. That is, aging is due to progressive damage to the organism from its internal and external environment.

Accumulation Theories.

According to some theorists, aging is caused by the accumulation of various harmful substances in the cells of the organism. All older cells contain a dark-colored, insoluble substance (lipofuscin), with the amount of this material increasing at a constant rate over time. (See Carpenter, 1965; Naeim & Walford, 1985; Strehler, 1978.) It is logical to assume that this "cellular garbage" interferes with cellular functioning, because it takes up space and serves no useful purpose and that it might even ultimately result in the death of the cell. But although this hypothesis is a tenable one, there is as yet no conclusive evidence in its favor (Rowlatt & Franks, 1978).

Cross-Linkage Theories.

A second possibility is that with the passage of time, harmful cross-linkages (bonds) develop between component parts of the same molecule or between two different molecules. Extracellular proteins (e.g., collagen) develop an increasing number of cross-linkages with increasing age, and collagen is related to the aging of the skin (as we have seen). This model posits that cross-linkages ultimately lead to severe oxygen deficiency and to other biochemical failures (Verzar, 1963; Bjorksten, 1968). However, the available empirical evidence concerning cross-linkages and aging is also inconclusive (Harman, 1981; Schofield & Davies, 1978).

Free Radical Theory.   A third nongenetic cellular theory attributes aging to the operation of "free radicals," or unstable chemical compounds that tend to react quickly with other molecules in their vicinity. These reactions are assumed to affect the structure and function of bodily enzymes and proteins, notably those proteins that are essential to the life of the cell. (See Harman, 1968; 1981; Scoggins, 1981.) However, experimental tests of free radical theory have not led to any definitive conclusions (Shock, 1977; Meier, 1984).

PHYSIOLOGICAL THEORIES

A third group of theories attributes aging to the failure of certain physiological systems, and to the resulting inability of these systems to coordinate important bodily functions. According to this model, a particular organ or system of the body is primarily responsible for repairing cells that can no longer reproduce themselves. When such "hot spot" organs wear out, cells can no longer be replaced, and the organism dies (Latham & Johnson, 1979).

Immunological Theories.   The immune system protects the body against invading microorganisms and against atypical mutant cells that may form within the body (e.g., cancer). It does so in two ways: by generating antibodies that react with the proteins of foreign organisms, and by forming special cells that engulf and digest the foreign cells.

Aging has a pronounced negative effect on the capabilities of the immune system. The production of antibodies peaks during adolescence and declines thereafter (Makinodan, 1974), and the ability to recognize mutated cells also declines with increasing age. Thus the increase in cancer rates among older adults, discussed previously, may well be due to failures of the immune system. In fact, some theorists define aging as a disease of the immune system. For example, one interesting hypothesis relates aging to the development of antibodies that act against normal and necessary bodily cells. (See Goodwin, 1981; Harrison, 1985; Walford, 1969; 1974; Weksler, 1981.) Although there is as yet little evidence that malfunctions of the immune system cause aging, this hypothesis is a viable one that deserves more widespread experimental testing.

Neuroendocrine Theories.   The neuroendocrine system is a complicated interactive system that includes a number of glands (e.g., pituitary, thyroid, pancreas, adrenal, ovaries, and testes) and the hypothalamus. Its function is to regulate various important bodily processes, such as metabolic rate, glucose and water level, and temperature.

The functioning of the endocrine system declines significantly with increasing age. For example, when blood sugar rises, the pancreas of older adults does not release sufficient insulin as quickly. (See Silverstone et al., 1957; Finch & Landfield, 1985.) This is one reason why diabetes is so prevalent among the middle-aged and elderly (see Figure 3.4). However, whether aging is actually caused by endocrine changes is not yet known.

AFTERWORD

Do we possess a built-in biological clock that governs the rate of aging and perhaps even the time of our death? Or do our cells undergo a gradual breakdown over time that is *not* genetically programmed, with aging due primarily to cellular wear and tear? Or is aging caused by the failure of certain physiological coordinating systems, such as the immune or endocrine systems?

As the preceding survey indicates, we do not yet know the answers to these questions. The theories we discussed represent only a sampling of those that have received research attention during the last few decades. Conceivably, there may be some truth in all of them. Because each one of these theories focuses on a different aspect of the aging process, they are not necessarily incompatible. Or we might find that some of these theories ultimately make a significant contribution to our understanding of aging, while others fall by the wayside as further empirical evidence is collected. Research into the causes of aging is still at an early stage, hence the large number of competing theories. But interest in this area is flourishing, so we may reasonably expect more conclusive findings to emerge in the not too distant future.

Lengthening Life

The quest for perpetual youth is as old as recorded history. People of various eras have tried to reverse the process of aging with magic, potions, sorcery, rituals, unusual diets, vitamins, and chemicals of various kinds.

Many of these procedures appear ludicrous by modern standards. The ancient Babylonians and Australian aborigines sought to prolong life by administering semen potions, or aphrodisiacs made from tigers' testes, to the feeble or dying. When the biblical King David was old and ill, his doctors prescribed close contact with a young female virgin, trusting that this would enable him to absorb her youth. The Taoists of 300 B.C. believed that men could achieve greater longevity by failing to reach sexual climax, thereby preserving their life essence, or semen. And the sixteenth-century explorer Ponce de Leon heard tales of a fountain in the Bahamas whose waters rejuvenated the aged, and he set out to find it. Navigation techniques not being very advanced in those days, he never did locate the fountain of youth. Instead, he accidentally discovered Florida, which ironically is now a major retirement area for the elderly. (See Segerberg, 1974; Trimmer, 1970.)

Despite centuries of efforts like these, there are as yet *no* scientifically accepted elixirs, drugs, or dietary supplements that will extend the length of

---

Myths About Aging

Physiological Aspects

Myth	*Best Available Evidence*
Our physiological processes remain at a fairly constant level of efficiency until we approach old age, at which time they undergo a drastic decline.	Most of our bodily functions reach their maximum capacity prior to or during early adulthood and begin a gradual decline thereafter.
Most adults proceed at much the same rate through a series of similar physiological stages.	Age-related physiological changes do *not* occur according to a strict timetable. Adults age at different rates, and such groupings as "the elderly" are more heterogeneous than is commonly believed.
Most adults past age 65 are so physiologically incapacitated that they must depend to a great extent on other people.	Helplessness and dependency are *not* characteristic of old age. Some 87 percent of adults over 65 are able to cope more than adequately with the demands of everyday living.
Taking large doses of antioxidants (or ginseng, or selenium, or pantothenic acid, or vitamin C) will extend the length of your life.	There are *no* drugs, pills, powders, vitamins, dietary supplements, or diets with proven antiaging capacities.

---

human life. There *are* ways to improve your chances of staying healthy and living longer, but these methods involve the more difficult course of changing your behavior.

MODERN QUESTS FOR THE FOUNTAIN OF YOUTH

People today are of course much more realistic about the possibility of lengthening human life—or are we? According to a recent investigation by the Select Committee on Aging of the House of Representatives, Americans spend more than *$2 billion per year* on unproven antiaging remedies (Meister, 1984). Some of these popular prescriptions are based on misrepresentations or overgeneralizations of gerontological research findings; others are pure quackery.

Antiaging Health Frauds

"Moon dust," promoted as a cure for arthritis and other afflictions, cost $100 for three ounces—and turned out to be just plain sand. The "miracle spike," a tube containing about a penny's worth of barium chloride (a chemical used in rat poison), was supposed to be worn around the neck as a cure for cancer and diabetes. It cost $300. The "Congo Kit," billed as a cure for arthritis, was actually two hemp mittens.

These are just three of several hundred worthless, unproven, and sometimes harmful products uncovered by a House subcommittee during a four-year investigation of quackery completed [in 1984]. . . . "We found the inventiveness of the quacks to be as unlimited as their callousness and greed," said Rep. Claude Pepper (D-Fla.), chairman of the House Aging subcommittee on health and long-term care. "We found promoters who advised arthritics to bury themselves in the earth, sit in an abandoned mine, or stand naked under a 1,000-watt bulb during the full moon. These suffering souls have been wrapped in manure, soaked in mud, injected with snake venom, sprayed with WD-40, bathed in kerosene. . . . [There is] a tremendous amount of money to be made in selling hope to the desperate." (*The Washington Post*, July 18, 1985, p. 1.)

Not all antiaging treatments are as bizarre as these examples. In this section, we will discuss some of the more plausible approaches.

Gerovital.   One purported antiaging drug, Gerovital (GH3), has been in use for more than 30 years. Its main ingredient is procaine hydrochloride, best known to Americans as the local anesthetic Novocain. Thousands of people believe in Gerovital and buy it where they can—England, Mexico, Jamaica, and other islands of the Caribbean. (Nevada is the only American state that has approved the clinical use of Gerovital.) Yet there is no reliable empirical evidence that Gerovital has any antiaging properties, although it does appear to be useful as a mild antidepressant (Schneider & Reed, 1985; Weg, 1983).

Antioxidants.   Some advertisements and popular best-sellers contend that life can be extended by taking large doses of **antioxidants**, compounds that block much of the damage to bodily proteins caused by free radicals. Although some laboratory experiments have obtained significant positive results with specially bred mice, there is as yet no convincing evidence that antioxidants will extend human life.

As we have seen, free radical theory remains controversial. Even if this theory is correct, the body's need for antioxidants can be met simply by eating a variety of nutritious foods, and there is no indication that surplus amounts will do a better job of fighting free radicals. Some antioxidant supplements are actually useless because they are digested before body cells can use them (e.g., superoxide dismutase, or SOD), and large doses of certain other antioxidants can be harmful (National Institute on Aging, 1984; 1989c; 1989d).

DNA and RNA.   Some proponents of DNA damage theory argue that supplements containing DNA and RNA will slow aging, cure senility, and treat skin and hair changes. Here again, there is no scientific evidence to support these claims (National Institute on Aging, 1984; 1989c). In fact, as we have seen, DNA damage is no longer regarded as a likely cause of aging.

Other Dietary Supplements.   Various other dietary supplements have been promoted as antiaging remedies. These include selenium, ginseng, para-aminobenzoic acid (PABA), pantothenic acid, and vitamins C and E.

Although selenium is an essential nutrient, there is no evidence that it reverses or retards the aging process, and excess amounts are toxic. Ginseng is notorious as an aphrodisiac and rejuvenator, yet there are no convincing empirical data to support these claims. Large doses of ginseng may well produce such side effects as nervousness, insomnia, gastrointestinal disorders, and elevated blood pressure. Huge doses of PABA do appear to darken gray hair, but also tend to cause nausea, vomiting, and blood disorders. Pantothenic acid is a component of Royal Jelly, the substance that turns female bees into long-lived fertile queens instead of short-lived sterile workers. This useful vitamin is present in so many foods that deficiencies are virtually impossible, making supplemental doses unnecessary. Nor is there scientific reason to believe that dietary supplements of vitamin C, or of any other vitamin, have any effects on the aging process (National Institute on Aging, 1989d).

Restricted Diets.   Yet another proposed method for extending life is to eat fewer calories while maintaining a nutritionally sound diet ("undernutrition without malnutrition"). Unlike other diets, this regimen is *not* discontinued when the dieter achieves the weight generally accepted as ideal, but is continued indefinitely.

Insofar as laboratory animals are concerned, the preponderance of research evidence does support this hypothesis. In some studies, rats and mice were fed a diet that was nutritionally adequate but severely restricted in calories. Although the growth of these animals suffered considerably, they had much longer average and maximum life spans than did control animals who were allowed to eat all they wanted. Milder caloric restrictions, begun early in life, have been found to produce moderate life extension with only slight reductions in growth. At present, however, there is no evidence that restricted diets will inhibit aging in humans. In fact, it would seem that the heaviest and thinnest members of a given cohort have the shortest survival rates and that those slightly over their ideal body weight live the longest. (See Schneider & Reed, 1985.)

Afterword.   The vast sums of money spent on purported antiaging remedies attest to the desperation with which some people regard the prospect of aging and death. At present, there are no liquids, pills, powders, or any other substances with proven antiaging capacities. There are some valid steps that can be taken to help ensure a longer life, however, as we will see in the following section.

LIFE-LENGTHENING BEHAVIORS

Psychological and social factors are now almost universally recognized as important determinants of human longevity. These include stress, personality variables, marital status, social relationships, and such psychological disorders as depression. These issues will be discussed in the chapters dealing with stress, interpersonal relationships, and adult psychopathology. Insofar as physiological factors are concerned, empirical evidence indicates that your chances of remaining healthy and living longer depend to a considerable extent on your own behavior.

Not Smoking. Smoking has been clearly related to oral and lung cancer, other pulmonary diseases, and cardiovascular disease. Conversely, ceasing or reducing the amount of smoking decreases the likelihood of premature death (e.g., Smith, Bierman, & Robinson, 1978; U. S. Public Health Service, 1988). Quitting smoking is desirable even for older adults: When a person stops smoking, benefits to the heart and circulatory system begin immediately, and the risk of heart attacks, strokes, and other circulatory diseases starts to decline (National Institute on Aging, 1989g). Quitting smoking will not reverse chronic lung damage, but it may slow this disease and help to prevent any further decline.

Recent evidence has shown that nonsmokers who breathe the smoke of others are more likely to develop smoking-related diseases, such as lung cancer and heart disease (Garland et al., 1985). For this reason, many organizations are restricting or eliminating the right to smoke (e.g., airlines and restaurants). In addition, there is increasing evidence that smoke in the home is a health hazard for babies and young children, as well as for those who suffer from asthma or heart disease (National Institute on Aging, 1989g).

Diet. Eating a balanced diet and maintaining a desirable weight will also increase your longevity. Obesity is related to diabetes, osteoarthritis, cardiovascular disease, and hypertension, and the effects of stress are greater among individuals who suffer from nutritional deficiencies. (See National Institute on Aging, 1989d; Weg, 1983.) Food and vitamins are *not* elixirs of youth, but appropriate nutrition will help to reduce the likelihood of harmful and fatal illnesses.

Exercise. Appropriate regular exercise helps to maintain cardiovascular health, strong muscles, and flexible joints, and to reduce hypertension and the amount of body fat. It may also enhance cognitive and motor performance. Conversely, the absence of even minimal exercise is related to reduced cardiovascular efficiency, a loss of bone calcium, and gastrointestinal problems. (See National Institute on Aging, 1989e; Spirduso & MacRae, 1990.)

Some skeptics contend that the beneficial effects of exercise are overrated. They point out that noted jogging authorities have suffered fatal heart attacks while engaging in their favorite sport (e.g., James Fixx). In laboratory studies with rats, however, both average and maximum life spans have increased significantly when exercise was begun early in life. (See Schneider & Reed, 1985.)

Conducting appropriately controlled research with human subjects is more difficult. Suppose that we compare one group of adults who exercise regularly with a second group of adults who do not exercise at all, and we find that the first group has a significantly longer life span. This does not necessarily mean that exercise improves longevity. Those adults who exercise frequently may have been healthier in the first place; they may have opted for more physical activity because they had an unusually high degree of vitality and energy. Similarly, those who avoid exercise may do so because they are less healthy and have less energy to expend.

In an attempt to resolve such problems, investigators at the Stanford University School of Medicine undertook what may well be the most comprehensive study ever to relate exercise and longevity. They traced the health and life styles of some 17,000 Harvard graduates, age 35 to 74, from the mid-1960s until 1978. The findings indicated that regular exercise lengthens human life by about one to two years on the average, although the amount of exercise required may well be considerable. For example, those ambitious enough to walk more than 35 miles per week reduced their risk of death by almost 50 percent. In contrast, the reduction in death rate was 11 percent for those who walked five miles or less. In general, the optimum expenditure of energy appeared to be about 3,500 calories per week, or the equivalent of six to eight hours of strenuous bicycling or singles tennis. Regimens that burned up more than 3,500 calories tended to cause injuries that negated most of the benefits derived from the exercise. (See *Newsweek*, March 17, 1986; *Time*, March 17, 1986.)

Low LDL Cholesterol.   **Cholesterol**, a fatty substance found in many parts of the body, is essential to our physical health. However, an excess of cholesterol may be deposited in the walls of the arteries over time, eventually clogging the arteries and impairing blood circulation. High levels of blood cholesterol therefore increase the risk of a heart attack. Technically, this cholesterol is known as *low-density lipoprotein (LDL) cholesterol*; it is what we try to reduce when we avoid foods that are "high in cholesterol" (e.g., liver, eggs, beef, chicken eaten with its skin).

Interestingly, there is a second, beneficial type of cholesterol. Higher amounts of *high-density lipoprotein (HDL) cholesterol* in the body have been associated with a *lower* likelihood of a heart attack, presumably because HDL carries cholesterol away from the arteries and to the liver for elimination (Assmann & Schulte, 1986; Frick et al., 1987). Conversely, *low* levels of HDL cholesterol are common among heart attack victims. Ways to increase the amount of this "good" cholesterol in the body include exercise (brisk walking, jogging, swimming, biking), a proper diet that avoids foods high in saturated fat (such as palm or coconut oil), and avoidance of smoking.

Other Factors.   Those who have regular health checkups tend to live longer; even serious illnesses can often be readily treated if caught in the early stages. The use of seat belts when riding in an automobile is also recommended by most authorities. Although there are occasional cases where seat belts have proved disadvantageous in an accident, the odds are much greater that they will help to avoid serious injury and even death. Alcoholic beverages should be used in moderation if at all, and should never be used when driving. The effects of alcohol on the brain change with increasing age, so a single drink will impair the cognitive functioning of an older adult more than it will a young person. Sufficient time for sleep, rest, and relaxation is also conducive to longer life. (See National Institute on Aging, 1984; 1989b; Scott & Mitchell, 1988.)

Afterword. These recommendations may seem trite or even sermonic. But they are effective, whereas the same cannot be said of the various antiaging remedies currently being sold on the open market. However, considerably more effort is required: Rather than merely consuming some magical antiaging substance, you must engage in and/or change various important behaviors.

How long will *you* live? Even if we omit the possibility of accidents, there is no scientific way to answer this question with any great degree of accuracy. However, some of the more important physiological, psychological, and social contributors to longevity have been incorporated into the questionnaire shown in Table 3.6. By answering these questions, you can obtain a *very approximate* guide to your personal longevity. More importantly, this questionnaire will help to improve your understanding of the factors that play a significant role in lengthening human life.

Table 3.6
Estimating your personal longevity.

1. Basic Life Expectancy.
If you were born in 1970, your basic life expectancy is 67 years if you are male and 75 years if you are female. Write down your basic life expectancy in the space at the right. (If you were born considerably before or after 1970 and wish to enter a more precise estimate, consult Table 1.2, Chapter 1, under the heading "Life Expectancy at Birth.")   _____

For each item that follows, decide how it applies to you and add or subtract the appropriate number of years from your basic life expectancy.

2. Current Longevity.
   A. If you are now in your fifties or sixties, add 10 years, since you have already proven yourself to be quite durable.   _____
   B. If you are now over age 60 and active, add another two years.   _____

3. Family History.
   A. If two or more of your grandparents lived to age 80 or beyond, add five years.   _____
   B. If any parent, grandparent, sister, or brother died of a heart attack or stroke before age 50, subtract four years. If instead any one of these relatives died from these diseases prior to age 60, subtract only two years.   _____
   C. Subtract three years of each case of diabetes, thyroid disorders, breast cancer, cancer of the digestive system, asthma, or chronic bronchitis among your parents or grandparents.   _____

   4. **Marital Status.**
      A. If you are married, add four years.   _____
      B. If you are over 25 and not married, subtract one year for every unwedded decade.   _____

   5. **Economic Status.**
      A. Subtract two years if your family income is over $40,000 per year.   _____
      B. Subtract three years if you have been poor for the greater part of your life.   _____

   6. **Physique.**
      A Subtract one year for every ten pounds you are overweight.   _____
      B. For each inch that your waist measurement exceeds your chest measurement,
         deduct two years.   _____
      C. If you are over 40 and *not* overweight, add three years.   _____

   7. **Exercise.**
      A. If your exercise is regular and moderate (e.g., jogging three times a week), add
         three years. But if your exercise is regular and vigorous (e.g., long-distance running
         three times a week), add five years instead of three years.   _____
      B. If your job is sedentary, subtract three years. But if it is active, add three years.   _____

   8. **Alcohol.**
      A. If you are a light drinker (one to three drinks a day), add two years. If instead you
         are a teetotaler, subtract one year. And if instead you are a heavy drinker (more
         than four drinks per day), subtract seven-and-a-half years.   _____

   9. **Smoking.**
      A. If you smoke cigarettes: less than one pack per day, subtract two years; one to two
         packs per day, subtract four years; two or more packs per day, subtract eight
         years.   _____
      B. Subtract two years if you regularly smoke a pipe or cigars.   _____

  10. **Disposition.**
      A. Add two years if you are a reasoned, practical person.   _____
      B. Subtract two years if you are aggressive, intense, and competitive.   _____
      C. Add three years if you are basically happy and content with life. If instead you are
         often unhappy, worried, and plagued by feelings of guilt, subtract three years.   _____

  11. **Education.**
      A. If you failed to complete high school, subtract two years. If instead you had four
         additional years of school after high school, add one year.   _____
      B. For a fifth year of school after high school, add two more years.   _____

  12. **Environment.**
      A. If you have lived most of your life in a rural environment, add four years. But if
         you have lived most of your life in an urban environment, subtract two years.   _____

  13. **Sleep.**
      A. If you typically sleep more than nine hours per night, subtract five years.   _____

  14. **Temperature.**
      A. If the thermostat in your home is set no higher than 68°F, add two years.   _____

  15. **Health Care.**
      A. If you have regular medical and dental checkups, add three years.   _____
      B. If you are frequently ill, subtract two years.   _____

The final figure entered above is the estimate of your personal longevity. Please note that
this is only a rough approximation. Although this questionnaire is based on factors known
to be correlated with longevity, these correlations are far from perfect, and the number of
years lived by any one individual may differ significantly from the estimated longevity.

Source: Schulz (1978, pp. 97–98).

Summary

AGE-RELATED PHYSIOLOGICAL CHANGES

Age-related physiological changes do not occur according to a strict time-table. Adults age at different rates, and such groupings as "the middle-aged" and "the elderly" are actually rather heterogeneous with regard to their physiological characteristics and capacities. Nevertheless, some important general trends can be identified.

The process of aging leaves clearly visible traces. Lines form in the forehead and elsewhere in the face. The skin becomes stiffer, less elastic, more spread out, and eventually loses its uniformity of color. Cranial hair becomes thinner and more gray or white. Height decreases by an inch or two, due primarily to years of coping with the effects of gravity. Weight increases from young adulthood to middle age, but tends to decline somewhat thereafter. Women's breasts sag. These changes are primarily cosmetic; they have no direct effect on our vigor, daily functioning, or health.

With increasing age, muscle tissue slowly declines in strength, tone, and flexibility. The cardiovascular, pulmonary, and excretory systems become less efficient. Our stamina decreases. The joints become more brittle and less flexible. Our ability to react quickly to stimuli declines significantly. These changes may cause some inconvenience or discomfort, but they are *not* incapacitating. The vast majority of older adults remain in their communities, suffer no significant limitations on their mobility, and cope more than adequately with the challenges of everyday living.

Aging does have one ominous physiological aspect: Because of the reduced efficiency of most bodily systems, older adults are more vulnerable to chronic disorders, diseases, and fatal illnesses and accidents. The most common chronic disorder is arthritis, which may take various forms. The primary symptom, pain in the joints, varies from mild to debilitating. A second major chronic disorder, hypertension, involves a consistent pattern of elevated blood pressure. Hypertension increases the likelihood of strokes and coronary heart disease. Older adults have relatively low accident rates, but the consequences of their accidents tend to be more severe. The probability of dying from cardiovascular disease, cancer, or a stroke increases dramatically after middle age. Despite these age-related problems, the majority of older Americans assess their health favorably.

THEORIES OF AGING

Although age-related physiological changes have been affecting humankind for thousands of years, scientists still do not know *why* we age. Various biological theories of aging have been proposed, no one of which has as yet achieved general acceptance.

Genetic cellular theories posit that age-related changes are programmed into the genetic structure of each species, much like a built-in biological clock. Some researchers contend that aging is caused by damage to DNA molecules, which control the formation of essential bodily proteins. Other theories focus on errors in the transmission of genetic information from the DNA molecules to the place where proteins are assembled, which is accomplished with the aid of RNA molecules.

Nongenetic cellular theorists reject the concept of an innate biological clock. Instead, they contend that aging is due to progressive cell damage from the internal and external environment (wear and tear). Such damage has been attributed to the accumulation of waste materials within the cells, to the formation of harmful cross-linkages between parts of the same molecule or between two different molecules, and to the operation of protein-destroying chemical compounds (free radicals).

According to a third group of theories, aging is caused by the failure of certain physiological systems to coordinate important bodily functions. Some researchers define aging as a disease of the immune system, which protects the body against harmful microorganisms and mutant cells. Other theorists relate aging to changes in the endocrine system.

At present, the available empirical evidence does not strongly support any of the aforementioned theories of aging. Research into the causes of aging is still at an early stage, but the great interest in this area suggests that more conclusive findings may well emerge in the not too distant future.

LENGTHENING LIFE

The quest for perpetual youth is as old as recorded history. People in ancient times tried to reverse or retard the aging process by resorting to magic, rituals, and potions; today, people spend billions of dollars on unproven antiaging treatments and dietary supplements. Despite centuries of effort (and some claims to the contrary), there are as yet *no* scientifically accepted drugs, liquids, pills, powders, chemicals, or vitamins that will extend human life. Empirical evidence does indicate that you can stay healthy and live longer by not smoking and avoiding the smoke of others, eating a balanced diet and maintaining a desirable weight, obtaining appropriate regular exercise, having regular health checkups, using seat belts when riding in an automobile, using alcoholic beverages in moderation if at all (and never when driving), and allowing sufficient time for sleep, rest, and relaxation.

Study Questions

1. "Societal attitudes toward aging and the aged have helped to create the fearsome image of old age that can be likened to punishment." To

which observable external changes does this statement refer? How debilitating to the individual are these changes? What changes in societal attitudes toward aging would you recommend? Do movies and television programs generally encourage or discourage positive societal attitudes toward aging?

2. Based on current research, at about what age is a person most likely to develop cardiovascular disease such as hypertension? Cancer? Arthritis? When is a person most likely to have a stroke? What does this imply about how the increasing number of older adults will affect (a) the health care professions; (b) society in general?

3. You decide to write a science fiction story in which someone finally discovers why human beings grow older, and then the character develops a method to retard the aging process and prolong life. Which of the theories of aging discussed in this chapter would you use as your point of departure? Why?

4. A friend wants to know what can be done in order to live longer. Based on the results of empirical research, what behaviors would you recommend? What behaviors would you strongly argue against? What aspects of your advice do you think would be most difficult for your friend to follow?

Terms to Remember

Antioxidants

Arthritis

Basal metabolism

Cancer

Cardiovascular disease

Chronic disorder

Deoxyribonucleic acid (DNA)

Genetic cellular theories of aging

Hypertension

Lipofuscin

Male pattern baldness

Neuritic plaques

Neurofibrillary tangles

Neurotransmitters

Nongenetic cellular theories of aging (wear and tear theories)

Osteoporosis

Physiological theories of aging

Ribonucleic acid (RNA)

Strokes

Chapter 4

Sensation and Perception

Joel Gordon / Joel Gordon Photography

One stereotype associated with old age is that of sensory deterioration. In fact, stage and screen comedians often portray the elderly as myopic and hard of hearing. Yet if our sensory and perceptual abilities decline as we grow through adulthood, this is surely no laughing matter. All information about our environment and many pleasurable (and painful) experiences come to us through our senses: perceiving and avoiding various obstacles while walking or driving, reading an interesting book, watching a favorite television program, observing if the weather is fair or foul, listening to some good music, engaging in friendly conversation, enjoying a tempting meal, or caressing a loved one, to cite just a few examples. We are so used to relying on our sight, hearing, and other senses that we typically take them for granted. Yet our physical capacities do tend to decline as we grow older, as we observed in the preceding chapter.

How do our sensory and perceptual abilities change with increasing age? Should you expect to suffer serious sensory losses on reaching old age, or only minor impairments that will have little effect on your daily functioning? Are some kinds of tasks more seriously affected by sensory losses than others, so that older adults should be advised to avoid certain activities or jobs?

This chapter deals with these issues: how we take in, organize, and experience the world around us and what important age-related changes occur in these processes. We will concentrate primarily on vision and audition, the two most widely researched senses. We will also discuss smell, taste, touch, and kinesthesis (the sense of position and movement, which can be a serious problem for some elderly individuals).

Vision

Declines in visual ability may well have important practical consequences for older adults. Gradually changing vision may be the reason for gradually decreasing mobility and independence, increased isolation, the occurrence of frightening visual impressions, and significant reductions in income (Yurick et al., 1984). As with other aspects of aging, however, the magnitude of age-related visual changes varies considerably from one individual to another.

THE ANATOMY OF THE VISUAL SYSTEM

The Lens.   Most visual sensations originate in some external object, which emits or (more often) reflects certain amounts and wavelengths of light. The **lens** of the eye bends the light rays that pass through it in order to project a suitably sharp, inverted image on the retina. The eye is able to focus on different objects because a set of muscles makes appropriate changes in the shape of the lens: It is flattened when the object is at a distance and thickened when the object is closer. These adjustments are known as **accommodation**. (See Figure 4.1.)

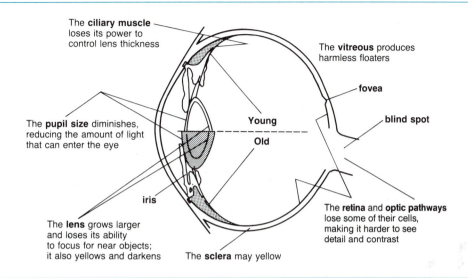

The **ciliary muscle** loses its power to control lens thickness

The **vitreous** produces harmless floaters

fovea

The **pupil size** diminishes, reducing the amount of light that can enter the eye

Young

Old

blind spot

iris

The **retina** and **optic pathways** lose some of their cells, making it harder to see detail and contrast

The **lens** grows larger and loses its ability to focus for near objects; it also yellows and darkens

The **sclera** may yellow

Figure 4.1
Anatomy of the eye: Major structures and anatomical differences between young and old. Source: Reproduced, with permission, from Weale, R., (1985) "What Is Normal Aging? Part XI: The Eyes of the Elderly." *Geriatric Medicine Today,* 4 (3): 29. Copyright 1985 by Med Publishing, Inc.

Interestingly, recent research suggests that the lens continues to grow and develop throughout the adult life span. New fibers continually cover older ones, similar to the growth rings found in tree trunks. Thus the lens contains cells derived from all age periods (Ohrloff & Hockwin, 1983; Tripathi & Tripathi, 1983).

The Iris. The **iris**, a muscle that surrounds the pupillary opening, controls the amount of light that enters the eye. It contracts when there is a significant increase in light and dilates when the illumination decreases, with the pupil changing size accordingly (the **pupillary reflex**).

The Retina. The **retina** serves a particularly important function: It transforms the incoming light energy into nerve impulses that can be communicated to the brain.

There are two kinds of photoreceptor cells in the retina, cones and rods. (See Figure 4.2.) **Cones** are most plentiful in the **fovea**, a small circular region located at the center of the retina, and more sparse toward the periphery. The cones make daytime vision possible because they respond to high levels of illumination, and they are also responsible for all sensations of color. **Rods** are completely absent from the fovea, and are more plentiful in the periphery of the retina. The rods make night vision possible, because they operate at low levels of illumination. However, they convey only colorless sensations. When your eyes take some time to adjust to a dark room after having been

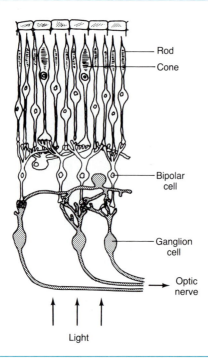

Rod
Cone
Bipolar cell
Ganglion cell
Optic nerve

Light

Figure 4.2
Anatomy of the eye: Cones and rods. Sources: Adapted from Gleitman (1983, p. 123); Coren et al. (1978).

exposed to bright light, the size of your pupils increases and you shift from cone vision to rod vision, a process known as **dark adaptation**. We need both kinds of receptors because the range of light to which we are exposed is enormous: The brilliant midday sun is *one hundred billion* times brighter than our absolute threshold, or the dimmest stimulus that the eye is capable of detecting. In all, the eye contains some 6 million cones and 120 million rods.

The Optic Nerve and Blind Spot.   The cones and rods report to the brain indirectly, through two intermediaries: bipolar cells and ganglion cells. The ganglion cells extend throughout the retina at one end and converge into a bundle of fibers at the other. This bundle leaves the eyeball as the **optic nerve**. The point where the optic nerve intersects the retina is known as the **blind spot** because it contains no receptors of any kind and cannot produce any visual sensations at all.

Visual Acuity.   Our visual system enables us to distinguish one object from another, an ability known as **visual acuity**. In daylight, visual acuity is the greatest in the fovea, where the cones are most densely bunched. Therefore, to see a particular object most clearly, you must move your eyes so that the object's image falls on both foveas. At night, however, you cannot see a faint star by looking at it directly. Rods are responsible for night vision, and there are none in the fovea. Under these conditions, you must look off at an angle and let the image of the star fall on the periphery of the retina—as experienced sailors know well.

AGE-RELATED CHANGES IN THE VISUAL SYSTEM

Long before old age, our eyes begin to undergo significant change. For example, the pupillary reflex responds more slowly after age 50, and the pupils do not dilate as completely. The lens becomes larger, more yellow, and less flexible after age 40. And the cornea, the transparent covering of the iris, decreases in luster by age 40 and increases in curvature and thickness past age 50 (Hunt & Hertzog, 1981). Some of these anatomical changes have important functional consequences.

Dark Adaptation.   As we grow older, our eyes adapt to the dark less rapidly and less effectively. (See Figure 4.3; *lower* threshold intensities indicate a *better* ability to see in the dark.) Middle-aged and elderly adults have considerably more difficulty dealing with sudden and pronounced decreases in illumination, as when going from bright sunlight into a darkened movie

Figure 4.3
Dark adaptation as a function of age and time in the dark.   Sources: Adapted from Hunt & Hertzog (1981); McFarland et al. (1960).

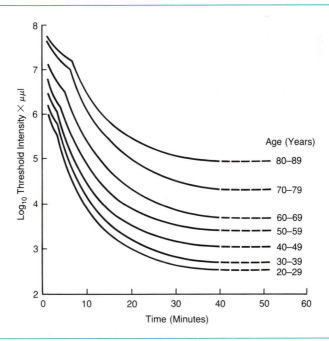

theater. Sudden increases in illumination are also troublesome, such as encountering the headlights of an oncoming car while driving at night. When designing environments for older adults, therefore, it is important to avoid abrupt transitions in light intensity, shadows, and glare (as might result from shiny floors or the chrome on wheelchairs).

In general, the middle-aged and elderly need a higher level of illumination in order to perceive visual stimuli as well as young adults. Thus, older adults are less efficient at tasks that must be performed under low illumination, such as detecting dimly lit signals or patrolling dark areas at night.

Accommodation.   The process of accommodation also deteriorates with increasing age, particularly between ages 40 and 55 (e.g., Bruckner, 1967). This reduced ability to focus on nearby objects *(presbyopia)* may well necessitate corrective measures, such as reading glasses or bifocals. Tasks like driving an automobile will also be more difficult, since we must often shift our focus back and forth from points far down the road to the gauges directly in front of us.

Visual Acuity.   Our ability to identify stationary objects (**static visual acuity**) shows a decided drop with age; the percentage of adults with 20/20 vision declines markedly after age 45. (See Figure 4.4.) Our ability to identify moving objects (**dynamic visual acuity**), such as credits on TV or road signs while driving, also decreases appreciably as we grow older, though not necessarily at the same rate as static visual acuity (Burg, 1966; Heron & Chown, 1967; Kosnik et al., 1988).

In one study, a group of young adults (mean age 33 years) and a group of elderly adults (mean age 66 years) were asked to identify a small road sign while in a moving automobile at night. Although the two groups were matched on static visual acuity, they performed very differently: The younger adults were able to read the sign at distances some 25 percent greater than the elderly subjects (Sivak, Olson, & Pastalan, 1981). This implies that older drivers will react more slowly to road warning signs and to other external stimuli because this task depends on dynamic visual acuity, an ability that has declined. The frequency of driving accidents has also been shown to be positively correlated with dynamic visual acuity, especially for older subjects (Hills, 1980). These findings suggest that the common eye chart is *not* sufficient to predict the performance of middle-aged and elderly adults on tasks like driving an automobile, because it measures only static visual acuity.

In some instances, degenerative changes in the retina may cause such severe difficulties that large-print books, magnifiers, and other visual aids are needed. However, these changes normally do not occur until extreme old age (Welford, 1980).

Color Sensitivity.   The yellowing of the lens after age 40 affects our ability to see certain colors, notably those at the blue-green end of the spectrum. The

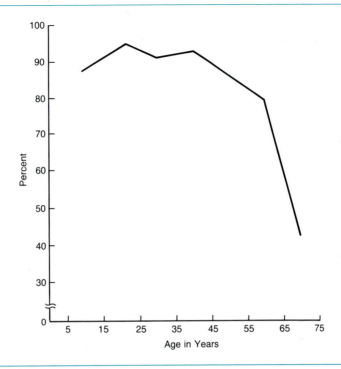

Figure 4.4
Percentage of population with 20/20 vision as a function of age. Sources: Hunt & Hertzog (1981); Department of Health, Education, and Welfare (1977).

effect is somewhat like viewing the world through yellow sunglasses: Older adults can discern yellows, oranges, and reds more easily than violets, blues, and greens. This is not a serious defect, but it can cause problems under some conditions (e.g., a tennis court illuminated at night with bluish light, or a white soup bowl on a white place mat). For this reason, the color controls on television sets in homes for the elderly must often be set at atypical values in order to make the hues appear more realistic.

The Quality of Visual Information Processing. The elderly have somewhat more difficulty recognizing shapes, numbers, letters, and words (Szafran, 1968). As a result, reading a sign or locating someone in a crowd may be more troublesome. The differences between younger and older adults are rather small, however, indicating that age is a relatively minor factor insofar as these visual abilities are concerned.

The Speed of Visual Information Processing. Numerous studies indicate that we process visual information more slowly as we grow older. In studies of critical flicker frequency, for example, subjects are typically shown a rapidly flashing light. Older adults require a significantly longer interval between the flashes in order to perceive that the light is not on continuously, indicating that the sensitivity of the visual system declines with age. A related experimental procedure is to show subjects a stimulus object, followed shortly thereafter by a masking stimulus that blocks it from view. Here again, the elderly require a significantly longer exposure time in order to identify the original stimulus. This implies that certain important activities, such as reading, will be done more slowly by older adults (Hunt & Hertzog, 1981; Kline & Szafran, 1975; Kosnik et al., 1988).

Some studies require the subject to locate a target object in a field of distracting stimuli as quickly as possible, a task that depends on both sensory processes and decision-making ability. (See Figure 4.5.) Adults age 60 and older perform such visual scanning tasks significantly more slowly than do young adults (e.g., Rabbitt, 1965; 1968; 1977; 1979). This is especially true if the subject must concentrate on other tasks simultaneously, as when the driver of an automobile must pick out the relevant information from a lengthy road sign while continuing to guide the car. However, there appears to be relatively little decline in visual scanning ability between ages 20 and 50. Thus, if an employer is seeking someone to proofread a manuscript in a brightly lit room, there would be little reason (insofar as this visual ability is concerned) to prefer a 20-year-old to a 40-year-old.

Alternatively, subjects may be asked to detect a target letter flashed on a display screen. Here again, elderly adults perform more poorly if the letter

As we grow older, it becomes more difficult to process visual information quickly. This is especially true when we must concentrate on two or more tasks simultaneously, such as trying to glean information from a lengthy road sign while maintaining a safe distance from the car in front. (Raymond Depard/Magnum Photos)

```
Z   N   O   R   E   X   V

L   A   I   Q   B   D   W

S   M   K   E   O   P   Y

E   L   A   X   R   V   Q

N   A   W   O   M   D   C

V   L   O   A   Y   K   J

B   Q   N   S   H   R   U
```

Figure 4.5
Sample visual scanning task.

Task: To mark each horizontal line that contains a "Q" under severe time pressure (e.g., there are 500 lines in all and a one-minute time limit).

may appear anywhere on the screen, forcing them to divide their attention But if the target letter always appears at the center of the screen, allowing subjects to focus their attention on a single spot, no significant age differences in performance are obtained. (See Plude & Hoyer, 1985; 1986.)

Afterword.   As we grow older, changes in the eye reduce the quality or intensity of the light that enters the retina. These changes imply that older people are in effect operating under poorer lighting conditions than are young adults, a decline that can be mitigated but not eliminated by increased illumination (Kline & Schieber, 1985; Welford, 1980).

Although the visual system changes considerably during adulthood, our eyes remain our most reliable sense. The deterioration that occurs is not drastic enough to incapacitate older adults, but it can make some visual tasks considerably more difficult. For example, if rapidly moving targets must be detected under conditions of low illumination, young adults will perform this task far better than the middle-aged or elderly. If instead the task requires rapid identification of single, motionless stimuli, young adults may be somewhat superior. But if the task is one of visual scanning, young adults will have little or no advantage over the middle-aged, although the elderly will be at a disadvantage. Thus the negative effects of aging on your visual system tend to be greater for tasks that are more complicated. However, appropriate training can improve the visual performance of older adults on some complicated tasks (Ball & Sekuler, 1986).

DISORDERS OF THE VISUAL SYSTEM

Though our visual system fares rather well with increasing age, a significant number of older adults do report that their ability to see is impaired. (See Table 4.1.)

Table 4.1

Percentage of persons reporting visual impairments by age and sex (United States, 1984).

	Age		
	65–74	75–84	85 and older
Male	9.7	16.7	25.0
Female	9.4	15.6	27.5

Source: National Center for Health Statistics (1986).

Common Eye Complaints.   As we observed in the preceding section, there is a gradual decline in our ability to focus on nearby objects after age 40. Presbyopia cannot be prevented, but it is easily compensated for with eyeglasses or contact lenses.

In bright light, you may observe tiny spots or flecks floating across your field of vision. These "floaters" are normal and usually harmless, although a sudden change in the type or number of spots may indicate a significant problem.

Sometimes the tear glands produce too few tears, resulting in itching and burning sensations or even reduced vision. Such dry eyes can be safely and effectively treated with prescription eyedrops ("artificial tears"). Conversely, excessive tears may result from an increased sensitivity to light, wind, or temperature, or from an eye infection or blocked tear duct. These problems are also readily treated and corrected (National Institute on Aging, 1983a).

Major Eye Diseases.   Cloudy or opaque areas may develop in part or all of the lens, inhibiting the passage of light and causing a significant decline in vision. (See Figure 4.6.) These **cataracts** usually form gradually, without pain, redness of the eye, or excessive tears; they are most common after age 60. Some recent research evidence suggests that cataract formation may be linked to enzyme modifications, or to changes in the characteristics of lens protein (Hoenders & Bloemendal, 1983; Lerman, 1983; Ohrloff & Hockwin, 1983). Some cataracts remain small enough to be safely ignored. Those large to cause significant problems can be surgically removed, a safe procedure that is almost always successful.

Glaucoma occurs when the fluid pressure in the eye becomes excessive, causing internal damage and gradually destroying one's vision. If glaucoma is detected in its early stages, however, it can usually be controlled well enough to prevent blindness. Common methods for this purpose include prescription eyedrops, oral medication, laser treatments, or perhaps surgery. As with cataracts, the initial stages of glaucoma seldom involve any pain or discomfort, so routine eye examinations of adults over 35 typically include a test for eye pressure (National Institute on Aging, 1983a).

NORMAL VISION—A person with normal vision or vision corrected to 20/20 with glasses sees this street scene. The area of the photographs is the field of vision for the right eye.

CATARACT—An opacity of the lens results in diminished acuity but does not affect the field of vision. There is no scotoma, but the person's vision is hazy overall, particularly in glaring light.

With cataracts, print appears hazy or lacking in contrast.

MACULAR DEGENERATION—The deterioration of the macula, the central area of the retina, is the most prevalent eye disease. This picture shows the area of a decreased central vision called a central scotoma. The peripheral or side vision remains unaffected so mobility need not be impaired.

With macular degeneration, print appears distorted and segments of words may be missing.

GLAUCOMA—Chronic elevated eye pressure in susceptible individuals may cause optic nerve atrophy and loss of peripheral vision. Early detection and close medical monitoring can help reduce complications.

In advanced glaucoma, print may appear faded and words may be difficult to read.

Figure 4.6
Effects of some major visual disorders. Source: Courtesy of Lighthouse Low Vision Service, © 1985, The New York Association for the Blind.

Most adults maintain good eyesight into their eighties and beyond, although corrective lenses may well be necessary. (Dan Chidester/The Image Works)

Most serious of all are the **retinal disorders,** which are the leading causes of blindness in the United States. In **senile macular degeneration,** a specialized part of the retina that is responsible for sharp central and reading vision (the macula) loses its ability to function effectively. Warning signs include blurred vision when reading, a dark spot in the center of one's field of vision, and distortion when viewing vertical lines. If detected early enough, senile macular degeneration may be amenable to laser treatments. **Diabetic retinopathy** occurs when small blood vessels that normally nourish the retina fail to function properly. As the name implies, this disease is one of the possible complications resulting from diabetes. The early stages of diabetic retinopathy are denoted by distorted vision, the later stages by serious visual losses. **Retinal detachment,** a separation between the inner and outer layers of the retina, has a more favorable prognosis: Detached retinas can usually be surgically reattached well enough to restore good, or at least partial, vision. This is probably the best known of the retinal disorders, due to media coverage of cases involving famous athletes (e.g., champion boxer Sugar Ray Leonard).

Afterword.   It is desirable to have a complete eye examination every two to three years, to permit the early detection of diseases like cataracts and glaucoma. This is especially true for those who have diabetes or a family history of eye disease. However, visual disorders are by no means inevitable with increasing age. Most of us maintain good eyesight into our eighties and beyond, albeit with the aid of corrective lenses in many cases. Furthermore, we also have the option of adapting the environment in ways that will maximize the visual competence of older adults.

Audition

THE ANATOMY OF THE AUDITORY SYSTEM

The Eardrum.   Auditory sensations are caused by physical movements in the external world, which disturb the surrounding air particles. These particles push other air particles in front of them, ultimately creating a chain reaction of sound waves that travel in all directions—much like the ripples that spread when a stone is thrown into a lake. Some of these sound waves are collected by the outer ear and funneled toward a taut membrane, the **eardrum,** which responds by vibrating. (See Figure 4.7.)

The Ossicles and Oval Window.   The eardrum transmits its vibrations across an air-filled cavity, the middle ear, by way of a mechanical bridge. This connecting link consists of three small bones (**ossicles**), which respond to the vibrations of the eardrum by moving in sequence. The third ossicle imparts the initial vibratory pattern to a membrane that separates the middle ear from the inner ear (the **oval window**).

Figure 4.7
Anatomy of the ear: Major structures.   Sources: Adapted from Gleitman (1983, p. 119); Lindsay & Norman (1977).

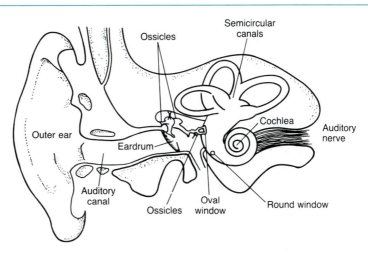

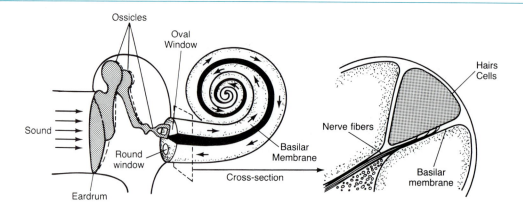

Figure 4.8
Anatomy of the ear: The middle ear and cochlea.   Sources: Adapted from Gleitman (1983, p. 120); Lindsay & Norman (1977); Coren et al. (1978).

The Cochlea and Auditory Nerve.   The movement of the oval window creates waves in the fluid that fills the **cochlea,** a coiled tube in the inner ear. The pressure resulting from these waves causes deformations in the **basilar membrane,** which bisects the cochlea throughout most of its length. (See Figure 4.8.)

The anatomical structures described thus far are merely accessories, which conduct and amplify the sound waves so that they can affect the true auditory receptors—**hair cells** lodged near the basilar membrane. The deformations of this membrane stimulate the hair cells by bending them, whereupon the cells communicate appropriate sound impulses to the brain via the **auditory nerve.** Thus our sense of hearing depends on mechanical pressures within the ear, yet it is capable of detecting stimuli that are far away. As a result, the auditory sense has been likened to feeling at a distance (Gleitman, 1983).

Loudness and Pitch.   The brain transforms physical sensations of sound into two psychological dimensions, **loudness** and **pitch.** Sounds are louder when the original movements in the environment are more intense, increasing the height (amplitude) of the resulting sound waves. Higher pitches are heard when the frequency of the sound waves is greater (i.e., when there are more waves per second). At higher frequencies, the sensation of pitch is determined by the place on the basilar membrane where the peak deformation occurs: The closer this maximum point is to one end of the membrane, the higher (lower) the pitch that we experience. At low frequencies, however, deformation is equal throughout the basilar membrane. Here, pitch is determined instead by the firing frequency of the auditory nerve. Finally, for moderate frequencies, pitch is probably related to both the place and firing frequency mechanisms.

The intensity of a sound, which we perceive as loudness, is measured in **decibels.** Zero decibels corresponds to our threshold of hearing; a whisper is about 20 decibels; normal conversation is approximately 60 decibels; shouting is about 100 decibels; and the loudest rock band on record registered some 160 decibels (which is about 20 decibels *higher* than the threshold of pain!). The frequency of a sound, which we perceive as pitch, is usually measured in **hertz** (or kilohertz, where one kHz = 1,000 hertz). The piano ranges from 27.5 hertz at its lowest note through 261.6 hertz (middle C) to 4,180 hertz at its highest note. Young adults can hear tones from 20 to 20,000 hertz, with the greatest sensitivity occurring at the middle of this region.

AGE-RELATED CHANGES IN THE AUDITORY SYSTEM

Sensitivity to Tones and Pitch.
Most often, methods for measuring our hearing use pure tones as the test stimuli. Losses in our ability to detect these tones begin to occur by about age 40, although pronounced changes are not evident until some time later (Fozard, 1990).

For example, the typical 30-year-old male can detect a 6 kHz tone (6,000 hertz) at a volume of about 4 decibels, which is softer than the rustling of leaves. Yet the same tone must be presented to the average 65-year-old man

Performers such as Eubie Blake serve as strong testament that high levels of sensory, motor, cognitive, and creative functioning can be maintained into very old age. (Ezio Peterson/UPI-Bettmann)

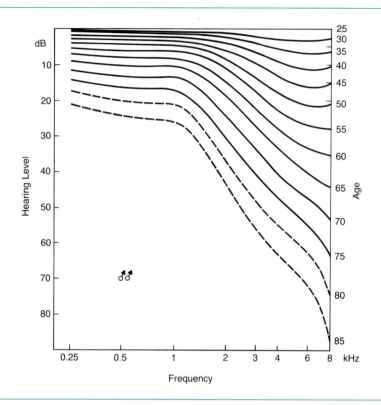

Figure 4.9
Ability to detect pure tones as a function of age and frequency (data for men only).   Source:
Adapted from Hunt & Hertzog (1981).

at approximately 40 decibels, the level of normal conversation, in order to be heard. (Average tone sensitivities for men in Western industrial society, as a function of age, are shown in Figure 4.9.) The greatest declines occur at frequencies above 2.5 kHz, due primarily to atrophy and degeneration of the hair cells and supporting mechanisms in the cochlea. To the extent that a job requires the detection and/or discrimination of middle- to high-frequency tones, many middle-aged and elderly adults may well be at a significant disadvantage. Older adults may also have more difficulty understanding words that are shouted, because this often increases the pitch of the voice as well as the loudness.

Speech Perception.   Our ability to perceive and understand speech also declines with increasing age, although the magnitude of this loss depends to a considerable extent on prevailing listening conditions. In one study (Bergman et al., 1976), speech perception was studied under three markedly different conditions:

- *Normal speech:* no background noise or interference.
- *Selective listening:* trying to understand one person's speech with competing voices in the background.
- *Interrupted speech:* trying to understand speech that is interrupted electronically several times per second, as might happen if a radio program were afflicted with intermittent static.

As shown in Figure 4.10, little decline was found in normal speech perception until after age 60. A somewhat greater decrement occurred in selective listening, amounting to about 10 percent between ages 20 and 50 and almost 20 percent by age 70. The greatest impairment was found in our

Figure 4.10

Ability to perceive speech under different listening conditions: Percent decrement from age 20 years. Source: Bergman et al. (1976), "Age-Related Decrements in Hearing for Speech: Sampling and Longitudinal Studies," *Journal of Gerontology, 31,* pp. 533–538. Reprinted by permission of the *Journal of Gerontology.*

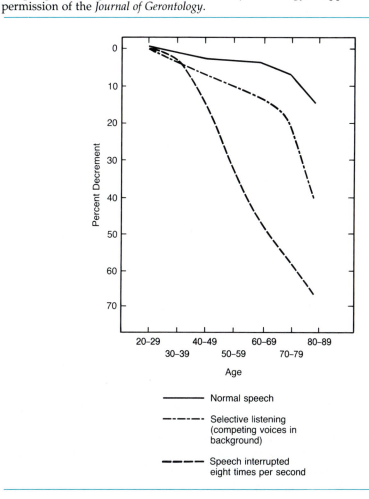

ability to perceive interrupted speech: This loss was approximately 35 percent between ages 20 and 50, and it reached 60 percent by age 70. These decrements are generally attributed to an increase in the time required by the auditory cortex to process the incoming information, and to changes in the peripheral nervous system. Such findings indicate the importance of securing good listening conditions, and improving the acoustic properties of buildings, where older adults are concerned. It may also be helpful to maximize visual communication cues, as by seating nursing home residents face to face in dining rooms and lounges so they can observe one another's lip movements and facial expressions.

Because the ability to perceive and understand speech differs from the ability to perceive pure tones, standard audiological evaluations now include tests of speech discrimination as well as tone discrimination. Where indicated by the subjects' symptoms, tests of more complex central auditory functions are also conducted. In view of these complications, hearing tests should be performed by a qualified audiologist, rather than by a hearing aid dealer or lay person. The trained audiologist is also able to assess the extent to which an individual is handicapped by the degree of hearing loss indicated by the test scores. This assessment requires an understanding of the subject's living and working environment.

Afterword: Aging versus Environment.   Compared to vision, our hearing suffers considerably more of a decline as we grow older. However, not all changes in the auditory system are due to increasing age. Certain environmental events can produce marked impairments in hearing, notably the exposure to intense high-frequency noise for a long period of time.

For example, significant noise-related hearing losses and even deafness are common among rock musicians (Kryter, 1970). When a large sample of Wisconsin residents was compared with members of a less technological (and less noisy) culture, Sudanese tribesmen, the latter showed much smaller losses in hearing with increasing age (Bergman, 1980). Cordless telephones, which have the ringer in the earpiece, and personal stereos, which deliver intense sound more directly to the eardrum through earphones, are currently being evaluated as potentially serious sources of hearing loss. In fact, it appears that the United States population as a whole is becoming increasingly hard of hearing: From 1940 to 1980, the incidence rate of deafness increased from under 200 per 10,000 to approximately 300 per 10,000 (Hunt & Hertzog, 1981).

If we were to consider only our own culture, we might erroneously conclude that substantial declines in hearing with increasing age are an inescapable part of the human condition. In actuality, however, both aging and our environment contribute to the hearing losses commonly found among middle-aged and elderly Americans. The atrophy of our auditory system is one price that we pay for living in a noise-ridden, industrialized society. To be sure, our society does pay some attention to preventing such losses: Employees who operate noisy machinery, and adults who practice with

handguns or rifles at firing ranges, may well be required to wear industrial earmuffs or earplugs. Yet given the prevalence of noise that we encounter, it is by no means unlikely that tomorrow's adult Americans will also experience significant hearing troubles, perhaps even more than we do today.

DISORDERS OF THE AUDITORY SYSTEM

A substantial number of older Americans report that they suffer from hearing impairments, men more so than women. (See Table 4.2.)

Presbycusis.   Some 13 percent of Americans over the age of 65 show advanced signs of **presbycusis**. This disorder involves a progressive loss of hearing in both ears for high-frequency tones, which is often accompanied by severe difficulty in understanding speech (Matlin, 1984). Presbycusis results from the deterioration of mechanisms in the inner ear; this may be caused by aging, long-term exposure to loud noises, certain drugs, an improper diet, or genetic factors. The onset of this disorder is gradual, and it typically becomes pronounced after age 50.

Hearing aids alone are unlikely to resolve this problem. They serve to amplify sounds in the external world, yet speech will remain distorted because of the inner ear degeneration. Speech reading, informational counseling, and hearing aid orientation are important aspects of comprehensive aural rehabilitation with patients suffering from presbycusis (Garstecki, 1981).

Conductive Hearing Loss.   **Conductive hearing loss** occurs when sound waves are unable to travel properly through the outer and middle ear. This disorder is caused by impediments in the ear, such as dense wax, excessive fluid, an abnormal bone growth, or an infection. Sufferers experience external sounds and other people's voices as muffled, but their own voices appear louder than normal. This disorder is less common than presbycusis and can usually be resolved through flushing of the ear, medication, or surgery.

Central Auditory Impairment.   Those who suffer from **central auditory impairment** have great difficulty understanding language. However, the ability to detect external sounds is not affected. This rare disorder is caused by

Table 4.2
Percentage of persons reporting hearing impairments by age and sex (United States, 1984).

	Age		
	65–74	75–84	85 and older
Male	30.0	39.9	58.3
Female	17.5	28.2	44.0

Source: National Center for Health Statistics (1986).

damage to the nerve centers within the brain, which typically results from an extended illness with a high fever, lengthy exposure to loud noises, the use of certain drugs, head injuries, vascular problems, or tumors. Unlike presbycusis, central auditory impairment may occur at any age; it may also interact with presbycusis in older adults. There is no cure for central auditory impairment, although rehabilitation by an audiologist or speech-language pathologist may be helpful in some instances (National Institute on Aging, 1983b).

Afterword. It has been estimated that 30 percent of all adults between the ages of 65 and 74, and 50 percent of those between 75 and 79, suffer some degree of hearing loss. In the United States alone, the total amounts to more than 10 million older people (National Institute on Aging, 1983b). In fact, hearing impairments rank second only to arthritis among the leading health problems of those over the age of 75 (Brock, Guralnik, & Brody, 1990).

Hearing disorders have significant practical consequences: failing to understand what other people are saying, which may significantly affect relationships with family and friends; letting a ringing telephone or doorbell go unanswered, and missing an important call; being unable to enjoy movies, plays, concerts, and television programs without closed captions; having to give up driving an automobile because the warning signal of an ambulance or fire engine cannot be heard. In addition, stimuli such as the plumbing sounds from another room provide an important auditory background that helps us to keep in touch with our surroundings. When hearing-impaired persons cannot detect these background stimuli, they may well become afraid to venture out into all but the most familiar environments. As a result, hearing losses have caused elderly people to be incorrectly diagnosed as confused, unresponsive, uncooperative, or even pathologically depressed, thereby denying them help that would have been readily available. Hearing impairments may even lead to true depression, with sufferers becoming so frustrated at their inability to communicate with other people (or so suspicious because others always seem to mumble incoherently) that they withdraw from social interactions (Weinstein & Ventry, 1982).

Despite these serious consequences, all too many adults steadfastly refuse to admit that they have a hearing problem. Whether this defensive behavior is due to fear, vanity, or misinformation, it is clearly unwise. Most hearing impairments are amenable to treatment, at least to some extent; so the best course is to face the issue squarely and seek appropriate medical assistance. The most common method for improving the hearing of elderly patients is through the amplification provided by an appropriate hearing aid (Rappaport, 1984). Hearing aids may take various forms, such as an instrument that hooks behind the ear, an amplifier built into the temple of a pair of eyeglasses, a device worn inside the ear, or a larger receiver carried in a shirt pocket. One or two hearing aids may be worn, depending on the extent and nature of the hearing loss.

Hearing aids do not restore hearing to normal, and the quality of sound obtained through a hearing aid is much different from what the healthy indi-

vidual hears without one. So older adults may well show some resistance to such aids, or have difficulty in adjusting to them. It may therefore be desirable to have the patient's spouse, or other close relative or friend, participate in the sessions with the audiologist and provide encouragement and support. Nevertheless, the benefits provided by the hearing aid are likely to be well worth the initial difficulties. Hearing is the sense most affected by aging, so it is important to be aware of the need for possible corrective action as one grows past middle age.

Taste and Smell

Our senses of taste and smell are closely interrelated. For example, both of these senses play an essential role in determining the desirability of various foods. It is therefore difficult to study these senses separately, although some researchers have sought to do so.

TASTE (GUSTATION)

Taste Sensitivity and Aging. Sensory researchers have identified four primary qualities of taste: sweet, bitter, sour, and salty. Taste sensitivity experiments typically present the subject with a solution based on one primary quality (e.g., a sucrose solution in the case of sweetness), and a separate quantity of water. The keener the subject's sensitivity to, say, sweetness, the smaller the concentration of sucrose that can be differentiated from plain water.

Several studies suggest that adults past age 50 have more difficulty detecting all four primary taste sensations (e.g., Byrd & Gertman, 1959; Cooper, Bilash, & Zubek, 1959; Schiffman, 1977). In general, however, the data are equivocal: Different research methods (such as stimulating the tongue with a weak galvanic current), or even the same methods used by different investigators, have at times produced conflicting results (Engen, 1977). This may be due in part to bias caused by factors related to age, such as poor health, which affect the taste sensitivity of older adults. The best recent evidence indicates that sensitivity to salt and sugar decreases with age, but only by small amounts (Bartoshuk & Weiffenbach, 1990). In addition, older adults are just as good as young adults at discriminating among different sensations that are above threshold (Bartoshuk et al., 1986).

Taste Preferences and Aging. Our senses of taste and smell discriminate more effectively among different substances (qualitatively) than among different concentrations of the same substance (quantitatively). Nevertheless, very little research has been conducted on age-related taste preferences. In one study, such different foods as corned beef and apples were liquefied in a blender to remove all textural cues; the results suggested that older adults dislike bitter stimuli more than younger subjects do (Engen, 1977).

SMELL (OLFACTION)

Olfactory Sensitivity and Aging.   Several studies have found that our ability to detect various odors declines with age (e.g., Kimbrell & Furchgott, 1963; Rous, 1969; Schiffman & Pasternak, 1979). In one recent study, 1,955 volunteers ranging in age from 5 to 99 were tested with 40 chemically simulated scents that included cinnamon, cherry, pizza, gasoline, tobacco, mint, soap, grass, lemon, motor oil, and root beer. The results suggested that olfactory ability is usually at its best between the ages of 20 and 40, begins to diminish slightly by age 50, and declines rapidly after age 70. Among subjects aged 65 to 80, some 60 percent suffered severe losses in olfactory sensitivity, and about 25 percent lost all ability to smell. For those over 80, the proportion with severe olfactory losses was 80 percent, and nearly one-half could not smell anything (*The Miami Herald*, Dec. 14, 1984).

Another study, based on two small samples of adults, age 18 to 26 and 66 to 93, found that the older group required a stimulus twice as strong in order to detect the smell of menthol (Murphy, 1983). Furthermore, it has been argued that age-related declines in olfactory sensitivity are related to declines in gustatory sensitivity. Murphy (1985) compared the ability of young adult women (mean age 19 years) and elderly women (mean age 71 years) to identify blended foods. When the subjects were allowed to use all of their senses, the younger group performed significantly better. But when the subjects were prevented from using their sense of smell by having their nostrils pinched closed, the performance of the younger group fell to the same level as that of the older group. The older subjects also had more difficulty with the cognitive aspects of this task, such as finding ways to name and recall these unusual odorless food stimuli (a topic that will be discussed in the next chapter).

One of the most extraordinary of all olfactory studies was conducted with the cooperation of *National Geographic* magazine. Each September 1986 issue contained an insert with six "scratch-and-sniff" samples, and a series of questions including "What is your age?" About 1.5 million readers took this test and sent in their answers, which may well be the largest sample on record. The results indicated that after age 70, the ability to smell the odorants declined with increasing age. Subjects in their fifties and sixties were just as likely as younger adults to detect that some odor was present, but they perceived it as less intense than it actually was and were less likely to name the odor correctly. Furthermore, the noxious odorants added to natural gas as a warning signal (mercaptans) were more difficult for older adults to detect and were perceived as less unpleasant. This implies that the elderly are significantly less likely to respond to dangerous gas leaks in their homes. Therefore, some theorists recommend that a different odor, to which older people are more sensitive (e.g., rose), be added to natural gas. (See Bartoshuk & Weiffenbach, 1990, pp. 438–439.)

As with taste, illness and injury can cause olfactory sensitivity to decline. If you have ever suffered from a severe respiratory infection or sinus disease,

Myths About Aging

Sensation and Perception

Myth	*Best Available Evidence*
The majority of elderly adults suffer such serious visual deterioration that they require major visual aids, such as large-print books and magnifiers.	Most of us maintain good eyesight into our eighties and beyond. (Eyeglasses or contact lenses may well be necessary, however, because the percent of adults with 20/20 vision does decline markedly after age 45.) Large-print books and magnifiers are normally not necessary until extreme old age.
The effects of aging are much the same for all visual tasks.	Some visual abilities decline significantly more with increasing age than do others. Tasks that involve perceiving objects that are dimly lit, moving, or masked by other stimuli become considerably more difficult after middle age, and locating a target object in a field of distracting stimuli becomes more difficult after about age 60. In general, the effects of aging are more pronounced on visual tasks that are more complicated.
The majority of elderly adults suffer such serious auditory deterioration that they have considerable difficulty perceiving speech and loud sounds.	Hearing is the sense most affected by aging, and there is some indication that the population of the United States is becoming increasingly hard of hearing. But serious hearing impairments are the exception rather than the rule, especially among those who obtain regular hearing checkups after middle age.
Those hearing losses that do occur among elderly Americans are due exclusively to aging.	The hearing losses suffered by Americans are caused in part by environmental conditions and events, notably the long-term exposure to such intense noise as rock music and loud industrial machinery. Thus some less technological cultures show considerably smaller losses in hearing with increasing age.

you probably experienced a temporary lapse in your ability to smell (and to taste). These lapses are more common among older adults, because the frequency of such illnesses increases with age. Alzheimer's disease, Parkinson's disease, and even mild head trauma can cause a permanent loss in olfactory sensitivity (Doty, Deems, & Stellar, 1988; Bartoshuk & Weiffenbach, 1990).

Olfactory Preferences and Aging.   Although the elderly appear to have different odor preferences than children, these differences are seen at about age 30 and cannot be attributed to aging (Engen, 1977). Here again, those elderly adults who report little difference among pleasant and unpleasant stimuli are likely to do so because of poor health rather than aging per se.

Afterword.   The available research evidence indicates that the sense of taste remains relatively stable with increasing age but that the sense of smell declines significantly. The latter finding has important implications for the safety of the elderly, as we have seen.

Somesthesis: The Skin and Kinesthetic Senses

THE SKIN SENSES

Data concerning the skin senses are sparse, often dated, and frequently contradictory. Furthermore, any decrements in somesthetic sensitivity among the elderly may well be due to the more frequent occurrence of disease and injury, rather than to aging per se.

Touch.   The importance of our sense of touch is easily taken for granted. Nevertheless, this sense is involved in many important behaviors: judging the smoothness of a piece of wood or the closeness of a shave, identifying a switch on the automobile console without taking one's eyes off the road, caressing a loved one. There is some indication that a small percentage of the aged experience a decline in touch sensitivity. Yet it has also been suggested that tactile sensitivity increases with age, because the skin of elderly adults deforms more easily and exposes more touch spots to external stimuli. (See, for example, Jalavisto, Orma, & Tawast, 1951; Zwislocki, 1960.)

Vibration.   Changes in vibratory sensitivity are helpful in diagnosing and assessing disorders of the nervous system. It appears that some older adults are significantly less sensitive than young adults to vibratory stimuli, particularly in the lower extremities (Goff et al., 1965; Perret & Regli, 1970). However, such decrements have not been shown to have any notable practical consequences for those individuals who do experience them.

Temperature.   The temperature sensitivities and preferences of older adults do not appear to differ in any significant way from those of younger subjects (Rohles, 1969). But the ability to cope with cold temperatures and maintain bodily warmth, and the ability to cope with hot environments, decline with increasing age (Finch, 1977; Krag & Kountz, 1950). This may explain in part why mortality rates increase among the elderly when there are sudden and extreme changes in ambient temperature.

Seasonal variation in mortality has been shown to occur in all American states, even those with temperate climates. (See Table 4.3.) This suggests that factors other than the acute effect of low absolute temperature contribute to these variations, such as abrupt temperature changes. The magnitude of the seasonal effect on mortality is large: During the coldest month of 1979 (January), there were approximately 20,000 more deaths from all causes and 12,000 more deaths from heart disease than for the warmest month (August). (See Anderson & Rochard, 1979; Collins et al., 1977.)

Pain. Given the increased likelihood of pathology among the elderly, any age-related changes in pain sensitivity would have important practical consequences. Perhaps for this reason, pain is the skin sense most often subjected to age-related studies. Unfortunately, these data are highly contradictory: Many studies report a marked decline in pain sensitivity with increasing age, numerous others find no such decrements (e.g., Harkins et al., 1986; Corso, 1987), and a few even report increased pain sensitivity among older adults (Kenshalo, 1977).

This issue may perhaps be resolved in part by examining sensitivity to different types of pain as a function of age. For example, it may be that older adults experience reduced pain sensitivity to superficial somatic pain, but show increased sensitivity and decreased tolerance to deep somatic pain (Newton, 1984).

KINESTHESIS

One important and distressing problem faced by the elderly is their susceptibility to falls, and the sometimes fatal complications that result. Such falls may be caused by dizziness, by muscular weakness, or by decreased input from the **kinesthetic** receptors that detect movements or strain in the muscles, tendons, and joints. Once again, however, the evidence is equivocal: There are studies that report little or no decline in kinesthetic sensitivity with advanced age and others that find some deterioration (Kenshalo, 1977).

AFTERWORD

Some older adults may experience some declines in somesthetic sensitivity. However, the great majority probably need not be concerned about the possibility of serious deterioration.

In comparison with vision, audition, taste, and smell, much less is known about the relationship between aging and the skin and kinesthetic senses. Whether this gap in our knowledge exists because the issue is relatively

Table 4.3
Average number of deaths per day, by age and month, in the United States (1979).

Age	Total	Month											
		January	February	March	April	May	June	July	August	September	October	November	December
All ages[1]	5,251	5,576	5,465	5,286	5,270	5,201	5,091	5,030	4,940	5,007	5,254	5,335	5,573
Under 45 years	603	576	580	590	588	610	625	634	614	619	602	599	603
45–64 years	1,159	1,237	1,211	1,173	1,173	1,156	1,134	1,123	1,105	1,093	1,153	1,158	1,196
65–74 years	1,233	1,304	1,290	1,249	1,245	1,224	1,192	1,178	1,164	1,165	1,233	1,252	1,302
75 years and over	2,254	2,457	2,382	2,273	2,262	2,209	2,138	2,093	2,056	2,128	2,265	2,324	2,472

[1] Includes figures for age not stated.
Source: Feinleib (1984).

unimportant (i.e., these other senses change very little as we grow older), or because researchers have found these questions to be too difficult or too uninteresting to investigate, is a question that is as yet unanswered.

Summary

VISION

The lens bends the light rays passing through it in order to project a suitably sharp image on the retina, and the iris controls the amount of light that enters the eye. The retina transforms light energy into nerve impulses with the aid of two kinds of photoreceptor cells: Cones are responsible for day vision and sensations of color, and rods are responsible for night vision. The shift from cone to rod vision is known as dark adaptation.

As we grow older, dark adaptation becomes less rapid and less effective. It becomes increasingly more difficult to focus on nearby objects, and to shift back and forth rapidly between far and near objects. The ability to identify both stationary and moving objects declines, with some older individuals experiencing greater losses in dynamic visual acuity. It becomes more difficult to discern colors at the blue-green end of the spectrum, and visual information processing takes place more slowly. These changes are not debilitating, but they do make certain tasks considerably more difficult to perform.

Common eye complaints include presbyopia, floaters, dry eyes, and excessive tearing. These problems are usually readily amenable to treatment. Major eye diseases include cataracts, glaucoma, and the retinal disorders, the last of these representing the leading causes of blindness in the United States. Although eye ailments are common enough to warrant complete examinations every few years, most older adults maintain good eyesight into their eighties and beyond, albeit with the aid of corrective lenses in many instances.

AUDITION

External sound waves are collected by the outer ear and funneled toward the eardrum, which responds by vibrating. These vibrations are then transmitted via the ossicles, oval window, cochlear fluid, and basilar membrane to the auditory receptors, the cochlear hair cells. The brain transforms physical sensations of sound into two psychological dimensions. The intensity of a sound, which we perceive as loudness, is measured in decibels. The frequency of a sound, which we perceive as pitch, is measured in hertz or kilohertz.

Losses in our ability to detect pure tones begin by about age 40, but do not become pronounced until some time later. The greatest declines occur at frequencies above 2.5 kHz. Declines in our ability to understand speech normally do not become pronounced until after age 50; the extent of these losses depends in large part on prevailing listening conditions. Hearing tests include tests of tone discrimination and speech discrimination, and should be conducted by a trained audiologist. Auditory losses may result from aging, from such environmental conditions as prolonged exposure to intense noise, and from various ear diseases.

Major auditory disorders include presbycusis, conductive hearing loss, and central auditory impairment. Audition is the sense most affected by aging: About 30 percent of all adults between ages 65 and 74, and 50 percent of those between 75 and 79, suffer some degree of hearing loss. Yet all too many older adults refuse to admit that they have a hearing problem, with the result that some have been incorrectly diagnosed as unresponsive, uncooperative, or even pathologically depressed.

TASTE AND SMELL

Several early studies suggested that adults past age 50 have more difficulty detecting all of the four primary taste sensations. However, the best recent evidence indicates that the sense of taste remains relatively stable with increasing age. Very few studies have dealt with age-related taste preferences; one experiment suggests that older adults have a stronger dislike for bitter stimuli than do younger subjects.

Data concerning age-related changes in olfactory sensitivity are more conclusive. Several recent studies indicate a reduced sensitivity to a number of different odors with increasing age, especially after age 70. For example, older adults are less likely to detect a gas leak because of their reduced olfactory abilities. Changes in odor preference are unlikely to occur after age 30. For both taste and smell, losses in sensitivity may also be caused by illnesses, such as upper respiratory infections and Alzheimer's disease.

SOMESTHESIS: THE SKIN AND KINESTHETIC SENSES

Data concerning the skin senses are sparse, often dated, and frequently equivocal: Some declines with increasing age have been observed in touch and vibratory sensitivity, and in the ability to cope with cold temperatures. Some studies report a marked decline in pain sensitivity with increasing age; others do not. Here again, decrements in sensitivity are probably due more to the increased likelihood of disease and injury at older ages than to aging per se.

One important problem faced by the elderly is their susceptibility to potentially fatal falls. There is some indication that this may be due in part to decreased input from the various kinesthetic receptors.

Little is known about the relationship between aging and the skin and kinesthetic senses as compared to vision, audition, taste, and smell. However, the growing research interest in these topics suggests that important new information may well become available in the not-too-distant future.

Study Questions

1. Based on the empirical evidence presented in this chapter, are middle-aged and elderly adults less competent at driving an automobile than younger adults? Which should take precedence: the need of older adults to engage in an activity (such as driving, so they can be independent and transport themselves) or the needs of society (to improve safety on the road, even if only slightly)?
2. How might a hearing disorder give the false impression of being a psychological disorder, or even result in a true psychological disorder? How might this information be useful when counseling an older adult to correct declines in hearing with an appropriate mechanical aid?
3. How have cross-cultural studies helped us to understand the reasons for declines in hearing with increasing age in the United States?
4. Why do some theorists recommend that a special odor be added to natural gas that is delivered to homes where elderly adults live?

Terms to Remember

Accommodation	*Frequency*
Auditory nerve	*Glaucoma*
Basilar membrane	*Gustation*
Blind spot	*Hair cells of the ear*
Cataracts	*Hertz*
Central auditory impairment	*Intensity*
Cochlea	*Iris*
Conductive hearing loss	*Kinesthesis*
Cones	*Lens*
Dark adaptation	*Loudness*
Decibel	*Olfaction*
Diabetic retinopathy	*Optic nerve*
Dynamic visual acuity	*Ossicles*
Eardrum	*Oval window*
Fovea	*Pitch*

Presbycusis
Presbyopia
Pupillary reflex
Retinal detachment
Retina
Retinal disorders

Rods
Senile macular degeneration
Somesthesis
Static visual acuity
Visual acuity

Chapter 5

Learning and Memory

Julie O'Neil/The Picture Cube

No one has ever seen memories, yet they pervade our everyday life. Memory makes it possible for you to recall your loved one's names and faces, what foods you like and where to obtain them, where you can safely sleep at night, how to do your job or perform your favorite sport, whether or not you liked last night's date or last month's vacation, previous events in the novel that you have not yet finished reading—and even your own identity, which depends on a continuous sense of self that links your past with your present. Without this invaluable ability, you would be forced to live from one disconnected moment to the next, trying to discover over and over again the information that would enable you to survive.

The ability to learn is also vital to our existence. Learning enables you to outgrow the dependency of infancy and childhood, and become a self-sufficient adult. Because you are able to learn, you can develop new skills and hobbies. You can profit from your painful or disappointing mistakes by switching to behaviors that are more rewarding. You can have a child and care for it properly, even though you have never done so before. You can move to a new city and become able to negotiate unfamiliar terrain without getting lost. You can acquire new friends, or pursue a new romance. Without the ability to learn, these activities would be impossible. Your knowledge would forever be frozen at a constant level; you would be unable to recognize potential new friends the next time you saw them, or to become familiar with street names and directions in your new home city. In fact, you would be unable to cope with *any* situation that you did not already know how to handle.

Because learning and memory are so essential to our survival, many older adults are frightened about the prospect of declines in these abilities—even more so than they are about possible sensory and physical impairments. These fears are intensified by the common stereotype of the forgetful and rambling older adult, which suggests significant memory declines in old age. They are also reflected in surveys of the elderly, many of whom report memory difficulties and expect this problem to become even worse with increasing age (Cavanaugh & Poon, 1989; Perlmutter et al., 1987).

In the preceding two chapters, we have seen that many of our physiological mechanisms do decline to varying degrees with increasing age; these include physical strength and endurance, circulation, respiration, excretion, audition, and vision. Memory and learning also depend to a considerable extent on physiological processes. Therefore, we must ask: What changes occur in these important cognitive functions as we grow older?

Learning and Memory Research: Basic Issues

METHODOLOGICAL PROBLEMS

The question posed in the preceding section is not an easy one to answer. One important problem is methodological.

Suppose that we try to determine the relationships among aging, learning, and memory by comparing the performance of younger and older adults on a variety of cognitive tasks (the cross-sectional method). There are various reasons why older adults might perform more poorly, other than declines in the ability to learn and remember. For example, middle-aged and elderly adults may be less motivated to do well on apparently meaningless laboratory tasks. Their educational level may well be lower than that of young adults. Their health may be significantly poorer. Or they may have had fewer recent opportunities to practice their cognitive skills because they have long since left school, or have retired from their jobs. That is, inferior performance by older adults could be due largely to cohort effects, rather than to aging. If instead we try to minimize cohort effects by conducting a lengthy longitudinal study, our results may prove to be obsolete when the study is completed some 10 or 15 years later; the field of learning and memory is currently undergoing continuous and extensive changes (Hartley, Harker, & Walsh, 1980; Hultsch & Dixon, 1990). For these reasons, obtaining accurate age-related data in the experimental laboratory can be a highly challenging task.

CONCEPTUAL PROBLEMS

The Distinction Between Learning and Memory. Another problem faced by researchers in this area involves the conceptual distinction between learning and memory, which is far from clear-cut. You cannot remember something unless you previously acquired at least some knowledge of it, a phenomenon that sounds very much like learning. Conversely, one common test of whether or not you have learned something is your ability to remember it at a later date. Thus experimental studies which purportedly deal with memory must of necessity also involve learning, and vice versa.

The Complexity of Learning and Memory. Learning and memory are more complicated constructs than might be apparent. Some years ago, for example, Tulving (1972; 1983) posited two distinct kinds of memory: **Episodic memory** records experiences in terms of time and place, and **semantic memory** involves our storehouse of general knowledge about the meanings of words, numbers, symbols, and their interrelationships.

If you recall that you ate a hamburger and french fries for lunch yesterday and remember where this meal took place, you are relying on your episodic memory. That is, you are remembering the time and place of a specific personal event, without making any effort to analyze or understand it. Your memory of what hamburgers and french fries are, where they come from, and how to calculate the bill is quite a different matter. You may readily recall that hamburgers are a form of meat obtained from livestock, and that french fries are made from a vegetable taken from the earth (potatoes), but it is very unlikely that you remember precisely when and where you first acquired this knowledge. These understandings are aspects of semantic memory, which is concerned with abstract and conceptual relationships.

Semantic memories tend to last much longer than episodic memories. You will probably always remember that potatoes grow in the ground and only become french fries later on, yet you may find it difficult or impossible to recall specific episodes from five years ago when you ate french fries. Understanding a concept often requires activating a larger network of facts and their relations than does merely noting when and where an event takes place. (Some important episodic memories may be long-lasting, however, such as the date and place of one's marriage.)

Nor does this appear to be the whole story. More recently, Tulving (1985) concluded that the nature of memory is still more complicated: There is a third form, which he calls **procedural memory**. This type of memory enables us to retain learned connections between stimuli and responses, and to deal adaptively with our environment, without necessarily recalling specific information from the past. An experienced baseball shortstop can field a ground ball and quickly throw it to the right base because he has done so many times before; he does not need to recall previous episodes involving grounders or understand the reasons for his play in order to follow the correct procedure. (In fact, if he tries to do so, he will undoubtedly take too long to make the play and the batter will be safe.) Procedural memory is evidenced only by making the correct overt response, whereas information from episodic and semantic memory can be consciously considered, elaborated upon, and used purposively.

Although not all theorists agree with this particular tripartite conception of memory, it does illustrate the complexities that we will encounter when we try to ascertain the relationships among aging, memory, and learning. (See Perlmutter et al., 1987.) As we will see, aging may well have quite different relationships to some kinds of memory and learning than to others.

AFTERWORD

To date, the two most influential models for studying learning and memory have been associationism and information processing. These theories have determined the kinds of research questions that have been asked in these areas, and the methods used to answer them. We will therefore begin this chapter by reviewing some of the major adult developmental findings in the realm of associationism. Although few modern psychologists would characterize themselves as associationists, these data are important because they provided the point of departure for more recent theories. Next we will investigate the currently more popular information-processing model. Our discussion will also touch on important practical issues, such as studies of everyday memory and methods for helping adults to improve their memory and ability to learn.

Associationist Approaches to Learning and Memory

As the name implies, **associationism** attributes all learning and memory to the association of stimuli and responses (S–R) that occur closely together in time. According to this model, learning consists of the formation and strengthening of these S–R bonds. Memory is evidenced when a stimulus is presented, and a response which has been previously associated with this stimulus (i.e., learned) is emitted. And forgetting results when the bond between a stimulus and a response grows weak or disappears.

To illustrate, consider Pavlov's famous experiment on classical conditioning. A dog was presented with a light (or tone); this was immediately followed by food, which caused the dog to salivate. After numerous repetitions of this procedure, the dog regularly salivated to the light alone. Because the light stimulus and the salivation response repeatedly occurred within a second or so of each other, a new S–R bond was formed between these elements. Similarly, some people fear the dentist's chair because of classical conditioning; this stimulus has repeatedly been associated with the pain and discomfort or having their teeth drilled. That is, and S–R bond has been formed between the dentist's chair and pain.

Since associationism defines learning and memory in terms of single S–R bonds, how can it explain more complicated forms of behavior? Simple S–R elements may be combined into a lengthy chain, wherein responses also serve as stimuli. Furthermore, associated stimuli and responses may be covert as well as overt. For example, suppose that you are trying to answer

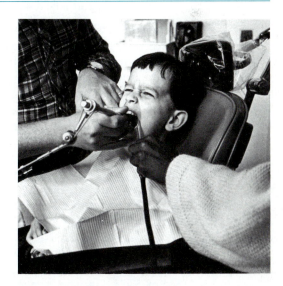

Some fears are due to classical conditioning, for example, when the stimulus of the dentist's chair has been repeatedly associated with the pain and discomfort of having one's teeth drilled. (Joel Gordon/Joel Gordon Photography)

an essay question on an examination. Your first response to this stimulus is to write down a word or sentence, which is possible because you have previously learned to associate certain aspects of this essay question with other information. This response then serves as a stimulus that elicits a subsequent response, such as writing down a second sentence (or perhaps deciding to erase what you have written and substitute a better alternative). Here again, you will be able to do this if you previously formed a strong S–R bond between these ideas. If not, the first sentence that you wrote down will not elicit any response, and you will unhappily conclude that you have forgotten the material (or that you failed to learn it well enough). Alternatively, the first sentence may be associated with information that you decide not to include in your answer because it is not relevant. But this information may be associated with yet another idea, which you do regard as suitable. This chain would then take the form S–r–s–R, where the small *r* and *s* represent the association that occurs only as a covert thought. Thus the simple building blocks formed by S–R bonds can be combined into highly complicated patterns.

Various forms of learning and memory have been explained in associationist terms. Much of the research on classical conditioning (and on Skinnerian operant conditioning, the second major type of conditioning) has been carried out with animals, mostly rats and mice (Woodruff-Pak, 1990). Although these studies may provide useful clues about age-related declines in humans, we will focus our attention on studies with humans. We will therefore limit our survey of associationism to two areas that are of particular gerontological importance: motor skill learning and verbal learning.

MOTOR SKILL LEARNING AND MEMORY

Definition.   **Motor skill learning** refers to any task wherein the subject must learn a sequence of bodily movements. Some motor skill tasks are fairly simple, such as unlocking a door or operating the ignition of an automobile. Often, however, the learner must associate various bodily responses with the perception of rapidly changing environmental stimuli. For example, driving an automobile in traffic requires you to make frequent changes in the pressure you exert on the gas pedal and brake, and in the position of the steering wheel, in response to what you observe in front of and around you.

Motor learning is also exemplified by buttoning your shirt, pouring juice into a glass without spilling any, hitting a baseball, brushing your teeth, playing a guitar, racking up a high score in a video game, typing, and countless other everyday activities. Associationists contend that motor skill learning involves a chain of S–R bonds but that the stimuli are often internal: The kinesthetic cues produced by your response at one stage of the sequence trigger the subsequent response.

Motor Skill Learning and Aging.   Many motor skills are acquired in childhood, adolescence, or early adulthood, and are practiced so often that they

become effortless and do not require conscious attention. These skills therefore tend to persist until very late in life.

For example, pilots between the ages of 40 and 60 have as few or fewer
accidents than younger pilots (Birren, 1964). Similarly, industrial workers
age 65 and over have fewer disabling accidents than employees age 25–34
(McFarland & Doherty, 1959; Sterns, Barrett, & Alexander, 1985). The one
notable exception concerns speeded responses: Older adults are more likely
to incur accidents caused by the failure to act quickly enough, such as being
hit by a moving object because they cannot get out of the way in time. But
when response speed is not a factor, the accident rate tends to decrease with
increasing age (King, 1955).

To be sure, there are some atypical and extremely complicated motor skills
that do decline to some extent with increasing age. Thus it is not unusual for
professional athletes and practitioners of certain arts to retire by middle age
because they can no longer perform effectively. But even here, there are many
well-known examples of individuals who continued to perform well at a
relatively advanced age: cellist Pablo Casals, pianist Arthur Rubinstein, and
golfer Sam Snead, to name just a few. For the most part, previously learned
motor skills are unlikely to deteriorate seriously with increasing age. (See
Welford, 1984.)

Although it is reassuring to find that our basic motor skills are not greatly
affected by aging, we must also ask how difficult it is for older adults to
acquire new motor skills. Some elderly individuals will be faced with such
tasks as learning to operate a wheelchair, and some may wish to take up golf
or other sports during retirement. Although research interest in this area has
waned in recent years, it does seem that older adults have greater difficulty
learning new motor skills, especially if cognition is required between the
visual input and the bodily response. (See Kay, 1954; 1955.)

VERBAL LEARNING AND MEMORY

A great deal of research on adult learning and memory has focused on verbal stimuli and responses, an area first investigated by Hermann Ebbinghaus
in the 1870s. Basing his ideas directly on associationism, Ebbinghaus concluded that memory consists of S–R bonds between various ideas or events.
He believed that using prose or poetry to test these associations would present formidable problems, since different excerpts might well differ considerably in difficulty. Therefore, Ebbinghaus developed his own stimuli: nonsense
syllables consisting of consonant/vowel/consonant combinations, such as
SEB, WUC, and LUP. (See Walsh, 1983.) In more recent verbal learning
research, single words are also often used as stimuli.

Serial and Paired-Associate Learning: Definitions.   In **serial learning**, the
subject is required to learn a list of words or nonsense syllables in the exact
order in which they appear. Examples of serial learning in everyday life
include learning the combination to a lock, memorizing a list of instructions

in the correct order (such as the directions to a friend's house), and knowing the sequence of stations you pass through when taking the commuter train home from work.

In some research studies, the subject is asked to reproduce the entire list from memory. More often, however, the subject must anticipate the item that follows a preceding one. That is, items on the list are presented one at a time, and the subject must quickly state the item that will appear next. Typically, items at the beginning of the list are easiest to recall; this is known as the **primacy effect**. Most difficult of all to remember are items in the middle of the list. Items at the end of the list are recalled more often than those in the middle (albeit not as readily as items at the beginning), a phenomenon referred to as the **recency effect**.

In **paired-associate learning**, on the other hand, pairs of items are used (e.g., SEB–GIF, WUC–ZEH, LUP–DOF). Real-life examples include associating an English word with the corresponding word in a foreign language, and memorizing the names of certain cities and the nickname of the National Football League team that plays in each one.

During the "study phase" of a paired-associate learning experiment, the subject is shown each of the S–R pairs; the time permitted to examine each pair is referred to as the **inspection interval**. This is followed by the "test phase": The left-hand member of each pair is presented by itself, and the subject must reply with the right-hand member before it is revealed by the experimenter a few seconds later. The time allowed the subject to respond to each item is known as the **anticipation interval**. The order of the pairs is usually changed on subsequent trials, but the specific items in each pair remain the same. (See Figure 5.1.)

For both serial and paired-associate learning, the difficulty of the task may be measured in two ways: the number of *trials* needed to learn the entire list without error, or the number of *errors* that are made until the list is learned perfectly. Memory may be indexed by the number of trials required on the following day to return to the previous level of accuracy.

Verbal Learning and Aging: I. Stimulus Rate.   Most studies of verbal learning and aging have been cross-sectional and are subject to the limitations of this type of research. Because learning and memory are unobservable processes, these abilities can only be inferred from **performance** on various tasks; and task performance may be influenced by cohort effects, individual differences, and other variables, as well as by genuine age-related changes in ability. Nevertheless, some fairly clear and important trends have emerged from this body of research.

First of all, older adults consistently perform more poorly on both serial and paired-associate learning tasks than do young adults (e.g., Arenberg, 1967; Arenberg & Robertson-Tchabo, 1977; Canestrari, 1963; 1966; 1968; Eisdorfer & Service, 1967; Zaretsky & Halberstam, 1968a; 1968b). To illustrate, findings from six paired-associate studies are summarized in Figure 5.2. Although there are some discrepancies insofar as specific patterns are

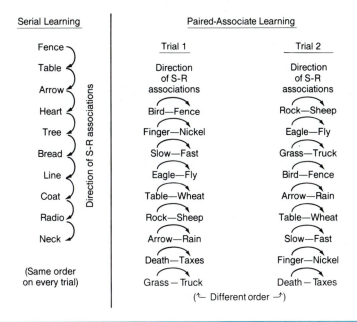

Figure 5.1
Comparison of serial learning and paired-associate learning.

concerned, all of these studies indicate a significant decline in performance with increasing age, sometimes beginning as early as age 30 or 40. Because such declines have been observed so frequently in empirical research, it has been widely concluded that they cannot be due solely to cohort effects or other forms of bias. Our capacity to learn and remember must decrease as we grow older, as least to some extent.

Why might this be true? One possible answer involves the ability of older adults to cope with speeded tasks: It has been found that the faster the rate at which the stimulus items are presented, the greater are the age-related differences in performance. (See Hultsch & Dixon, 1990.) In one study (Canestrari, 1963), a sample of young adults (age 17–35) and a sample of older adults (age 60–69) were required to learn three lists. Each list was presented at a different pace:

- *Fast pace:* Inspection and anticipation intervals of 1.5 seconds.
- *Slow pace:* Inspection and anticipation intervals of 3.0 seconds.
- *Self-paced:* Unlimited inspection and anticipation intervals. Subjects could take all the time they needed to examine each pair during the study phase and to respond to each item during the test phase.

Although the younger group performed better under all three conditions, the most striking age differences occurred at the fast pace. (See Figure 5.3A.)

When stimuli were presented every 1.5 seconds, the older group made many more errors of omission. Their performance suffered not because they usually gave wrong words as answers, but because they often failed to provide any response at all. Conversely, older adults fared better in the self-paced condition because they took significantly more time than did the younger group, especially during the test phase. Subsequent research has confirmed that longer anticipation intervals reduce age differences in performance on paired-associate tasks, although middle-aged and elderly subjects rarely perform as well as young adults even when there is no time pressure of any kind (e.g., Monge & Hultsch, 1971; Salthouse, 1982).

Similar findings have also been obtained from serial learning experiments. When items in the list are presented at a faster rate, all subjects perform more poorly. But the adverse effects are greater for older adults, especially those past middle age (Arenberg, 1967; see Figure 5.3B).

These data suggest that older adults perform more poorly on learning and memory tasks because they cannot respond as quickly. We will return to this hypothesis later in this chapter, when we discuss research based on the more recent information-processing approach to learning and memory.

Figure 5.2

The relationship between age and performance on paired-associate learning tasks.   Source: Adapted from Salthouse (1982, p. 126).

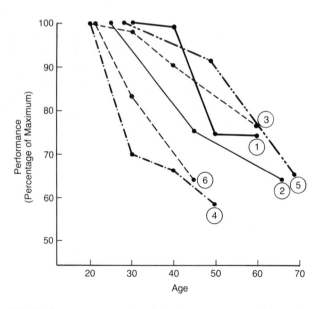

Note. Performance scores are expressed as a percentage of the maximum score across all ages. The circled numbers refer to different experiments: (1) Canestrari, 1968; (2) Gladis & Braun, 1958; (3) Hulicka, 1966; (4) Monge, 1971; (5) Smith, 1975; (6) Thorndike et al., 1928.

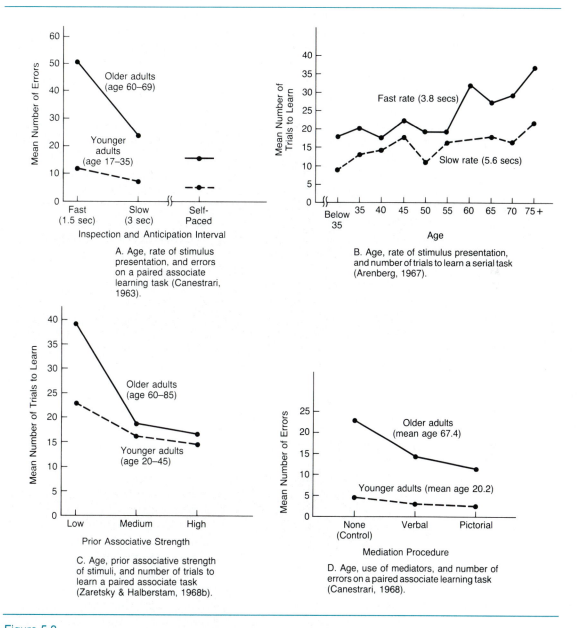

A. Age, rate of stimulus presentation, and errors on a paired associate learning task (Canestrari, 1963).

B. Age, rate of stimulus presentation, and number of trials to learn a serial task (Arenberg, 1967).

C. Age, prior associative strength of stimuli, and number of trials to learn a paired associate task (Zaretsky & Halberstam, 1968b).

D. Age, use of mediators, and number of errors on a paired associate learning task (Canestrari, 1968).

Figure 5.3
Aging and verbal learning: Some typical research findings. Source: Adapted from Kausler (1982, pp. 378, 381, 385, 387).

Verbal Learning and Aging: II. Mediators. Paired-associate studies have shown that the relationships among aging, learning, and memory also depend on how often the items in each pair have been associated in the past. Older adults perform much more poorly than young adults when the paired items are low in prior associative strength, such as *finger–nickel*; but they are at less of a disadvantage if each pair consists of commonly associated items, such as *slow–fast* or *eagle–fly* (Canestrari, 1966; Kausler & Lair, 1966; Zaretsky & Halberstam, 1968a; 1968b). In one study, older adults (age 60–85) averaged approximately 40 trials to learn the task when the prior associative strength of the paired items was low, whereas younger adults (age 20–45) required only about 23 trials. But when the prior associative strength of the paired items was high, the superiority of the younger group dropped to approximately three trials. (See Figure 5.3C.)

Findings like these led verbal learning researchers to posit the importance of **mediators**, or intervening links between the stimulus and response that can serve as an effective aid to learning and memory. For example, the *finger–nickel* association might be more easily acquired and recalled by using the verbal mediator "five," because there are five fingers on each hand and a nickel is worth five cents. Thus, if the subject silently says "five" when presented with this pair during the study phase, this mediator may make it easier to remember that the correct response is "nickel." Or the mediator might take the form of a pictorial image, with the subject visualizing a finger holding a nickel (Paivio, 1971). Apparently, older adults do not use mediators as often or as well as do younger adults (Canestrari, 1968; Hulicka & Grossman, 1967; Poon, Walsh-Sweeney, & Fozard, 1980). This makes little difference when the prior associative strength of the paired items is so high that mediators are not needed (e.g., *slow–fast*), but places older adults at a significant disadvantage when the paired items are so dissimilar that a mediator would be helpful.

If older adults are provided with specific training in the use of mediators, such as mnemonic devices, there is some improvement in their performance on paired-associate tasks. This is especially true when pictorial mediators are used. (See Figure 5.3D.) But even with this assistance, older adults are still unable to match the performance of young adults.

Similar findings have also emerged from serial learning research (Bugelski, Kidd, & Segmen, 1968; Miller, Galanter, & Pribram, 1960). For example, if the list to be learned consists of ten items, subjects may first be asked to learn a series of rhymes involving the numbers one through ten (e.g., "one is a bun," "two is a shoe," "three is a tree"). Then, when the serial list is presented, the learner is advised to form a distinctive image of the first word interacting with a bun. For example, if this word is *car*, the subject might envision a sandwich consisting of a bun piled high with lettuce, tomato, and a Chevrolet. Similarly, each of the other nine rhymes helps the subject to form a pictorial image that will make it easier to recall the corresponding item on the list. Or subjects may be asked to imagine a trip through a familiar environment, such as their own home, and to key an image of each word on the list to a distinctive location. Thus *car* (the first word on the list) might be visualized in the hallway, *horse* (the second word on the list) in the living room, and so forth. Once this has been done, the subject recalls the list by mentally traveling the route once again in the same order and naming the object found at each location. These strategies have been used effectively with both young and old subjects, although young subjects usually perform better. (See Bower, 1970; Kliegh & Baltes, 1987; Mason & Smith, 1977; Yesavage & Sheikh, 1989.)

These results suggest that there may be a genuine loss in mediational ability with increasing age, possibly due to physiological deterioration in the central nervous system, and that this loss is in part responsible for the inferior performance of older adults on learning and memory tasks. It is possible, however, that the poorer mediational ability of older adults may be due partly or largely to disuse. The use of mediators may be most common fairly early in life, as when college students use this technique to increase the amount of material that can be recalled on an examination. If so, younger generations may perform better on paired-associate and serial tasks because they have had more recent practice with the use of mediators. Whatever the reason, this issue has also exerted a strong influence on more recent learning and memory research—as we will see later in this chapter.

Afterword.   The findings of verbal learning studies have stimulated a great deal of modern research. Therefore, the traditional associationist approach to the study of learning and memory was the logical place to begin our search for age-related differences. Serial and paired-associate learning tasks are similar to some forms of real-life learning, as we have seen. So it is not surprising that associationist research has made important contributions to our understanding of the relationships among aging and learning and memory.

However, the associationist approach also has its limitations. As we observed at the outset of this chapter, psychologists now believe that there are several distinct kinds of memory. Thus the associationist assumption that serial and paired-associate tasks tap *the* ability to learn and remember now appears to be a serious oversimplification.

Although serial and paired-associate tasks do have real-life analogues, they are still artificial laboratory procedures. It has been argued that even if there is a true age-related decline in our ability to recall lists of unrelated items, this decrement may have little or no bearing on our ability to perform such everyday functions as gleaning new information from the daily newspaper or remembering the events in a novel that we began a few nights ago. That is, serial and paired-associate tasks may be low in **ecological validity**: These findings may not apply very well to the behavior of men and women in their natural environments.

Nonsense syllables and unrelated single words may even be perceived as so irrelevant by older adults that they strongly object to the experiment, and do not care how well (or how poorly) they perform. For example, Hulicka (1967; Hulicka & Weiss, 1965) tried to administer a paired-associate task to subjects age 65–80, using two letters as stimuli and single words as responses (e.g., *TL–insane*). This experiment suffered an extremely high dropout rate, with many of these elderly subjects refusing to make the effort to learn "such nonsense." But they carried out the task willingly when it was made more meaningful, as by using occupation names as stimuli and personal surnames as responses (e.g., *lawyer–Johnson*). The poorer performance of older adults when meaningless stimuli are used is a common research finding, although there are exceptions (e.g., Hanley-Dunn & McIntosh, 1984). For these reasons, some researchers have sought to measure the relationships among aging, learning, and memory by using more meaningful material, such as coherent sentences and paragraphs. This significant methodological change has also been accompanied by efforts to develop theoretical models that are more appropriate to this form of research.

Because of criticisms like these, most modern theorists have turned to alternative conceptions of learning and memory. The most notable of these is the information-processing approach, which is based on the principles that underlie modern electronic computers.

Information-Processing Approaches to Learning and Memory

INTRODUCTION

The **information-processing model** distinguishes between two major aspects of learning and memory: *structure* and *process*. **Structural theories** focus on the ways in which information is organized in the human brain, or how our memory banks are constructed. **Process theories** emphasize the mental activities that we perform when we try to put information into memory (learn), or make use of it at some later date (remember).

Structural Theories.   In an effort to understand how human memory is structured, some psychologists have tried to glean important clues from the design of electronic computers. Like human beings, computers can store remarkable amounts of information for long periods of time.

Computers possess several different kinds of memory. There is an input or peripheral buffer memory, which stores incoming information until enough data has been read into the computer for the analysis to begin. A working memory holds the information being actively analyzed by the computer. And the core memory stores large amounts of inactive information for later use. Accordingly, one prominent theory posits that there are three distinct types of human memory-storage structures:

1. *Sensory Memory:* The very brief persistence of a visual, auditory, or other form of sensation after the stimulus is withdrawn. Sensory memories last for perhaps a fraction of a second after the presentation of a stimulus, and are a nearly exact replica of that stimulus. However, if the information is not

converted to some more durable form, it will be quickly lost (Bourne, Domin-owski, & Loftus, 1979).

2. *Primary Memory* (also referred to as "short-term memory" and, more recently, as "working memory"): Memories that last from one or two seconds up to about half a minute. When someone talks to you, you can understand the meaning of each sentence because the initial words are still fresh in your mind when the end of the sentence is reached, even though you may well forget the entire conversation shortly thereafter. Or you may be introduced to someone at a party and retain this name long enough to say it while shaking hands, but be unable to recall it half an hour later. Or you may look up a number in the telephone directory and remember it long enough to dial it accurately, get a busy signal, and then have to look up the same number again because you can no longer recall it (and have neglected to write it down).

These common experiences suggest that the ability to remember information for very short periods of time is distinctly different from the capacity for longer-term memories. In this structural theory, therefore, primary memory is conceptualized as a temporary and limited-capacity storage system. It holds relatively little information at any one time, and the information that it contains decays very rapidly.

What can be done to prevent this material from being lost completely? If the information in primary memory is rehearsed or elaborated upon, as by repeating it several times, it will enter secondary memory. The process of rehearsal and elaboration that enables information to proceed from primary memory to secondary memory is called **encoding**. (See Smith & Fullerton, 1981; Poon, 1985.) As we will see later in this chapter, old persons exhibit substantial encoding deficits when compared to younger persons.

3. *Secondary Memory* (also referred to as "long-term memory"): Memories that last from one or two minutes to many years. You have a great many of these memories at your disposal: your name, birth date, and other biographical data; similar information about your loved ones; various facts and abstract relationships that enable you to perform well on a job or in school; geographical data about the city, state, and country in which you live; recollections of experiences that you have had in the recent and distant past; information concerning your hobbies, such as what happened in a novel you began last night or yesterday's baseball scores; and much more.

If secondary memory covers such a wide range of briefer and longer-lasting information, why do you need a sensory and a primary memory at all? Without sensory memories, brief though they are, you would lose track of incoming information too quickly for any of it ever to be remembered. Sensory memories occur automatically, without any effort on your part, and they preserve information in your nervous system just long enough for it to undergo further processing. If you pay *attention* to this information, it is read out from sensory memory and enters the next stage in the processing system—primary memory.

Primary memory plays an important role in the control and assimilation of information. If you tried to store all of the immense amount of data that reaches you through your senses, you would be inundated with so much data that you could not function at all. That is, too much information that arrives too rapidly will overload your cognitive system. For example, you would undoubtedly find it impossible to understand what a friend is saying while simultaneously trying to read a book and note the baseball scores being announced on a radio sportscast. Primary memory narrows down the information at your disposal to manageable limits because its storage capacity is very small (as we will see later in this chapter). Older data are frequently expelled to make room for new data, thereby making it easier for you to decide which information is important enough to be committed to secondary memory.

To illustrate, suppose that you are introduced to a group of twelve strangers at a party. Your primary memory will probably not be able to store all of these names at once. Instead, you may recall only four or five names. Faced with this more manageable input, you might then choose to focus on one name belonging to an attractive member of the opposite sex and repeat this name to yourself several times, with this rehearsal making it more likely that the name will enter your secondary memory (and that you will recall it later on). And this choice may be influenced by some useful feedback from your secondary memory, as when you recall some prior experiences with attractive members of the opposite sex that proved to be very pleasant.

This structural model is summarized in Figure 5.4. It assumes that human memory consists of three fixed structures, each of which represents one stage in the processing of the information that reaches us through our senses. Each form of memory has a particular function and a typical length of time during which information is stored therein. (See Table 5.1.) One appealing aspect of

Figure 5.4
A structural model of learning and memory.

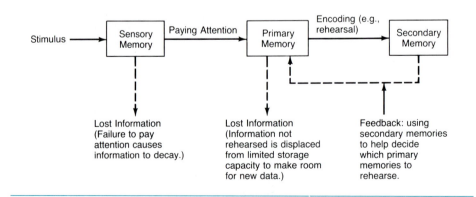

Table 5.1

A comparison of sensory memory, primary memory, and secondary memory.

Characteristic	Sensory Memory	Primary Memory	Secondary Memory
How information is entered	Without effort	Paying attention	Encoding (e.g., rehearsal)
How information is maintained	Not possible	Continued attention	Continued rehearsal, organization of the information
Form of information	Literal copy of input	Acoustic, visual, or semantic codes	Abstract symbols and their relationships (e.g., meanings)
Capacity	Large	Small (3–7 items)	Enormous
Duration of information	About one-quarter second (iconic memory); one-quarter to five or six seconds (echoic memory)	From one or two seconds to about half a minute	From one or two minutes to many years
Function	To preserve information until it can be consciously processed	To maintain active control of cognitive activity	To store information for later use
How information is forgotten	Decay	Decay and interference	Decay, interference, poor retrieval strategies
Computer analog	Input (buffer) memory	Working memory registers	Core memory; peripheral storage (e.g., disks, tapes)

this model is that it emphasizes a well-known and important aspect of human learning and memory, namely that some memories last considerably longer than others. It has proved to be very influential in learning and memory research, especially during the 1950s and 1960s.

More recently, however, this model has been found to have some significant flaws. (See, for example, Craik & Lockhart, 1972; Schneider & Shiffrin, 1977.) Although this is a structural theory, it also defines how information proceeds from one memory structure to another. That is, you presumably must pay attention to the information in sensory memory for it to proceed to primary memory, and you must rehearse the information in primary memory for it to enter secondary memory. This is a question of process, not structure. As researchers explored such issues further, many came to believe that the three structures are not nearly as functionally separate as this model implies. Instead, they concluded that process is more important than structure. That is, longer-lasting information is *not* shifted from one memory structure to another. It endures in memory because the individual has processed it more deeply, as by understanding its meaning rather than merely repeating it over and over. To these psychologists, then, learning and memory are better conceptualized in terms of process theories.

Process Theories. The act of remembering depends on three basic processes. First of all, to remember anything, you must first have learned it. For example, suppose you take an examination in French and are asked to translate the word *heureux*. Unless you previously learned that this word means "happy," you cannot possibly remember the answer during the test. This initial process is known as **acquisition.**

The second process is that of **retention**, wherein the information is filed away for future use. Your French test may occur days or weeks after the acquisition period, so you must retain the meaning of *heureux* until it is time to demonstrate your knowledge.

The third process, **retrieval**, concerns your efforts to dredge up a particular memory from all the others that you have acquired. You may be unable to translate *heureux* during the examination, yet you spontaneously remember the answer a few hours later without consulting your French text. This information must have been stored in your memory at exam time, since you did no subsequent studying of any kind. You acquired and retained it, but were unable to retrieve it.

Previously stored material can be retrieved in two ways. In **recall** tasks, you must produce the correct answer by searching your memory for the correct word or words (as in our example). In **recognition** tasks, you are shown various possible answers and must choose the correct one. Recall is considered to be a more demanding test of retrieval than is recognition, as you undoubtedly know from your experience with essay versus multiple-choice examinations.

Notice once again the intimate relationships between learning and memory. If you cannot remember important information during an examination, the problem might be one of retrieval: You learned the material but could not remember it during the examination, possibly because you were anxious or fatigued or because the answers you needed became confused with other information. However, the problem might instead be one of acquisition: You never really learned the material. You may not have studied very effectively; perhaps you merely read through the assigned chapters once, or you stared at the text while allowing your attention to wander to other matters. Conversely, if your studying was thorough enough so that you clearly understood what you read (as, for example, if you rewrote it in your own words), you are much more likely to remember this information during the examination. According to this theory, then, memory depends in part on how deeply you process the material in question. Understanding its meaning will produce much longer-lasting memories than just paying attention to it or rehearsing it repeatedly.

To illustrate, one sample of subjects was asked to participate in an experiment that was described as an investigation of perception and reaction time. Words printed in all upper-case or all lower-case letters were presented very briefly via a tachistoscope, one at a time (e.g., *friend, CRATE, table*) and the subjects were required to answer yes or no questions about each word as quickly as possible. At the shallowest level of processing, subjects were asked to indicate whether the physical structure of a word was lower-case type or upper-case type; this required only a brief scanning of the stimulus. To obtain a deeper level of processing, subjects were questioned about the sound of a word (e.g., "Does the word rhyme with *blend*?"). The deepest level of processing was induced by having subjects answer questions about the semantic features of a word (e.g., "Does the word fit this sentence: 'He met a ——— in the street'?"). Afterwards, to their complete surprise, subjects were tested for their ability to recognize the words used in the experiment. The results indicated that deeper levels of processing produced more durable memory traces: The semantic questions led to significantly better recognition than the phonemic questions, which in turn led to significantly better recognition than did the questions dealing only with the physical structure of the words (Craik & Tulving, 1975; see Figure 5.5). Thus, as we

Figure 5.5
A depth-of-processing model of learning and memory.

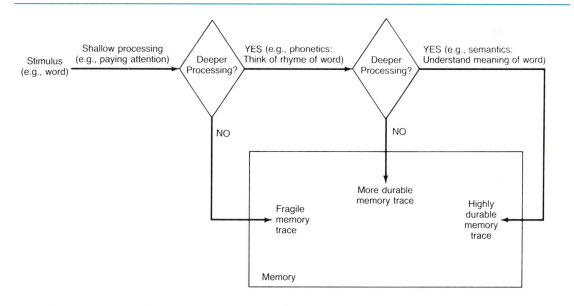

noted at the outset of this chapter, information processed in terms of many meaningful relationships (e.g., semantic memories) tends to last longer than information processed less thoroughly (e.g., episodic memories).

Although process theories are currently more popular than structural theories, useful age-related data have been derived from both structurally oriented and process-oriented research. We will therefore devote some attention to both models in the pages that follow.

STRUCTURAL CONSIDERATIONS: I.   SENSORY MEMORY

By temporarily preserving the physical characteristics of a stimulus, even for a fraction of a second, **sensory memory** retains information just long enough for you to process it. The capacity of the sensory memory storage systems is relatively large; you take in much more information with a single glance than you can possibly use. But sensory memories rarely interfere with one another because their duration is so brief, so it is rather easy to distinguish among them.

Definition: Iconic and Echoic Memory.   **Iconic memory** is a type of sensory memory that is based on the visual system (Neisser, 1967). It is the peripheral information store that maintains a faithful representation of a visual stimulus for less than one second after this stimulus is removed. In one noted study, three-by-four arrays of letters were presented to subjects via tachistoscope for 50 milliseconds (Sperling, 1960):

L   V   R   D

Z   P   S   Q

M   X   T   F

Immediately after each array was withdrawn from view, subjects were asked to name all 12 letters (the method of "whole report"). This typically proved to be impossible, and subjects averaged only about four to five correct letters per array. Yet many subjects also reported that they actually saw more letters, but could no longer remember them an instant later when asked what they had seen. This suggested a most interesting possibility: A visual mental picture (*icon*) of the entire array was formed in the subject's memory, but it faded away so rapidly that only four or five letters could be recalled.

To test this hypothesis, a modified version of this experimental procedure was used. Subjects were now asked to name only one row of letters, with this row not specified until a fraction of a second after the array disappeared (the method of "partial report"). A high-frequency tone was used to request the top row, a middle-frequency tone specified the second row, and a low-frequency tone designated the bottom row. Under these conditions, the performance of the subjects was nearly perfect. But when there was so much as a one-second delay between the removal of the array and the designation of the row to be recalled, performance dropped to the usual level of about 40 percent correct (Sperling, 1960). These results clearly indicated that the entire icon must be available for an instant in sensory memory, enabling subjects to scan it and recall the designated row of letters. Subsequent research has estimated the duration of iconic memory to be approximately one-quarter of a second (e.g., Haber & Nathanson, 1968; Haber & Standing, 1969; 1970; McCloskey & Watkins, 1978).

A second important type of sensory memory is based on the auditory system. **Echoic memory** is the peripheral information store that maintains a faithful representation of an auditory stimulus for a very brief period after this stimulus is removed (Neisser, 1967; Rumelhart, 1977). The auditory analog of Sperling's procedure utilizes a cleverly designed set of stereophonic earphones: Subjects simultaneously hear one list of letters (or numbers) in the left ear, a different list in the right ear, and a third list that appears to be coming from the middle of the head because it is presented binaurally. Typically, each list is three items long. When the whole report method is used, subjects are asked to name all nine items. If instead the partial report method is used, subjects are informed visually whether to report the list from the left ear, the right ear, or the middle. Here again, the partial-report method produces significantly better performance than does the whole-report method, indicating that a substantial number of these auditory items are briefly retained in echoic memory (Darwin, Turvey, & Crowder, 1972).

Echoic memories last somewhat longer than iconic memories. There duration in the preceding experiment was approximately two seconds, but other estimates have varied from one-quarter of a second to as much as five or six seconds (e.g., Crowder & Morton, 1969; Crowder & Prussin, 1971; Crowder & Raeburn, 1970; Massaro, 1972; Routh & Mayes, 1974).

Sensory Memory and Aging. Insofar as iconic memory is concerned, adults over age 60 do tend to have considerable difficulty with Sperling's partial-report task. However, this is *not* due to decrements in sensory memory. The rapid shifting of attention becomes more difficult with increasing age (Chapter 4), and older adults apparently cannot focus their attention on the designated row fast enough to retrieve it before the iconic memory trace fades (Walsh & Prasse, 1980). Also, the elderly deal with this task inefficiently; they focus too strongly on the top row of letters in the array (Salthouse, 1976). Since sensory memory occurs automatically, without any effort on our part, these task difficulties are irrelevant to the question at hand. They represent methodological sources of bias, which make it virtually impossible for Sperling's task to reveal the true relationship between aging and iconic memory.

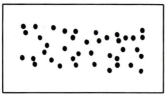

First Stimulus

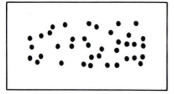

Second Stimulus

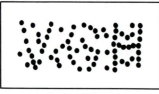

First and Second
Stimuli Superimposed

Figure 5.6
An experimental method for determining the duration of iconic memory. Source: Adapted from Eriksen & Collins (1967).

In order to obtain valid age-related data in this area, researchers have had to devise tasks that make fewer demands on the subjects' attention and response strategies. One good alternative is to briefly expose two successive stimuli, with the interval between them varying from a small fraction of a second to one or two seconds. The goal is to determine the largest inter-stimulus interval for which the two stimuli are perceived as connected, rather than as separate and distinct. This provides an indication as to the maximum duration of the iconic memory trace, or how long it can last and obtrude on the second stimulus. For example, suppose that both the first and the second stimulus consist of a series of meaningless dots. When the two stimuli are superimposed, however, they form a recognizable nonsense syllable such as *VOH*. (See Figure 5.6.) If these stimuli are presented a half-second apart, and if the subject correctly reports the nonsense syllable, the iconic memory trace of the first stimulus must have persisted for half a second (Eriksen & Collins, 1967). And if the iconic memory trace lasts significantly longer for younger adults than for older adults, we may reasonably conclude that this form of memory does decline with increasing age. In general, however, research in this area has found that iconic memory is largely unaffected by aging. (See, for example, Amberson et al., 1979; Kline & Baffa, 1976; Kline & Orme-Rogers, 1978; Kline & Schieber, 1981; Walsh & Thompson, 1978.)

As compared with iconic memory, the methodological problems involved in testing the relationship between aging and echoic memory are even more formidable. Because older adults more often suffer from significant hearing impairments than from visual disorders (Chapter 4), it can be difficult to distinguish between age-related declines in echoic memory and decrements caused by poor health. However, the available evidence suggests that echoic memory is also largely unaffected by aging (e.g., Arenberg, 1968; 1976; Crowder, 1980; Parkinson & Perey, 1980).

As we observed previously in this chapter, older adults have greater difficulty with highly speeded learning and memory tasks. However, it has been shown that older adults do *not* suffer any significant slowing of iconic or echoic memory (Cerella, 1985).

In sum: There appears to be no significant relationship between aging and the capacities of iconic and echoic memory. (There is virtually no age-related research dealing with any other form of sensory memory.) If there is any truth to the common belief that our ability to learn and remember declines significantly with increasing age, the reasons must lie elsewhere.

STRUCTURAL CONSIDERATIONS: II.   PRIMARY MEMORY

Definition.   The function of **primary memory** is to hold a sufficiently small amount of information for conscious processing. Therefore, the storage capacity of this "working memory" is extremely limited; it has been estimated at only about three to seven unrelated letters, digits, or words (Baddeley, 1970; Craik, 1971; Murdock, 1967; Watkins, 1974). Primary memories are also of very brief duration, lasting from one or two seconds up to about half a minute. You typically encounter a great deal of information while driving to school or work, reading the daily newspaper, or simply observing the environment, yet you forget much of this information a few moments later.

In recent years, the concept of **working memory** has become a popular way to describe how information is regulated in primary memory. Working memory consists of both a limited capacity storage system, like primary memory, and a central executive capable of selecting or manipulating the information in primary memory (Baddeley, 1981; Hultsch & Dixon, 1990). Thus primary memory is somewhat like the loading platform of a warehouse: Items must first pass through this register before they can enter secondary memory, only a limited number of items are handled at any one time, and old items are quickly cleared away so that new items can be processed. And working memory is the superintendent who is responsible for making sure that each item is sent to its proper location.

Primary Memory and Aging.   There are several different ways in which primary memory might be adversely affected by aging. We will consider each of these in turn.

Does the storage capacity of primary memory decrease with increasing age? Conceivably, middle-aged and elderly adults might be able to store even less information in primary memory than do young adults. One experimental procedure commonly used to test this hypothesis is the **digit-span test:** The subject is read a sequence of digits, which must immediately be repeated back in the same order. The stimuli may vary from as few as two or three digits to as many as twelve or more, and the number of digits that the subject can reliably report reflects the storage capacity or his or her primary memory. Various studies have found that age differences in performance on this task are small or nonexistent, indicating that primary memory capacity remains stable as we grow older (e.g., Botwinick & Storandt, 1974; Craik, 1968a; Drachman & Leavitt, 1972; Talland, 1968).

Corroborating evidence comes from a second methodological approach, the **free-recall task**. The subject is presented with a series of items (usually common English words, sometimes nonsense syllables), which are to be recalled in *any* order. Enough items are presented so that the subject cannot remember all of them. This task produces a somewhat different form of recency effect than is the case with serial learning: The last few items in the list are recalled first. This is attributable chiefly to primary memory, although the very last item may be recalled from sensory memory. Therefore, if older adults have significantly more difficulty recalling the last few items than do young adults, this would suggest that the storage capacity of primary memory declines with increasing age. However, this does not appear to be the case. Older adults perform as well as young adults in this regard, indicating once again that age differences in the storage capacity of primary memory are minimal (Craik, 1968b; Raymond, 1971; see also Craik, 1977).

Does the duration of primary memories decrease with increasing age? As a second possibility, older adults may forget the information in primary memory more quickly than do young adults. This issue has been widely researched, using a simple but ingenious procedure. Subjects are given one nonsense syllable to remember for from 1 to 18 seconds. To prevent them from rehearsing the syllable during this interval (which would enable it to enter secondary memory), they are then immediately presented with a 3-digit number, and they must count backwards by threes from this number until the time comes to recall the syllable (e.g., 346, 343, 340, 337, and so on). As the retention interval increases from 1 to 18 seconds, performance declines sharply, indicating once again the brief duration of primary memories (Brown, 1958; Peterson & Peterson, 1959). However, various studies have shown that performance on this task is not greatly affected by aging. That is, older adults are able to retain information in primary memory for about as long as do young adults (e.g., Elias & Hirasuna, 1976; Kriauciunas, 1968; Mistler-Lachman, 1977; Puglisi, 1980).

Are age differences in performance significantly greater on more difficult primary memory tasks? Tasks that involve primary memory can be made considerably more difficult by requiring that subjects not only store, but also process (e.g., rehearse), the information presented to them. Such tasks are thought to tap working memory.

For example, suppose that the digit-span test is modified so that the subject must repeat the stimulus digits in reverse order: If the stimulus is 5 3 8 4 7, the correct response is 7 4 8 3 5. In marked contrast to the results obtained with the standard digit-span test, performance on this task does decline significantly with increasing age (Botwinick & Storandt, 1974).

A second possible way to tap the capacity of working memory is by emphasizing response speed. (Recall that verbal learning research found age differences in performance to be significantly greater on highly speeded tasks.) In one study, subjects age 19–21, 33–43, and 58–85 were shown a set of 1, 3, 5, or 7 digits. Immediately thereafter, a single digit was presented, and subjects were asked to decide as quickly as possible whether this test item was or was not included in the original set. The larger the number of items in the set, the slower were the responses of all subjects, and the greater was the disadvantage of the two older groups. (See Figure 5.7.) This suggests that

Figure 5.7

Aging and performance on a speeded primary memory task.   Source: Adapted from Anders, Fozard, & Lillyquist (1972).

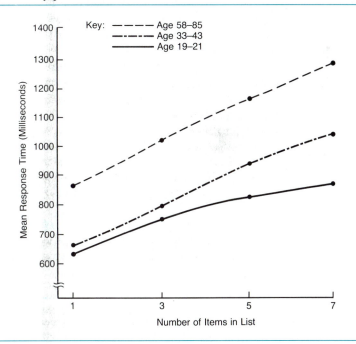

older adults search primary memory for specific information more slowly than do young adults. However, the oldest group performed most poorly even when there was only one item in the original set and virtually no searching was required. Thus other factors must also influence the performance of middle-aged and elderly subjects on this task, such as how quickly the test digit is perceived and encoded (Anders, Fozard, & Lillyquist, 1972; see also Sternberg, 1966; 1969).

In sum: The first two lines of research discussed above clearly indicate that the storage capacity of primary memory, and the duration of the information in it, are largely unaffected by aging. However, this conclusion is based on studies in which subjects were asked to perform relatively undemanding tasks. If tasks are used that tap working memory by requiring more active processing (e.g., rehearsal), younger adults perform significantly better (Craik, Morris, & Gick, 1989).

STRUCTURE AND PROCESS: SECONDARY MEMORY

Conceptual Issues. **Secondary memory** stores information in terms of abstract symbols and their relationships, and is capable of retaining data for from one or two minutes to a great many years. The capacity of secondary memory is enormous; it includes the information that enables you to speak, read, recall your name and age, learn a part in a play, remember what you had for dinner or saw on television last night, and much more. Some indication as to the capacity of secondary memory can be gleaned from the fact that the average college student possesses a reading vocabulary of approximately 50,000 words, as well as large amounts of other information. (See Craik & Lockhart, 1972; Gleitman, 1983.)

When older adults complain of marked deterioration in their ability to recall important information, they are typically referring to secondary memory. For example:

A 73-Year-Old Former Interior Decorator

Mrs. W. is a physically healthy, articulate, and intelligent woman. During the past few years, however, her memory has become a serious problem. The Seattle Center Coliseum is a famous building in her home city, and she has visited it in the past, yet she can no longer recall its name. Instead, she must refer to it in such roundabout terms as "that great big thing where everyone goes to watch things." Similarly, Poland and Russia are "that place and the other, larger one to the east of it." At first, her memory lapses were small; but now she even has trouble remembering the names of furniture or colors, information that she used to work with every day. "It gets worse every year, every month," she says. "If it continues to do that, I wonder when I won't be able to remember anything." (*The Seattle Times*, Jan. 29, 1982, p. B1.)

A Noted Musician

Composer Aaron Copland encountered considerable difficulty while writing his autobiography at an advanced age. "I have no trouble remembering everything that happened 40 to 50 years ago—dates, places, faces, and music" Copland claims. "But

I'm going to be 90 my next birthday, November 14, and I find I can't remember what happened yesterday." Copland's problems with secondary memory are clearly indicated by the fact that he actually would be only 80 years old on his next birthday. (Kausler, 1982, p. 397.)

Are these examples unusual and extreme, suggesting the early stages of a dementia, or do they indicate what will befall most of us in old age? Before we can investigate this important issue, we must first mention a troublesome conceptual problem: Insofar as secondary memory is concerned, the distinction between structure and process has become blurred.

As we have seen, structural theory explains longer-lasting memories in terms of *where* they are stored (that is, in secondary memory). In contrast, process theory explains longer-lasting memories in terms of *how* you deal with the information (you process it more deeply, as by understanding its meaning). Nevertheless, various psychologists have hypothesized that older adults perform more poorly on tasks that involve secondary memory (a structural concept) because they do not encode or retrieve the information as well as do young adults (process concepts). Other psychologists have argued that age-related differences in secondary memory are due to the speed with which the information is processed. Therefore, the following discussion will perforce include both structural and process concepts.

Secondary Memory and Aging: I.   Acquisition, Retention, and Retrieval.   One of the clearest findings in the field of aging and memory is that the secondary memory of older adults is inferior to that of young adults (Hultsch & Dixon, 1990; Light, 1990; Walsh, 1983). In an effort to explain these age-related declines, some researchers turned their attention to the basic processes of acquisition, retention, and retrieval. Retention was soon eliminated as a potenial cause (Craik, 1977; Hultsch & Craig, 1976), so research in this area focused on the two remaining alternatives: The observed age-related declines in performance may occur because the information is not stored or encoded in secondary memory (problems of acquisition), or because the information exists in secondary memory but is not accessible at the time when it is supposed to be recalled (problems of retrieval).

To study acquisition, experimental tasks were chosen that presumably minimized the importance of retrieval. Some of these tasks involved recognition, a relatively easy test of retrieval. Another common procedure is the **cued-recall task:** Subjects must learn a list of words, but they are helped to retrieve the correct answers by being given such clues as the first letter, a rhyme, or a synonym of each word. Presumably, if older adults perform significantly more poorly on these tasks than do young adults, this would suggest that the observed age-related declines in secondary memory are due primarily to problems of acquisition. When researchers wished instead to study retrieval, the more demanding free-recall task was often used. Poorer performance by older adults on this task would presumably imply that age-related declines in secondary memory are due primarily to retrieval problems. Various studies using these procedures found that both acquisition

Myths About Aging

Learning and Memory

Myth	*Best Available Evidence*
Most old persons suffer from severe memory impairments and cannot remember such basic information as the names of their loved ones and where they live.	Secondary memory does decline significantly with increasing age, but usually not to this extent. Memory impairments of this magnitude typically result from severe illnesses, such as Alzheimer's disease or other dementias (Chapter 11). Memory declines in healthy middle-aged and elderly adults are likely to take the form of absentmindedness, such as forgetting what one said an hour ago and repeating it to the same listener or deciding to do something ten minutes from now and then forgetting to do so.
Most middle-aged and elderly adults conform to the maxim, "You can't teach an old dog new tricks."	This is true only for certain kinds of tasks. Older adults perform more poorly on tasks that involve learning new motor skills, the cognitive reorganization of material between the stimulus and the response, dividing attention among several tasks simultaneously, and highly speeded tasks. On many other kinds of tasks, middle-aged and elderly adults are capable of significant amounts of learning.
Because of age-related declines in memory and learning, most older people should not be given complicated and challenging jobs.	While older adults do perform more poorly on difficult memory tests, most jobs are not as demanding. So older adults can usually do well by relying on their experience.

and retrieval are adversely affected by aging (e.g., Botwinick & Storandt, 1974; Craik, 1968b; 1977; Drachman & Leavitt, 1972; Erber, 1974; Hultsch, 1975; Laurence, 1967a; 1967b; Smith, 1977; 1980).

The basic assumption underlying this body of research is that acquisition and retrieval can be studied independently. Unfortunately, this assumption now appears to be untenable (Hartley, Harker, & Walsh, 1980). As we observed previously in this chapter, acquisition and retrieval are very closely related: You cannot remember something (retain and retrieve it from memory) unless you have first learned (acquired) it, although more thorough acquisition makes retrieval easier. Furthermore, there is some indication that older adults acquire information in different ways than do young adults (as we will see). For these reasons, it is extremely difficult to hold retrieval constant and study acquisition alone, or to hold acquisition constant and study retrieval alone. This means that despite the research efforts previously described we cannot determine whether the common age-related declines in secondary memory are due more to problems of acquisition or problems of retrieval. Therefore, let us turn to research strategies that seek to explain these declines in other terms.

Secondary Memory and Aging: II. Organization Strategies. One good way to improve the acquisition and retrieval of secondary memories is by organizing the information. To remember some 15 items on a shopping list, for example, you might sort them into such categories as meats, vegetables, desserts, and beverages. (See Figure 5.8.) If, instead, the items to be

Figure 5.8
Effective organization as an aid to learning and memory.

A. Unorganized Material

Verbal Information: A Shopping List				*Numerical Information:* Scores on a 10-Point Quiz					
Pound cake	Potatoes	Cola	5	9	7	10	6	5
Broccoli	Lamb	Corn	8	4	7	2	8	8
Steak	Pudding	Chicken	10	7	8	5	7	9
Juice	Hamburger	Bacon	6	10	7	5	10	7
Peas	Milk	Pie						

B. Organized Material

Meat	*Vegetables*	*Score*	*Frequency*
Steak	Potatoes	10	4
Hamburger	Broccoli	9	2
Chicken	Peas	8	4
Lamb	Corn	7	6
Bacon		6	2
		5	4
		4	1
Desserts	*Beverages*	3	0
Pound cake	Cola	2	1
Pudding	Milk	1	0
Pie	Juice	0	0

Note: When presented with stimuli like these for a fixed period of time, most people will learn and recall more when the information is organized.

remembered do not have any obvious common features, they can be organized by using verbal or pictorial mediators (as we observed in our discussion of verbal learning). Conceivably, then, older adults may perform more poorly on secondary memory tasks because they do not organize the information as effectively as do young adults.

To test this hypothesis, Hultsch (1971) asked adults age 20–29, 40–49, and 60–69 to sort a list of words into categories and then recall the words. Control groups matched on age inspected the words for the same number of trials, but did not perform the sorting task. The results showed that sorting significantly improved the performance of the two oldest groups, albeit not to the level achieved by the youngest subjects. (See Figure 5.9.) Apparently, older subjects who were not instructed to organize the material by sorting it into categories tended not to do so on their own. (See also Hultsch, 1974; Mandler, 1967.)

Corroborating evidence has been obtained from the free-recall task. Subjects in one study were given various lists of words to learn, some of which were much more similar than others (e.g., *horse—monkey—elephant* versus *cow—table—necklace*). Age differences in performance proved to be significantly smaller on lists that contained conceptually related words, suggesting

Figure 5.9
The effect of improved organization (sorting) on the recall of words as a function of age.
Source: Adapted from Hultsch (1971).

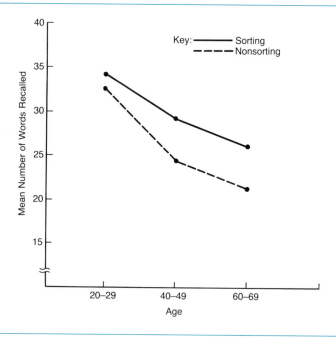

once again that older adults do not spontaneously organize unrelated items (Laurence, 1967b).

Although there are some exceptions to these findings (e.g., Laurence, 1966), we may conclude that the failure to use effective organization strategies is partly responsible for the poorer performance of older adults on secondary memory tasks. This accords well with the verbal learning studies discussed previously, which showed that older adults do not use mediators as often or as well as do young adults. One possible reason is that organization requires considerable more mental effort at more advanced ages, a hypothesis that will be examined further in the following sections.

Secondary Memory and Aging: III.   Depth of Processing.   Another way to produce longer-lasting memory traces is by processing the information more deeply. As illustrated in Figure 5.5, understanding the meaning of a word (semantics) represents a deeper level of processing than does knowing the sound of the word (phonemics), while phonemic encoding requires a deeper level of processing than does merely observing the physical characteristics of the word. This suggests a third possible reason for the observed age differences in performance on secondary memory tasks: Older adults either cannot or do not choose to process information as deeply as do young adults.

This hypothesis has been supported by various empirical data. In one study, four groups of younger and older adults were given lists of unrelated nouns. One group was asked to count the number of letters in each word, and a second group was instructed to make up a rhyme for each word (shallow processing). A third group generated appropriate adjectives for each word, and a fourth group formed a mental image of each word and rated it for vividness (deep processing). Afterward, all subjects were given an unexpected free-recall test of the list of nouns. For those subjects who performed the shallow-processing tasks (letter counting and rhyming), there were no significant age differences on the free-recall test. But for subjects who carried out the tasks requiring deeper processing (generating adjectives and forming images), young adults recalled significantly more of the nouns than did older adults. That is, the older subjects were less proficient at building strong memory traces through deeper processing (Eysenck, 1974).

Further evidence for the importance of depth of processing comes from a study by Craik and Simon (1980). Younger and older adults were presented with lists of sentences that contained key words to be recalled later on, such as "the highlight of the circus was the clumsy *bear*" or "the lock was opened with the bent *pin*." Then, during a cued-recall test, subjects were given either the specific adjective used in each sentence ("clumsy," "bent") or a general description of the correct answer ("wild animal," "fastener"). The adjective cues proved to be a more effective aid to retrieval for the younger subjects, whereas the general descriptions led to better recall for the older adults. This implies that the younger adults processed the information more deeply;

they remembered "clumsy" and "bent" because they encoded the context in which the key words appeared. Conversely, the older adults did not pay attention to the context and encoded only the key words, just as though only these words had been presented. Because of this shallower processing, their retention was relatively poor, and they needed a broader clue in order to recall the information. This study also found that on cued-recall tasks, phonemic cues (the first two letters of the word to be recalled) were more helpful to older adults than were semantic cues (synonyms). This indicates once again that older adults typically encode information at relatively shallow, phonemic levels.

Why do older adults fail to process information as deeply as do young adults? According to the **attentional deficit hypothesis**, our capacity to pay attention to stimuli declines considerably by old age. Older adults must therefore expend more mental effort to process information more deeply, with the result that they are less likely to do so (Craik, 1977; Craik & Byrd, 1982; Craik & Simon, 1980; Rabinowitz, Craik, & Ackerman, 1982). For example, if subjects must perform two or more tasks simultaneously, the need to divide attention in this way proves to be much more demanding for older than for younger adults. (See Guttentag, 1985.) This age-related decline in the total attentional capacity that is available for information processing may be due to biological changes. Or younger adults may profit from more recent opportunities to practice similar mental tasks, as on school examinations.

Although the attentional deficit hypothesis has merit, there is an important exception: Greater skill may compensate for increased age. Deep processing need not always require greater effort, as when repeated practice enables some of these responses to become nearly automatic (Bransford et al., 1980). Whatever the underlying reasons may be, shallower processing is one major reason for the poorer performance of older adults on secondary memory tasks.

Secondary Memory and Aging: IV. Speed of Processing. As might be expected in an area as complicated as learning and memory, not all psychologists agree with the depth-of-processing model. In our survey of research on verbal learning and primary memory, we observed that older adults have considerably more difficulty with speeded tasks. According to some psychologists, structural changes in the nervous system have much the same effect on secondary memory. These theorists argue that differences in processing strategies are relatively unimportant. Rather, older adults perform more poorly on secondary memory tasks because they cannot process the information as quickly, both during acquisition and retrieval (Birren, 1974; Salthouse, 1980; Waugh & Barr, 1980).

Various studies indicate that this theory exaggerates the importance of speed of processing. Older adults do not necessarily fare better when stimuli to be retained in secondary memory are presented at slower rates of speed, implying that a lack of sufficient encoding time is *not* a sufficient explanation for age-related differences in performance (Craik & Rabinowitz, 1985). Nor are the responses of older adults on free-recall or cued-recall tasks necessarily slower than those of young adults (Macht & Buschke, 1984). While our cognitive processes undoubtedly do operate more slowly as we grow older, such changes represent only one of the factors responsible for age-related decrements in performance on secondary memory tasks.

Afterword. Insofar as secondary memory is concerned, older adults do not acquire or retrieve information as well as do young adults. They do not organize information as effectively. They do not process information as deeply. And the speed at which they process information is slower.

Since the evidence reviewed in the preceding pages was primarily cross-sectional in nature, these findings may have been partly influenced by cohort effects. Nevertheless, it is reasonable to expect some troublesome impairments in secondary memory as you grow toward old age. You are also likely to encounter such lapses in your dealings with older adults. Memory impairments may also result from various illnesses, such as Alzheimer's disease, strokes, alcohol or drug abuse, and mental illness, as well as from deficiencies in physical fitness, nutrition, education, and prior opportunities to use memory skills (Perlmutter et al., 1987).

To what extent do such impairments affect the everyday lives of older adults? This is not an easy question to answer, as we will see in the following section.

THE ISSUE OF ECOLOGICAL VALIDITY

As was the case with verbal learning research, the information-processing studies discussed above have been criticized on the grounds of low ecological validity. These studies typically used such tasks as remembering lists of unrelated single words, which is not a common activity in everyday life. Conceivably, the skills tapped by these tasks may differ significantly from the ability to recall the contents of a novel, the names of important people and places, or other meaningful material. (See, for example, Neisser, 1978; 1982.) Therefore, some researchers have used experimental tasks that are more similar to everyday activities in order to study the relationship between aging, learning, and memory.

Connected Discourse: Sentences and Paragraphs. To improve the ecological validity of information-processing research, some investigators have replaced the usual lists of unrelated words with meaningful sentences or paragraphs. When long passages are used, exact reproduction is not required; subjects are allowed to paraphrase, or to recall the basic ideas in their own words. For example, if a paragraph includes the statement "no casualties were reported," full credit is given if the subject recalls that "there were no casualties." If artificial laboratory tasks do exaggerate the relationships among aging and learning and memory, age differences in performance should be considerably smaller when these more meaningful stimuli are used.

Insofar as learning is concerned, one study presented younger and older adults with 215-word and 957-word passages. The older subjects had significantly greater difficulty understanding this material, as measured by multiple-choice recognition tests (Taub, 1976). It is not clear whether these age-related differences in comprehension are limited to adults who are average in verbal ability (Taub, 1979) or whether they also occur among highly educated and verbally superior adults (Finkle & Walsh, 1979). In general, however, the ability to comprehend meaningful discourse does appear to decline with increasing age.

Older adults also have more difficulty remembering meaningful sentences and paragraphs. To be sure, the earlier research evidence in this area is somewhat equivocal. Some researchers compared the ability of younger and older adults to recall normal sentences, foolish near-sentences (e.g., "The Declaration of Independence sang overnight while the cereal jumped by the river"), and random groupings of words. Not surprisingly, the younger subjects performed significantly better on this secondary memory task. But age differences were *greatest* when the normal sentences were used, despite the better ecological validity (Botwinick & Storandt, 1974; Craik & Masani, 1967). However, when subjects were asked to recall the major idea(s) in a sentence rather than the exact words, age differences in performance were reduced (Till & Walsh, 1980; Walsh & Baldwin, 1977; Walsh, Baldwin, & Finkle, 1980). When longer passages were used to test memory (e.g., 60–300 words), older adults sometimes performed more poorly than young adults on both free-recall and recognition tasks (Cohen, 1979; Gordon & Clark, 1974; Taub & Kline, 1978), but other studies found no significant age-related differences (Meyer et al., 1979a; 1979b).

After a recent review of the literature, however, Light (1990) concluded that the ability to recall meaningful material does decline with increasing age. Although older adults understand single words just as well as younger adults do, they are more likely to forget the earlier material in a complicated sentence or paragraph. Thus older adults are at a greater disadvantage if the structure of a sentence is particularly difficult, if there are many ideas and concepts to be learned, if irrelevant materials must be ignored, or if the ideas are presented in an order that is difficult to follow (so that the material must be reorganized in order to be understood).

So we see once again that learning and memory are closely interrelated. When older adults must contend with complicated material, one memory failure may result in an inability to learn and lead to another memory failure later on. That is, being unable to remember earlier material may deprive older adults of a background against which to interpret new material and prevent them from understanding, learning, and remembering what follows. This implies that material written for older adults should be particularly clear and to the point—which, incidentally, is sound advice when writing for younger adults as well.

Spatial Memory.   Most adults readily learn and remember how to proceed from one place to another without getting lost, as when going from home to the supermarket, to school, or to work. This task may appear to be a simple one, yet it actually involves a complicated set of behaviors: We must know where we wish to go, how best to reach our destination, and where to make various changes in direction while en route. Since spatial learning is considerably more involved than recalling single words, and because older adults typically perform much more poorly on more difficult tasks, it is likely that our ability to negotiate our environment declines appreciably with increasing age.

To test this hypothesis, young and elderly adults were asked to recall as many buildings as they could in their local downtown area. All subjects were also required to locate familiar buildings on a grid. On both tasks, the elderly subjects demonstrated significantly less knowledge about their geographical environment than did young adults (Evans et al., 1984). As with verbal stimuli, older adults appear to organize this information less effectively, making retrieval more difficult. Other studies have also found significant age differences in spatial memory, using such tasks as placing drawings of buildings in the proper position on a maplike display and finding one's way in an unfamiliar building (Ohta & Kirasic, 1983; Perlmutter et al., 1981).

Declines in spatial memory pose a particular problem for the institutionalized elderly (notably those suffering from Alzheimer's disease), who may wander off and be unable to find their way back to familiar surroundings. One study focused on residents of a nursing home who ranged in age from 72 to 93 years, were ambulatory, had adequate vision, and were cognitively alert. Most of these subjects had difficulty identifying the location of various places in the nursing home, with this problem more common among the older residents. By comparison, a small group of college undergraduates who spent a mere 40 minutes touring the nursing home achieved consistently better identification scores than did the elderly adults who had been living there for some time (Weber, Brown, & Weldon, 1978). This implies that such institutions must do more to help residents learn and become comfortable with their environment, as by providing distinctive furnishings or other cues in different areas.

Memory for Everyday Tasks.   Other researchers have sought to resolve the problem of ecological validity by designing experimental tasks that resemble common daily activities, such as keeping appointments. To illustrate, ten young adults (age 22–37) and ten older adults (age 65–75) were instructed to telephone the experimenter once a day at a fixed time of their own choice. They were told that if they called more than five minutes late, they would be considered to have missed the appointment. A telephone answering service

Research evidence clearly indicates that the secondary memory of older adults is inferior to that of younger adults. One good way to combat the effects of such declines, and to deal more effectively with daily activities, is by using such external aids as memoranda and shopping lists. (Pamela Price/The Picture Cube)

recorded the day, time, and caller. This proved to be one of the few studies wherein the performance of the older adults was clearly superior: The young subjects much more often called late, or forgot their appointments entirely. Even when random and irregular calling times were substituted, making the task more difficult, the older adults still remembered significantly more appointments than did the young adults (Moscovitch, cited by Harris & Morris, 1984). The older subjects were apparently more motivated to perform well on this task, so they made greater use of such external aids as writing down the appointment times on a sheet of paper and keeping it in plain sight.

In general, however, studies that have used everyday tasks support the conclusion stated previously: Older adults have more difficulty remembering complicated material, even if this material is high in ecological validity. In one study (Morrell, Park, & Poon, 1990), a sample of young adults (age 18–22) and a sample of older adults (age 59–85) were tested for their ability to learn and remember the information on the labels of prescription medicine bottles. This is clearly an ecologically valid task, because patients who cannot understand or recall such instruction as "one capsule three times per day" or "take this medicine only with milk or food" are likely to suffer unpleasant consequences. Subjects were shown bottles with labels that contained only words, and bottles with labels that included both words and pictures specially designed to enhance understanding. (See Figure 5.10.)

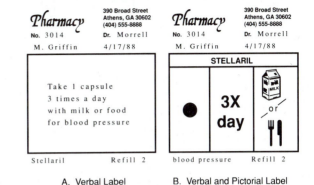

Figure 5.10
Prescription labels used in the 1990 Morrell et al. study. Source: The *Journal of Gerontology, 45,* pp. 166–172. Copyright © The Gerontological Society of America.

The information on the labels was a simplified version of medical instructions that had actually been prescribed by a physician and dispensed by a pharmacist. Not surprisingly, the younger adults recalled more of the prescription information than did the older adults, regardless of the type of label. But the older subjects performed significantly *worse* when the labels contained both words and pictures, presumably because the mixture of verbal and pictorial messages was more complicated. These results therefore suggest that a well-organized verbal label, without pictures, is best for older adults.

Afterword: Improving Learning and Memory.   Taken as a whole, the research findings discussed previously suggest that the case of Mrs. W. is an extreme one; most elderly adults need not expect to undergo this degree of memory deterioration. Nevertheless, we are likely to encounter at least some troublesome impairments in learning and memory as we grow toward old age. What can be done to help older adults cope with these decrements, and to deal more effectively with their daily activities?

One possibility is to provide formal training in the use of organization strategies, such as categorization and mediators. (See, for example, Poon, Walsh-Sweeney, & Fozard, 1980.) Such training does tend to improve the performance of older adults on learning and secondary memory tasks, albeit not to the level achieved by young adults. But if the attentional deficit hypothesis is correct, and the mental energy that powers our cognitive activity declines with increasing age (as physical energy certainly does), older adults may find it too difficult to deal with secondary memory tasks that require sustained amounts of attention.

Rather than relying solely on internal memory aids (that is, mental strategies designed to enhance learning and recall), a better approach may be to encourage the use of such external aids as notebooks, diaries, and electronic memory devices. As we have seen, this proved extremely helpful in the

Moscovitch telephone appointment study. B.F. Skinner, the noted behaviorist, offers some useful recommendations in this regard:

Improving Memory Through Intellectual Self-Management: B.F. Skinner's Advice

[Suppose that] ten minutes before you leave your house for the day, you hear a weather report: it will probably rain before you return. It occurs to you to take an umbrella . . . but you are not yet able to execute [this behavior]. You can solve that kind of problem by executing as much of the behavior as possible when it occurs to you. Hang the umbrella on the doorknob, or put it though the handle of your briefcase, or in some other way start the process of taking it with you.

Here is a similar intellectual problem: in the middle of the night it occurs to you that you can clarify a passage in the paper you are writing by making a certain change. At your desk the next day you forget to make the change. Again, the solution is to make the change when it occurs to you, using, say, a notepad or tape recorder kept beside your bed. The problem in old age is not so much how to have ideas as how to have them when you can use them. A written or dictated record, consulted from time to time, has the same effect as the umbrella hung on the doorknob. . . . In place of memories, memoranda. (Skinner, 1983, p. 240; see also Skinner & Vaughan, 1983.)

Skinner also offers useful strategies for dealing with potentially awkward social situations. If he is with his wife and cannot recall the name of an acquaintance, and there is some chance that she could have met this person, he simply says to her: "Of course, you remember . . . ?" By prearrangement, before it becomes apparent that he has forgotten the name, the wife interrupts with "Yes, of course. How are you?" The acquaintance may not recall ever having met the Skinners, but will hopefully be too unsure of his or her memory to raise any questions. When speaking, elderly adults should use simple sentences, so that they don't forget key ideas in the course of a lengthy digresssion. Or if older adults are having a conversation and fear that they will forget a clever idea by the time their turn to speak arrives (and they are too polite to interrupt!), they can keep repeating this material silently to themselves until the other person has finished talking.

Skinner himself put his own advice to good use, drawing on strategies like these to continue writing scholarly works right up to his death at age 86. Thus the memory decrements that do occur with increasing age need not always have a detrimental effect on overt behavior—provided, of course, that one is sufficiently determined and resourceful.

AFTERWORD: THE COMPETENCE OF OLDER ADULTS IN EVERYDAY LIFE

The research discussed in this chapter clearly indicates that the cognitive abilities of learning and memory, notably secondary memory, decline significantly with increasing age. However, gerontologists who have gone out of the research laboratory and focused on the real world have noticed a striking paradox: A great many older adults seem to cope quite well with everyday tasks and perform capably even in difficult and important jobs. In fact, adults in their sixties and seventies are seldom perceived as less cognitively competent than adults in their twenties and thirties, and many of the most responsible and demanding leadership positions in our society are routinely held by late middle-aged or older adults (Salthouse, 1990). As Schludermann et al. (1983) observed, after administering a battery of neuropsychological tests to 558 business executives of different ages,

> [Older business] executives seemed to function very adequately in high managerial positions which required judgment and complex decision making. Yet their performance level on neuropsychological tests, those measuring the most complex cognitive functions . . . was close to that of brain-damaged patients. (p. 153)

Thus there is a major discrepancy between the way older adults perform in most laboratory research experiments and their performance in many important real-life situations. How can this be explained?

Self-Selection.   Most of us have some control over our own lives and actions. We therefore tend to avoid more stressful and difficult tasks (at which we are likely to fail), choosing instead activities at which we are more skilled (and which are more likely to provide us with rewards). The 65-year-old corporation president and the 55-year-old professional golfer on the senior tour are probably engaging in activities that they do very well. Even if their ability to learn and remember has declined with increasing age, they are performing tasks at which they are more competent than most adults of any age. That their performance may have been even better when they were younger does not alter this fact.

Overly Demanding Laboratory Tasks.   Research experiments on learning and memory usually tap the upper limits of performance. Gerontologists who are interested in finding age differences are likely to devise procedures that unearth such differences, rather than mundane activities that are performed equally well (or equally poorly) by most adults. The typical everyday task is less demanding, and does not require adults to perform at the very peak of their abilities. Thus, although laboratory experiments may paint a relatively accurate picture of certain declines in cognitive functioning, the practical implications of these declines may be considerably less important. (See also Salthouse, 1990.)

Experience.   Most research experiments on learning and memory use tasks that are unfamiliar to the subjects, so that the "potentially confounding" effects of prior experience will be eliminated. But when the factor of experience is negated, older adults lose one of their most valuable assets. Age and experience are of course positively correlated, and such well-known maxims as "experience is the best teacher" indicate how important this factor can be. So it should not be surprising when older adults perform competently on everyday and work activities, in which they can draw on their experience, yet suffer when compared with younger adults on laboratory tasks that they have never seen before.

Substantial memory declines do afflict some individuals, as we have seen. Research on learning and memory can help us to understand and deal with those declines that do occur. But the stereotype of the forgetful and inept older adult, mentioned at the outset of this chapter, must be regarded as yet another of the many myths that pervade the field of gerontology.

Summary

Learning and memory are closely interrelated. You cannot remember something unless you previously acquired some knowledge of it, and one common test of whether or not you have learned something is your ability to remember it at a later date. Also, learning and memory are complicated and unobservable processes. We must draw inferences about them based on the performance of subjects on experimental tasks, which we can observe directly.

ASSOCIATIONIST APPROACHES TO LEARNING AND MEMORY

Associationism attributed all learning and memory to the association of stimuli and responses that occur closely together in time. Although this conception was most popular a few decades ago, it has provided an important point of departure for more modern theories.

Motor skill learning refers to any task wherein the subject must learn a sequence of bodily movements. Many motor skills persist until very late in life because they are acquired during childhood, adolescence, or early adulthood, and are practiced so often that they become nearly automatic. The primary exception occurs with tasks that require speeded responses, on which older adults perform more poorly. The capacity to develop new motor skills does decline with increasing age, especially with regard to complicated tasks.

A great deal of associationist research on learning and memory has focused on verbal stimuli and responses. In serial learning, the subject is required to learn a list of words or nonsense syllables in the exact order in which they are presented. In paired-associate learning, pairs of words or nonsense syllables are used, and the subject must learn to reply with the second member of the pair when presented with the first member. On both kinds of tasks, older adults consistently perform more poorly than do young adults. Possible reasons are that older adults cannot respond as quickly, and that there is a significant loss in the ability to rehearse or organize the information (and to resort to other mnemonic strategies) with increasing age.

More recently, associationist theory has been criticized on several grounds. Serial and paired-associate tasks would seem to ignore certain important aspects of learning and memory, such as semantic memory. These tests also appear to be low in ecological validity. Modern theorists have therefore sought to develop alternative conceptions of learning and memory, the most notable of which is the information-processing approach.

INFORMATION-PROCESSING APPROACHES TO LEARNING AND MEMORY

The information-processing model is based on the principles that underlie modern electronic computers. Although this analogy is only a rough one, it serves to emphasize the importance of encoding, storing, and retrieving information for the purposes of solving problems, taking action, and acquiring new information. Structural information-processing theories focus on the ways in which information is stored and organized in the human brain, whereas process theories emphasize the mental activities that we perform when we try to learn or remember information.

The most prominent structural theory posits that there are three distinct types of memory storage systems: sensory memory, primary memory, and secondary memory. Information must first pass through sensory memory in order to reach primary memory, and must pass through primary memory in order to enter secondary memory. Sensory memory very briefly preserves the physical characteristics of a stimulus, so that we have just enough time to select information by paying attention to it. This form of memory is relatively unaffected by aging. Primary memory holds a sufficiently small amount of information for conscious processing, and retains this material for at most half a minute. To the extent that the information in primary memory is complicated and taps the capacity of working memory, older persons perform more poorly. Secondary memory stores information in terms of abstract symbols, has an enormous capacity, and is capable of retaining data for many years. Performance on secondary memory tasks also declines significantly with increasing age.

According to process theory, there is only one kind of memory storage system, and the duration of memory traces depends on how deeply or thoroughly we process the information. The act of remembering depends on three basic processes: acquisition, retention, and retrieval. Insofar as secondary memory is concerned, older adults do not acquire or retrieve this information as well as do young adults. It is very difficult to study acquisition and retrieval independently of each other, however, so researchers have been unable to determine which of these processes is more affected by aging. Information-processing research has confirmed that older adults perform more poorly on secondary memory tasks because they do not organize the material as effectively as do young adults, as by using categories or mediators. Older adults also do not process information as deeply as do young adults, which results in less durable memory traces. Our capacity to pay attention to stimuli may decline with increasing age, with the result that older adults must expend more mental effort to process information more deeply. The poorer performance of older adults on secondary memory tasks may also be due in part to the showing of our cognitive processes as we grow older, although this is at most only one of the factors responsible for the observed age differences.

In an effort to improve the ecological validity of laboratory research, some investigators have instead used experimental tasks that are more similar to everyday activities. The ability to comprehend and recall meaningful discourse, such as sentences and paragraphs, does appear to decline as we grow older. Significant age-related decrements have been found in spatial learning and memory, which has important implications for the well-being of the institutionalized aged.

As a whole, the research reviewed in this chapter indicates that there is a significant decline in secondary memory with increasing age. However, these decrements need not always have a detrimental effect on overt behavior. Training in the use of organizational categories and mediators may help older adults to improve their performance on learning and memory tasks, while intellectual self-management and the use of external aids can enable older adults to deal effectively with their daily activities. Furthermore, laboratory research may well have exaggerated the practical importance of declines in learning and memory. A great many older adults cope quite well with everyday tasks and perform capably in difficult and important jobs, because they choose activities at which they are skilled and can draw upon their greater experience.

Study Questions

1. Research on verbal learning typically uses rather artificial tasks, such as memorizing lists of nonsense syllables or unrelated words. How, then, have researchers been able to derive useful information about aging and changes in learning and memory? What efforts have been made to improve the ecological validity of such studies? Has this led to more useful research results?

2. How might the use of mediators help you to remember more of the material that you learn in this course, and improve your examination scores?

3. How might deeper processing of the material that you learn in this course help you to remember more of it, and improve your examination scores? How would you go about processing this information more deeply?

4. What aspects of memory decline the most with increasing age? What are the practical consequences of these declines? What can be done to help remedy the effects of these declines?

5. Why may laboratory research on learning and memory underestimate the competence of older adults to deal with real-life situations? What changes in research design might help to resolve this problem?

Terms to Remember

Acquisition	*Paired-associate learning*
Anticipation interval	*Performance*
Associationism	*Primacy effect*
Attentional deficit hypothesis	*Primary memory*
Cued-recall task	*Procedural memory*
Depth-of-processing model	*Process theory*
Digit-span test	*Recall*
Echoic memory	*Recency effect*
Ecological validity	*Recognition*
Encoding	*Retention*
Episodic memory	*Retrieval*
Free-recall task	*Secondary memory*
Iconic memory	*Semantic memory*
Information-processing model	*Sensory memory*
Inspection interval	*Serial learning*
Long-term memory	*Short-term memory*
Mediator	*Structural theory*
Motor-skill learning	*Working memory*

Chapter 6

Intelligence, Creativity, and Wisdom

Hazel Hankin/Stock, Boston

Among the most admired of human characteristics are intelligence, creativity, and wisdom. More intelligent people can perform important mental behaviors more easily, and are more likely to succeed in school or in various professions. Creative individuals have made monumental contributions to virtually every area of human endeavor, including music, art, literature, the physical and social sciences, inventions, and recreation. Wisdom is widely regarded as a highly desirable characteristic, if not a very common one.

The relationship between these variables and aging is therefore of considerable importance. Will your capacity for intelligent thought decline markedly as you grow older? Should you expect to lose much of your capacity for original, creative work as you grow past middle age? Will you become more wise later in life? Such issues have a significant bearing on the satisfactions you are likely to experience during adulthood.

In this chapter, we examine gerontological data dealing with intelligence, creativity, and wisdom. First, however, we must survey the efforts that have been made to define these important but complicated variables.

The Meaning of Intelligence

THE PROBLEM OF DEFINING INTELLIGENCE

What is **intelligence**? The general meaning of this concept is well known: It refers to the range of behavior from dull to bright, slow-witted to quick-witted, stupid to clever. High intelligence presumably makes it easier to use words and numbers correctly, to remember substantial amounts of information, and to reason out the solutions to problems of various kinds.

Nevertheless, it is extremely difficult to state an exact definition of intelligence. Are there several primarily separate forms of intelligence (e.g., verbal, numerical, spatial), so that an individual may be considerably brighter in some areas and duller in others? Or is intelligence a general phenomenon that has a similar effect on all mental activity? Although the very first model of intelligence adopted the latter hypothesis (Spearman, 1904), most modern psychologists prefer the former approach. Yet they disagree as to whether intelligence consists of two or three distinct abilities, half a dozen, or perhaps even as many as 150. (See, for example, Anastasi, 1976; Cunningham, 1987; Guilford, 1984; Schaie, 1990.)

The concept of intelligence is also subject to cultural issues. People who come from different countries, societies, ethnic groups, and/or socioeconomic groups are likely to undergo markedly different experiences and training during their formative years. Thus the meaning of intelligence may well vary from culture to culture.

Furthermore, it is not always easy to distinguish between intelligence and related variables. Consider the stereotype of the aged guru, who passes on priceless secrets about life to those who seek such knowledge. This individual would generally be regarded as unusually wise, rather than intelligent. Yet it is only recently that developmental researchers have taken a keen interest in the concept of wisdom (e.g., Clayton & Birren, 1980; Sternberg, 1990). Or, consider a musical genius like Beethoven, who was unquestionably creative. Is it reasonable to regard him as unintelligent, simply because he may not have scored particularly high in verbal and mathematical ability?

For these reasons, we will not attempt to formulate a word-for-word definition of intelligence. Instead, we will explicate the meaning of this concept by discussing several different approaches to its measurement.

CONCEPTUALIZING INTELLIGENCE: THE PSYCHOMETRIC APPROACH

Historical Background.   Prior to the twentieth century, the nature of intelligence was very poorly understood. In these unenlightened times, intelligence was measured with such physiologically oriented tests as muscular strength, sensitivity to pain, visual and auditory acuity, and reaction time.

The pioneering step in defining intelligence as we know it today was taken by a French psychologist, Alfred Binet. By 1900, most industrialized nations had established compulsory elementary education. This new requirement presented a formidable problem: Some children might well be mentally retarded and in need of special education classes. Others might only appear to be backward because they came from an intellectually impoverished home, and would be quite able to cope with regular classes. How, then, could truly dull children be identified? To deal with this problem, the French minister of public instruction appointed a special committee, of which Binet was a member. Their solution, achieved in 1905, ushered in the **psychometric approach** to intelligence: They decided to develop an objective diagnostic instrument to assess each child's intellectual capacity.

Binet and his collaborator, Theodore Simon, assumed that intelligence is a general aptitude that relates to many kinds of mental functioning (Binet & Simon, 1905). Their landmark test included cognitive tasks that varied widely in content and difficulty: copying a drawing, repeating back a string of digits, recognizing coins and making change, explaining why certain statements are absurd. Binet also assumed, correctly, that intelligence increases with age until maturity. Therefore, in the 1908 revision of his test, he arranged the items according to age level. First, the difficulty of each item was determined by administering the test to some 300 normal children between the ages of 3 and 13 years. Then, items passed by 80 percent to 90 percent of children of a specific age (e.g., 7 years) were grouped at that age level. This made it possible to express a child's cognitive ability in terms of **mental age (MA)**. For example, suppose that a child passes all items through the six-year level, half of those at the seven-year level, and no others. This child's mental age is equal to 6 years plus an additional half year, or 6.5 years.

The Intelligence Quotient (IQ).

If a 5-year-old child has a mental age of 6.5, and a 9-year-old has a mental age of 8.0, which one is more intelligent? Although the former child has a lower MA, this child's performance is well above the level expected from his or her chronological age (CA). Conversely, the latter child is performing at a level below the average of his or her age group. To make such comparisons easier, a German psychologist, William Stern, proposed the use of the **intelligence quotient (IQ)** in 1912:

$$IQ = MA/CA \times 100$$

In the preceding example, the first child has an IQ of $(6.5/5) \times 100 = 130$, indicating superior intelligence. The IQ of the second child is $(8.0/9) \times 100 = 89$, which is below average. An average IQ occurs when $MA = CA$, and it is equal to 100.

Problems in the Measurement of Adult Intelligence.

The well-known intelligence quotient, which was devised for use with children, is badly flawed as an index of adult intelligence. Intelligence does not grow forever, any more than height does, but our chronological age consistently increases. If this intelligence quotient were to be used with adults, it would seem as though we all become shockingly dim-witted as we grow toward old age.

To illustrate, if your MA is 18.0 years and your CA is 12 years, your IQ is an impressive 150. There may be some decline in your intelligence with increasing age (an issue to be discussed later in this chapter), yet you will surely remain quite bright throughout your life. But if your MA remains at about 18 years by the time your CA reaches 54 years (which is by no means unlikely), your IQ would be 33, a value that indicates severe mental retardation! Obviously, this is an absurdity.

One possible alternative is to use mental age as the index of adult intelligence. In the preceding example, your MA remains at about 18 years, which does give a more accurate picture. This procedure is suitable for some kinds of research; but it provides no indication of whether your intelligence is above or below average, let alone how far above or below. Thus a popular alternative is to compare an individual's test score to the average score obtained by a sample of adults of the same age, using such statistical procedures as means, standard deviations, standard scores, and percentile ranks.[1]

For example, suppose that your score on an intelligence test is one standard deviation above the mean of your age group. This places you in the

---

[1] For a discussion of these and other basic statistics, see Welkowitz, Ewen, and Cohen (1991).

top 16 percent of that group. A score that is two standard deviations above or below average represents the top or bottom 2 percent. Because the standard deviation on some prominent intelligence tests is approximately 15, these scores are sometimes translated into **deviation IQs**: 115 represents one 15-point standard deviation above the average of 100 (and therefore places you in the top 16 percent of your age group), 130 represents two standard deviations above average, 90 represents two-thirds of a standard deviation below average, and so on. Note that although the popular concept of IQ is retained, mental age plays no part at all in these calculations; all that is involved is the comparison of a subject's test score to the mean score of his or her age group.

Tests like Binet's equate intelligence with educational aptitude. Because the original purpose of these tests was to predict the academic success of children, the test constructors defined high intelligence in terms of the capacity to do well on classroom tasks. If those who obtained higher test scores received higher grades in school, and those who scored lower received lower grades, the test was assumed to be a valid measure of intelligence. Insofar as adults are concerned, however, this rationale may well be inappropriate. Most middle-aged and elderly adults have long since left school, and have little need for purely academic talents. Also, one's success or failure in life cannot be evaluated in terms of such simple criteria as letter grades.

As an alternative, some attempts have been made to devise tests of adult intelligence that are based on real-life situations (e.g., Demming & Pressey, 1957; Gardner & Monge, 1977; Schaie, 1978: Scheidt & Schaie, 1978). The items on these tests may deal with such issues as where to look in the yellow pages of the telephone directory if you want to buy an Airedale, the title of a person who baptizes a baby, how best to drive a car in rush-hour traffic, and a knowledge of the major diseases that afflict the elderly—a type of intelligence that is now referred to as "practical intelligence" (Schaie, 1990). This is quite different from such common intelligence test items as repeating back a string of digits, explaining the meaning of the word "tantamount," or identifying the author of *Huckleberry Finn*. There is some indication that older adults may be at less of a disadvantage when these innovative tests are used, but this issue is still essentially unresolved. This research area is still in its infancy, and it is plagued with criterion problems: It is difficult to find an external standard that can be used to validate the test and show that high scores do signify high intelligence, now that school grades are not relevant.

In sum: The psychometric approach has contributed substantially to our understanding of intelligence. But some significant problems do arise when this approach is used to measure the intelligence of adults, especially older adults. Therefore, we may well ask: What alternatives to the psychometric approach currently exist?

CONCEPTUALIZING INTELLIGENCE: OTHER APPROACHES

The Piagetian Approach.   Jean Piaget, the noted Swiss child psychologist, devoted considerable attention to the development of human intellectual processes. Rather than dealing with the usual verbal and mathematical abilities, Piagetian theory is concerned with various innovative concepts. For example, "object permanence" involves the child's awareness of the identity and continuing existence of objects when they are seen from different angles, or are out of sight. "Conservation" concerns the child's ability to recognize that an attribute of an object remains constant even though its perceptual appearance changes, as when the same quantity of liquid is poured into differently shaped containers.

The Piagetian approach is an influential one in developmental psychology. But this theory deals primarily with childhood (especially early childhood), as does the large majority of related empirical research. Some attempts have been made to test Piagetian ideas with adult subjects, but these have had only limited success. Few longitudinal studies have been carried out. Older adults frequently perform more poorly than younger people in cross-sectional studies (Clayton & Overton, 1973), but this is a finding that is difficult to explain.

The Piagetian approach has led investigators to ask important questions about intellectual growth throughout adulthood, such as how we deal with ambiguity or contradiction and how emotional or subjective factors affect our thinking. (See, for example, Commons et al., 1989; Hooper, Hooper, & Colbert, 1984; Labouvie-Vief, 1985; Labouvie-Vief, Devoe, & Bulka, 1989.) At present, however, there is not enough empirical research available in this area for any firm conclusions to be drawn.

The Information-Processing Approach.   Some investigators have tried to link individual differences in intellectual ability with such cognitive processes as learning, memory, and attention, as measured by the kinds of laboratory tasks discussed in the preceding chapter. These theorists argue that the hard-to-define concept of intelligence is best explained in terms of differences on these more fundamental, better-understood variables. Thus people who are "more intelligent" may actually be better learners, may acquire new information and retrieve data from memory more efficiently, or may be better able to pay attention to the task at hand. (See, for example, Hunt, 1978; 1980.)

Some studies do suggest that scores on intelligence tests are positively correlated with performance on certain laboratory tasks, including serial learning and free recall. But considerably more research is needed in order to evaluate the merits of the information-processing approach to intelligence.

Afterword.   Although the psychometric approach to intelligence suffers from various conceptual and methodological problems, it has produced most of the available gerontological research evidence. Therefore, our investigation of the relationships between aging and intelligence will perforce be couched primarily in terms of test scores.

Intelligence and Aging

WAIS STUDIES

The Wechsler Adult Intelligence Scale. The intelligence test most often used with adults is the **Wechsler Adult Intelligence Scale**, or **WAIS** (Wechsler, 1958). Like most modern psychologists, Wechsler conceptualized intelligence as consisting of a number of different abilities. He was particularly concerned with Binet's emphasis on verbal skills: One can presumably be intelligent yet not overly proficient in the English language. Wechsler sought to remedy this defect by devising an intelligence test that consisted of two types of scales, **verbal** and **performance**. Each of these includes a number of subtests, as summarized below and shown in Figures 6.1 and 6.2.

Verbal Scales

1. *Information:* 29 questions covering a wide variety of information that is readily available to adults in our culture, but excluding specialized or academic knowledge.

Figure 6.1
Test items similar to WAIS verbal subtests.   Source: Modified from Gleitman (1983, p. 393).

Information
1. Who wrote *Huckleberry Finn?*
2. Where is Finland?
3. At what temperature does paper burn?
4. What is entomology?

Arithmetic
1. How many 22 cent stamps can you buy for two dollars?
2. If two oranges cost 37 cents, what will a dozen oranges cost?
3. How many hours will it take a cyclist to travel 60 miles at a rate of 12 miles per hour?

Digit Span
1. Repeat these numbers in the same order: 7—1—6—2—2—8—3.
2. Repeat these numbers backwards: 9—4—1—5.

Comprehension
1. Why should we obey traffic laws and speed limits?
2. Why are antitrust laws necessary?
3. Why should we lock the doors and take the keys when leaving a parked car?
4. What does this saying mean: "Kill two birds with one stone."

Similarities
1. In what way are a hammer and a screwdriver alike?
2. In what way are a dog and a plant alike?
3. In what way are coal and gasoline alike?

Vocabulary
1. What does "careful" mean?
2. What does "tantamount" mean?

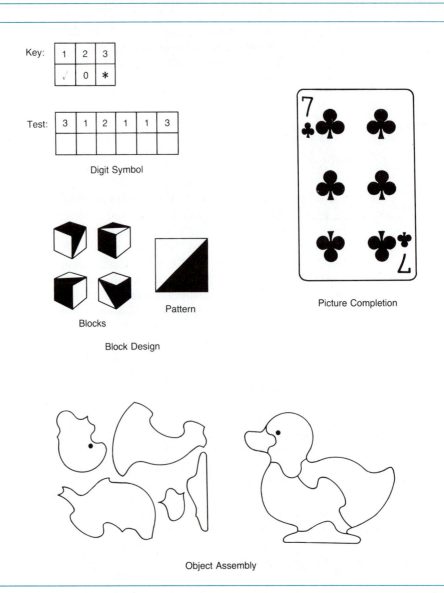

Figure 6.2
Test items similar to WAIS performance subtests.   Source: Modified from Gleitman (1983, p. 393).

2. *Comprehension:* 14 items dealing with the necessity for certain actions or rules, the meanings of proverbs, and so on.
3. *Arithmetic:* 14 problems involving elementary school arithmetic, to be solved without using paper and pencil.
4. *Similarities:* 13 items involving the way in which two things are alike.

5. *Digit Span:* Repeating back sequences of from three to nine digits in the order presented, and repeating back sequences of from two to eight digits backwards (as discussed in the preceding chapter).
6. *Vocabulary:* Stating the meaning of 40 unrelated words, presented both orally and visually and in order of increasing difficulty.

Performance Scales

7. *Digit Symbol:* The subject is provided with a key that contains nine symbols paired with the nine digits. Using this key, the subject has 1½ minutes to fill in as many symbols as possible on the answer sheet.
8. *Picture Completion:* Identifying the missing component in a common picture. There are 21 pictures, which vary in difficulty.
9. *Block Design:* The subject is given a set of identical one-inch blocks whose sides are red, white, or half red and half white, and must assemble them so that the pattern on top matches a specified design.
10. *Picture Arrangement:* A set of cards, each of which contains a picture, must be rearranged in the proper sequence so as to tell a story (as though a comic strip in the daily newspaper were cut into separate panels and presented out of order, but without any dialogue). There are eight such items, which vary in difficulty.
11. *Object Assembly:* Four rather simple jigsaw-type puzzles, wherein pieces must be put together to form a flat picture of a familiar object.

Notice that the verbal subtests focus on the subject's store of knowledge in various areas: general facts (historical, literary, biological), how to deal competently with one's environment, arithmetical operations, the meanings of words. Only the arithmetic test has a time limit. In contrast, the performance subtests deal with primarily unfamiliar material and place a heavy emphasis on response speed. All of these subtests are timed, and bonus points are awarded for unusually fast solutions. Scores on the WAIS may be expressed simply in terms of points (raw scores), which is usually best insofar as aging research is concerned, or converted into deviation IQs.

The Classic Aging Pattern. When the relationship between aging and WAIS scores is investigated with cross-sectional studies, a fairly consistent pattern emerges. Both verbal and performance scores peak at a relatively early age (verbal scores by the mid-twenties, performance scores by the late teens), and then decline steadily with increasing age. These decrements are typically small on the verbal scales and much more pronounced on the performance scales, a phenomenon known as the **classic aging pattern**. (See Figure 6.3.)

Among the verbal scales, the similarities and digit span subtests suffer the greatest declines with increasing age, but the remaining four subtests show little change. Conversely, substantial decrements are found on all of the performance scales. (See, for example, Botwinick, 1967; 1977; Doppelt & Wallace, 1955; Jones, 1959.) For this reason, IQ scores on the WAIS are age graded: The same score yields a higher IQ at an older age. For example, suppose that a 22-year-old achieves a performance score of 60 points. This individual's peer group has a fairly high mean, so the score of 60 translates into a deviation IQ of only about 112. But if a 71-year-old obtains a score of 60, this is equivalent to a deviation IQ of 140, since this older adult belongs to an age group with a much lower mean.

How much reliance can be placed on these findings? Cross-sectional studies are likely to *overstate* the extent of age-related declines in WAIS scores because they do not control for cohort effects. Older adults may well be at a disadvantage on the WAIS because education and test taking were not stressed as much during their youth. They may obtain lower scores because they have considerably greater test anxiety, or because they are less familiar with the required facts and skills, rather than because their intelligence is lower. Accordingly, many modern researchers prefer to investigate the relationship between aging and intelligence by using longitudinal studies. But while this approach has definite advantages, it is no panacea, for it is likely to *understate* the extent of age-related declines in WAIS scores. Less capable subjects tend to drop out over the course of a longitudinal study, which

Figure 6.3
WAIS classic aging pattern.   Sources: Jones (1959); Kausler (1982, p. 574).

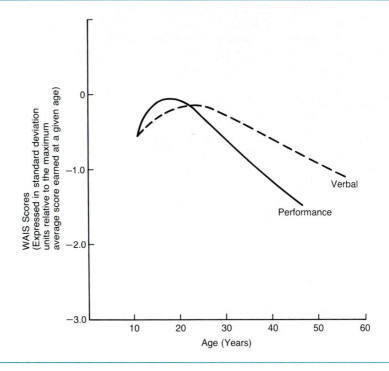

In the WAIS Block Design Performance Scale, the subject is asked to assemble the blocks so that the pattern on top matches the design on the printed card. This subtest is timed; bonus points are awarded if the solution is reached with extraordinary speed. (Sepp Seitz/Woodfin Camp & Associates)

inflates the group mean in later years (the phenomenon of selective attrition, discussed in Chapter 2). Thus, it is hardly surprising that the declines in WAIS scores reported by these studies tend to be small, and often negligible. Some longitudinal studies even report modest increases in WAIS scores with increasing age, at least on the verbal scales. (See, for example, Siegler & Botwinick, 1979.)

Partly because there is no ideal research method, the field of aging and intelligence has been rife with controversy and debate. However, there is increasing agreement that scores on intelligence tests do decline with increasing age, at least to some extent; researchers have produced a substantial amount of empirical data bearing on this issue. Some interesting (albeit anecdotal) support is also provided by the following case history:

Reminiscences of a Prominent Psychologist

D. O. Hebb, a noted psychologist in the field of learning and perception, retired in 1977. Hebb found that on reaching his 60s and 70s, he retained his addiction to difficult crossword puzzles, which draw primarily on previously acquired information [*crystallized intelligence*, discussed later]. But he gradually lost interest in solving mathematical brain teasers, which require the juggling of new ideas [*fluid intelligence*]. As Hebb put it: "I'm not quite senile, not yet. I can still keep up appearances, and there are points on which I can still outtalk younger colleagues. But—between you and me, privately—the picture is one of a slow, inevitable loss of cognitive capacity." (Hebb, 1978, p. 23.)

So let us now examine the research evidence to evaluate the significance of these age-related declines.

FLUID AND CRYSTALLIZED INTELLIGENCE

Definition.   Intelligence is often conceptualized in terms of a number of specific intellectual abilities: verbal, numerical, reasoning, spatial relations, memory, and so forth. In contrast, one influential theory argues that psychological knowledge has not yet advanced far enough for us to identify the precise mental abilities that comprise intelligence (Cattell, 1940; 1963; Horn, 1970; 1978). Instead, this approach distinguishes between two general kinds of intelligence. **Fluid intelligence** involves the capacity to use unique kinds of thinking in order to solve unfamiliar problems, rather than merely drawing on previously acquired information. For example, one aspect of fluid intelligence is measured with items like these:

> In each of the following problems, there are four four-letter combinations. Three of the combinations in each group are alike in some way. Which combination does *not* belong in each group?[2]
>
> 1.   VWXY   JKLM   PRTU   BCDE
> 2.   HDOR   GDOR   LDOR   EDOR
> 3.   MRCW   OUIE   XLVQ   TODI

Notice that the abilities tapped by this test are relatively unaffected by prior education and classroom learning. In contrast, **crystallized intelligence** involves the knowledge that has been acquired through education and acculturation. It is typically measured by using tests of vocabulary, information, and mechanical knowledge, all of which draw on one's acquired store of information. Thus crystallized intelligence is determined largely by personal experiences and intentional learning, while fluid intelligence is determined primarily by heredity and incidental learning. Both kinds of intelligence do involve some similar processes, however, such as perceiving relationships among objects, abstract reasoning, concept formation, and problem solving. Also, it is quite possible for a single test to tap both fluid and crystallized intelligence. An example is the verbal analogies test (e.g., TOE is to FOOT as FINGER is to ?), which draws on both acquired knowledge about the meanings of words and an inherent ability to perceive semantic relationships.

Relationship to the Classic Aging Pattern.   How does this theory relate to the WAIS? The WAIS verbal scales are concerned primarily with acquired information, which is the hallmark of crystallized intelligence. Conversely,

---

[2]Answers: 1. PRTU (letters not in sequence); 2. LDOR (should be FDOR to continue the reverse sequence H-G-?-E followed by DOR); 3. TODI (not either all consonants or all vowels). Since these are hypothetical items only, other answers may be possible.

the performance scales would seem to deal mainly with fluid intelligence. If we assume that the two types of intelligence become more and more independent of one another as we grow older, then the WAIS verbal and performance scores should indeed demonstrate different aging patterns.

Is this assumption a plausible one? Crystallized intelligence reflects our accumulated store of knowledge, which is likely to remain relatively stable or even increase as we grow older. That is, we should acquire enough new knowledge to equal or exceed that which we forget, especially since we inhibit forgetting in many areas by refining and applying what we know. Conversely, fluid intelligence is a more innate capacity. It does involve incidental learning, but also requires the use of an efficient brain and nervous system. Since our physiological capacities are known to degenerate with increasing age, a corresponding decline in fluid intelligence is to be expected (Horn & Donaldson, 1980).

This rationale leads to the conclusion that crystallized intelligence should remain stable or even increase with increasing age, at least through about age 70, whereas fluid intelligence should decline during adulthood. (See Figure 6.4.) And this is essentially what occurs in the classic aging pattern: WAIS verbal scores (which reflect crystallized intelligence) show much smaller declines than do performance scores (which reflect fluid intelligence).

Figure 6.4

Hypothesized age changes for fluid intelligence and crystallized intelligence. Source: Kausler (1982, p. 586).

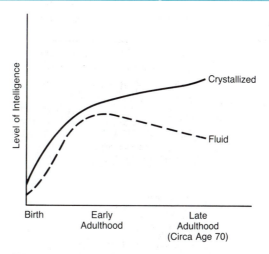

Note. This figure illustrates only the *hypothesized* age changes for fluid and crystallized intelligence, in accordance with the text discussion. Some research evidence does support this hypothesis, but considerably more is needed before definitive conclusions can be drawn.

This also implies that declines in fluid intelligence may be compensated for by gains in crystallized intelligence, resulting in little if any loss in functioning. Some evidence does indicate that fluid intelligence declines and crystallized intelligence increases as we grow older, although some of these data are based on specially designed tests of fluid intelligence rather than on the WAIS. (See, for example, Cunningham et al., 1975; Hayslip & Sterns, 1979; Horn & Cattell, 1967; Kausler & Puckett, 1980; Sands, Terry, & Meredith, 1989.)

Some WAIS studies have found that for adults aged 70 and older, score declines are of about equal magnitude on both the verbal and performance scales, and are much greater than for younger subjects (e.g., Eisdorfer & Wilkie, 1973). Why might the classic aging pattern not apply to the very old? Conceivably, those over 70 are more affected by retirement and declining health, and are therefore more likely to become socially isolated. (See Chapter 8.) As a result, their opportunities to acquire new information are more limited; they forget more than they learn; and their store of information decreases, resulting in a marked decline in crystallized intelligence. There is some indication that both fluid and crystallized intelligence do follow a similar pattern of deterioration in very late adulthood, reversing the earlier trend shown in Figure 6.4 (e.g., Baltes et al., 1980). However, considerably more research is needed to evaluate this hypothesis.

As might be expected in the controversial realm of intelligence, not all psychologists agree with the fluid-crystallized distinction. In fact, one noted critic has even characterized these concepts as "fanciful" (Guilford, 1980). Nevertheless, this conception does offer an interesting theoretical explanation for the pattern that is so often observed when WAIS scores are related to aging.

THE INFLUENCE OF EXTRANEOUS VARIABLES

In the preceding pages, we have been careful to state that *test scores* change with increasing age. However, these score changes may not necessarily reflect an equal change in *intelligence*. The observed declines in test performance may instead be exaggerated (or, less often, deflated) by the operation of certain **extraneous variables.**

Education and Test Anxiety.   As we observed earlier in this chapter, tests like the Binet and WAIS equate intelligence with educational success. Formal schooling is much more widespread today than it was 50 years ago. Therefore, older adults tend to have fewer years of education than do younger adults.

Since many of the WAIS verbal scales emphasize material taught in the classroom, the aged are likely to be less familiar with the required information. And since less schooling also implies less experience with examinations, older adults tend to be more anxious about taking an intelligence test. They are also less efficient at devising appropriate test-taking strategies, such as guessing freely when there is no penalty for doing so. Furthermore, many elderly individuals have heard a great deal about declines in intelligence with increasing age. Thus they are likely to be concerned about the possibility of becoming senile and to fear that their scores on the WAIS will reveal this. Accordingly, even well-educated older adults may well experience debilitating test anxiety. Some even refuse to take the test at all (Whitbourne, 1976; see also Birren & Morrison, 1961).

The evidence in this area provides support for those who attribute age-related declines in WAIS scores to cohort effects, rather than to aging. To a significant extent, older adults obtain lower test scores because they have had less formal education and/or are higher in text anxiety, rather than because their intelligence is lower. Thus the declines in test scores obtained by the early cross-sectional studies, which are particularly vulnerable to cohort effects, would seem to exaggerate the declines in intelligence that occur with increasing age.

Cautiousness. Some theorists have suggested that older adults are overly cautious, and that this is the primary reason for their failure to guess on an intelligence test even when it is to their advantage to do so. (There is no penalty for guessing on the WAIS.) However, the preponderance of research evidence does *not* support the hypothesis that cautiousness increases as we grow older. (See Chapter 7.) Therefore, this inefficient test-taking behavior of the elderly appears to be due more to anxiety, which may lead to excessive cautiousness in this particular situation.

Health. Most of us find it harder to perform well on cognitive tasks when we are ill. Since the elderly are more prone to disease and injury than are younger adults, some of the age-related declines in intelligence test scores may reasonably be attributed to poor health.

One study found that for subjects age 65 to 91 years, even mild illnesses were associated with lower scores on most WAIS scales, especially the performance scales (Botwinick & Birren, 1963). For another sample with a mean age of about 76 years, hearing losses were significantly related to lower WAIS scores, notably on the information and vocabulary subtests (Granick, Kleben, & Weiss, 1976). A number of studies have found that adults who were at greater risk of contracting cardiovascular disease tended to show declining intelligence test scores at an earlier age (Hertzog et al., 1978; Manton, Siegler, & Woodbury, 1986).

Although the preponderance of the research evidence indicates that poor health adversely affects the test performance of the elderly, there are some exceptions. Schultz et al. (1986) found that hypertensives did not perform as well on the WAIS as did normotensives, but the differences were small and clinically insignificant. Mild elevations in blood pressure have even been related to modest *increases* in WAIS and other intelligence test scores over a ten-year period, although subjects with very high blood pressure did tend to obtain lower scores (Eisdorfer, 1977; Hertzog et al., 1978; Wilkie & Eisdorfer, 1977). Possibly the extent to which an adult's functioning is impaired may be more relevant than merely having an illness: A hearing loss that makes it difficult to understand the examiner's questions may well be more disadvantageous than a heart disease that is in remission and does not greatly affect one's daily activities.

It has also been suggested that a significant decline in cognitive functioning occurs a few years prior to death, which is reflected by a sharp drop in intelligence test scores (Kleemeier, 1962). This **terminal drop hypothesis** has been supported by a number of studies (e.g., Baltes & Labouvie, 1973; Riegel & Riegel, 1972; Riegel, Riegel, & Meyer, 1967; Steuer et al., 1981). However, several studies either have failed to obtain any evidence in favor of terminal drop, or have found the relationship between WAIS scores and death to be statistically significant but of little practical importance (Botwinick et al., 1978; Palmore & Cleveland, 1976). There is also some disagreement as to whether the sum of all verbal and performance scores should be used to measure terminal drop (Reimanis & Green, 1971), or only the scores on certain subtests (Jarvik & Falek, 1963). These controversies have been attributed in part to sampling and statistical errors, such as studies that did not begin to take measurements far enough in advance of the subjects' deaths (Siegler, 1975).

One interesting approach to the study of terminal drop has been developed by Suedfeld and Piedrahita (1984). They analyzed published letters written by 18 eminent individuals, all deceased, during the last ten years of their lives. Each letter was scored for the degree of cognitive complexity reflected therein. Some of the noted personages whose writings were included in this study died from prolonged illnesses (e.g., Lewis Carroll, Sigmund Freud, Aldous Huxley, Franz Kafka, D. H. Lawrence, Napoleon I, Queen Victoria), but others died quite suddenly (Louis Brandeis, Robert Browning, Gustave Flaubert, Franz Liszt, Walter Raleigh). The results obtained from both groups supported the terminal drop hypothesis, albeit in somewhat different ways: The sudden-death group suffered a drastic decline in the cognitive complexity of their writings during their last year of life, but the protracted-illness group showed a substantial decline in cognitive complexity during the five years prior to their deaths. The available evidence in this area is not unequivocal, but it appears that a substantial drop in intelligence test scores and/or in the cognitive complexity of one's writings may indeed forecast the occurrence of death within a few years.

Fatigue.   There is some indication that older adults fare more poorly on long intelligence tests because they become tired more quickly (Furry & Baltes, 1973). Thus shorter test segments and more frequent rest pauses may be necessary with the elderly.

Response Speed.   As we have seen, you must respond quickly on some WAIS subtests in order to obtain a high score. Because older adults perform more poorly on speeded tasks, some critics contend that they face an unfair disadvantage on these subtests. But other theorists argue that response speed reflects the functioning of the central nervous system, is related to cognitive ability, and should be an aspect of tests given to the aged.

Various studies have shown that if the digit symbol and picture arrangement subtests are administered without any time limits at all, the typically large age-related declines on these subtests do *not* disappear, although they are reduced. (See, for example, Doppelt & Wallace, 1955; Klodin, 1976; Storandt, 1976; 1977.) Whether response speed should be regarded as an extraneous variable is open to question, but it is only partly responsible for poorer test performance among the elderly.

Other Factors. Some factors have been found to be related to higher scores on intelligence tests. These include a higher level of education, income, and occupational status; a more complicated job, or exposure to some other stimulating environment; a lengthy marriage to an intelligent spouse; and more flexible, less rigid attitudes during middle age. (See Schaie, 1990.)

Afterword.   The variables discussed in this section are important for two reasons. First, they help us to understand why some older adults perform more poorly on intelligence tests than do other older adults. Those who suffer from certain illnesses tend to score lower than those who do not; those who are more prone to fatigue (perhaps because they are in inferior physical condition) tend to score lower than those who are not; those who become anxious because they lack test experience tend to score lower than those who remain calm because they are familiar with written tests. Variables such as health, fatigue, and anxiety are thus directly related to some of the variation in scores that occurs among individuals who take intelligence tests.

Also, as we have seen, these variables may bias the relationship between aging and intelligence. It is in this sense that they are "extraneous." If older adults score lower than young people partly because of such factors as illness, fatigue, and anxiety, then these *test score* differences will overstate— perhaps considerably—the actual differences in *mental ability*, or the extent to which mental ability declines with increasing age.

Psychological testing is not an exact science. No test is perfectly reliable or valid: The best test usually will not produce identical scores for the same person on two different occasions, even if there has been no change at all during this time, nor will it measure a concept like intelligence without tapping at least some undesired attributes as well. We can indeed glean useful and important information about intelligence at various ages from score changes on well-constructed tests. But we must remember that these score changes are also influenced by the operation of various extraneous variables, so they do not necessarily reflect an equal degree of change in intellectual ability.

OTHER FINDINGS AND ISSUES

Longitudinal Studies Using Other Intelligence Tests.   Although the WAIS is the most popular test of adult intelligence, it is by no means the only one. As noted previously in this chapter, some studies of aging and intelligence have utilized specially designed tests of fluid intelligence. Other studies have focused on such measures of intelligence as the Army Alpha, a verbal test first used during World War I for the screening and placement of new recruits. Still other studies have used the test of Primary Mental Abilities (Thurstone, 1938; Thurstone & Thurstone, 1941), which includes subtests dealing with verbal comprehension, numerical ability, word fluency (e.g., naming as many words as possible beginning with the letter *T*), spatial relations, memory, perceptual speed, and general reasoning ability.

As was the case with the WAIS, these longitudinal studies report smaller score declines with increasing age than do cross-sectional studies. In some of these studies, those decrements that were found did not begin until after age 50. For example, in the Seattle Longitudinal Study, the PMA was administered to a large number of adults over each seven-year interval between the ages of 25 to 81 years. The results indicated a gain until the late thirties or early forties, followed by stability until the mid-fifties or early sixties. From age 53 to 60, average declines in PMA scores were quite small and were statistically significant only for the numerical ability and word fluency subtests. Only after age 60 did more general score declines occur (Schaie, 1990; see also Owens, 1966; Schaie & Labouvie-Vief, 1974). We may conclude that insofar as longitudinal research is concerned, the results obtained from other intelligence tests do not contradict those derived from the WAIS.

Practical Intelligence.   Some theorists argue that an important aspect of intelligence is not measured by the WAIS, PMA, or other conventional tests: namely, the practical application of intellectual skills to everyday activities. For example, a person who is higher in **practical intelligence** should be able to find desired items more quickly and efficiently in the yellow pages or when shopping at the local supermarket, and be able to drive more competently in rush-hour traffic. Thus practical intelligence is *not* the same as specialized expertise (as in the case of a nuclear physicist or television repair person), because it involves common tasks that do not require special training. (See Cavanaugh, 1990; Schaie, 1990.)

As we observed earlier in this chapter, some researchers have attempted to devise tests of practical intelligence that are based on real-life situations (e.g., Demming & Pressey, 1957; Garner & Monge, 1977). Alternatively, judges may be asked to rate whether a person behaves competently in a particular situation. One such study used judges who were experts in the field of intelligence and judges who were laypersons (Sternberg et al., 1981).

Both sets of judges agreed that practical intelligence consists of three major factors: *problem-solving ability*, which involves reasoning logically, seeing all aspects of a problem, and making good decisions; *verbal ability*, which includes speaking in an articulate manner, having a good vocabulary, and reading with a high rate of understanding; and *social competence*, which involves accepting others for what they are, admitting one's mistakes, and showing interest in the world at large.

Research in this area is still in its infancy, and we cannot as yet draw firm conclusions regarding the relationship between practical intelligence and aging. It does reflect an increasing awareness that many different types of skills are involved in what we call "intelligence."

Initial Level of Ability. Some theorists have suggested that if you achieve a superior score on an intelligence test as a young adult, you will suffer less of a decrement later in life than will those whose scores are average or below. However, the research evidence concerning this hypothesis is equivocal. Some studies report that an individual's initial level of ability is not significantly related to subsequent changes in test scores (e.g., Eichorn, 1973; Eisdorfer, 1962; Troll, Saltz, & Dunin-Markiewitz, 1966). Other studies have found that young adults with higher test scores do show smaller declines with increasing age (Bayley & Oden, 1955; Blum & Jarvik, 1974; Riegel, Riegel, & Meyer, 1967; Siegler & Botwinick, 1979). Still other findings suggest that it is the less capable subjects who experience smaller decrements as they grow older (Baltes et al., 1972).

In view of these contradictions, any conclusions in this area must await the results of future research. It does appear that those young adults who are high in intelligence are likely to remain so throughout their lives, although their margin of superiority in some intellectual areas may grow smaller relative to other adults of the same age.

Training and Test Scores. Some efforts have been made to devise and evaluate training methods for improving the test scores of the elderly. These interventions have achieved only modest success, and have not eliminated score differences between older and younger adults. For example, one study found that training improved the test performance of elderly subjects with regard to one form of fluid intelligence, but not numerous others (Plemons, Willis, & Baltes, 1978).

AFTERWORD

In the preceding pages, we have reviewed a considerable amount of evidence dealing with aging and intelligence. Although controversy and debate abound in this area, some general conclusions do appear to be warranted by the available empirical data.

Myths About Aging

Intelligence, Creativity, and Wisdom

Myth	*Best Available Evidence*
There is a universal decline in intelligence with increasing age. Thus you are very likely to suffer serious and widespread deterioration in intellectual ability during your old age.	Some intellectual abilities do show significant decrements as we grow older, especially after middle age. But the declines in other abilities are small and do not appear to have much effect on one's daily functioning. Age-related changes in intelligence test scores may not accurately reflect true changes in intelligence because of cohort effects, extraneous variables, selective attrition, and/or other methodological problems. The majority of elderly adults do *not* suffer extreme deterioration in intelligence, although some losses may be expected in such areas as perceptual integration, response speed, and certain aspects of memory.
If you have not made any creative contributions by about age 40, you probably never will.	Creativity does tend to peak prior to middle age but numerous important creative works have been produced during the latter part of the creator's life.

First, cross-sectional studies present an overly pessimistic picture of the extent to which intelligence declines with increasing age. These studies are particularly vulnerable to cohort effects and to the operation of various extraneous variables.

Longitudinal studies tend to underestimate the extent of age-related declines in intelligence. Such studies are vulnerable to selective attrition, to the operation of extraneous variables, and to other problems inherent in the measurement of change. (See Chapter 2.) However, longitudinal studies do appear to present a more accurate picture of the relationship between aging and intelligence. There is increasing agreement that most intellectual abilities begin to decline in the sixties. The declines on perceptual speed tasks are quite large, whereas decrements on other tasks are small but significant. Conversely, stability or even increases are typical during the twenties and thirties. Relatively little is known about the course of intelligence during the forties and fifties, and more research is needed in this area. (See Cunningham, 1987.)

Intelligence is not a unidimensional concept. It includes a variety of intellectual abilities, many of which change at a different rate with increasing age.

You may well notice declines in certain abilities as you grow past middle age, such as memory (Chapter 5), response speed, and perceptual integration. You may also find that some of these declines become more pronounced when you reach old age. But so long as you are fortunate enough to avoid a serious organic brain disorder, grave concern about the possibility of widespread deteriorations in intelligence during your life span does *not* appear to be warranted.

The Meaning of Creativity

Creativity may be defined as the solution to a problem of significance to society that is original, unusual, ingenious, and relevant. Examples may be found in virtually every area of human endeavor: a Beethoven developing a new form of symphony, a medical researcher who discovers a badly needed vaccine, a writer who produces a dramatically important work of fiction or nonfiction, an inventor who devises an innovative and effective industrial machine or home appliance, and so forth.

Creativity is *not* the same as intelligence, nor can it be measured with the kinds of tests discussed previously in this chapter (e.g., Thurstone, 1951). Researchers have used two primary methods to study creativity and aging: the psychometric approach and the creative performance approach.

THE PSYCHOMETRIC APPROACH

Convergent and Divergent Thinking.
We typically conceptualize the solution to a problem in terms of a single correct answer. Examples of such **convergent thinking** include deducing the identity of the murderer in a mystery story, determining the answer to a problem in elementary algebra, deciding on the correct bid in a game of bridge, or answering a multiple-choice examination question correctly. In each of these cases, various clues and data are presented, and the respondent must narrow down the many possibilities to one and only one answer.

Although convergent thinking is very common in our society, it is by no means the only type of problem solving. In fact, creativity is more closely related to the ability to produce many different and unusual answers to a problem (**divergent thinking**). Suppose that you are asked to list 20 different uses for a newspaper, other than the obvious one of reading it. Some answers are very common and would not be regarded as creative, such as using the newspaper to start a charcoal fire or to line a garbage pail. To qualify as original, a response must be one that is practical but given by few people, such as using the newspaper to cut out words for a kidnapper's ransom note. The more original answers that one can produce, the more creative the individual.

Convergent thinking often leads in a smooth and uninterrupted fashion to the correct answer. In contrast, creativity typically occurs in unanticipated bursts of illumination. The creative individual usually does spend a considerable amount of time totally immersed in the problem, but this frequently fails to produce the desired result. The individual then puts the problem aside for awhile, often with some discouragement, only to find that the needed creative thoughts arrive suddenly and spontaneously during this rest period. Most often, crucial creative insights do not occur at the composer's piano, scientist's laboratory, or writer's desk. Instead they may take place while one is enjoying a peaceful walk in the woods, a ride in a carriage, a warm bath (as in the famous case of Archimedes' "Eureka, I have found it!"), or even a night's sleep (with the solution appearing in the form of a dream). Paradoxically, then, *not* thinking consciously about a problem (at least for a while) may be the best way to arrive at a creative solution.

Psychometric Measures of Creativity.   No one measure of creativity has achieved the widespread acceptance and popularity accorded to the WAIS. As a further illustration of the difference between creativity and intelligence, consider these tests of divergent thinking devised by Guilford (1967):

- *Word Fluency:* Write as many words as possible containing a specified letter. The letter may appear anywhere in the word.
- *Expressional Fluency:* Write a meaningful four-word sentence, where each word must begin with a specified letter (e.g., W_____ A_____ M _____ S _____).
- *Alternate Uses:* List as many uses as possible for a specified object (e.g., a newspaper), other than the most obvious one.
- *Ideational Fluency:* Given a specified category (e.g., "things that will burn"), name as many things as possible that belong in that category.
- *Plot Titles:* Given a one-paragraph description of a short story plot, write a brief, interesting, and relevant title for that story.
- *Consequences:* Given a hypothetical event (e.g., people no longer need or want sleep), list as many consequences of this event as possible (e.g., no more alarm clocks).
- *Making Objects:* Using only a given set of figures (e.g., circle, triangle), draw a specified object (e.g., a face, a lamp).
- *Match Problems:* Given a set of matchsticks that form a pattern (e.g., two rows of three square boxes), remove a certain number of matchsticks so as to produce a specified result (e.g., remove three matchsticks to reduce the number of boxes from six to four).

Nevertheless, intellectual ability is by no means wholly unrelated to creativity. For example, after numerous possible solutions have been produced by divergent thinking, it is still necessary to use your cognitive capacities to evaluate these alternatives and decide on the best one. Also, to make a creative contribution in fields like music, literature, medicine, and science, you must first be able to understand and deal with the basic concepts and principles of these disciplines. But it is quite possible to be creative without having the ability to obtain high scores on intelligence tests, or to do very well on intelligence tests yet not be particularly creative.

THE CREATIVE PERFORMANCE APPROACH

As an alternative to the psychometric approach, some researchers have obtained data about actual creative achievements and the ages at which they were made. That is, by following the careers of noted painters, composers, writers, inventors, and scientists, we can observe directly the quality and quantity of their creative contributions throughout their adult lives. (See Simonton, 1990.)

To be sure, reasonable people will sometimes disagree as to whether a particular work is creative. More often, however, a consensus is likely to emerge; few would dispute the creativity of Monet's *Water Lily* series or Beethoven's Ninth Symphony. Thus the creative performance approach seeks to ascertain the relationship between creativity and aging, without having to contend with such troublesome psychometric issues as reliability and validity.

Creativity and Aging

RESEARCH FINDINGS

The Psychometric Approach.
Almost without exception, longitudinal studies using psychometric measures have found that the capacity for divergent thinking declines with increasing age. The peak usually occurs during the late thirties, with no significant increases during the last half of life. (See for example Alpaugh & Birren, 1977; Cornelius & Caspi, 1987; Simonton, 1990.)

However, psychometric studies in this area suffer from an important methodological problem. Just because a particular measure has been labeled a "creativity test" does *not* necessarily mean that it measures real-life creativity! As we observed in our discussion of intelligence, some theorists argue that the ability to repeat back a string of digits or to explain the meaning of the word "tantamount" may not be strongly related to an older adult's ability to solve important practical problems. Similarly, stating a large number of unusual uses for a newspaper may not be strongly related to the ability to produce a creative novel or symphony. The test constructor must show that the instrument in question is valid—that it does in fact measure creativity, rather than something else—and, unfortunately, the validity coefficients for such tests tend to be fairly low or even negligible (Simonton, 1990). Therefore, let us now turn to information about aging and creativity that has been derived from the creative performance approach.

The Creative Performance Approach. Anecdotal evidence may seem to indicate that creativity at older ages is fairly common. For example, painter Claude Monet began his *Water Lily* series at age 73. Benjamin Franklin invented the bifocal lens at age 78. Sophocles wrote *Oedipus Rex* at age 75. George Bernard Shaw wrote his first play at age 48. And Bach and Beethoven produced some of their most creative works toward the latter part of their lives (Denny, 1984).

To understand the relationship between aging and creative performance, we must examine a creator's production throughout his or her entire adulthood. Such studies have shown that creativity typically rises fairly rapidly, reaches a peak, and then declines. The precise location of the peak depends on the specific field of endeavor. Creative contributions in lyric poetry, pure mathematics, and theoretical physics peak relatively early, usually around the early thirties or even the late twenties, and decline sharply thereafter. In contrast, creative contributions in history, philosophy, and writing novels show a more gradual increase, peak by the late forties or even the early fifties, and decline more gradually thereafter (Simonton, 1990, 1991; see Figure 6.5). People who are creative and productive early in life tend to be creative throughout their lives, but their performance does decline after the peak has been reached. In fact, assuming that the person lives to late middle or old age, the output during the last decade of his or her career is likely to be about half that of the peak years. (See, for example, Lehman, 1942; 1953; 1956; 1958; 1960; Lyons, 1968; Simonton, 1990; Zusne, 1976.)

Creative people tend to be extremely productive. Edison did not invent only the light bulb and the phonograph; all told, he held 1,093 patents. And although Einstein may be best known for his theory of relativity, he could claim 248 publications at the close of his career (Simonton, 1988). At one

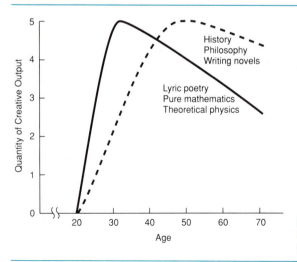

Figure 6.5

Creativity as a function of age. Source: Based on Simonton (1990).

Some studies suggest that creativity declines after age 40, but there are many famous exceptions. For example, painter Claude Monet did not begin his noted Water Lily *series until age seventy-three.* (The Bettmann Archive)

time, it was believed that age-related declines in the quantity of creative productions differed considerably from age-related declines in the quality of such works. More recently, however, it has been shown that when suitable methodological precautions are taken, as by calculating age curves separately for major and minor works, the age curves for quantity and quality are virtually identical (Simonton, 1988; 1990.) Apparently, those periods in a creator's life that yield the most masterpieces also produce many less memorable works. So the quantity and quality of creative productions during the course of adulthood are closely related: The more (fewer) works a creator generates during a particular time in his or her life, the more (fewer) that are truly creative.

Extraneous Variables. As was the case with intelligence, some theorists argue that observed declines in creative performance may be exaggerated (or, less often, deflated) by the operation of certain extraneous variables. That is, a change in the *number of creative contributions* with increasing age may not necessarily reflect an equal change in the *capacity for creativity*.

For example, as creative people grow older, they may be more likely to be promoted to positions that remove them from active participation in their disciplines. A creative college chemist or psychologist may become a department head or dean, be required to devote most of the work day to administrative matters, and have little time for original work. If this is a common occurrence, promotions would then be an extraneous variable that would bias the relationship between aging and creativity. Alternatively, creative performance may decline with increasing age simply because it is not adequately reinforced; some awards, such as the Nobel Prize, are often given decades after the appearance of the works that they commemorate. As behaviorist psychologists have shown, delaying a reward until long after the behavior in question is a poor way to maintain that behavior. At present, however, there is little research evidence to support the hypothesis that extraneous variables exert a significant effect on the relationship between aging and creativity.

AFTERWORD

Each of the approaches to the study of creativity and aging has its strengths and weaknesses. The psychometric approach strives for objectivity, but the validity of written measures of creativity has been questioned. The creative performance approach deals directly with actual works, but it requires subjective judgments as to what is or is not creative. Some works of considerable merit and originality have not been recognized as such for many years after they first appeared—sometimes, not until long after the creator's death.

Despite these important differences, the empirical evidence obtained from these approaches is rather consistent. Both the quality and the quantity of creative performance increases during young adulthood, peaks fairly early in life, and declines thereafter, with the precise nature of the age curve depending on the specific field of endeavor. Although there are numerous anecdotes of major creative works produced during middle and old age, such creators usually were even more productive during their twenties and thirties.

In sum: If you are creative as a young adult, you will probably continue to be so as you grow older, but you should expect to produce fewer works (good and inferior) after middle age. Keep in mind, however, that quite a few great masterpieces have been produced during the latter part of life—which is surely reason enough to reject an overly pessimistic outlook regarding the relationship between creativity and aging.

Wisdom: An Emerging Research Area

What is **wisdom**? Most people agree that wisdom develops over time: Older people are wiser than younger people. In many cultures, a popular image of the wise person is that of the experienced, enlightened, and respected elder. Yet we all know older people who are not wise, and young people who are "wise beyond their years." Is the stereotype of the wise old person an accurate one? What exactly does it mean to be wise, and how does one become wise?

Historically, wisdom has been viewed as an ability that is passed from one generation to the next through social interaction. (Eastcott-Momatiuk/The Image Works)

HISTORICAL VIEWS OF WISDOM

Historical views have emphasized three main dimensions of wisdom. Wisdom is first of all a *cognitive process:* a way to obtain and process information. From ancient times, philosophers and writers have stressed that being wise is not the same as having a great deal of specialized knowledge or being extremely intelligent. Wise persons do have a good intellect and superior reasoning ability. But they also possess good judgment and the ability to learn from past mistakes. Thus wise people do not simply know a lot; they act effectively on their environment, and their effectiveness increases over time because they are willing to admit their errors and able to learn from them. (See Sternberg, 1990.)

Wisdom is also a *virtue,* or a pattern of behavior that society values highly. The wise person understands cause-and-effect relationships, and is therefore able to help others find the correct path. That is, rather than giving up in confusion or lamenting that "the fates are against me" when things go wrong, the wise person understands why and is able to plan appropriate remedial action.

Finally, wisdom is a *good:* a personally desirable condition. Wisdom is rewarding for its own sake. Without it, many other aspects of life will not be as pleasurable. Wisdom helps us to get pleasure from health, satisfaction from fame, and good use out of wealth. People who lack wisdom may achieve temporary success; but they may then try so hard for yet another triumph that they lose all pleasure in what they are doing. Alternatively, they may become embittered when they fail. They may squander the wealth they have acquired on things that do not bring them any real happiness. In contrast, wisdom brings with it an intense joy. As the philosopher Montaigne observed, "The most manifest sign of wisdom is a continual cheerfulness: her state is like that of things in the regions above the moon, always clear and serene."

MODERN VIEWS OF WISDOM

It is only recently that behavioral scientists and other researchers have become interested in the concept of wisdom (e.g., Clayton & Birren, 1980; Sternberg, 1990). Consistent with earlier views, most modern researchers agree that being wise is not the same as being intelligent, at least as assessed by standardized intelligence tests. Having a keen intellect or possessing large amounts of information may help one to be wise, but other important characteristics are also necessary. (See Table 6.1.)

Table 6.1
Facets of wisdom: Views suggested by various researchers.

How Wisdom Develops	Characteristics of a Wise Person
Through extensive experience and the acquisition of knowledge.	Intelligent, emphatic.
By integrating conflicting types of information in a growth-oriented way.	Has exceptional insight, gives good advice.
By developing logical reasoning and shrewdness.	Realizes that knowing is uncertain, that he or she may err, and that all questions cannot be answered.
By learning to integrate cognitive and emotional matters, an ability that increases with increasing age.	Is generally competent, has good judgment and good communication skills.
By developing the ability to synthesize opposing views with what one already knows, rather than ignoring them—an ability that increases with increasing age.	Probes for knowledge, seeks truth; is not dismayed by ambiguous information that lacks a clear-cut right answer.
By striving for a balance between knowing and doubting, an ability acquired primarily through supportive interpersonal relationships rather than aging.	Understands self and others; is intuitive.
	Solves own problems effectively, advises others; may manage social institutions.

Source: Modified from Birren & Fisher (1990).

In particular, the wise person must be able to integrate cognitive material with experience and emotional material in order to make good decisions at an individual and societal level. An individual who is guided solely by intellect in making decisions, and does not also draw upon his or her experiences and feelings, would *not* be regarded as wise, regardless of how high he or she might score on an intelligence test. Also, wise persons recognize their own fallibility. They realize that they may err, that all questions cannot be answered, and that certain aspects of life are unpredictable. Thus one indication of a person who lacks wisdom is a cocky, "know-it-all" attitude. Finally, most researchers agree that experience, and therefore age, are related to the acquisition of wisdom. Wisdom develops over time, and it is therefore more likely to be found among older adults. (See Sternberg, 1990.)

AFTERWORD

Researchers have made some progress in defining wisdom. Although no one definition is currently accepted as correct, there is some agreement as to the meaning of this important variable. But there are very little data regarding such issues as how to measure wisdom and the relationship between wisdom and aging. With the increasing research interest in this area, we may reasonably expect that further information will be forthcoming in the near future.

Summary

THE MEANING OF INTELLIGENCE

Intelligence refers to the range of behavior from dull to bright, slow-witted to quick-witted, stupid to clever. High intelligence presumably makes it easier to use words and numbers correctly, to remember substantial amounts of information, and to reason out the solution to problems of various kinds. Intelligence is not a unitary concept; it includes a number of specific intellectual abilities. However, it is extremely difficult to state an exact definition of intelligence.

The psychometric approach, which was originated at the beginning of the twentieth century by Alfred Binet, involves the use of formal psychological tests to define and measure intelligence. The well-known intelligence quotient is unsuitable for use with adults, so deviation IQs or similar measures are commonly used in aging research. A major problem with tests like Binet's is that they equate intelligence with educational aptitude. Insofar as adults are concerned, this rationale may well be inappropriate: Most older adults have long since left school, and their success or failure in life cannot be evaluated in terms of such simple criteria as letter grades. Unfortunately, this difficulty is not easily resolved.

Some of the theoretical alternatives to the psychometric approach include the Piagetian approach and the information-processing approach. However, virtually all of the available empirical evidence concerning aging and intelligence has been provided by the psychometric approach.

INTELLIGENCE AND AGING

The intelligence test most often used with adults is the Wechsler Adult Intelligence Scale (WAIS), which consists of six verbal scales and five performance scales. Numerous studies have found that both verbal and performance scores peak by about age 18 to 25 and then decline steadily with increasing age. These decrements are typically small on the verbal scales and much more pronounced on the performance scales, a phenomenon known as the classic aging pattern. For this reason, deviation IQ scores on the WAIS are age graded: The same score yields a higher IQ at an older age.

There is no ideal research method for studying intelligence and aging. Cross-sectional studies are likely to overstate the extent of age-related declines in WAIS scores, since they do not control for cohort effects. Longitudinal studies are likely to understate the extent of age-related declines in WAIS scores because they are vulnerable to selective attrition and other methodological problems concerning the measurement of change. In view of these uncertainties, it is hardly surprising to find disagreements among researchers regarding the relationship between intelligence and aging.

One theory distinguishes between two general kinds of intelligence. Fluid intelligence involves the capacity to use unique kinds of thinking in order to solve unfamiliar problems, and is believed to decline with increasing age. Crystallized intelligence involves the knowledge that has been acquired through education and acculturation, and presumably remains stable up to about age 70. These age trends are similar to the WAIS classic aging pattern, since the verbal subtests deal primarily with crystallized intelligence and the performance subtests emphasize fluid intelligence.

Changes in test scores may not necessarily reflect an equal change in intelligence. The observed declines in test performance may instead be influenced by such variables as the amount of education, test anxiety, health, and fatigue. These variables are directly related to some of the variation in scores that occurs among individuals who take intelligence tests, but they are also "extraneous" variables because they may exaggerate (or, less often, understate) the relationship between aging and intelligence. Insofar as health is concerned, a sharp drop in intelligence test scores may well forecast the occurrence of death within a few years (terminal drop).

Longitudinal studies using other intelligence tests have not markedly contradicted the results obtained from the WAIS. Researchers have also taken an interest in practical intelligence, which refers to the practical application of intellectual skills to everyday activities and which may not be measured by typical intelligence tests. They are also studying the relationship between initial level of ability and subsequent changes in intelligence test scores with increasing age, and whether age-related declines in test scores can be reversed by appropriate training.

The early cross-sectional studies dealing with aging and intelligence presented an overly pessimistic picture of age-related declines in intelligence. Longitudinal studies tend to underestimate the extent of age-related declines in intelligence, but appear to present a more accurate picture. There is increasing agreement that most intellectual abilities begin to decline in the sixties, especially those involving perceptual speed. Conversely, stability or even increases are typical during the twenties and thirties. Although losses in some intellectual abilities are to be expected with increasing age, grave concern about the possibility of widespread deterioration does not appear to be warranted.

THE MEANING OF CREATIVITY

Creativity may be defined as the solution to a problem of significance to society that is original, unusual, ingenious, and relevant. It pertains to virtually all areas of human endeavor.

Researchers have used two primary methods to study the relationship between creativity and aging. The psychometric approach involves the use of written tests: These most often focus on the ability to produce many different and unusual answers to a problem (divergent thinking), rather than the ability to find one right answer to a problem (convergent thinking). Commonly used measures of divergent thinking include such subtests as word fluency, alternate uses, consequences, and match problems. In contrast, the creative performance approach involves obtaining data about actual creative achievements and the ages at which they were made. Thus the quantity and quality of creative contributions is observed more directly, by studying the creator's performance throughout his or her adult life.

CREATIVITY AND AGING

The psychometric approach strives for objectivity, but the validity of written measures of creativity has been questioned. The creative performance approach avoids this problem because it deals directly with actual works, but it requires subjective judgments as to what is or is not creative. Despite these differences, the empirical evidence obtained from both approaches indicates that both the quality and quantity of creative performance increases during young adulthood, reaches a peak (during the early thirties or late twenties for some fields of endeavor, during the late forties or early fifties for other fields), and declines thereafter. There is not sufficient evidence to conclude that extraneous variables affect the relationship between creativity and aging. The quantity and quality of creative productions during the course of adulthood are closely related, and the age curves are similar. Quite a few major creative works have been produced during middle and old age, but these creators were usually even more productive earlier in life.

WISDOM: AN EMERGING RESEARCH AREA

Wisdom is a desirable personal characteristic that involves a good intellect, good reasoning ability, good judgment, the realization that one may err and that all questions cannot be answered, the ability to learn from past mistakes, being able to solve one's own problems and give good advice to others, and understanding self and others. Most researchers agree that experience, and therefore age, is related to the acquisition of wisdom. Research in this area is still in its very early stages, and much more work needs to be done regarding the meaning of wisdom and its relationship to aging.

Study Questions

1. Why is the intelligence quotient (IQ) *not* suitable for use with adults? What alternative measures are preferable? What does this imply about our ability to formulate a precise definition of intelligence?
2. Would you prefer to be higher in fluid intelligence or higher in crystallized intelligence for purposes of: (a) doing well on a classroom examination? (b) writing a novel? (c) inventing an important new product? (d) learning a foreign language? If you took an appropriate test, would you expect to score higher in fluid intelligence, higher in crystallized intelligence, or about the same in both? Why?
3. Would you prefer to be better at convergent thinking or at divergent thinking for purposes of: (a) writing a novel? (b) identifying the murderer in a mystery novel? (c) trying to decide why a former friend doesn't seem to like you anymore? If you took an appropriate test, would you expect to score higher in convergent thinking, higher in divergent thinking, or about the same in both? Why?
4. Based on the research data presented in this chapter, do the people who are most creative concentrate on creating just one or two works during their peak years in order to produce a true masterpiece? Or do they create many different works, including some that are inferior? What does this imply about the nature of creativity?
5. How does wisdom, as defined in this chapter, differ from intelligence and creativity? Of these three variables (intelligence, creativity, wisdom), which is least common in this country? Why might this be true?

Terms to Remember

Classic aging pattern

Convergent thinking

Creative performance approach

Creativity

Crystallized intelligence

Deviation IQ

Divergent thinking

Extraneous variable

Fluid intelligence

Intelligence

Intelligence quotient (IQ)

Mental age (MA)

Performance scales (subtests)

Practical intelligence

Psychometric approach to creativity

Psychometric approach to intelligence

Terminal drop hypothesis

Verbal scales (subtests)

Wechsler Adult Intelligence Scale (WAIS)

Wisdom

Part III

Personality and Social Development

Table 8.1

Attitudes of a middle-class, middle-aged sample toward various age-related characteristics (1965).

Characteristic	Age Range Designated as Appropriate or Expected	Percent of Sample Agreeing	
		Men (N=50)	Women (N=43)
Best age for a man to marry	20–25	80	90
Best age for a woman to marry	19–24	85	90
When most people should become grandparents	45–50	84	79
Best age for most people to finish school and go to work	20–22	86	82
When most men should be settled on a career	24–26	74	64
When most men hold their top jobs	45–50	71	58
When most people should be ready to retire	60–65	83	86
A young man	18–22	84	83
A middle-aged man	40–50	86	75
An old man	65–75	75	57
A young woman	18–24	89	88
A middle-aged woman	40–50	87	77
An old woman	60–75	83	87
When a man has the most responsibilities	35–50	79	75
When a woman has the most responsibilities	25–40	93	91
When a man accomplishes the most	40–50	82	71
When a woman accomplishes the most	30–45	94	92

Source: Neugarten et al. (1968).

Americans who become widowed or suffer a stroke at age 65 to 70, or who get married for the first time at age 25. Conversely, an event is **temporally non-normative** if it occurs at an atypical age. In our society, becoming widowed or suffering a stroke at age 35, or getting married for the first time at age 45, are temporally non-normative life events.

A second good way to classify life events is according to their frequency, regardless of age. Thus an event is **statistically normative** if it happens to the majority of individuals in a given culture. Most people in this country experience marriage and retirement at some point in their lives, so these life events are statistically normative. In contrast, few Americans of any age suffer from strokes or spinal cord injuries, or are lucky enough to win a state lottery. Therefore, these life events are **statistically non-normative**.

If we combine these dimensions, the result may be depicted as a two-by-two table. (See Table 8.2.) Note that whether an event is *temporally* normative or non-normative depends solely on the *age* at which it occurs. Conversely, whether an event is *statistically* normative or non-normative depends solely on *how many people in that culture* experience that event at some point in their lives. (See Schulz & Rau, 1985.)

IMPLICATIONS

Virtually all of us experience some life events from each of the four cells in Table 8.2. By definition, however, most of us spend most of our time dealing with statistically and temporally normative events. These events are the most common, so they are also the ones for which friends, loved ones, and society are best prepared to offer any necessary assistance. For example, experienced college counselors and professors are likely to understand and help resolve the scholastic and emotional problems of the 20-year-old student, and widowhood support groups are generally effective for those over 60.

What of those relatively few adults who experience an unusually large number of non-normative life events? Because these events are by definition rare and unpredictable (albeit perhaps more interesting), friends, relatives, and society are less likely to know how to provide appropriate help. Thus, a woman who is widowed at age 25 may have no friends who can give her appropriate emotional support, because they are all too young to have

Table 8.2

Classifying major life events according to temporal and statistical normativity.

	Temporally Normative	Temporally Non-normative
Statistically Normative	Getting married for the first time at age 25	Getting married for the first time at age 45
	Becoming widowed at age 65	Becoming widowed at age 35
	Retiring at age 65	Retiring at age 40
	Having first child during late twenties	Having first child at age 45
Statistically Non-normative	Suffering stroke at age 65	Suffering stroke at age 35
	Spinal cord injury at age 18–30	Spinal cord injury at age 55
		Winning state lottery (any age)

Source: Schulz & Rau (1985, modified).

undergone a similar experience. A 45-year-old man who enters college for the first time may prove to be somewhat of a puzzle to his counselor and professors. An adult who marries and has children late in life may have some difficulty dealing with teachers and other parents, who do not expect a 6-year-old child to have a 50-year-old father and a 40-year-old mother. Or a person who suffers a spinal cord injury at any age may find that this rare event leaves friends feeling helpless and confused, and unable to respond effectively. In fact, adults who must deal with many non-normative life events (and the corresponding stress) may well be more likely to suffer physical illness, psychopathology, or even premature death.

A further discussion of stress and non-normative life events will be deferred until Chapter 10. The remainder of this chapter concentrates on those life events that are statistically normative, including marriage and parenting.

Adult Friendships

Some social scientists prefer to explain the behavior of friends, lovers, spouses, and families in roughly similar terms. But while friendships may vary from casual to loving, even the best and closest of these would seem to differ in many significant respects from an intimate relationship with one special person. In accordance with those theorists who support the latter view, we will treat friendship and marriage in separate sections.

DEFINITION

What characteristics define a friend? How does a friend differ from a casual acquaintance, or from someone you know well but who does not seem to belong in this desirable category? In order to be a friendship, a relationship between two people must be

- *Voluntary.* The relationship is entered into freely and without coercion.
- *Mutual.* Both persons contribute to the relationship, and both derive benefits from it.
- *Flexible.* Behaviors change to meet the needs of the persons. For example, one person may be supportive at some times and in need of support at other times.
- *Terminable.* The relationship may be ended at any time.
- *Equal and reciprocal.* Neither person consistently adopts a superior role, as by trying to manipulate the relationship or refusing to share important information.
- *Emotional.* Both parties contribute their feelings to the relationship. These feelings represent an involvement in the total personality of the other person.

(See Brown, 1981; Matthews, 1986.) By these standards, a person who consciously keeps secrets from another individual would *not* be considered a friend. For example:

A Friendship Betrayed

A magazine editor told . . . how upset he was when his closest friend, a man he had gone to high school with, withheld from him the fact that he had cancer "until he was practically on his deathbed. I tried to respect that; I know he was suffering and had his own reasons for not telling me, but—it sounds terrible, I know—I was hurt . . . like he'd let me down." (Brenton, 1974; Matthews, 1986, p. 26)

No maliciousness was involved; in fact, the terminal patient may well have been trying to spare the editor's feelings. Yet concealing this vital information violated the elements of reciprocity and total personal involvement, so it proved harmful to the friendship.

STYLES OF ADULT FRIENDSHIPS

Even when a friendship satisfies these criteria, it may be expressed in different types of behavior. Matthews (1986) concludes that there are three basic friendship styles: independent, discerning (or discriminative), and gregarious (or acquisitive).

The Independent Style.
Adults who develop the **independent style of friendship** do not regard anyone else as a best friend, or even as a close friend. Although they do share good times with other people, they emphasize their self-sufficiency and maintain a certain psychological distance from others:

The Independent Style of Friendship

[A woman]   I am a very private person. I always lived by the rule "no explain, no complain." When you say too much you are revealing too much about yourself. You should retain a little bit of your privacy and thereby you get pride and you get self-discipline. The very private things you keep to yourself.

[A man]   Oh, I consider all of [the people in my retirement complex] to be friends. There are some that I wouldn't give you a dime a dozen for them. But still you participate in the stuff that we do here. You have to go along with them, but I wouldn't call them friends.

[A man]   I love friends. I love people. But I've been stung by friends, and I could never place myself in the position where I'd say, "Well, he or she is a *very* good friend of mine." I won't let myself get hurt anymore. (Matthews, 1986, pp. 35, 39)

These adults do not want or expect their friendships to be intimate. They give the impression of being surrounded by a sea of people, none of whom are closer emotionally than the others.

The Discerning Style.
Adults who develop the **discerning style of friendship** have a small number of friends to whom they feel close and regard as very important:

The Discerning Style of Friendship

[A woman]   I formed a very close friendship in high school within a group of girls . . . and there was a really close friendship with one of these girls . . . Another friend was a close friend in college and I married her brother, so that friendship was maintained. . . . We have a lot of more casual friends, for instance, that we play bridge with and that sort of thing, but not the type of friends that you are totally unreserved or honest with, that you can . . . say how you really feel about something. I'm pretty on guard most of the time with most people.

[A man]   [My best friend and I] had a lot of what we considered very serious discussions, you know, about our lives and the future and what our goals might be and that sort of thing. . . . We had a lot of interesting times together, had a lot of fun together. He had a good sense of humor as well as a rather keen mind and we had a very enjoyable time. We were very close. . . .

[A man]   There's one couple . . . we've known each other a long time, but I don't consider [the man] a friend. I guess there'd be lots of people you'd put in that category. Yes, you are glad to see each other and they know you, but you wouldn't just on the spur of the moment call them up or they call you. . . . (Matthews, 1986, pp. 45–47)

These adults draw a clear distinction between close, trusted, long-term friends and more casual, impersonal acquaintances.

The Gregarious Style.   Adults who develop the **gregarious style of friendship** feel close to a fairly large number of people. There may be a core of half a dozen friends whom they describe as very special, and another group of several dozen people whose company they enjoy:

The Gregarious Style of Friendship

[A man]   Sometimes it's hard to draw the line between acquaintances and friends, but there must have been, I'd say, fifty or so of them anyway, that I considered good friends, played cards with, just a lot of companionship.

[A woman]   In the past three or four years we've met several couples that we see fairly often. Otherwise you become isolated. And the ones that die and the ones who move out of town, unless you make friends you're isolated. You have to make a conscious effort to make friends. (Matthews, 1986, pp. 53, 55)

These adults are also optimistic about the prospect of acquiring new friends in the future.

THE PURPOSES OF ADULT FRIENDSHIPS

Why do adults have friends? What sort of people are we likely to choose as our friends? The answers to these questions are by no means simple ones, because friendships can serve various important purposes.

Interpersonal Similarity.   The popular notion that opposites attract one another may hold true in rare instances, but it is *not* generally supported by

Adult friendships take many different forms and are a central feature of adult lives. (Joel Gordon/Joel Gordon Photography)

empirical evidence. Instead, we are usually attracted to those who have similar beliefs, values, and personalities. A man who engages in the discerning style of friendship put it this way:

> A friend in my opinion is somebody who has similar ideas. For me it means he would have to love classical music. He would have to have an interest in art, not in artists, but like to go to museums. Read good books, love nature, somebody you could have a serious talk [with], not just, "How is your car?" (Matthews, 1986, p. 48; see also Griffitt, 1974; Kandel, 1978; Lowenthal et al., 1975)

People who resemble us may be easier to communicate with and relate to because they tend to perceive events in similar ways. Or it may be reassuring to see our own characteristics and opinions reflected, and thereby implicitly endorsed, by someone else.

Psychological Support.   Not all studies support the importance of interpersonal similarity. Some findings suggest that while we may at first be drawn to those who resemble ourselves, long-term friendships actually depend far more on psychological support: A good friend is one who makes you feel good, and is there when needed. In the words of one woman,

> [My friends] always called me when [my son] was [terminally] ill. They never asked me because they knew if I wanted to talk about it, I'd talk. But they never questioned me. Because at the time I wasn't always able to talk about it. And they knew if they asked me at the wrong time, they didn't know what they were going to get back. But they knew enough so if I talked about it, they listened. And they're still my friends today. (Matthews, 1986, p. 78; see also Bailey, Finney, & Heim, 1975; Troll & Smith, 1976)

Thus mutual trust, and feeling comfortable with one another, may ultimately prove to be more important determinants of friendship than similarity. As we have seen, however, even close friends may find it difficult to offer effective psychological support in the case of non-normative life events.

Self-Disclosure. One vital aspect of a close and trusting friendship is **self-disclosure**, or revealing information about ourselves that we would normally keep secret. As we observed in the case of the cancer patient and magazine editor, the refusal to make such self-disclosures can seriously jeopardize a friendship.

Most of us seem to need at least one confidant with whom we can safely share our innermost thoughts and feelings, especially those which seem particularly vulnerable to criticism by other people (e.g., Candy, 1977; Lowenthal & Haven, 1968). The loss of this important confidant may even lead to depression, while maintaining this relationship makes it easier to survive other crises and personal disasters.

Physical Attractiveness. To many psychologists, an individual's inner personality is much more important than mere physical characteristics. Yet even in our psychologically enlightened era, physical attractiveness remains an attribute of prime importance. It is a major determinant of success in our society (Berscheid & Walster, 1974), and it significantly affects most people's perception of the ideal friend (Dion, Berscheid, & Walster, 1972; Walster et al., 1966). A man who is seen with a good-looking friend, especially a female, is likely to enjoy increased stature in the eyes of his friends and associates (Sigall & Landy, 1973). Apparently, then, many of us still assume that what is beautiful is good and worthwhile.

However, those of us who are less than beautiful need not despair. Research has shown that for both same-sex and cross-sex friendships, people tend to choose those who are approximately similar in physical attractiveness (e.g., Cash & Derlaga, 1978; Murstein & Christy, 1976; Shanteau & Nagy, 1979). That is, most adults normally do *not* pursue friendships with the most physically attractive candidates. Instead, we select those similar enough to ourselves so that our overtures are less likely to be rejected.

Intelligence and Competence.   We tend to prefer friendships with people who are intelligent and competent, perhaps because such individuals are more likely to provide us with effective support and assistance. In fact, in the long run, intelligence may be an even more important component of personal attractiveness than physical characteristics (Gross & Crofton, 1977; Solomon & Saxe, 1977).

Other Factors.   We value friends who are psychologically and emotionally stimulating, and who introduce us to enjoyable new experiences. We are also likely to choose friends who are usually pleasant and agreeable; who clearly like and approve of us; and who live close to us, making them more accessible on those occasions when we need a friend (Backman & Secord, 1959; Kaplan & Anderson, 1973; McCormick, 1982).

Less is known about the choice of cross-sex versus same-sex friendships. Traditionally, cross-sex friendships have been viewed with marked suspicion: Can they really be platonic, or must a sexual element inevitably intrude? At present, there is relatively little research dealing with this issue. Married couples appear to resolve this problem by associating primarily with other couples, with the presence of the other spouse presumably allaying any fears of infidelity (Hess, 1972).

FRIENDSHIPS AND AGING

Most of the available information about friendships and aging has been obtained from cross-sectional studies. Therefore, these data must be interpreted with caution.

Number of Friendships.   The number of friends one has, especially close friends, appears to remain relatively stable throughout adulthood (e.g., Antonucci, 1984; Babchuck, 1978–79; Lowenthal et al., 1975). One of the rare longitudinal studies in this area, which focused on a sample of men from age 50 to age 64, also found no significant decline in the number of friendships during these years (Costa, Zonderman, & McCrae, 1983). However, there is some indication that casual friendships may become less common with increasing age. We also appear to change our best friends frequently during young adulthood, but only rarely after middle age. (See Fischer, 1982; Fischer et al., 1977; Stueve & Gerson, 1977.)

How do adults manage to maintain about the same number of friends as they grow older? Some friendships last for years because the participants are highly committed to the relationship, and go to great lengths to ensure its continuation (e.g., traveling hundreds of miles to visit a friend who has moved away; frequent telephone calls or letters). Other friendships endure without much effort because of favorable circumstances, as when the individuals live very near one another. Furthermore, even when an adult friendship does end, this may not be a permanent loss. Most often, such friendships end by quietly fading away, rather than by being actively terminated. (For example, one person may move to a distant city.) These passive endings are usually regarded as no one's fault, so there is no residue of hard feelings, and the friendship may well be reactivated at a later date. Finally, even when a friendship is irrevocably lost, an older adult is likely to have formed numerous acquaintances over the years. This provides a pool of prospects from which a new friend can be developed. (See Matthews, 1986.)

These findings indicate that as we grow through adulthood, we do *not* suffer an increasing shortage of good friends. We do sift through our various interpersonal relationships, and retain those that we value the most.

Purposes and Benefits. Some data indicate that adults past middle age interact with their friends less often, while increasing the amount of time spent with relatives (Stueve & Fischer, 1978). Yet other studies report that for adults age 55 and over, the frequency of contact with close friends is significantly related to satisfaction with life in general, whereas the frequency of contact with family members is not (e.g., Arking, 1976; Blau, 1981; Graney, 1975; Larson, 1978; Palmore, 1981; Spakes, 1979; Wood & Robertson, 1978).

Why should close friendships be so beneficial for older adults? Although relatively little research attention has been devoted to this issue, it would seem that psychological support is particularly important. Adults of all ages who receive such support from their friends cope better with various adverse life events, including physical disabilities, losing a job, and widowhood. Asking a close friend for help may be easier than calling on one's adult children, which appears to involve a greater loss of independence (Lee, 1985). And it is likely to succeed. The amount of psychological support that is provided by close friends does not appear to decline appreciably with increasing age, at least insofar as normative life events are concerned. (See Antonucci, 1984; Cobb & Kasl, 1977; Kasl & Berkman, 1981; Schulz & Decker, 1983.) There is even some indication that close friends can give effective support in the case of some non-normative life events, such as rape and cancer (Burgess & Holmstrum, 1978; Vachon et al., 1977). Although these specific events are rare ones, they are not wholly dissimilar from illnesses or injuries in general, which most friends have some experience in dealing with.

Some studies also suggest that adults of all ages who have more friends and social contacts enjoy lower mortality rates and better mental health (Berkman & Syme, 1979; Hirsch, 1981; House, Robbins, & Metzner, 1982; McKinlay, 1981; Mitchell & Trickett, 1980). Similar findings have also been obtained for older white males with numerous social ties (Blazer, 1982; Schoenbach et al., 1986). Overall, the evidence strongly indicates that having friends and social relationships is important for physical and mental health, even though a few investigators have obtained no significant relationship between the number of friends and psychological well-being (Lieberman, 1982; Schaefer et al., 1981).

Afterword.   All in all, research evidence provides little support for the stereotype of the friendless and lonely older adult. Although this unfortunate picture is undoubtedly accurate in some instances, it represents the exception rather than the rule. To be sure, the number of casual friends that one has may well decrease to some extent with increasing age. But most adults do not suffer any appreciable decline in the number of close friends as they grow through adulthood, or in the amount of psychological support that is received from these friends.

Love, Marriage, and Divorce

Love is probably the ultimate form of interpersonal relationship. Yet throughout most of recorded history, the meaning of love has been shrouded in mystery. Until recently, most social scientists regarded love as too intangible, complicated, and unscientific (and much too personal and controversial) to study empirically (Berscheid & Walster, 1978; Wrightsman & Deaux, 1981). The subject of love is no longer shackled with these taboos and doubts, and researchers have begun to take a serious interest in this most important phenomenon.

CONCEPTIONS OF LOVE

As might be expected of an area that has only recently been subjected to empirical research, there is as yet no single definition of love that is wildly accepted by social scientists.

Passionate and Companionate Love.   According to Walster and Walster (1978), there are two kinds of love. **Passionate love** is characterized by total absorption in another person, intense physiological arousal, and moments of ecstasy and complete fulfillment. In contrast, **companionate love** is highlighted by affection for those who are closely involved in our lives. Companionate love tends to be more common than passionate love, and is more typical of long-term relationships.

D-Love and B-Love.   Abraham Maslow, a noted personality theorist, has posited a different dichotomy of love. **D-love** ("deficiency love") takes the form of a selfish need to receive love from other people, and is often accompanied by anxious and manipulative efforts to win the loved one's affection. Nevertheless, D-love is not wholly undesirable. This need must be satisfied in order for us to develop unselfish **B-love** ("being love"), which is nonpossessive, giving, honest, and richer and more enjoyable than D-love. That is, if we do not receive sufficient love at some periods in our lives, we will be unable to give genuine love to other people (Maslow, 1968; 1970).

The Art of Loving. Other personality theorists regard love as a phenomenon that transcends mere one-to-one relationships. To Erich Fromm, the "art of loving" involves four main aspects: a genuine caring for and giving to other people, an accurate knowledge of their true feelings and wishes, a respect for their right to develop in their own way, and a sense of responsibility toward all humanity:

> Love is not primarily a relationship to a specific person; it is . . . an *orientation* of *character* which determines the relatedness of a person to the world as a whole . . . If I truly love one person I love all persons, I love the world, I love life. (Fromm, 1956/1974, pp. 38–39)

According to Fromm, everyone has the capacity for genuine love. However, fulfilling this potential is very difficult. We all begin life as wholly self-centered (narcissistic) infants, and pathogenic experiences in later life can cause us to revert to this immature state. Authoritarian parents who use the child to fulfill their own frustrated ambition for social or professional success, or parents who are overly pessimistic, joyless, narcissistic, or physically abusive, may well cause the child's healthy ability to love to be replaced by narcissistic tendencies (Fromm, 1941; 1947; 1956).

Psychometric Conceptions. How can we determine empirically if someone is in love with a given person? Simply asking this individual if he or she is in love, and receiving a yes or no answer, would seem to be a rather inaccurate and unscientific approach. A more detailed alternative has been developed by Rubin (1970), who constructed two nine-item scales. One of these is designed to measure romantic love, the other to tap how much the other person is liked:

Sample Love-Scale Items	Sample Liking-Scale Items
"I would forgive _____ for practically anything."	"I think that _____ is unusually well adjusted."
"If I could never be with _____ , I would feel miserable."	" _____ is the sort of person who I myself would like to be."
"I feel that I can confide in _____ about virtually everything."	"Most people would react very favorably to _____ after a brief acquaintance."

Subjects are asked to indicate the extent of their agreement with each item, using a scale ranging from 1 (most negative) to 9 (most positive). In one study, 158 college couples who were dating but not engaged were asked to complete these scales twice: once with respect to their dating partner, and once with respect to a close friend of the same sex. The results indicated that there is a conceptual distinction between romantic love and liking. The data also revealed significant differences in the nature of the relationships formed by men and women: Women included more liking in their love relationships, and more loving in their liking (friendly) relationships. That is, women liked their love partners, and loved their same-sex friends, more than men did (Rubin, 1970; see also Booth, 1972).

LOVE AND MARRIAGE

The Development of Love.
Many relationships that end in marriage proceed through a fairly standard sequence: casual dating, more frequent dating, going steady, informal engagement (being "engaged to be engaged"), and—ultimately—formal engagement. As the relationship progresses, the initial, idealized image of the loved one yields to a more realistic appraisal of the other's strengths and weaknesses (Pollis, 1969). Apparently, "love is blind" only at the outset.

In any loving relationship, different factors tend to be important during different stages. The early attraction is typically based on superficial aspects, such as physical attractiveness. In later stages, however, we are more likely to value opportunities for self-disclosure, similar beliefs, and similar levels of emotional maturity. When a relationship is relatively new, self-disclosure is usually limited; few deeply personal matters are shared with one's partner. Only gradually do we become willing to confide our innermost thoughts and feelings to the one we love (Adams, 1979; Altman & Taylor, 1973; Levinger, 1974; 1978).

There also appears to be an inverse relationship between attraction and attachment. Attraction is high during the early stages, due to novelty and intrigue; but attachment is low, since there has not yet been sufficient time to develop firm emotional bonds. If the relationship should end at this time, the couple will normally experience only temporary unhappiness and disappointment. As the relationship continues, the novelty and corresponding attraction decreases, while the attachment becomes much more powerful. Thus a breakup during this later period can cause emotional pain that is never completely overcome.

Enduring Love: Marriages That Last.
Why do some loving relationships survive for many years? A recent study focused on 351 couples who remained married for 15 years or more, 300 of whom reported that they were happily married. The most frequently cited reason for the enduring relationship was: "My spouse is my best friend" (Lauer & Lauer, 1985; see Table 8.3). Liking one's spouse as a person, meaningful communication and self-disclosure, openness, trustworthiness, caring, and giving were considerably more important to a lasting marriage than passionate love. Other factors that were typical of lengthy marriages included recognizing and accepting the spouse's faults, believing that marriage is a long-term commitment, and avoiding displays of intensely expressed anger. The following quotes were typical:

Table 8.3

Why marriages endure: Reasons most often given by a sample of 351 couples married for at least 15 years, in order of frequency.

Men	Women
1. "My spouse is my best friend."	1. "My spouse is my best friend."
2. "I like my spouse as a person."	2. "I like my spouse as a person."
3. "Marriage is a long-term commitment."	3. "Marriage is a long-term commitment."
4. "Marriage is sacred."	4. "Marriage is sacred."
5. "We agree on aims and goals."	5. "We agree on aims and goals."
6. "My spouse has grown more interesting."	6. "My spouse has grown more interesting."
7. "I want the relationship to succeed."	7. "I want the relationship to succeed."
8. "An enduring marriage is important to social stability."	8. "We laugh together."
9. "We laugh together."	9. "We agree on a philosophy of life."
10. "I am proud of my spouse's achievements."	10. "We agree on how and how often to show affection."

Source: Lauer & Lauer (1985, abridged).

A Man Married for 24 Years:

"[My wife] isn't perfect. But I don't worry about her weak points, which are very few. Her strong points overcome them too much." (p. 24)

A Man Married for 20 Years:

"Commitment means a willingness to be unhappy for awhile. I wouldn't go on for years and years being wretched in my marriage. But you can't avoid troubled times. You're not going to be happy with each other all the time. That's when commitment is really important." (p. 25)

A Man Married for 36 Years:

"Discuss your problems in a normal voice. If a voice is raised, stop. Return after a short period of time. Start again. After a period of time both parties will be able to deal with their problems and not say things that they will be sorry about later." (p. 26)

Virtually all of these couples preferred peaceful interactions; only one couple reported that they often yelled at each other. Interestingly, sex was far down the list of reasons for a happy marriage. Although sexual relations were important to these couples, fewer than 10 percent regarded sex as one of the primary factors keeping the marriage together. However, the men and women in this study placed considerable emphasis on sexual fidelity. One wife who had been married 27 years stated that she could resolve almost any problem with her husband given enough time, but infidelity "would probably not be something I could forget and forgive" (p. 26).

Paradoxically, then, a relationship that may have originated primarily because of passionate love is likely to require strong elements of friendship and companionate love in order to endure. As these investigators concluded, "The redemption of difficult people through selfless devotion may make good fiction, but the happily married people in our sample expressed no such sense of mission. Rather, they said, they are grateful to have married someone who is basically appealing and likable" (Lauer & Lauer, 1985, p. 24).

Role Factors in Marriage.

In 1983, a *Newsweek* cover story emphasized the increasing prevalence of "househusbands." According to empirical research during the late 1970s, however, the demise of the traditional housewife role has been greatly exaggerated.

Many couples do tend to share household duties while they are childless. But this egalitarianism usually does not continue after the first child is born, even if both spouses are working. Instead, the need to earn more money and the generally higher income potential for men drives the husband to concentrate on his career, leaving the wife to assume primary responsibility for the home and family. As a result, couples with children are likely to adopt traditional roles: The wife does most of the housework, prepares the meals, and takes care of the children; the husband may make minor house repairs, shovel snow, mow the lawn, and take out the garbage (Campbell, Converse, & Rodgers, 1976; Hoffman & Manis, 1978; Pleck, 1977). Conversely, shared duties and role equality are most often found in childless marriages.

Marriage and the Empty Nest.

The time that a married couple spends together after the last child leaves home, up until the death of one spouse, is known as the **empty nest**. According to folklore and popular literature, this is a painful time for most parents—particularly women, who supposedly lament that their all-important role of mother is all but gone. How much truth is there to this common belief?

During this decade, the duration of the empty nest period has increased considerably. In 1900, it lasted for only about two years and often occurred during the couple's old age. Due to such recent trends as smaller families, the closer spacing of children, and a longer life span, the empty nest now lasts for an average of 13 years. Nevertheless, recent data do *not* support the prevailing stereotype. Couples are likely to view the departure of their children in mostly favorable terms. True, there is some sense of loss. But there is also relief from the relentless responsibility of daily child rearing, more opportunities to indulge personal interests, and increased freedom and privacy, which result in markedly improved marital relationships and individual well-being (Barber, 1989; Hagestad, 1980). Although exceptions undoubtedly exist, the "pain of the empty nest" must be regarded as yet another of the myths that pervade the field of adult development and aging.

Caring for a Seriously Ill Spouse.   When an older parent becomes seriously ill (as from cancer, heart disease, or Alzheimer's disease), care is most often provided by the adult offspring. We will discuss this issue later in this chapter, in the section dealing with intergenerational relationships.

As married couples grow old, it is not uncommon to find that one spouse becomes chronically ill or disabled. As a result, one spouse becomes the caregiver for the other. The spouse who most often has to provide such care is the wife; the husband is usually older, and men have shorter life expectancies. Caregiving for a major illness goes far beyond the bounds of normal care, and can be extremely burdensome. The wife's personal life suffers greatly; since she lives with the patient, her privacy and leisure activities are severely restricted. Her emotional involvement with the patient tends to be even greater than that of the children because of her longer personal relationship with him. As a result, the negative impact of a major illness is even greater on caregiving wives than on grown children who serve as caregivers. There are also some positive effects, however: increased self-esteem because of her patience, compassion, courage, and strength in such difficult circumstances, and feeling appreciated by her husband and closer to him. Interestingly, the few husbands who care for seriously ill wives appear to function quite well; they are better able to put limits on the amount of care that they provide by relying more on supportive family members and professional services. (See Biegel, Sales, & Schulz, 1991; Schulz et al., in press; Williamson & Schulz, in press.)

DIVORCE

Demographics.   The preceding sections have emphasized the more pleasant aspects of marital relationships: being attracted to another person, learning to share our innermost feelings, liking as well as loving one's spouse. However, marriage is not without a certain degree of risk. Each year, the blissful expectations of more than one million American couples are shattered by divorce. The divorce rate in this country has increased consistently during the past three decades and doubled between 1968 and 1978, with the result that the average duration of a marriage in the United States is currently 9.4 years. In fact, divorce has become statistically normative (more or less); it terminates one of every two marriages (Glick, 1979; Lauer & Lauer, 1985).

Divorce is most common among adults aged 30 to 45 and among black females. (See Figure 8.1.) Youthful marriages, where both the man and woman are younger than age 21, are significantly more likely to end in divorce than marriages after the age of 30. Nevertheless, the elderly are far from immune. Among Americans age 65 and older, more than half a million are divorced, and approximately 10,000 new cases are registered each year. As we will see in Chapter 10, divorce among the elderly may well be even more stressful and pathogenic than widowhood.

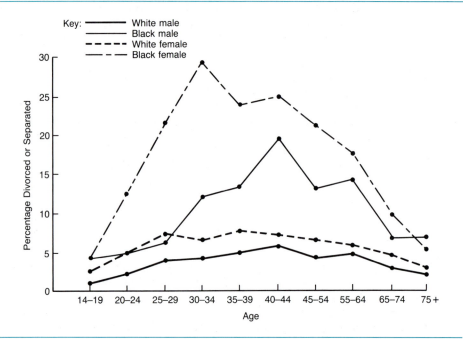

Figure 8.1
Divorce rate as a function of age and ethnic group.   Source: U.S. Department of Commerce, Bureau of the Census (1976).

Causes of Divorce.   As we have seen, couples with happy marriages tend to regard one another as best friends. In contrast, those headed for divorce are likely to have arguments that become increasingly severe. Instead of one spouse backing off when the other is upset and initiating peace-making overtures, anger and rejection are met with greater anger and rejection. This causes the conflict to escalate and increases the likelihood of leaving permanent emotional scars. (See Raush et al., 1974.)

Other common causes of divorce include alcoholism, desertion, brutality, and adultery (Bennett, 1984; see also Table 8.4). The personality of each spouse is also an important consideration, for those with a strong commitment to maintaining the marriage are more likely to do so even in the face of serious obstacles (as we have seen).

The increasing divorce rate in this country may also be due in part to the easing of divorce laws and the establishment of "no fault" divorces, where incompatibility and breakdown of the relationship are accepted as sufficient grounds. Also, since women have made greater inroads into the workplace during the last half century (Chapter 9), their financial status has improved. Thus, not as many women must remain mired in an unhappy marriage in order to survive economically. For these reasons, the increased divorce rate in this country is not entirely negative; it may well indicate that more people can now extricate themselves from relationships that have become unbearable.

Stages of Divorce. Divorced people tend to proceed through several behavioral stages, much like a rite of passage (Chiriboga, 1979). At first, they prefer to nurse their psychological wounds in isolation, so they segregate themselves from other people. Next, they experience a period with no clear social identity; they are no longer married, but not yet truly single. During the first few months after the divorce is granted, many men who were fed and cared for by their wives must now learn to prepare their own meals and keep the house clean. Conversely, many women must learn those tasks which were formerly performed by their husbands, such as having the car repaired or balancing the checkbook. The ex-spouses spend much of this time in dealings with one another, often arguing bitterly over financial matters. However, not all of these interactions are negative. One study found that some 12 percent of divorced couples had sexual relations with one another during the first two months following the divorce, and most stated that they would turn first to their ex-spouses if they needed help handling a crisis (Hetherington, Cox, & Cox, 1976). Ultimately, divorced individuals do begin to seek out other people and reestablish themselves socially.

The Effects of Divorce. Divorce is usually a traumatic experience. There is some indication that when one spouse favors and initiates the divorce, this individual is more likely to establish a satisfactory life in the future, whereas the other spouse tends to suffer long-lasting emotional scars. On the whole,

Table 8.4
Why marriages end: Reasons most often given for divorce.

Reasons Women Give		Reasons Men Give	
1. Communication problems	70%	1. Communication problems	59%
2. Basic unhappiness	60%	2. Basic unhappiness	47%
3. Incompatibility	56%	3. Incompatibility	45%
4. Emotional abuse	56%	4. Sexual problems	30%
5. Financial problems	33%	5. Financial problems	29%
6. Sexual problems	32%	6. Emotional abuse	25%
7. Alcohol abuse by spouse	30%	7. Women's liberation	15%
8. Infidelity by spouse	25%	8. In-laws	12%
9. Physical abuse	22%	9. Infidelity by spouse	11%
10. In-laws	11%	10. Alcohol abuse by self	9%

Source: Adapted from Cleek & Pearson (1985).

however, divorce would seem to affect women more deeply than men. Only 14 percent of divorced American women are awarded alimony, and fewer than half of these receive it regularly; 44 percent are awarded child support, with fewer than half receiving it regularly (*McCall's*, Sept. 1976). Thus, despite the improving financial status of women in this country, numerous divorcees must either find ways to support themselves (and their children, if any) or else accept a markedly reduced standard of living. Older women are likely to have particular difficulty in this regard because their generation was not as tolerant of women in the workplace, making it less likely that they ever developed any income-producing skills. In contrast, divorced men are usually employed, so they can continue to derive income and satisfaction from their work.

Furthermore, establishing a satisfying heterosexual relationship may well be particularly difficult for divorced older women. There are more single women than single men, so divorced women are less often asked by friends to serve as blind dates or unattached party guests. The woman is most likely to gain custody of the children, and to become anxious about their reactions to and possible jealousy of any dates and sexual relationships that she may have. Thus it is hardly surprising that divorced women (and single men) show the most symptoms of stress in our society (Douvan, 1979).

The effect of divorce on children varies with their age, and with the parents' ability to cope with the resulting problems. Young children tend to blame themselves for the divorce, to worry about being abandoned, and to have fantasies that their parents will reconcile. Adolescents are likely to experience initial anger and turmoil, but are generally better able to cope with the divorce. There is also some evidence that after a divorce, parents are less affectionate with their children, adolescent girls become more promiscuous, and boys are more feminized. (See Anthony, 1974; Hetherington, 1972; Hetherington, Cox, & Cox, 1977; Hetherington & Duer, 1972; Kelly & Wallerstein, 1976; Wallerstein & Kelly, 1974; 1975; 1976.) However, children in single-parent families appear to function better than children in families with two parents where there is frequent conflict (Rutter, 1979).

Divorce can be a shattering experience for the husband as well. It has been argued that divorce laws and decrees are often unfair not only to women, but also to men. Some fathers report that their efforts to gain joint custody of the children involved years of expensive legal wrangling and caused so much hard feeling that the relationship with the children was seriously impaired. Others contend that they are denied proper visitation by their ex-wives, presumably due to the latter's anger and bitterness. As one fathers'-rights activist put it, "I've seen some men sobbing away, so overcome by the system . . . The system is so stacked against men that they don't fight" (*Time*, Nov. 24, 1986).

Nevertheless, if a marriage is truly unbearable and if the couple's religious and personal beliefs permit, the least of evils may well be to end it and give each spouse the opportunity to find happiness elsewhere. In any case, it appears that divorce will remain a common phenomenon for the foreseeable future.

Remarriage.   The emotional pain caused by a broken marriage does not prevent many adults from trying again. More than 20 percent of the current marriages in this country include at least one spouse who has been married previously (Bowers & Bahr, 1989).

The probability of remarrying decreases with increasing age for both men and women. (See Figure 8.2.) However, remarriage rates are much lower for older women than for older men. As we observed in Chapter 1, there are

Figure 8.2

Remarriage rates of previously divorced men and women, by age.   Source: Vital and Health Statistics (1989).

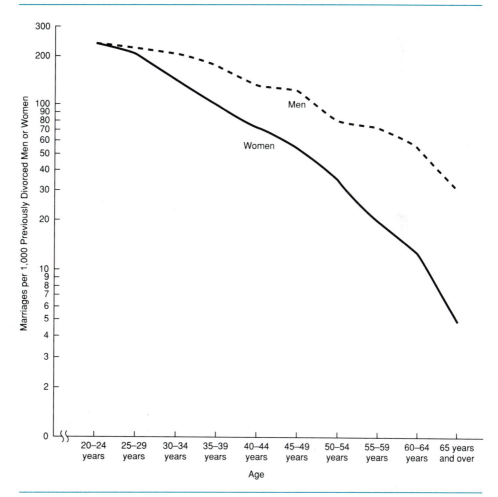

many more unmarried older women than unmarried older men (see Figure 1.6). Also, older men have more latitude in their choice of spouse: Social custom looks with disfavor on women who marry much younger men, but not the reverse. Thus remarried men tend to be more satisfied with their marriages than are remarried women, who have a smaller pool from which to select and are more likely to settle for less desirable partners. (See Bowers & Bahr, 1989.)

In general, those who remarry later in life have more stable and satisfying marriages than do those who remarry as young adults. One reason is that older adults can draw on greater experience as to what makes a relationship successful, by combining practical with romantic considerations. (See Bahr & Peterson, 1989.)

Afterword: Intimate Relationships and Aging.   Empirical data indicate that it is disadvantageous to marry too early; youthful marriages are more likely to end in divorce. Also, divorces are most common between the ages of 30 and 45. For the most part, however, it is difficult to draw any age-related conclusions with regard to marriage and divorce. Some adults find marriage to be an increasing source of love and fulfillment as they grow older, but others experience increasing conflicts that make continuation of the marriage virtually impossible. Some useful clues as to why marriages endure or fail have been unearthed by social scientists; but these factors involve the personality, motivation, and interpersonal behavior of the spouses, rather than age per se.

The relationship between love and aging is also far from clear, partly because adults pursue many diverse courses insofar as intimate relationships are concerned. Some marry young; some do so later in life. Some marry once, for better or worse; some marry numerous times. Some eschew marriage altogether and remain single throughout their lives, possibly engaging in a number of loving relationships along the way. And some find fulfillment from homosexual relationships, rather than heterosexual ones. We can only conclude that the love adults derive from intimate relationships does not necessarily decline in quantity or quality with increasing age, at least not until old age makes the death of the loved one more likely. The negative relationship between age and the capacity for sexual expressions of love has also been exaggerated, as we will see in the following section.

Sexuality and Aging

HETEROSEXUAL RELATIONSHIPS

Research Problems and Prevailing Stereotypes.   As was the case with love, human sexuality has only recently been subjected to much empirical research. This is also an extremely personal and sensitive area, and it is one that poses significant conceptual and methodological problems. For example, should researchers define heterosexuality solely in terms of intercourse? If so, should sexual behavior be measured in terms of frequency (number of coital acts per week or month), percentages (how many adults of a given age still participate in sexual intercourse), or level of intensity (degree of physical arousal and excitement)? Or perhaps a sound definition of human heterosexual behavior should also include less overt behaviors, such as thoughts, fantasies, wishes, and affectionate touching. But is behavior that does not end in orgasm truly sexual? When does friendly caressing turn into sexual foreplay?

To complicate matters further, it has been argued that we engage in sex for many reasons. The most obvious motives are sexual desire and the need to satisfy biological and reproductive drives. But sex may also be used to obtain affection and intimacy, to exert power over another person, to escape boredom, to make up with a loved one after a fight, to gratify feelings of pride and self-esteem, and to confirm one's masculinity or femininity (Neubeck, 1972).

Until recently, very little was known about the relationship between sexuality and aging. And since no one knew much about the sexual desires and behaviors of the middle-aged and elderly, it was widely assumed that there was nothing to know—that is, that older adults did not and should not have any interest in sex. In one early study that used a sentence completion task, a sample of college students most often stated that "sex for most old people is negligible, unimportant, and past" (Golde & Kogan, 1959). More recently, the majority of a sample of 646 college students concluded that their parents had sexual intercourse no more than once a month, and some 25 percent of this sample believed that their parents had abandoned sex completely (Pocs et al., 1977). These views are so incorrect as to be ludicrous, yet they are by no means limited to laymen. When middle-aged and elderly patients complain of sexual difficulties or disinterest, some physicians respond with supposedly humorous statements like "Well, what can you expect at your age?" or "Maybe you've had as much [sex] as you're going to get!" (Labby, 1984). This smug and insensitive attitude is likely to feed the patient's loss of sexual self-confidence, thereby creating a self-fulfilling prophecy: Sex in later adulthood becomes impossible because the individual believes that it is abnormal and impossible. All too many older adults accept this erroneous stereotype, abandon any efforts to engage in sex, and miss out on some of the major interpersonal satisfactions and rewards that their lives still have to offer.

During the last few decades, however, we have become increasingly aware that there is indeed sexual life after middle age. To be sure, some adults have ambivalent feelings about sex and welcome advancing age as an excuse to abandon it. More often, however, the fear of losing the capacity to obtain sexual pleasure and intimacy is a very powerful one. As an anonymous sage once observed, "Sex doesn't make you live longer, it only makes you want to!" (Labby, 1984, p. 183). Thus, insofar as many middle-aged and older adults are concerned, it is fortunate that empirical data about sexuality and aging have begun to allay such fears.

Young Adulthood.   Most researchers define sexual behavior as that which results in or is intended to result in orgasm, notably coitus. By this definition, young men tend to be more sexually active than young women. Some 44 percent of men and 30 percent of women report having had sexual intercourse by age 16, with these figures increasing to 95 percent for men and 81 percent for women by age 24. Similarly, the median age for the first act of coitus has been estimated as 18 for men and 20 for women. (See Hunt, 1974; Sorensen, 1973; Wilson, 1975.)

There is some indication that the frequency of sexual behavior has increased during the past few decades, especially among younger adults and younger women. (See Figure 8.3.) This increase is a cohort effect. Social standards have changed considerably during the last half century; sexual behavior is now more accepted (and expected). As a result, younger generations are undoubtedly more willing to report (or even to exaggerate) their sexual activity. As psychologist Rollo May has observed, "[Whereas] the Victorian nice man or woman was guilty if he or she did experience sex, now we are guilty if we *don't* (1969, p. 40). Conversely, couples who grew up during the

Figure 8.3
Frequency of sexual intercourse among married couples, 1940s and 1970s.   Source: Mussen, Conger, Kagan, & Geiwitz (1979).

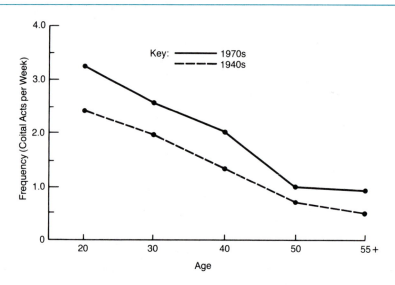

more conservative 1940s are more likely to favor modesty and to understate the extent of their sexual behavior. It has also become more acceptable for women to state openly that they have sexual desires and interests, due in part to the efforts of female advocacy groups.

Figure 8.3 also indicates that the frequency of sexual behavior among married couples does decrease from young adulthood to middle age. This is due in part to environmental constraints: Many couples have children during this period, and the rigors of night feedings or the presence of an active child or teenager may well make some reduction in sexual activity more convenient. Aging is also partly responsible for this decrease, particularly insofar as men are concerned.

Male Sexuality and Aging.   Numerous studies have found that male sexual activity declines with increasing age. The peak of male potency occurs during the late teens, although the first substantial drop in interest and desire is not usually not experienced until about age 50 (Pfeiffer, Verwoerdt, & Davis, 1972). A second significant drop in the number of men who remain sexually active has been reported to occur at about age 70 to 80. However, there is some disagreement as to the extent of this decline. In various studies, some of which were longitudinal, the percent of men who remain sexually active at older ages has been estimated as follows:

At age 60: 53–60 percent*; 95 percent

At age 70: 45 percent*; 70 percent*; 70 percent

At age 78: 25 percent*
            (* = longitudinal study)

(See Hegeler, 1976; Kinsey, Pomeroy, & Martin, 1948; Pfeiffer, 1974; Pfeiffer, Verwoerdt, & Wang, 1968; 1969; Verwoerdt, Pfeiffer, & Wang, 1969.)

The results of a cross-sectional study of men age 45 to 69, all of whom were members of a medical group insurance plan, are shown in Table 8.5. Although older men were less sexually active, 76 percent of the oldest group continued to have sexual intercourse one or more times per month (Pfeiffer, Verwoerdt, & Davis, 1974). Some more recent studies suggest that levels of male sexual activity after middle age remain even more stable (George & Weiler, 1981). It has also been estimated that 60 percent of married couples where both spouses are between ages 60 and 70 have intercourse at least occasionally (Busse & Blazer, 1980), as do 25 to 30 percent of couples past age 75 (McCary, 1978). Few researchers have focused on men over 80, but some instances of sexual intercourse by men age 90 or even older have been reported (*National Geographic*, 1973).

These data point to two significant conclusions. As age increases, fewer men are sexually active, and those who are active are less so than younger men. Nevertheless, a substantial number of men continue to engage in sex throughout much or even all of their adult lives. Although aging does appear to be

Table 8.5
Frequency of sexual intercourse reported by men and women in a medical group insurance plan.

	Percent Reporting Intercourse					
Group	Not at All	Once a Month	Once a Week	2–3 Times a Week	More than 2–3 Times a Week	Percent Still Sexually Active
Men, Age						
46–50	00	05	62	26	07	100
51–55	05	29	49	17	00	95
56–60	07	38	44	11	00	93
61–65	20	43	30	07	00	80
66–70	24	48	26	02	00	76
Women, Age						
46–50	14	26	39	21	00	86
51–55	20	41	32	05	02	80
56–60	42	27	25	04	02	58
61–65	61	29	05	05	00	39
66–70	73	16	11	00	00	27

Note: For men, N=261; for women, N=231. There were at least 41 subjects in each subgroup.
Source: Pfeiffer, Verwoerdt, & Davis (1972).

partly responsible for declines in sexual capacity and interest among men, an important question remains: Why are some older men still sexually active, while others are not?

Factors Affecting Male Sexual Activity. As a man grows older, several physiological changes begin to occur in response to overt sexual stimulation. It takes two to three times longer to achieve full penile erection, and direct physical stimulation by the partner may well be necessary. Ejaculation is significantly less forceful. The volume of seminal fluid decreases. And more time is required following orgasm before another erection is possible (Burt & Meeks, 1985; Masters & Johnson, 1966; 1970).

If a partner fails to understand the nature of these changes, the couple's sex life may be adversely affected. For example, instead of attributing the man's desire to have sex without ejaculation to the effects of aging, the woman may erroneously conclude that he does not find her attractive or that he is having an affair with someone else. On purely physiological grounds, however, there is no reason why these changes should have a profound effect on the man's sexual activity, nor is there any scientific support to date for the idea of a male menopause (Kolodny, Masters, & Johnson, 1979).

More importantly, men who have had more sexual experiences early in life tend to remain more sexually active during middle and old age. This has been referred to as the "use it or lose it" syndrome (Solnick & Corby, 1983;

see also Pfeiffer & Davis, 1972). As Masters and Johnson put it: "The most important factor in the maintenance of effective sexuality for the aging male is consistency of active sexual expression. . . . For the male geriatric sample . . . those men currently interested in relatively high levels of sexual expression report similar activity levels from their formative years. It does not appear to matter what manner of sexual expression has been employed, as long as high levels of activity were maintained" (1966, pp. 262–263). Conversely, extended periods of abstinence pose a serious risk to the sexual functioning of the older male. Therefore, if the man's partner becomes unavailable (as through hospitalization), masturbation may be a valuable way of maintaining sexual capacity and interest.

A second determinant of sexual activity among older men is physical health. Men who are (or who believe they are) in poor health are significantly less likely to engage in sexual intercourse (Pfeiffer & Davis, 1972). Sex is unappealing when one does not feel well, and ill health is more common at older ages. However, the general belief that intercourse is likely to precipitate fatal heart attacks in older men is *not* supported by empirical data. Although sexual activity is somewhat stressful, deaths during intercourse are rare and account for only 1 percent of sudden coronary fatalities. It has also been argued that some seven out of ten such deaths occur during extramarital affairs, and are due largely to the accompanying guilt and anxiety (Butler & Lewis, 1976). And other investigators have concluded that the oxygen cost during sexual intercourse is no greater than when climbing a flight of stairs, walking briskly, or performing ordinary tasks (Hellerstein & Friedman, 1970). Even adults who have had heart attacks can usually resume sexual activity upon recovery, possibly with the aid of nitroglycerin (or other coronary dilator) ten minutes prior to intercourse if angina is unusually likely (Labby, 1984).

Third, the sexual desires of older men may be inhibited by negative attitudes. As we observed at the outset of this section, all too many men accept the stereotype of the sexless older adult and erroneously conclude that they can no longer function effectively in this area. One or two failures to sustain an erection may therefore lead to a vicious circle: The resulting performance anxiety makes it progressively more difficult to enjoy sex, and the ensuing failures produce still more performance anxiety. Other attitudes that may lead to a decline in sexual activity include possible monotony resulting from many years of sex with the same partner and worries about work and career problems (Masters & Johnson, 1970).

In sum: Men are more likely to remain interested in sex through middle and old age if they enjoyed sex more often during young adulthood (or even if they merely had sexual experiences more often), if they are in good health, and if they believe that they can indeed maintain effective sexual behavior as they grow older.

Female Sexuality and Aging. In marked contrast to men, women reach their sexual peak in their mid-thirties and suffer relatively little loss in capacity thereafter. To be sure, middle age does bring some physiological changes: Lubrication of the vagina decreases, the vaginal walls lose elasticity, more precoital stimulation may be required, orgasmic experiences may be somewhat slowed, and menstrual periods eventually cease (Burt & Meeks, 1985). However, there is no evidence that these changes cause any significant decline in female sexual capacity. For example, although menopause may inhibit sexual desire if the woman (erroneously) believes that it must, the resulting freedom from the possibility of unwanted pregnancy may produce a reduction in anxiety and greater sexual satisfaction. Also, although the duration and intensity of orgasmic episodes may be reduced, the subjective levels of sensual pleasure appear to continue unabated. As Kinsey et al. (1953) put it, "[There is] no evidence that the female ages in her sexual capacities"; while Masters and Johnson (1966) concluded that "there is no time limit drawn by the advancing years to female sexuality." Orgasmic response has been observed in women age 70 to 80 and older (Kleegman, 1959; Solnick & Corby, 1983).

Nevertheless, the number of women who remain sexually active and the frequency of these activities decrease substantially with increasing age. In the study reported in Table 8.5, for example, the percentage of women who engaged in sexual intercourse declined from 86 percent at age 46–50 to 27 percent at age 66–70. And fewer women than men in each age group remained sexually active, with the greatest differences occurring in the oldest groups. Similarly, other studies have found that only 20 to 40 percent of 60-year-old women and 15 to 30 percent of 70-year-old women engage in sex (Newman & Nichols, 1960; Verwoerdt, Pfeiffer, & Wang, 1969). Thus, while the sexual *capacity* of women declines relatively little with increasing age, their sexual *activity* decreases markedly and is significantly lower than that of men of similar ages. How can this apparent paradox be explained?

Factors Affecting Female Sexual Activity. Numerous studies have found that female sexual activity depends to a large extent on the presence of a socially acceptable and sexually capable partner, such as a healthy spouse. Thus marital status is an important predictor of sexual activity among older women, but not among men (e.g., Kinsey et al., 1953; Pfeiffer & Davis, 1972; Pfeiffer, Verwoerdt, & Davis, 1972; Pfeiffer, Verwoerdt, & Wang, 1968; 1969).

American women marry men who average four years older, and who are therefore likely to become ill and/or lose interest in sex before the woman does (Newman & Nichols, 1960). Furthermore, women in our society live longer than men, so there are many more widows than widowers. (See Table 1.2; Figure 1.6.) For these reasons, middle-aged and elderly women are much more likely to be without an appropriate sexual partner than are older men. In fact, some 53 percent of women past age 65 are widows, while there are approximately 30 single men for every 100 single women over 65. Thus the woman's superior sexual capacity at older ages proves to be a dubious benefit, since her sexual activity is likely to be limited by the declining health or death of her (usually older) male partner. According to Kinsey et al. (1953), "[The decrease in sexual activity among women is] controlled by the male's desires, and it is primarily his age rather than the female's loss of interest or capacity which is reflected in this decline."

Women who enjoy sex more during young adulthood, and those who experience more coital orgasms, are more likely to remain sexually active in later life (Christenson & Gagnon, 1965; Pfeiffer & Davis, 1972). However, mere frequency of intercourse during early adulthood is not significantly related to female sexual interest and activity after middle age. Also, in contrast to men, physical health appears to have little influence on the sexual functioning of older women (Solnick & Corby, 1983).

Problems of the Institutionalized Elderly.   Negative stereotypes and the loss of sexual interest are particularly common among institutionalized men and women. In one nursing home, 49 percent of the residents agreed that "sex over 65 is ridiculous" (Kahana, 1976).

Although this decline in sexual activity is due to ill health in some instances, it is furthered by the attitudes and actions of many nursing home personnel. Few institutions provide sufficient privacy for sexual intercourse, and many ignore the desires of nonmarried residents by segregating men and women and/or ridiculing any expressions of sexual interest (Solnick

All too many men and women in nursing homes are denied this couple's opportunity for love and affection because of the misguided b265elief that the aged should not be interested in intimacy. (Frank Siteman/The Picture Cube)

& Corby, 1983; see also Burnside, 1975; Schlessinger & Miller, 1973). Conversely, ending the isolation of male and female residents tends to produce better social adjustment, a richer social life, reduced anxiety, and at least some increases in pleasurable sexual activity (Silverstone & Wynter, 1975; Wasow, 1977). At present, however, the sexual rights of the institutionalized elderly remains an essentially unresolved issue.

Afterword.   Elsewhere in this chapter (and in this book), we have had to conclude that the relationship between aging and important aspects of human behavior is ambiguous. Here, the evidence is clear. Male sexual capacity and interest decline to some extent with increasing age, especially after about age 70, but this decrement is not nearly as great as has been widely believed. The sexual capacity of women decreases relatively little as they grow through adulthood, but the frequency of their sexual activity declines even more than that of men. Women tend to marry men who are older and who are therefore likely to become ill and/or die before the woman does. So women are much more often without a socially acceptable and sexually capable partner.

Nevertheless, many men and women remain sexually active throughout much or all of adulthood. According to Comfort (1974, p. 442), "Most people can and should expect to have sex long after they no longer wish to ride a bicycle." The findings discussed above have led to profound changes in our conception of sexual behavior among older adults. Even more importantly, these discoveries should enable many older adults to liberate themselves from the shackles of negative stereotypes and self-defeating doubts and to enjoy the pleasures of this most intimate form of interpersonal relationship.

HOMOSEXUAL RELATIONSHIPS

Less is known about the relationship between aging and homosexual activity, possibly because homosexuality has long been regarded as a form of mental illness. In 1973, however, the American Psychiatric Association removed homosexuality from the official list of mental disorders. Currently, homosexuality is considered a mental disorder only if the individual is distressed about his or her homosexuality and would prefer to be more heterosexual (American Psychiatric Association, 1987).

Whatever the reasons, the status of this area resembles that of research on heterosexuality and aging some 50 years ago. According to one common stereotype, homosexual males supposedly find aging to be particularly stressful, lonely, and depressing:

The Myth of the Aging Male Homosexual

One popular myth about the older male homosexual is that he "no longer goes to bars, having lost his physical attractiveness and his sexual appeal to the young men he craves. He is over-sexed, but his sex life is very unsatisfactory. He has been unable to form a lasting relationship with a sexual partner, and he is seldom sexually active anymore. When he does have sex, it is usually in a 'tearoom' (public toilet). He has disengaged from the gay world and his acquaintances in it. He is retreating further and further into the 'closet' . . . He is labeled 'an old queen,' as he has become quite effeminate." (Kelly, 1977, p. 329)

There are few empirical studies dealing with such issues, however, and the minimal data that do exist offer little support for the prevailing stereotypes. Older homosexual males tend to report that they are still sexually active, and that their sexual relationships are quite satisfactory (Kelly, 1977; Kimmel, 1977). Some of these subjects stated that sex became less important as they grew older, but others indicated that their sex lives were now more satisfying than in young adulthood. Virtually all preferred contacts with men of similar ages, rather than with young men. There was also some indication that aging was not overly depressing for these homosexual men because they had previously learned how to cope with living alone, and because they had developed a network of friends on whom to rely for social and sexual companionship.

Data concerning homosexual women are even more sparse, although one study suggests that gay females tend to discontinue sexual activity at an early age (Christenson & Johnson, 1973). If homosexuality continues to be regarded with increasing tolerance, future research may well shed more light on the relationship between this form of interpersonal behavior and aging.

Intergenerational Relationships

PARENTS AND ADULT CHILDREN

As we observed in Chapter 1, more people are living to an older age than ever before. Many of these aging individuals are parents; some 81 percent of middle-aged and elderly adults have living children (Atchley & Miller, 1980). Since it is statistically normative to have children prior to age 35, most of the children of older Americans are also adults. During the past few decades, therefore, the relationship between parents who are past middle age and their adult children has become increasingly important.

There are two major issues for us to explore in this area. First, are adult children likely to ignore their aging parents in order to put their own interests and children first? That is, does parenthood become significantly less satisfying as one grows past middle age? Second, ill health is more common at older ages. Elderly parents may therefore become partly or wholly dependent on their adult children because of health problems ranging from gradually increasing arthritic disability to a sudden fall that fractures a hip or the ravages of Alzheimer's disease (Chapter 11). How well do those in an intergenerational relationship cope with the demands posed by an elderly parent who requires considerable care?

Myths About Aging

Interpersonal Relations

Myth	*Best Available Evidence*
Middle-aged and elderly adults have significantly fewer friends than do young adults.	The number of casual friendships does decline to some extent with increasing age. But older adults have as many close friends as do young adults, and these relationships contribute significantly to their overall life satisfaction.
The years after the last child leaves home (the "empty nest") is a time of considerable emotional pain, particularly for women.	The relief from the responsibility of daily child rearing, greater opportunities to indulge personal interests, and increased freedom and privacy most often lead to improved personal well-being.
Few middle-aged adults, and virtually no elderly adults, have any interest in sex.	Many adults remain sexually active throughout much or all of adulthood. The sexual capacity of men does decline with increasing age, but not as much as has been widely believed. There is no evidence that aging has any important effects on the sexual capacity of women.
Sexual intercourse should be avoided by men past middle age because it is very likely to precipitate a fatal heart attack.	Deaths during sexual intercourse are very rare. Such deaths account for no more than 1 percent of all sudden coronary fatalities, and it has been alleged that the majority occur during extramarital affairs and are due in large part to anxiety and guilt.
A century ago, elderly parents and their children lived together more often because families were more caring. The modern family is much more isolated, both geographically and emotionally.	There has been no significant change in the mutual caring shown by the American family. A century ago, elderly parents did live with their children more often, but this was due primarily to financial necessity; there was no social security system or variety of private pension plans. Today, more elderly parents live alone because they want to and can afford to do so, but most live no more than a half-hour away from at least one adult child.
Most parents age 65 and older are neglected by their adult children who never visit them, or who callously place them in nursing homes at the slightest provocation.	Approximately 80 percent of parents over age 65 see at least one of their adult children every one to two weeks. Most families place elderly parents in nursing homes only as a last resort, and with the utmost reluctance.

Frequency of Contact.   According to popular belief, elderly parents are grossly neglected by their children—or, even worse, are callously placed in nursing homes at the slightest provocation and promptly forgotten. This notion is supported by two of the most pervasive cultural myths in this country, which live on even though they are fallacious. The first of these myths holds that at some unspecified point in the past (perhaps circa 1900), the American family was far more devoted to one another than is the case today:

The Myth of the Classical Devoted Family

This myth portrays the family of some 100 years ago as "a pretty picture of life down on grandma's farm. There are lots of happy children, and many kinfolk live together in a large rambling house. Everyone works hard. . . . All boys and girls marry, and marry young. Young people, especially girls, are likely to be virginal at marriage and faithful afterward. Though the parents do not arrange their children's marriages, the elders do have the right to reject a suitor and have a strong hand in the final decision. After marriage, the couple lives harmoniously, either near the boy's parents or with them, for the couple is slated to inherit the farm." (Goode, 1963, p. 6)

The second, related myth is that the modern American family has become isolated, and that today's children take much worse care of their parents than was the case in the "good old days":

The Myth of the Modern Isolated Nuclear Family

According to this myth, today's family has "fewer children, and they are economic liabilities rather than assets. They leave the nest at a relatively early age, marry without parental approval or guidance, receive training (at parental expense of course) for occupational advantage in a direction that takes them away from their parents. Contact is limited to occasional letters and obligatory telephone calls on holidays; exceptions to these patterns occur only when the children need money. As the parents experience the inevitable decrements of advancing age, such as widowhood and failing health with the attendant economic exigencies, the children are concerned but not motivated to do anything about it because they are too wrapped up in their own problems; too busy with their own careers, children, and mortgages to spare the time or resources their parents need. . . . [This implies that] if middle-aged children paid more attention to their elderly parents, the parents would be less lonely, better adjusted, happier, and more satisfied with their lives." (Lee, 1985, pp. 22, 26)

These myths have been soundly contradicted by empirical data. It is true that since 1900, the proportion of adults past age 65 who live with their children has declined from about 60 percent to approximately 10 percent (Smith, 1979; White House Conference on Aging, 1981). And many more elderly adults now live alone, especially women (Kobrin, 1976; Michael, Fuchs, & Scott, 1980; Soldo, Sharma, & Campbell, 1984). However, this does *not* mean that modern elderly parents are more often neglected by their children. The financial status of the aged has improved dramatically during the last 50 years (Chapter 9), so today's older adults can better afford to maintain their independence and live by themselves. Although it was much more common for parents to live with their children circa 1900, there is no evidence that they *wanted* to; they may well have had little choice in an era that had no social security system or private pension plans (Lee, 1985). Supporting this position is the fact that parents who currently live with their children tend to have extremely low incomes, indicating that they have chosen this course primarily because they cannot afford anything else (Lawton, 1980; Soldo, 1979).

Even though fewer parents now live *with* their children, the number who reside *near* at least one adult child has increased. As of 1975, more than half of all older Americans with children lived within ten minutes' distance of at least one child, and some 75 percent were no more than a half-hour away (Shanas, 1979). Thus the frequency of contact between today's older parents and their adult children is quite high. In one study of subjects in the United States, Britain, and Denmark, over 80 percent of all elderly parents saw at least one of their adult children during the preceding week (Shanas et al., 1968). More recent findings are similar: Some 55 percent of older parents saw one adult child within the previous 24 hours, while approximately 80 percent did so during the past one to two weeks (Harris & Associates, 1975; 1981; Shanas, 1979).

Even when elderly parents become seriously ill, their children maintain frequent contact. About twice as many aged parents are cared for by relatives as are placed in nursing homes and other institutions (Shanas, 1979). Most residents of nursing homes either have no close relatives to call upon because they never married or have outlived their children, or are so ill that they cannot be cared for at home. Rather than relegating their elderly parents to nursing homes at the slightest excuse, today's adult children typically regard institutionalization with the utmost reluctance and take this step only as a last resort.

Quality of Contact.   Frequent contact does not in and of itself ensure a rewarding interpersonal relationship. However, research data have also shown that most older parents and adult children have highly positive feelings for one another. In fact, many of these parents feel close enough to their children to use them as confidants (e.g., Atchley & Miller, 1980; Harris & Associates, 1975).

These relationships are motivated by a sense of duty, and are likely to involve the provision of mutual aid. This may take the form of housework, advice, moral support, babysitting, or financial assistance, with the last two of these more often provided by the parents. Thus it appears that many elderly parents continue to provide for their children whatever they can, for as long as they can (normally, at least through age 75). In turn, adult children support their parents when the latter's health or financial condition deteriorates.

Caring for an Elderly Parent.   It is becoming increasingly likely that adult children will have to care for an elderly, infirm parent. The "old-old" are the

Adult children are often the primary care providers to their disabled parents. (David Wells/The Image Works)

most rapidly growing segment of the American population, and the lingering geriatric and terminal illnesses are now the rule rather than the exception (Chapters 11 and 12). To be sure, a lucky few have parents who retain much of their health and independence even in old age:

An Autonomous Elderly Couple

Mr. R., age 98, is troubled by arthritis and some hearing loss, but he still cooks for himself in his New Jersey home. His wife, age 96, can no longer see well and has grown forgetful, but she still does her own shopping. Their 69-year-old married daughter lives a half mile away, and finds it a simple matter to care for her parents. "There are just some little things to worry about," she says, "like whether he locked the back door at night, or has he checked the windows in case of a storm." (*Newsweek,* May 6, 1985)

More often, however, caring for an elderly parent is far more difficult. The demands made on adult children in such situations can be extremely severe, as the following case histories indicate (*Newsweek,* May 6, 1985):

Intergenerational Conflict

Mr. J.'s ailing mother stayed at his home for two months. She had a falling out with his wife during this time, and also expressed displeasure with him. Even though he is 55 years old, "to her I'm still a child," he says. "Of course I try to resist that, but she doesn't think I have enough sense to turn out the lights. She thinks I'm irresponsible. When I go to light the stove, she gives me hell until I've properly disposed of the match."

A Blind, Paralyzed Widow

Mrs. L., a 79-year-old widow, is blind and paralyzed on one side of her body. Her two adult daughters have to put her to bed and get her up each day, dress her, move her to the dining room, and feed her. On weekends they take her to park to sit in the sun, or to visit their married sister. The daughters have no time for any private life; neither has married.

A Partly Paralyzed, Incontinent Man

Mr. B. is 85 years old, partly paralyzed, and incontinent. His 60-year-old son hired a home attendant to care for his father, but the attendant found the task far too rigorous and quit in a week. Reluctantly, the son decided on a nursing home. "I had to either make that decision or keep changing his diapers myself," he says. He visits his father two to three times a week, but comes away depressed. "It would be good if Dad died," he says bluntly. "I don't see anything in him that shows me that he's comfortable."

How well does the modern family respond to such challenges? Numerous studies show that today's adult children (primarily daughters) are expending considerable effort, and are incurring substantial costs, to help their elderly parents in time of need. For example, 87 percent of one sample of 700 elderly persons received at least half of the help they needed from their children or other relatives (Morris & Sherwood, 1984; see also Cicirelli, 1981; Moon, 1983; Schulz, Tompkins, & Wood, in press; Shanas, 1980; Stoller, 1983; Stoller & Earl, 1983). According to some estimates, the average American woman will spend 17 years raising children and 18 years helping aged parents (*Newsweek*, July 19, 1990). In fact, the care provided by children (and other kin) has helped to prevent or at least postpone the institutionalization of many elderly parents (e.g., Branch & Jette, 1983; Brody, 1978; 1981; Cantor, 1980).

Nevertheless, such kin networks are not without serious problems. Caring for an ill elderly parent can be so demanding that even the most loving, considerate child suffers considerable resentment and guilt (e.g., Cantor, 1983). Young parents who have only recently begun to recover from the financial and emotional strain of rearing their own child, or who must still contend with these burdens, may well find it difficult to cope with a parent who is now almost as helpless as an infant. Furthermore, seeing one's formerly authoritative and powerful parent become childishly dependent can prove to be psychologically disturbing. Those children who live far from their parents may be spared this daily anguish, but they must contend with the tactical problems of trying to help from a distance and with the guilt evoked by not being present. As a result, caregivers are three to four times more likely than their elderly parents to report symptoms of depression and anger (Schulz, Visintainer, & Williamson, 1990). Women are particularly vulnerable in this regard, because it is the daughter who most often assumes primary responsibility for the elderly parent. If she is also working and a mother, she may well find that this trio of responsibilities leaves her with so little time for leisure and recreation that her health and well-being decline.

Secondly, elderly parents may be less willing to receive help from their children than the children are to provide it. Independence and autonomy are highly valued in our society, and the elderly are no exception. In one study, for example, the majority of elderly adults differed significantly from young adults by stating that they would rather pay a professional for assistance than ask a family member (Brody et al., 1983). Elderly parents know that their adult children have their own lives to live, and that caring for an invalid is demanding and disruptive. Therefore, they may regard it as demeaning and distasteful to become dependent on their children. Those who take this course may well do so because they have (or believe that they have) no other choice, and at considerable cost to their self-esteem and desire for independence (Lee, 1985). Also, parents may find it less pleasant to live with their children because they have much more in common with people of their own age.

These problems are likely to become even more severe in the not-too-distant future. It has been estimated that by the year 2040, the number of Americans over age 85 will increase from the present 2.2 million to nearly 13 million and that the number over 65 will grow from 26 million to 66.6 million. (See Chapter 1.) In about 50 years, then, we may find a large number of old-old adults being cared for by old relatives, which may well be too great a strain for all concerned.

Afterword.   Since family caregivers are likely to need help coping with ill parents, and since elderly parents are likely to fare better psychologically if they are not forced to depend on their adult children, formal support groups would seem to be desirable. Virtually every part of this country does have an agency on aging, which provides basic information and assistance with regard to home health services and other problems. But once a family member assumes in-home responsibility for an elderly parent, the United States government takes a hands-off approach. Medicare does *not* provide for respite care, where a qualified professional fills in for the family caregiver for a few days. Nor does Medicare cover chronic long-term nursing home care, which currently costs about $18,000 per year. Caring for the ill elderly is at present a prominent issue among this country's health policy planners, so some form of federal assistance may perhaps be forthcoming in the foreseeable future.

Empirical data clearly show that today's adult children are doing an outstanding job of caring for their elderly parents. But demographic data indicate that this problem may soon become so widespread as to make outside support essential.

GRANDPARENTING

The increasing human life span has also produced more modern families that span three, or even four, generations. Becoming a grandparent is now more common in middle age than in old age, and may even occur as early as age 40 (Butler & Lewis, 1976; Kivnick, 1982). As a result, today's children and young adults are likely to have at least some contact with one or more grandparents. It has been estimated that 75 percent of all elderly adults have living grandchildren, and that today's children can expect to live half their lives as grandparents (Peterson, 1989).

Grandparents are often pictured as having warm and close relationships with their grandchildren, partly because they can enjoy the pleasures of these interactions without having to shoulder parental responsibilities. We have all heard stories of grandfathers who go fishing with their grandsons on a regular basis, grandmothers who spend part of each day teaching their granddaughters to sew or bake cookies, and grandchildren who tenderly care for an aging or ill grandparent. Although some researchers have focused on issues like these, there are very few empirical data dealing with grandparenting.

Frequency of Contact. There is no indication that modern grandparents are being neglected by their grandchildren. Among Americans over age 65 who have living grandchildren, about 75 percent see their grandchildren at least once every week or two, some 50 percent do so every few days (Harris & Associates, 1975).

Although grandparent–grandchild interactions are frequent, they are usually peripheral in the lives of both parties. As with elderly parents and adult children, grandparents most often live apart from their grandchildren (Atchley, 1977). Interactions between grandparents and grandchildren typically take the form of special events, such as an outing or a telephone call, rather than occurring routinely within the household. "The rocking-chair grandparent is no longer an appropriate image; neither is the child carer, cookie baker, or fishing companion" (Troll, 1980, p. 476; see also Hagestad, 1985).

Quality of Contact. Some researchers have sought to determine the typical ways in which grandparents behave toward their grandchildren. In one classic study (Neugarten & Weinstein, 1964), interviews of 70 middle-class sets of grandparents revealed five specific styles of behavior:

1. *Formal:* Maintaining a clear distinction between parent and grandparent. Although these grandparents were interested in their grandchildren, they limited their assistance to occasional gifts or babysitting. This style was more common among grandparents past age 65.

2. *Fun-seeker:* Enjoying mutually pleasurable activities with the grandchildren; being informal and playful.

3. *Surrogate Parent:* Assuming the mother's parental responsibilities because she worked outside the home, or was otherwise unable to care for her children. This style was determined by necessity rather than by choice; grandparents preferred not to become surrogate parents unless there was no good

Grandparenthood provides a rewarding opportunity to indulge one's grandchildren without the responsibilities that burden a parent. (UN Photo)

alternative. The surrogate parent was almost always the grandmother, rather than the grandfather.

4. Reservoir of Family Wisdom: Assuming an authoritarian position and dispensing information, advice, and resources to the grandchildren. A relatively rare style that was more often adopted by grandfathers than by grandmothers.

5. Distant Figure: Maintaining little contact with the grandchildren, except for such occasions as birthdays or holidays.

More recently, Kivnick (1982) investigated the ways in which being a grandparent are meaningful and rewarding. Some 286 grandparents completed a lengthy questionnaire, and the responses were subjected to the mathematical procedure of factor analysis. The results indicated that grandparenthood is rewarding for several reasons. There is the opportunity to *spoil and indulge* one's grandchildren, since grandparents are usually not burdened by the same responsibilities as parents. Grandparenthood provides a form of *immortality through clan,* since the grandparent leaves behind not only children but also grandchildren. Grandparents enjoy receiving the grandchild's respect as a wise, helpful *valued elder.* Grandparenthood also facilitates a *reinvolvement with one's personal past,* as by recalling relationships with one's own grandparents. However, grandparenthood is more central in the lives of some grandparents than others.

Other researchers have focused on the ways in which grandparents and grandchildren seek to influence one another's attitudes and styles of life. Many grandparents pass along recommended religious, social, and vocational values to their grandchildren (Cherlin & Furstenberg, 1985; Troll & Bengtson, 1979). This may be done through such methods as storytelling, giving friendly advice during an outing or visit, or working together on special projects. In turn, grandchildren may introduce their grandparents to such recent cultural innovations as new toys or styles of dress, thereby helping the grandparents to reduce their feelings of alienation from an ever-changing world. However, there is usually an unspoken agreement to protect the relationship by avoiding topics likely to cause conflict. For example, during the 1960s, grandparents and radical student grandchildren were unlikely to discuss such volatile issues as hair length and clothing preferences. These mutually avoided, sensitive areas have been referred to as "demilitarized zones" (Hagestad, 1978).

Despite efforts like these, social scientists have been unable to agree on standard styles of grandparenting. One possible reason is that grandparents may vary in age from 40 to 100 or more, and grandchildren may vary from newborn infants to age 60 or older. There may well be little common ground between the way a 50-year-old adult treats a 2-year-old child and the behavior of an 80-year-old adult toward a 16-year-old adolescent, even though both cases involve interactions between a grandparent and a grandchild. For example, some data indicate that grandparents age 50 to 70 show more positive emotions about their grandchildren than do grandparents in their forties and eighties (Troll, 1980). Thus grandparent–grandchild interactions may be too idiosyncratic to be described in terms of generally applicable styles. (See Bengtson & Robertson, 1985.)

Legal Responsibilities and Rights of Grandparents.   As we observed earlier in this chapter, divorce has become very common in this country. This can pose considerable problems for grandparents, who may become caught in the middle of the marital conflict. The legal responsibility of grandparents is extensive—they can be sued for grandchild support in many states. Yet their legal rights are very few; grandparents have virtually no standing insofar as visitation or adoption of their grandchildren is concerned (Wilson & DeShane, 1982). Because parents tend to function as gatekeepers by limiting or encouraging grandparent–grandchild interactions, a bitter ex-wife or ex-husband can and may prevent grandparents from ever seeing a cherished grandchild.

Theories of Interpersonal Behavior

In the preceding pages, we have concentrated primarily on the *what* and the *how* of adult interpersonal relationships: what happens to the number of friendships with increasing age, how grandparents behave toward their grandchildren, whether older parents and their adult children interact frequently, and so on. In addition, social scientists are keenly interested in explaining *why* adults behave as they do toward other people.

For example, we have seen that elderly parents are considerably more reluctant to seek help from their adult children than the children are to provide it. Why should this be so? The fear of disrupting the children's lives is a sensible explanation, but a very specific one. A more general theoretical argument might be that people are uncomfortable with relationships wherein power is markedly unequal. Few individuals enjoy receiving a great deal from a loved one or close friend, while being unable to give anything in return. According to this theory, then, adults who are unable to maintain a fairly equal amount of give-and-take in an interpersonal relationship will dislike this relationship and tend to avoid it. (See Lee, 1985.) Theories like this one have the potential advantage of explaining a wide range of adult interpersonal behavior, rather than dealing only with a specific example.

During the past three decades, social scientists have proposed several such theories to explain the interpersonal behavior of older adults. Devising a useful theory is not an easy task, and no one of these theories is as yet regarded as clearly superior to all of the others.

EXCHANGE THEORY

Definition.   Our relationships with other people may bring us material or nonmaterial rewards. For example, we may receive compliments that increase our self-esteem, entertainment, attention and affection, a valued gift, or obedience. We may also incur various costs, such as having to endure boredom or irritation, suffering anxiety (as on a first date), spending money, or investing time (which might otherwise be devoted to useful solitary activities). That is, interpersonal relationships can be viewed as processes wherein the people involved try to maximize the rewards and minimize the costs.

According to **exchange theory**, interpersonal interactions will be initiated and continued so long as they are sufficiently rewarding for both parties— that is, if the rewards exceed the costs (Dowd, 1975). At any given moment in an interpersonal relationship, the rewards enjoyed by each party are unlikely to be precisely equal. However, the person who is currently gaining more from the relationship is obligated to try and restore a more equal balance in the future. If, instead, one individual is consistently unable to provide sufficient rewards, the other is likely to terminate the relationship because the costs are too great. An interpersonal relationship involves give-and-take, and it will not survive if one individual gives or receives too little (that is, if the relationship is imbalanced).

Exchange Theory and Aging.   Because the elderly tend to have less power and fewer resources than younger adults, their interpersonal relationships are particularly likely to be imbalanced. The only apparent recourse is to use compliance as a reward and to yield consistently to the wishes of the other person. This ultimately results in a serious loss of self-respect, however, whereupon the elderly are likely to withdraw from social activity. According to exchange theory, then, the aged presumably engage in fewer interpersonal relationships because of their inability to reward other people and maintain balanced interactions.

Conceptual Difficulties.   There are several conceptual difficulties with the exchange approach. First of all, intrinsic, self-determined rewards can compensate for the absence of any specific returns from another person. Some individuals continue to interact with the elderly on the grounds of duty, charity, or a genuine interest in the aged, even though they obtain no extrinsic rewards at all. This implies that interactions that are imbalanced in terms of extrinsic rewards may continue to exist, rather than terminating as exchange theory predicts. (See Schulz & Manson, 1984.)

In addition, the effective reward and cost value of any interpersonal interaction is deceptively difficult to calculate. Our satisfaction with an interaction depends to a great extent on how the associated rewards and costs compare to our prior expectations, rather than on their absolute value. If, for example, we receive moderate rewards from an interpersonal interaction, we will tend to be happy if we expected very little but rather unhappy if we expected a great deal, even though the amount of the reward is the same in both cases.

Exchange theory has raised some interesting issues. However, these conceptual difficulties indicate that it cannot be accepted as a definitive explanation of the interpersonal behavior of the aged.

REFERENCE GROUP THEORY AND SOCIAL COMPARISON THEORY

Definition.   According to reference group theory, we use important other people as a frame of reference to evaluate our behavior, attitudes, values, and beliefs (e.g., Blau, 1981; Merton, 1957). In particular, **social comparison theory** states that we all possess a basic drive to evaluate our abilities and opinions (Festinger, 1954).

When possible, we base these self-assessments on appropriate objective evidence: A college student may conclude that he is poor in mathematics or art because he consistently obtains low grades in these subjects, or an athlete may decide to try out for the Olympics because she has won ten consecutive matches in the hundred-yard dash. However, many important questions lack objective answers (e.g., "How happy am I, and how good is my life?" or "Am I doing as well professionally, financially, or socially as I should be?"). In the absence of clear objective standards, we perform our self-evaluations by comparing ourselves with other people. If we rate ourselves favorably compared to others, we will tend to feel satisfied and content. But if we conclude that others are much better off, we are likely to become unhappy and depressed.

Social Comparison Theory and Aging.

The reference group that we use for our self-evaluations is likely to vary depending on the specific attribute that we are evaluating; it may even be a group from our past, rather than the present. In order to apply social comparison theory to the elderly, therefore, we must first ask a question: With whom do they typically compare themselves? If the institutionalized aged base their self-evaluations primarily on other elderly residents, who are more or less equal in most important respects, dissatisfaction is unlikely. But if the elderly usually compare themselves to younger people, or to their own status of years ago, they will probably be unhappy. The many real declines that they have experienced, as in living conditions, financial status, physical capacities, and daily routine, will make their present circumstances seem considerably inferior (Schulz, 1982; Schulz & Manson, 1984).

Only indirect evidence is available concerning this issue. Numerous studies indicate that both the institutionalized and the noninstitutionalized aged do *not* differ significantly from younger adults in morale, well-being, and level of depression (Larson, 1978; Zemore & Eames, 1979). We may therefore infer that negative social comparisons are not a serious problem for the aged. They apparently adjust their expectations to realistic levels, rather than dwelling on people who are more fortunate or on their own past.

DISENGAGEMENT AND ACTIVITY THEORIES

Definition.

According to **disengagement theory**, there is a process of mutual withdrawal between the aged and society (Cumming & Henry, 1961). Elderly individuals withdraw from society because they realize that their capacities have diminished, and because they wish to protect themselves as much as possible from failure and rejection. Society withdraws from the elderly because it needs to replace them with younger, more capable persons in order to remain vibrant and viable. This mutual disengagement takes the form of a decrease in the number and diversity of contacts between the aged and society, and is assumed to be universal, inevitable, and mutually satisfying.

Almost from its inception, disengagement theory sparked a controversy that has persisted for more than a decade. The major opposition has come from proponents of **activity theory**, which posits that the social activity of the elderly is positively correlated with their satisfaction with life (Lemon, Bengtson, & Peterson, 1972). Activity theory does agree with disengagement theory in one respect: As we grow older, our social activity is assumed to decrease. But activity theory states that this decrease is *dissatisfying*, and that those older adults who are exceptions to this rule are happier. In contrast, disengagement theory predicts that reduced social activity is *satisfying* to the aged.

Conceptual Difficulties.   Choosing between these diametrically opposed theories would seem to be an easy task, but this is not the case. Both views are supported by a sizable amount of research evidence, and the same data has, at different times, been interpreted as favorable to both theories. Since one test of a good theory is that it can be effectively disconfirmed (and discarded), and since this does not appear to be true for activity theory and disengagement theory, we may reasonably conclude that both of these theories are at least somewhat flawed (Hochschild, 1976; Schulz & Manson, 1984). It has been argued that both theories are not stated precisely enough for them to be convincingly disconfirmed even if they are incorrect, and that they fail to take into account the complicated nature of the interactions between the elderly and society. Although disengagement theory and activity theory have stimulated some important research, neither one appears valid enough to fully explain the interpersonal behavior of the elderly.

AFTERWORD

Because theories are by definition tentative explanations about reality, they often appear to be frustratingly inaccurate. However, they serve an important purpose. Established facts are often lacking in scientific work, and a theory offers guidelines that will serve us in the absence of more precise information. Although some of the theories previously discussed appear to be marred by conceptual flaws, all have points of interest and importance. Furthermore, these theories tend to be more complicated than our overview might indicate. Therefore, the interested reader is encouraged to obtain more information by consulting the original sources cited in the preceding pages.

Summary

CLASSIFYING MAJOR LIFE EVENTS

Most of us experience many major life events between birth and death. One useful way to classifying these events is according to the age at which they occur: An event is temporally normative if it occurs at an age that is typical for most people in that culture, and temporally non-normative if it occurs at an atypical age. A second good way to classify life events is according to their frequency, regardless of age: An event is statistically normative if it happens to the majority of individuals in a given culture, and statistically non-normative if it is experienced by relatively few people. Non-normative events are likely to be quite stressful, and adults who must deal with many such events are more vulnerable to physical and psychological illnesses or even premature death.

ADULT FRIENDSHIPS

Adult friendships have been defined as voluntary, mutual, flexible, terminable, equal, reciprocal, and emotional. Three basic styles of friendship have been identified. The independent style involves a lack of best or close friends, personal self-sufficiency, and maintaining psychological distance from other people. The discerning style involves drawing a clear distinction between a small number of close, trusted friends and casual acquaintances. The gregarious style involves psychological closeness with a fairly large number of people and optimism about the prospects of making new friends.

Friendships can serve a variety of important purposes. They provide opportunities for self-disclosure, and furnish us with psychological support. We tend to choose friends who have similar beliefs and personalities; who are physically attractive, intelligent and competent, pleasant and agreeable, and emotionally stimulating; who like and approve of us; and who live close to us.

Although casual friendships tend to become less frequent with increasing age, the number of close friends that one has remains relatively stable throughout the adult life span. Apparently, as we grow older, we sift through our interpersonal relationships and retain those that we value the most. Close friendships contribute significantly to the well-being and overall life satisfaction of older adults. Because of the well-known "generation gap," the elderly are likely to have more in common with people of similar ages than with their children. Also, asking a close friend for help would seem to involve less loss of independence than calling on one's adult children.

LOVE, MARRIAGE, AND DIVORCE

Various conceptions of love have been proposed by social scientists. These include such distinctions as passionate love versus companionate love, D-love versus B-love, and narcissism versus genuine love. Efforts have also been made to measure love psychometrically, using written questionnaires.

Many relationships that end in marriage proceed through a fairly standard sequence that begins with casual dating and ends with formal engagement. In any loving relationship, different factors tend to be important during different stages. It also appears that there is an inverse relationship between attraction and attachment, with many long-term loving relationships becoming more placid over the years. Among couples married for many years, the most commonly cited reason for the enduring relationship is, "My spouse is my best friend." Other factors typical of lengthy marriages include meaningful communication and self-disclosure, openness, trustworthiness, caring, believing that marriage is a long-term commitment, and avoiding displays of intensely expressed anger. Families with children tend to follow traditional marital roles, with the wife doing the housework; role equality is most often found in childless marriages. The years after the last child leaves home (the "empty nest") most often lead to improved personal well-being and marital relationships because of the relief from the responsibility of daily child rearing, greater opportunities to follow personal interests, and increased freedom and privacy. When the husband becomes seriously ill, the negative impact is even greater on caregiving wives than on grown children who serve as caregivers.

Marriage entails some risk; approximately one of every two marriages ends in divorce. Divorce is most common among adults age 30 to 45, black females, and those who married prior to age 21. Yet more than half a million Americans age 65 or more are divorced, with many new cases registered each year. Common causes of divorce include drunkenness, desertion, brutality, adultery, and increasingly bitter arguments. Divorced people tend to proceed through several behavioral stages, ranging from isolation to reestablishing social contact. Divorce is typically a traumatic experience for all concerned, most notably women and the spouse who did not initiate the divorce. But it may be argued that if a marriage is truly unbearable, the least of evils may well be to end it and give each spouse the opportunity to find happiness elsewhere. The emotional pain caused by a broken marriage does not prevent many adults from remarrying; more than 20 percent of the current marriages in the United States include at least one spouse who has been previously married.

SEXUALITY AND AGING

Until recently, very little was known about the relationship between sexuality and aging. As a result, it was widely assumed that there was nothing to know—that is, that older adults had no interest in sex. During the past few decades, however, we have become increasingly aware that there is, indeed, sexual life after middle age.

Insofar as young adults are concerned, men tend to be more sexually active than women. There is some indication that the frequency of sexual behavior has increased during the last few decades, especially among younger adults and young women, although these data are inflated by cohort effects. The frequency of sexual behavior among married couples does tend to decrease from young adulthood to middle age, but this is due largely to such environmental constraints as the presence of young children.

Male sexual capacity has been found to decline with increasing age, but not nearly as much as had been widely believed. There is likely to be a significant drop in sexual ability and interest at about age 50, and again at about age 70 to 80. As age increases, fewer men are sexually active, and those who are active are less so than younger men. Nevertheless, a substantial number of men continue to engage in sex throughout much or even all of their adult lives. Men are more likely to remain interested in sex through middle and old age if they engaged in sex more often during young adulthood, if they are in good health, and if they believe that they can maintain effective sexual behavior as they grow older.

There is no evidence that aging causes any significant declines in female sexual capacity. However, sexual activity among women does decrease markedly with increasing age. Since women tend to marry men who are older, and since men tend to die at a younger age, women are more likely to be without a socially acceptable and sexually capable partner. Women who enjoy sex more during young adulthood are more likely to remain sexually active in later life, provided that an appropriate partner is available.

At present, the sexual rights of the institutionalized elderly remains an essentially unresolved issue. Nor is much known about the relationship between aging and homosexual behavior.

INTERGENERATIONAL RELATIONSHIPS

Contrary to popular belief, modern American families are no less caring than were families of some 100 years ago. It is true that since 1900, the number of elderly parents who live with their children has declined markedly. But the financial status of the aged has improved dramatically during the past 50 years, so today's older adults can better afford to maintain their independence and live by themselves. In fact, the number of older parents who reside near at least one adult child has increased over the years. Thus today's adult children see their elderly parents often, and expend considerable effort and money to help their parents in time of need. Children typically regard the institutionalization of an aged parent as a last resort, and the caregiving they provide has helped to prevent or at least postpone it in many instances.

Nevertheless, the demands of caring for an ill parent can cause even the most loving and dedicated child to become resentful and guilty. There is also some indication that elderly parents are less willing to receive help from their children than the children are to give it, primarily because this loss of independence is demeaning. Since the number of old-old and old adults is expected to increase dramatically during the next fifty years, the problem of caring for the ill elderly is likely to become particularly acute in the not-too-distant future.

There is no indication that grandparents are being neglected by their grandchildren; contact is frequent, albeit typically peripheral in the lives of both. Although some researchers have tried to establish the ways in which grandparents behave toward their grandchildren, it appears that such interactions are too idiosyncratic to be described in terms of generally applicable styles. Divorce may pose a problem to grandparents, since their legal responsibilities are great while their rights are very few.

THEORIES OF INTERPERSONAL BEHAVIOR

Social scientists are also interested in explaining why adults behave as they do toward other people, and various theories have been devised for this purpose. Exchange theory views interpersonal relationships as processes wherein the people involved seek to maximize their rewards and minimize their costs.

This theory posits that the elderly engage in fewer interpersonal relationships because they are unable to reward other people and maintain balanced interactions. However, this theory suffers from important conceptual difficulties.

Social comparison theory states that we all possess a basic drive to evaluate our abilities and opinions, and that we often perform these self-assessments by comparing ourselves with other people. However, negative social comparisons do not appear to be a serious problem for the aged.

Disengagement theory posits a process of mutual and satisfying withdrawal between the aged and society. In contrast, activity theory holds that any substantial decrease in interpersonal activity among the elderly is dissatisfying to them. Although both of these theories have stimulated important research, neither one appears valid enough to stand alone as an explanation of adult interpersonal behavior.

Because theories are, by definition, tentative explanations about reality, they often appear to be frustratingly inaccurate. But established facts are often lacking in scientific work, and theories offer guidelines that will serve us in the absence of more precise information. All of these theories have points of interest and importance, and have contributed to our understanding of aging and interpersonal behavior.

Study Questions

1. Why is an event likely to be more stressful if it is temporally non-normative, such as beginning college at age 50 or becoming widowed at age 35? Is a statistically non-normative event, such as having a stroke, likely to be even more stressful if it is also temporally non-normative? Why or why not? Have you ever experienced an event that was temporally or statistically non-normative? How stressful was this event?
2. Of the purposes of adult friendships discussed in this chapter, which ones are most important to you when forming a friendship? Are all of these purposes satisfied by one close friend, or do different friends satisfy different purposes? Which style of friendship do you prefer from a friend? Which style (if any) best describes your behavior? Which of your current friends is most likely to be your friend 20 years from now? Why?
3. Of the various reasons why marriages endure (as presented in this chapter), which would be most important to you when deciding whether or not to marry someone? What advice would you give to a friend who is seeking a marriage partner and wants to significantly reduce the probability of divorce?
4. Based on the empirical evidence presented in this chapter, what advice would you give to a middle-aged person who wants to maintain a satisfying sexual relationship with his or her spouse? Would your recommendations differ for males and females?

5. According to current research data, are families of today more isolated and less devoted to one another than families of 100 years ago? What changes in our society might have created a false impression in this regard?

Terms to Remember

Activity theory

B-love

Companionate love

D-love

Discerning style of friendship

Disengagement theory

Empty nest

Exchange theory

Gregarious style of friendship

Independent style of friendship

Passionate love

Self-disclosure

Social comparison theory

Statistically non-normative life event

Statistically normative life event

Temporally non-normative life event

Temporally normative life event

Chapter 9

Work and Retirement

People work for many reasons. The most obvious of these is financial: Work enables us to support ourselves and our families. In addition, work may be interesting for its own sake. A writer, a carpenter, or a mechanic may derive considerable satisfaction from creating an innovative book, a well-crafted piece of furniture, or a finely tuned automobile engine. For many people, work supports their self-esteem and sense of identity. Society expects men in particular to hold a job, and accords greater respect to certain types of workers (e.g., physicians and judges). In fact, when a person is asked "Who are you?", occupation is one of the most frequently given answers. Work also offers important social rewards and punishments, because it involves interactions with co-workers, supervisors, subordinates, and/or clients. If you are male, you are likely to work during half of your life; if you are female, for approximately two to three decades. Modern men and women spend more years at work than did their counterparts in 1900, particularly women. (See Figure 9.1.)

Because work is such a major aspect of human endeavor, the relationship between work and aging is of considerable importance, and there are various interesting and provocative issues for us to consider. With so many more of us living to old age, there may well be an increase in the number of middle-aged and older adults who wish to work. Are these older adults poorer employment risks? That is, are they likely to perform more poorly, to develop negative attitudes that will interfere with organizational goals, or to become injured or ill? Or are older adults as competent as younger employees, but more likely to be the targets of unfair stereotypes and prejudice? Are more women of various ages seeking employment instead of motherhood? How does this affect their satisfaction with their adult years?

Most people expect they will someday retire from the world of work. Is this likely to be a painful experience? Are retirees more likely to suffer major psychological and physical disorders, or even death, because they are no longer needed at work? Does retirement cause such a severe drop in income that the retiree's standard of living declines substantially? Should retirees expect an increase in marital difficulties now that they must spend day and night with their spouses? As these questions indicate, our discussion of work and aging must also include the issue of retirement.

This chapter focuses on three major areas: first, work and its relationship to age and gender; second, retirement, its dynamics, and its likely effects on retirees and their families; and third, the economic future of the elderly in this country, including the role of Social Security, Medicare, and Medicaid.

Work and Adult Development

INTRINSIC AND EXTRINSIC ASPECTS OF WORK

Work affects the quality of our lives in two important ways. One is direct, or **intrinsic**, and involves our satisfaction and dissatisfaction with the events

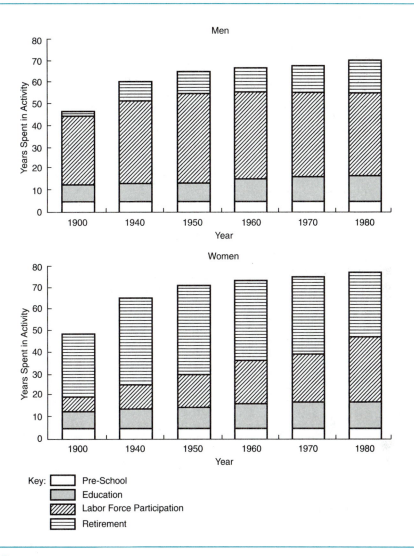

Figure 9.1
Life cycle distribution of education, labor force participation, retirement, and work in the home: 1900–1980.   Source: U.S. Senate Special Committee on Aging (1987–1988).

that take place on the job. The other is indirect, or **extrinsic**, which refers to the influence of work on such nonwork areas as home and family life (Kahn, 1981; Rice, 1984).

Intrinsically, work may be engrossing and self-fulfilling or tedious and unpleasant. Extrinsically, work may or may not provide good housing, food, clothing, education for one's children, and recreation. Some individuals value the intrinsic aspects of work more highly; some are more concerned with the extrinsic aspects. Nevertheless, work has a pronounced effect on our overall well-being. (See Figure 9.2.)

Low-level and low-income jobs may compel an employee to live in meager surroundings, subsist on bare necessities, and endure a boring and tedious workday. Higher level positions tend to provide a better standard of living and more interesting work, but are not always extrinsically advanta-

Figure 9.2

Relationships among work variables, quality of life at work, quality of life away from work, and overall quality of life.   Source: Modified from Rice (1984).

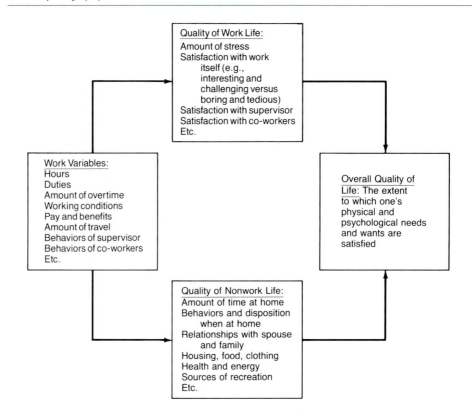

Note. Any single work variable may affect the quality of work life only or the quality of both work and nonwork life. Also, any single work variable may have effects that are positive, negative, or both. For example, more overtime may lead to better housing (through greater income), but also to less time at home and poorer health. A change to more challenging and interesting duties may improve both the quality of work and nonwork life (because the employee is happier), or it may improve the quality of work life but have an adverse effect on the quality of nonwork life (because the employee neglects the family to spend more time at work, resulting in more marital strife).

geous; such jobs may have an adverse effect on an employee's family relationships because they are so stressful and time consuming. In one study (Evans & Bartolomé, 1980), some 40 percent of the wives of managers reported that their husbands' stress at work spilled over into their home lives:

The Relationship Between the Quality of Work Life and the Quality of Nonwork Life

"What annoys me is when he comes home tense and exhausted," observed the wife of one manager who was in her early thirties and had been married for eleven years. "He flops into a chair and turns on the TV. Or else he worries and it drives me up the wall. If he's happy, that's OK. But three years ago he had a very tough job. He was always at the office, even weekends. We had no holidays at all and he was always tense at home—when he was home, that is.... I think he should get out of the commercial U.S.A.-type rat race." Another manager had been dissatisfied with his job for many years. His fifty-year-old wife commented: "I think that his work has an enormous effect on our family life, but he doesn't. We've often had violent arguments about it. He considers himself as one of those men who doesn't rant and rave and destroy his family, even when he is having problems at his work. And there I agree.... Instead, he closes up like a shell. Total closure.... He just doesn't exist. He's completely absent. It's quite clear that you can't reproach him for being disagreeable or aggressive, but it's just as bad in its way.... It's a big burden for a wife to bear."

If the employee's job satisfaction is high, there may instead be a positive spillover into the home and family life. According to one wife, "[My husband] really enjoys his work.... It's so much easier to live with someone who is happy." However, an intense interest in the job may provoke marital strife because the employee spends too little time with the spouse. "My wife feels that I should work less hard, travel less, and be content with a smaller salary," said one manager. "Sure, we don't need the money that much, but that isn't the point. What she doesn't realize is that I work for the satisfaction that it gives me. If I didn't work as hard, I'd be much less satisfied. I'd be miserable when I'm at home, and things would be even worse than now."

Thus the relationship between work and aging is important not only because we spend so much of our lives at work, but also because work significantly affects our satisfaction with life in general.

WORK AND AGING

Job Performance.   As we observed in Chapter 4, some sensory and physiological capacities decline significantly with increasing age. For jobs that require these abilities, corresponding age-related decrements in performance may also be expected. To illustrate, airline pilots who reach age 60 are legally prohibited from flying commercial airplanes because of declines in sensory and processing abilities.

Aging appears to have little detrimental effect in some professional and artistic fields, and may even be related to improved performance. As we observed in Chapter 6, people who are highly creative in early adulthood tend to remain so as they grow older. In fact, artists and musicians often do their best work late in life: Dali, Monet, Picasso, and Arthur Rubinstein made outstanding contributions during their sixties, seventies, and eighties.

Conversely, deteriorating physical skills force most professional athletes to retire by age 35 or 40. The most productive years for mathematicians occur during their twenties and thirties, and their performance declines markedly with each decade. Therefore, even the greatest mathematicians must spend most of their lives burdened with the knowledge that they have passed their prime. Age-related decrements in job performance are also found in other physical sciences. When Nobel laureate I. I. Rabi was asked about the age at which physicists tend to run down, he replied:

> It very much depends on the individual. . . . I've seen people run down at thirty, at forty, at fifty. I think it must be basically neurological or physiological. The mind ceases to operate with the same richness and association. The information retrieval part sort of goes, along with the interconnections. I know that when I was in my late teens and early twenties, the world was just a Roman candle—rockets all the time. . . . You lose that sort of thing as time goes on. . . . Physics is an otherworld thing; it requires a taste for the unseen, even unheard of. . . . These faculties die off somehow when you grow up. . . . Profound curiosity happens when children are young. . . . Once you are sophisticated, you know too much—far too much. (Gardner, 1983, p. 154)

The research evidence in this area is equivocal, which may well be due in part to the limited information provided by chronological age (Chapter 2). Some studies of workers at various job levels do find significant declines in performance with increasing age, but numerous others do not. For example, one study investigated 1,572 design and development engineers from age 21 to 60 and above. Rated job performance was highest for those in their thirties, and declined for each successive five-year age group. But educational experience and job complexity were more closely related to performance rating than was age, and a significant number of engineers continued to be highly rated throughout their careers (Graves, Dalton, & Thompson, 1980; see also Atchley, 1985; Doering, Rhodes, & Schuster, 1983).

The most justified conclusion appears to be that age often bears little or no relationship to job performance, but that some exceptions may be expected in certain jobs and professions. Nor does there seem to be much truth to the old maxim that "you can't teach an old dog new tricks." Rather, the greater experience of older workers often makes it easier for them to adapt to the requirements of related job situations.

Job Satisfaction.   Throughout much of history, work was regarded as a necessary evil: arduous and demanding, valued for the extrinsic benefits that it provided, and rarely (if ever) gratifying for its own sake. To cite one famous example, a major attraction of the biblical Garden of Eden was the lack of any need to work; Adam was punished for eating the forbidden fruit by being told by God, "In the sweat of thy face shalt thou eat bread" (Holt, 1982).

This gloomy conception of work has changed considerably during the last half century, facilitated in part by the discoveries of industrial social psychology. Research has shown that if an organization takes the trouble to make the workplace more conducive to the needs and wants of its employees, it may

In most occupations, work performance does not decrease with age. (Nina Winter/The Image Works)

well reap such benefits as reduced absenteeism and turnover—and perhaps improved production as well, although the relationship between job satisfaction and productivity has proved to be considerably more complicated than might be expected. (See, for example, Vroom, 1964.) Also, as our society has become more concerned with humanitarian issues, we are less willing to accept the belief that an activity that occupies so much of our time and energy should cause extensive dissatisfaction. Although there are more than a few employers who still retain the traditional concept of work, the importance of intrinsic job variables has achieved widespread acceptance (as we have seen). Thus the concept of **job satisfaction** currently encompasses such aspects as the work itself (e.g., interesting versus boring), opportunities for autonomy and control (such as the freedom to decide how to do your work), chances for advancement, and relationships with the supervisor and co-workers, as well as such traditional aspects as pay, fringe benefits, working conditions, and job security (e.g., Kahn, 1981; Smith, Kendall, & Hulin, 1969).

The importance of some of these work variables appears to vary from early to late adulthood. One study found that young adults were more concerned with such intrinsic factors as chances for advancement, recognition and approval, and enjoyment of their work. Older employees tended to be more concerned with pay, working conditions, and company policy regarding such issues as coffee breaks and absenteeism (Rosenfeld & Owens,

1965). In another study dealing with engineers age 20 to 69, younger adults once again proved to be more interested in opportunities for promotion and for professional and personal development, whereas older workers were less willing to move to a new city. However, such aspects of the job as pay increases, feeling a sense of accomplishment, working on challenging projects, and having good relations with one's supervisors were important to young and old workers alike (Breaugh & DiMarco, 1979). Although the findings in this area are somewhat equivocal, opportunities for promotion and developing one's skills appear to be more important to young adults than to middle-aged and older workers.

In general, however, the relationship between aging and job satisfaction is far from clear. Some theorists have suggested that this relationship is *U*-shaped: Satisfaction is initially high for the new employee because of a honeymoon effect, declines as time goes by and reality sets in, and then increases because the worker forms more accurate expectations of the rewards that can be derived from the job (e.g., Morse, 1953). Other investigators have reported a more or less linear relationship between age and job satisfaction, with older employees tending to be more satisfied (Hulin & Smith, 1965). The data are too equivocal to permit any firm conclusions, but there is no convincing evidence that older workers tend to be less satisfied with their jobs than younger adults or that they are more likely to develop morale problems (Doering, Rhodes, & Schuster, 1983). If anything, the reverse appears more likely to be true: Very dissatisfied younger adults may well quit and find jobs more to their liking before they reach more advanced ages, but middle-aged and older workers are likely to have so much difficulty finding new jobs that they learn to be satisfied with what they have.

Health and Absenteeism.   Older workers are less likely than young adults to be injured on the job. But when they do sustain an injury, they are more likely to be disabled and to require more time to recover (Doering, Rhodes, & Schuster, 1983). Older workers are also less likely to be absent than younger workers, but there is an important exception to this trend: Those who suffer from chronic ill health have higher rates of absenteeism because they require more time to convalesce. These findings imply that, rather than rejecting older job applicants out of hand, organizations can obtain valuable employees by ascertaining the health of these applicants relative to the requirements of the job (Quirk & Skinner, 1973).

Problems of the Older Worker.   The U.S. Department of Labor defines a "mature" worker as one at or past the age of 40. In many respects, these older workers face significantly greater problems than do young adults.

Older employees are less likely to lose their jobs than are younger workers, due in part to their seniority. However, they find it much more difficult to obtain a job if they do become unemployed. To be sure, the Age Discrimination in Employment Act of 1967 prohibited the denial of employment to applicants over 40 because of their age. And in 1986, the Act was amended to prohibit job termination on the basis of age, at any age. Furthermore, many older adults are highly competent, have positive attitudes, and are less likely to be injured or absent than are young employees. Nevertheless, severe **age discrimination** still exists in the world of work.

Between 1979 and 1983, the number of age discrimination complaints increased by some 300 percent, and more than $24.6 million was awarded by the courts to over 5,000 individuals because of violations of the ADEA (Atchley, 1985). By 1986, the number of age discrimination complaints reached 27,000 (J. H. Schulz, 1988). Furthermore, there is good reason to believe that these figures seriously understate the actual extent of job-related age discrimination. Many people undoubtedly fail to file for damages because they are unaware of the protection offered by the ADEA, because they erroneously believe that it is extremely difficult to file a complaint, or because they despair of ever proving that their rejections were due to age. Case histories like this following are far from uncommon:

A 59-Year-Old Master Printer

In December of 1956, a large printing company that published several popular magazines ceased operations and closed its plant. Seniority thus offered no protection to Mr. H., a master printer with 42 years of experience. Mr. H. had very strong ties to his present community; he had been born there, many of his relatives and all of his friends lived there, and he was active in his church and in local politics. To remain there, he was willing to change professions and to accept significantly less money than he had made as a printer. Jobs were available in local manufacturing companies, and his skills would have made it easy for him to adapt to their machinery. Nevertheless, he could not secure employment. Understandably bitter, he reluctantly opted for early retirement at age 62. (Atchley, 1985, pp. 189–190)

Such age discrimination appears to be due in part to negative stereotypes about older workers. In one study, a sample of 42 business students was asked how they would deal with various job problems:

- A recently hired shipping room employee who seemed unresponsive to customer calls for service.
- Whether to terminate or retain a computer programmer whose skills had become obsolete.
- Whether to transfer an employee to a higher-paying but more demanding job.
- Whether to hire someone for a position that required not only knowledge of the field, but also the capacity to make quick judgments.
- Whether to honor a request from a production staff employee to attend a conference dealing with new theories and research relevant to production systems.
- Whether to promote an employee to a marketing job that required fresh solutions to challenging problems, and a high degree of creative and innovative behavior.

When the employees in these situations were described as "older," they were more likely to be fired or turned down for the job or promotion than when they were characterized as "younger." Since the work-related qualifications of these hypothetical employees were otherwise identical, the adverse treatment could only have been due to age. (See Rosen & Jerdee, 1976a; 1976b.) Although this study dealt only with students, research evidence also indicates that managers unfairly stereotype older workers as resistant to change, uncreative, slow to make decisions, and untrainable.

Age discrimination is also caused by the nature of organizational fringe benefits. Pensions for older workers are more costly to employers, because contributions must be spread over a shorter period. Health insurance costs are also considerably higher for those age 45 to 65 than for young adults. (See Taggart, 1973; Zillmer, 1982.) Employers may therefore reject older applicants or try to phase out older workers so as not to incur these greater expenses, even though the ADEA prohibits justifying such decisions on the grounds of high pension costs.

In sum: Despite legal safeguards, age discrimination is still a problem in the world of work. All too many older workers are unfairly denied the opportunity to earn needed income, fulfill their potentials, satisfy their need for self-respect, and enjoy the other rewards that the workplace has to offer. And all too many short-sighted organizations fail to improve their production and profits because they refuse to employ these potentially competent, valuable workers.

Midlife Career Changes.   If changing jobs is so difficult for those over 40, midlife career changes would seem to pose even greater problems. Some popular periodicals and scientific researchers contend that midlife career changes are fairly common (e.g., Sarason, 1977; Siegler & Edelman, 1977). However, there is little statistical evidence to support this conclusion (Atchley, 1985).

According to one study, which focused on men in their thirties and forties, midlife career changes are most often due to three factors: failing to realize one's potential in the first career, finding a new career that is potentially more satisfying, or changing one's life goals due to such events as divorce, widowhood, or sudden unemployment (Clopton, 1973). But another study of managerial and professional men age 34 to 54 indicated that such career changes are more often due to external causes, such as losing one's old job, rather than to the employee's wishes and intentions. Some 34 percent of this sample changed careers solely because of external circumstances; another 26 percent experienced external pressures and also wanted to change careers. Only 17 percent changed their careers just because they wanted to (Thomas, 1977). Given the prevalence of age discrimination in the workplace, it would seem that midlife career changes may not be as feasible as some theorists believe.

Afterword.   The study of work and aging is more problematic than might be apparent. Job satisfaction is a multidimensional variable, and there is some indication that aging is more closely related to some facets than to others (e.g., the importance of chances for advancement). Job productivity is also a multidimensional variable: The quality of an individual's work is not necessarily related to the quantity that he or she produces, and many jobs lack any obvious or easily obtainable quantitative measure of performance (e.g., teaching, clinical psychology, politics). In fact, the problem of determining satisfactory criteria of job performance has often proved to be a major stumbling block in industrial psychology research. When we also recall the limitations of chronological age as an index of human capacities, it is hardly surprising that relatively few clear relationships between aging and work variables have emerged from the research literature. Instead, such variables as job level and job complexity appear to be more important than age per se. Older workers are likely to be more experienced, to have reached higher level positions, and to have more challenging and demanding jobs, and it is these aspects that are more closely related to their job performance and satisfaction.

Insofar as age discrimination at work is concerned, more definitive conclusions are justified. It is eminently fair to exclude older workers from jobs that they can no longer perform adequately because of physiological or physical deterioration. Some would also argue that providing more jobs for older workers would reduce the number of openings available to young adults, who are more likely to need the income from work to support their families. Our economic society is a complicated one, and justifiable attempts to reduce unfairness to one group may inadvertently cause other groups to suffer. Nevertheless, adults in their forties and early fifties still have much of their work lives ahead of them. Many of these individuals have a strong desire to work and are as or more competent than young adults. To discriminate against these employees solely because of age is not only illegal and harmful to the individual, but also likely to cost the organization valuable and productive workers.

GENDER DIFFERENCES

Demography.   The **labor force** consists of all people who are employed, plus those who are unemployed but are looking for work. Because our society has long regarded men as the primary breadwinners and women as the primary child rearers, it is not surprising to find considerably more men in the labor force. In 1980, for example, the labor force included almost 90 percent of men between the ages of 20 and 24, and from 90 percent to 95 percent of men between 25 and 54. The corresponding figures for women ranged from 65 percent to 70 percent. (See Figure 9.3.)

As with men, women work for many reasons. Historically, the most important of these is economic: Many women must work to support themselves

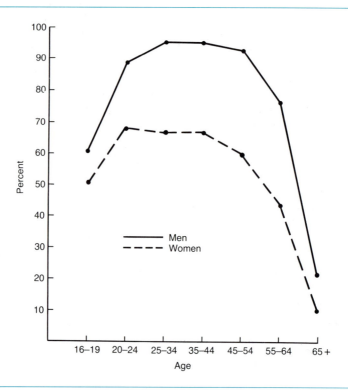

Figure 9.3
Percent of men and women in the labor force, 1980.   Source: U.S. Bureau of the Census (1981).

(and perhaps their children as well), including the divorced (Chapter 8) and the poor. Because non-whites are more likely to be economically disadvantaged than are whites, the work force has traditionally included many more non-white women than white women, although these rates have tended to converge during the last three decades (U.S. Senate Special Committee on Aging, 1986).

More recently, the increasing emphasis on individual rights has been reflected in pressures for more equal job opportunities for women. Our society has to some extent relinquished the stereotype that, except in cases of dire financial need, the woman's place is in the home. Women have felt increasingly free to join the work force in order to express their independence, to provide a second income that will enable their families to enjoy some of the more expensive pleasures in life, or to fulfill their potentials and need for achievement. Thus, there has been an increase in the percent of working women during the last half century, although this trend has leveled off to some extent in recent years. Whereas only 25 percent of those at work in 1940 were women, this figure increased to 33 percent by 1958, to 41 percent by 1978, and to 44 percent by 1984. Women have made considerable gains in some occupations once dominated by men: Between 1972 and 1981, the proportion of accountants who were women rose from 22 percent to 38 percent, women economists from 12 percent to 25 percent, and women bartenders from 28 percent to 48 percent (*Newsweek*, April 22, 1985). However, women have made fewer gains with regard to managerial and administrative positions. (See Table 9.1.) Also, women working full time in 1983 earned only 64 percent of what men did, a figure that has remained fairly steady for decades.

The Comparable Worth Controversy.   To some theorists, the lower pay typically received by women is a clear sign of **sex discrimination.** They argue that employers are paying men significantly more for much the same work and/or are denying women access to higher level and more lucrative positions. It has therefore been suggested that the demands and difficulty of various jobs be rated numerically, so that pay can be determined solely according to this criterion and men and women will receive comparable pay for comparable work.

Other theorists have taken strong exception to this proposal. They point out that women are much more likely than men to discontinue their work in order to bear and raise children, which has a negative effect on their seniority and chances for advancement. Statistical data indicate that women as a group have fewer years of experience and less seniority than do men (*Newsweek*, April 22, 1985). Also, if the mother chooses to return to work after the child is born, she may prefer a lower-level and less demanding job so that she can spend more time at home. These critics generally agree that there is sex discrimination in the workplace, but they contend that the best way to alleviate this problem is by allowing pay to fluctuate freely in accordance with the supply and demand for the jobs in question.

The issue is likely to remain a controversial one. Because of the difficulty of evaluating the demands made by different jobs, as well as the opposition

Table 9.1
Jobs held by men and women during 1958, 1968, and 1978 (in percents).

Year	All Jobs		Managerial and Administrative Jobs		Clerical Jobs	
	Men	Women	Men	Women	Men	Women
1958	67.3	32.7	13.6	5.0	6.9	30.1
1968	63.4	36.6	13.6	4.5	7.1	33.8
1978	58.8	41.2	14.0	6.1	6.2	34.6

Source: U.S. Bureau of the Census, Social Indicators III (1980).

Women have made considerable gains in some occupations once dominated by men and have achieved some important positions. But they have made less progress in other areas and may well be paid less than men for the same type of work. (Bettye Lane/Photo Researchers, Inc.)

to such programs, it seems unlikely that an effective system for determining comparable worth will be forthcoming in the near future.

Career and/or Motherhood.   As Figure 9.3 indicates, the majority of young women seek some form of employment. More than 50 percent of women age 16 to 19, and approximately 70 percent of women age 20 to 24, belonged to the labor force in 1980. Some of these women opt for full-time careers, and some leave the labor force permanently in order to raise a family. Various studies have shown that women who elect to work full time are no less (or more) satisfied with their adult years than are those who opt for motherhood (e.g., Baruch & Barnett, 1980; Blood & Wolfe, 1960; Wright, 1978). As Carl Jung, the noted psychiatrist, once observed: "The shoe that fits one person pinches another; there is no universal recipe for living" (1931, p. 41).

Still other women choose to combine work and family roles, either for financial reasons or because they enjoy their jobs and do not wish to abandon them. Research evidence indicates that married women who work enjoy better mental health than those who do not, but they also experience greater interrole conflicts than do male workers. This is apparently due to the fact that the woman's multiple roles tend to be salient simultaneously, whereas the man's multiple roles are more likely to operate sequentially. That is, the woman's family responsibilities normally continue throughout the day, so she is more likely to encounter situations where she must be at work yet take care of home and children at the same time. Conversely, the man can more often concentrate solely on work during the day and pursue family activities during the evening. (As we observed in the preceding chapter, the role of the "househusband" has been greatly exaggerated. After the first child is born, the husband typically seeks to earn more income, and the wife assumes primary responsibility for family matters.) Thus married women who work perceive the home as more of a burden and are more likely to cite scheduling conflicts as a source of problems, whereas working men more often view their home environment as a support system (Hall, 1975; Kessler & McCrae, 1981; Sekaran, 1983; Staines & Pleck, 1983; Welch & Broth, 1977). The working married woman is particularly likely to experience interrole conflicts if she has young children, if her decision to work is not supported by her husband, if she works for many hours during the week, and if she has a higher level of career aspiration (Gore & Mangione, 1983; Holahan & Gilbert, 1979a; 1979b).

Afterword.   The stereotype that the woman's place is in the home has been shattered by empirical data: Women who choose to work are no less satisfied with their adult lives than are women who opt to raise a family, nor is there any indication that they are, in general, less competent employees than are men. However, women who elect to combine work and family roles may find it difficult to meet their obligations in both areas. Although sex discrimination is still a significant problem in the workplace, the influence of women at work has increased considerably during the past four decades—and is likely to continue to do so in the future.

Retirement

Leaving the world of full-time work involves financial, psychological, and physical changes. For most people, retirement brings a reduction in annual income. Work can no longer be used to gratify the retiree's self-esteem and need for achievement. The opportunity for social interactions with co-workers, supervisors, and subordinates is no longer available. And instead of spending some eight hours per day in the work environment, the retiree must now either remain at home or find other activities to fill the day.

Thus it is not uncommon to hear about people who retire and then die unexpectedly within weeks or even days, presumably because they cannot cope with this major life change. Less extreme but equally prevalent are anecdotes about retirees who require psychiatric help because they feel useless and depressed, or because they cannot tolerate having to spend both day and night with their spouses. Nevertheless, these stories do not necessarily indicate that retirement causes ill health. Retirement may instead *result from* an existing physical or mental disorder. Most people do not retire until age

60 or later, and health tends to decline toward the end of the adult life span. If some adults choose to retire because poor health makes it too difficult for them to function at work, and if their disorders become considerably more serious or even terminal in subsequent months, it is clearly erroneous to conclude that an otherwise healthy individual was made ill by retirement. (Compare with the discussion of stressful life events in Chapter 10.)

Also, as we have seen, work may be valued more for its extrinsic than its intrinsic aspects. It may be boring and stressful, rather than interesting and enjoyable, yet serve as an essential source of income. For some, or even many jobs, then, retirement may represent more of a relief than a deprivation. In this section, we will seek to determine whether the supposedly adverse effects of retirement are supported by research evidence, or whether these beliefs are merely more of the myths that pervade the field of adult development and aging.

OVERVIEW

Definition. **Retirement** can be defined in various ways. Some theorists regard any person who performs no gainful employment during a given year as retired. Others apply this definition only to those who are currently receiving retirement pension benefits. And still others consider anyone who is not employed full time, year round, as retired.

For purposes of the present discussion, a retired person is one who is *not* employed at a *full-time* paying job *and* who receives at least some income from a pension due to prior employment. Thus retirement is an *earned* reward, one that results from having previously been a member of the labor force. Also, retirement does not necessarily mean a total separation from the world of work. Some retirees opt for part-time jobs or choose to do some work on a self-employed basis, as we will see later in this chapter.

Demographic Considerations: Mandatory Versus Voluntary Retirement. The proportion of older people who retire has increased dramatically since the turn of the century. In 1900, approximately 60 percent of men over 65 were actively employed. By 1986, however, this figure dropped to 16 percent.

Some might attribute this decline primarily to mandatory retirement policies, which require an employee to retire at a specific age (e.g., 65 or 70). However, the empirical evidence indicates otherwise. In 1978, the Age Discrimination in Employment Act was amended to prohibit mandatory retirement before age 70 in most sectors of the economy. Surprisingly, however, this did *not* produce a substantial increase in the number of older workers. In fact, between 1970 and 1986, the percent of men age 65 to 69 in the labor force decreased from 39 percent to 25 percent. A decline also occurred for men 60 to 64 years old, from 73 percent to 55 percent. (See Table 9.2.) Thus, even though adults are now able to work for more years than ever before, more and more are opting for **early retirement.** Only about 4 percent

Table 9.2
Labor force participation rates by age, sex, and race: 1986.

Sex and race	50–54 years	55–59 years	60–64 years	65–69 years	70+ years
Total male	88.9	79.0	54.9	25.0	10.4
Total female	62.0	51.3	33.2	14.3	4.1
White male	89.8	79.8	55.7	25.3	10.7
White female	62.0	51.0	33.1	14.3	4.1
Black male	81.1	70.8	45.9	21.0	7.2
Black female	62.1	52.9	33.3	13.9	4.6

Source: U.S. Senate Special Committee on Aging (1987–1988).

to 7 percent of those who retire are compelled to do so against their will because of age (Parnes & Nestel, 1981; Reno, 1971; 1972; J. H. Schulz, 1974).

Another recent trend involves part-time work and the elderly. Many people like the option of part-time employment after age 65, and empirical data indicate that such an option is increasingly available. (See Figure 9.4.)

Apparently, then, mandatory retirement does *not* force many well-qualified and willing employees to leave work prematurely. We must therefore look elsewhere to ascertain the reasons for the increasing popularity of early retirement.

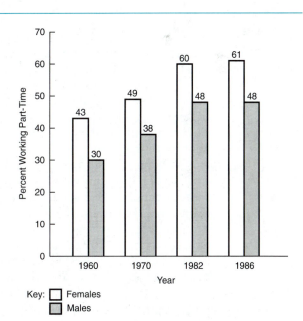

Figure 9.4
Percent of persons 65 years old and over who work part-time. Source: Based on U.S. Senate Special Committee on Aging (1987–1988).

THE PRE-RETIREMENT YEARS

Attitudes Toward Retirement.   Almost all working adults expect to retire someday, usually before age 65. The majority of young and middle-aged workers probably do not think about retirement to any great extent. However, most employees past age 45 who do speculate about retirement view it as positive and desirable (e.g., Goudy, 1981; Prentis, 1980).

Some cross-sectional studies suggest that there is a significant negative relationship between age and attitudes toward retirement. However, this finding is due to cohort effects rather than to aging: More recent generations are more accepting of retirement. In 1951, for example, the majority of steelworkers believed that retirement was justified only if an employee was physically unable to continue working. But by 1960, the same majority concluded that retirement is a benefit that they deserve for having worked for so many years (Ash, 1966). Of considerably more importance than age is the worker's financial status: The higher the income that one expects to receive during retirement, the more favorable are the attitudes toward this life event.

How prevalent are optimistic views of retirement? Approximately 67 percent of employed adults do *not* anticipate financial problems during retirement, even though they also expect retirement to reduce their incomes by up to 50 percent from preretirement levels (Atchley, 1985). Few employees take concrete action to ensure that their retirement income will be adequate; only about 4 percent to 8 percent of men age 60 and older participate in formal retirement preparation programs (Beck, 1984; Harris & Associates, 1975; 1981). However, there is no indication that this lack of formal preretirement planning has any substantial impact on postretirement well-being.

Factors Affecting the Decision to Retire.   Because mandatory retirement policies affect only a very small number of employees, the decision to retire must often be due to other reasons. These include the employee's job level and job satisfaction, age discrimination and employer pressures to retire, actual and self-perceived health, the expectation of a more enjoyable life, and the influence of one's family, friends, and co-workers.

Those who hold higher-level jobs tend to regard retirement more favorably because of their sound financial position, but they are also more likely to postpone retiring because they find their work to be too enjoyable. As Dr. Charles B. Huggins, 81-year-old Nobel Prize-winner in physiology and medicine, put it, "Why should I retire as long as I love my work and can still do it well? I'm not a furniture mover, you know. . . . Research has always been my pleasure as well as my job. There is nothing that matches the thrill of discovery" (*The Wall Street Journal*, March 10, 1983). Employees with low-level jobs are also likely to put off retirement, but for reasons that are primarily financial. These workers favor retirement in theory, because their jobs are typically dull and routine, but they often cannot afford it because of their low income and poor pension plans. Consequently, middle-level employees are the ones most likely to choose early retirement. They tend to have adequate retirement programs, and don't enjoy their jobs enough to want to continue working past the minimum retirement age. (See, for example, Atchley & Robinson, 1982; Streib & Schneider, 1971.) A common expectation of these workers is that life will be more satisfying if they retire.

Age discrimination is also a factor in the decision to retire early, as we have seen. Employers may well refuse to hire qualified job applicants who are past middle age; or they may find various ways to let older workers know that their continued presence on the job is no longer desired, by transferring them to less attractive positions or treating them with less respect and consideration. As a result, older employees and job applicants may reluctantly decide that early retirement is their only feasible option.

Since older workers do suffer declines in certain physical and physiological capacities, and since they are more likely to become disabled when they do sustain injuries on or off the job, some may be compelled to retire because they find that the job has become too demanding. Most men who opt for early retirement under Social Security cite health as their reason for doing so (Reno, 1971). However, this finding probably cannot be accepted at face value: To some employees, health is undoubtedly a more socially acceptable reason for retiring early than admitting that they just don't want to work anymore (J. H. Schulz, 1988). For those who reach the normal retirement age of 65 or 70, health issues appear to have little effect on the decision to retire (Palmore, George, & Fillenbaum, 1982).

Family and peer pressures may also influence the decision to retire. Some spouses and children may want the employee to retire at an earlier age, but others may not. An adult who lives in a leisure community populated primarily by retirees may experience peer pressure to conform, whereas another employee who lives among full-time workers may face precisely the opposite pressures (Atchley, 1976).

Afterword.   Some workers do choose early retirement because they sincerely believe that their health is inadequate, or because of employer, family, or peer pressures. Some are forced to retire because they have reached a specific age. We do not mean to minimize the plight of those who find their work to be psychologically or financially rewarding, yet who are compelled against their wishes to retire. Nevertheless, research evidence clearly indicates that retirement is most often a welcome, desired event. The majority of employees retire voluntarily because they expect to enjoy life more as a result, and because they anticipate few financial problems. In fact, more and more adults are choosing early retirement for these reasons. Let us now ascertain whether these positive expectations are likely to be realized.

RETIREMENT AND ITS EFFECTS

Phases of Retirement.   Some theorists have suggested that retirees tend to proceed through a series of distinct psychological and emotional stages (Atchley, 1976; 1982; 1985). Retirement may well begin with a euphoric and busy *honeymoon* phase, during which the individual eagerly tries to do many of the things that were ruled out by full-time work (such as extended travel). This intense activity may be followed by a period of letdown or *disenchantment*, especially if the individual's prior expectations of retirement were unrealistically positive.

Disenchanted with Retirement

Mr. A., a 64-year-old former data technician for the U.S. Postal Service, found that retirement was not the paradise he had expected. "I spent the first eight months [of retirement] fixing up my lawn and house," he observed. "Then I ran out of things to do." Similarly, Mr. D., a 68-year-old retiree, found that "three years of loafing were all I could take." (*The Wall Street Journal*, March 2, 1983)

These retirees must now take stock of themselves and their life situation, adjust to the realities of retirement, and seek out appropriate new activities. If this *reorientation* phase is successful, the retiree then settles into a predictable and generally satisfying *retirement routine*. Such retirees accept the limitation brought on by advanced age, keep busy to at least some extent, are self-sufficient, and manage their own affairs. Very few choose to isolate themselves from other people; most want to retain at least some social contacts, especially with their families (Chapter 8). But there are retirees who cannot resolve the reorientation phase successfully, and who remain in a state of disenchantment even after some years have passed. Finally, some elderly adults become so ill that they can no longer function independently; they are more properly described as sick or disabled rather than retired (the *termination* phase). A few may instead terminate retirement by returning to full-time work.

These phases are not intended to represent an inevitable sequence. Some retirees may not experience some phases, or they may encounter them in a different order. For example, death may claim a retiree before the termination phase is reached. Some retirees may not have enough money for the activities involved in a honeymoon period, and may therefore omit this phase. Several cross-sectional studies suggest that many retirees proceed directly from the honeymoon phase to the retirement routine, without suffering a period of disenchantment (e.g., Atchley, 1976; 1982). Other retirees may prefer to indulge in a period of *rest and relaxation* either immediately after retirement, or following the honeymoon period. This inactivity typically gives way to boredom and restlessness, however, whereupon the retiree enters the reorientation phase and must face the challenge of establishing a satisfactory daily routine.

Research evidence concerning this phase model is sparse and somewhat equivocal. Some tentative findings indicate that enthusiasm does tend to be high immediately after retirement, and that some degree of emotional letdown or reassessment is likely during the second or third year of retirement (Adams & Lefebvre, 1981; Ekerdt, Bossé, & Levkoff, 1985; Haynes, McMichael, & Tyroler, 1978). Other studies have failed to find any evidence of a honeymoon effect (Beck, 1982). Perhaps the most important inference to be drawn from the phase model is the fact that although some retirees ultimately experience strong and prolonged feelings of disenchantment, many others do not. That is, some adults find it considerably easier to adjust to retirement than do others. Why is this so? How do successful retirees make this period more satisfying and rewarding? The answer appears to involve several important aspects of the individual's life style prior to retirement: financial status, degree of social and recreational activity, and health.

Financial Effects. Some early cross-sectional studies have suggested that retirement produces a substantial drop in income, so much so that the retiree's standard of living and satisfaction with life are adversely affected. However, this conclusion has now been shown to be inaccurate. One longitudinal, multivariate, and large-sample study analyzed data obtained from six extensive research programs, which spanned from 2 to 10 years and comprised a total of more than 23,000 men and women age 45 to 70 and older. The results indicated that financial differences between retirees and those who are still working are due in large part to differences in the amount of preretirement income, rather than to retirement per se. Early retirement does have more of an adverse financial effect than later retirement, since the individual must usually accept a smaller income in order to begin collecting benefits sooner. But when preretirement level of income is statistically controlled, most of the purported negative financial consequences of retirement turn out to be small or insignificant (Palmore, Fillenbaum, & George, 1984). Although there is a drop in income at retirement, the typical retired household is no more likely than the employed household to feel economically strapped or to draw upon savings (McConnel & Deljavan, 1983). As Sylvester J. Scheiber, the research director of the Employee Benefit Research Institute in Washington, D.C., has observed: "The idea that the word 'aged' is synonymous with 'poor' is a myth" (*The Wall Street Journal*, Feb. 21, 1983).

A similar conclusion has been reached by the President's Council of Economic Advisers, which recently reported that the financial status of retirees has improved markedly during the last 30 years. Most elderly people today live in homes that are paid for, with enough money to enjoy their leisure years (*Time*, Feb. 18, 1985). In fact, due in part to the automatic cost-of-living increases in Social Security payments that began in 1974, America's senior citizens have received *greater* percentage increases in their average annual incomes during the past decade than did those below age 65.

> *Finances and Retirement: A Typical Example*
>
> "I hear all these retired folks complaining that they don't have this and they don't have that," says Mr. H., a 74-year-old retired shipping clerk. "I'm not pinched. . . . My house is paid for. My car is paid for. Both my sons are grown up. I don't need many new clothes. Every time I go out and eat somewhere, I get a senior citizen's discount. This is the happiest period of my life. These are my golden years." (*The Wall Street Journal*, Feb. 21, 1983)

The picture is by no means entirely bright, however. Those with lower-level jobs and poor fringe benefits may well find themselves in serious financial difficulty during retirement. This is particularly true for those who are low in education and/or have been the object of prejudice in the workplace, such as blacks and women:

An Economically Disadvantaged Retiree

Mrs. B. is a black 72-year-old widow who lives in a senior citizen's housing project in Washington, D.C. She once worked as a janitor, a job that provided minimal retirement benefits. Now she barely scrapes by on her annual Social Security income of $3,800, plus $800 from her late husband's veteran's pension. "It's just terrible," she says. "Social Security payments are so low that they don't even want you to have enough money to eat or to buy medicine. . . . Social Security benefits may go up $15, but the cost of everything I need has already gone up $15 or $20." (*The Wall Street Journal*, Feb. 21, 1983)

Here again, however, preretirement characteristics rather than retirement per se were primarily responsible for Mrs. B.'s financial difficulties. In fact, many low-level and minority group employees earn so little income that retirement has virtually no financial effect; their pay is essentially replaced by food stamps and other age-related income supports. As the authors of one longitudinal study concluded, "the presence of these supports, and the finding that retirement had no adverse effects on the [incomes of black men], forcibly indicates how low their work-related income must have been" (Fillenbaum, George, & Palmore, 1985).

In sum: Although the aged were indeed an economically disadvantaged group some 30 years ago, this is no longer true. For this reason, some observers have become critical of Social Security. As *Time* magazine reported: "Providing decent living standards for the elderly puts a great burden on younger people. Today's workers are paying for benefits to retirees that far exceed contributions the retirees made during their working years. An individual who goes on Social Security [in 1985] has put about $50,124 into the system during his lifetime. If he gets the average 1985 payment of $594 a month, it will take seven years to recoup that" (*Time*, Feb. 18, 1985).

However, there is another side to the story. Even as recently as 1984, older Americans had a lower economic status than other adults in our society. (See Figure 9.5.) Furthermore, the economic status of the elderly is far more varied than that of any other age group. Although some older adults have substantial financial resources, a surprising number have practically none. (See Figure 9.6.) Comparisons of average figures may therefore be misleading, with the high values for some retirees obscuring the fact that quite a few elderly adults are below or just barely above the poverty level (U.S. Senate Special Committee on Aging, 1986). Thus there is a significant number of elderly individuals who suffer serious financial problems during retirement.

Whether the younger generation is supporting the elderly to an unfair extent is a highly controversial issue. (See the boxed excerpt on pages 299–301.) The economic status of the aged is likely to remain a source of keen political debate. However, the stereotype of the elderly retiree who

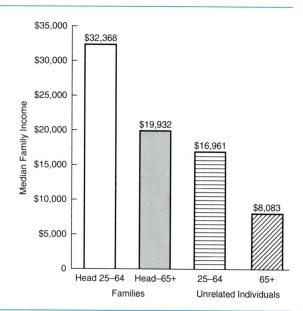

Figure 9.5
Median family income as a function of age for families and for unrelated individuals (1986). Source: U.S. Senate Special Committee on Aging (1987–1988, p. 57).

lives from hand to mouth on a meager fixed income, resides in a drab and dingy apartment, and struggles desperately to secure the bare necessities of life must be emphatically rejected in light of the available research evidence.

Activity versus Boredom. Here again, the general picture is an optimistic one: The majority find retirement to be a busy and satisfying period. In particular, those individuals who developed enjoyable hobbies and recreational activities prior to retirement are most likely to enjoy their years away from full-time work. However, those who had few avocations during their working years may well find that retirement is disenchanting and depressing. Thus a county coordinator of adult and community education in Florida observes: "Our biggest battle is loneliness. A lot of people dream about paradise. They sell their homes and move here. After the drapes are up and the carpets are down, paradise can turn into a living hell if they don't find something to do" (*The Wall Street Journal*, March 2, 1983).

Those retirees who do become bored and disenchanted may seek to resolve their problems by joining a senior center and developing new interests. Or, part-time work may prove to be an effective and rewarding way to keep busy. One Florida retirement community is filled with elderly gas station attendants, grocery store baggers, retail clerks, and owners of small businesses. Most of these older adults are paid at or near the federal minimum of $4.25 per hour, yet they value this opportunity to be active.

We may conclude that there is a close relationship between an individual's preretirement and retirement life styles. Those who begin retirement with many avocational (or vocational) activities that they want to pursue are likely to find this time of life to be full and rewarding. Conversely, those with few hobbies and non-job social activities during their working years may well find that they have far too much time on their hands during retirement. (Compare with the discussion of the stability of personality during adulthood in Chapter 7, and the social life-styles of the elderly in Chapter 8.)

Figure 9.6
Percent of elderly people below the poverty level, by selected characteristics, 1986.   Source: U.S. Senate Special Committee on Aging (1987–1988).

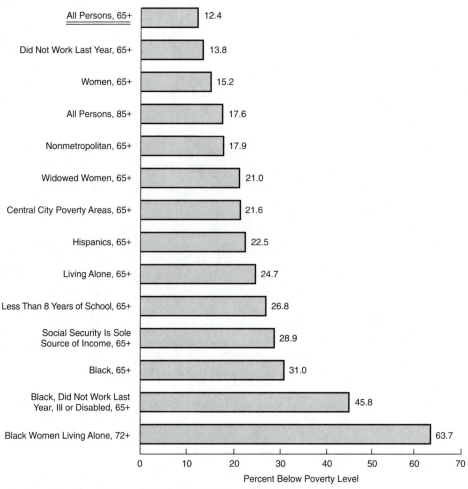

Note. Poverty level for elderly two-person families in 1986 was $6,630; poverty level for elderly individuals in 1986 was $5,255.

The War Between the Generations

The Financial Status of the Retired: Conflicting Opinions

By Joseph A. King[1]

Not long ago, while waiting on line at our local movie theater, I tuned in to the conversations of the people around me. Ahead were two couples—in their late 60s, I think—chatting about their grandchildren, tax-free municipal bonds and, at one point, the expensive Gucci bag one of the ladies was clutching. Behind me several students who attend the college I had taught at for 21 years talked about the horrendous cost of textbooks, the fare increase on the Bay Area Rapid Transit and their inability to find a decent one-bedroom apartment for less than $500 a month.

The ticket office opened. The two elderly couples—who, I gathered from my eavesdropping, lived in the luxury retirement community of Rossmoor in Walnut Creek—stepped up and paid $2.50 a ticket: half price. Having just turned 60, I qualified for the discount, too. The youngsters behind me paid the full $5.

This minor incident got me to thinking about the old and the young in America and about some inequities in our system. I am a recently retired person and, though not yet 65, I already receive substantial discounts at restaurants and theaters. In a few years I will get a double exemption on my income tax and a 90 percent discount on our public-transit system. My income from pension and investment is several times above the poverty level and growing. My mortgage payment is $128 per month, a trifle, on a 30-year note, at 6 percent with 10 years to go. My four children have completed college, are out on their own, and my disposable income now far exceeds what it was when my wife, Betty, and I were raising them. The government, the capitalist establishment and the

[1] King taught English at Diablo Valley College in Pleasant Hill, California, for 21 years. He retired in May of 1985.

Good Lord have been magnificent to us.

I do not think that Betty and I, or the well-to-do couples who preceded us into the movie theater on discounted tickets, are an insignificant segment of that class of people deceptively and plaintively labeled "senior citizens" in political debate. History has never been kinder to us. We have lots of money. In 1984 the poverty rate of those 65 and over was 12.4 percent and lower than the national average of 14.4 percent. We have lots of votes. Few politicians dare irritate us; aspiring young ones pander to us. We are a formidable political lobby.

Nasty backlash: We also have one of the most effective public advocates on our side—the venerable Claude Pepper, Democrat of Florida. A liberal of the old New Deal school who has served 38 years in the Senate and the House of Representatives, always as a spokesman for the underdog, Claude Pepper has been a hero of mine for a long, long time. I deplored his loss of a Senate seat after a Red-baiting campaign during the McCarthy era. I cheered his resurrection as a member of the House. But now his activities worry me. With triple-focus glasses, two hearing aids, a pacemaker in his chest and a plastic valve in his heart, he is promoting a bill that prohibits mandatory retirement at 70. At 85 the chairman of the powerful Rules Committee, member of the Select Committee on Aging, fiercely defends federal supports for senior citizens even as young heads of households with mortgage payments of $1,000 per month try their damnedest to get a solid footing in the work force and to raise their families. Even as college students with marginal incomes pay increased transit fares for the privilege of sitting next to Rossmoor residents in Guccis who pay 10 cents on the dollar. Even as a fifth of all American children live in households below the poverty line.

What really worries me is the distinct possibility, indeed the inevitability, of a nasty backlash by the young against the old. This backlash awaits only the emergence of ambitious politicians willing to set one generation against another. I fear they will find a field ready for demagogues to conquer—troops of young people who have much justice on their side. For the liberal assumption that most old folks are poor and needy has become only a half-truth.

Legal responsibility: Those who wage war against the heartless oppressors of the aged will remind us, for sure, that there is a large number of really poor seniors who exist on pitifully small pensions, social security and supplemental-security-income allowances. Yes, their number is great, but I also know that many are also beneficiaries of outside resources, especially in the form of unreported help from their children. They have no legal responsibility to support their parents, yet many children do so generously if surreptitiously, so that seniors can have it both ways: aid from the state and gifts.

The larger picture is not one of the young voluntarily helping the old, but of the transfer of income to the elderly. The fact is that 12 percent of the population, those 65 and over, receives 50 percent of all government expenditures for social services. We seniors end up with the cash, the disposable income, while our progeny are taxed and shortchanged. This is certainly a turnabout, something rather new, I think, in a society which believes that each generation should do better than the one before.

I'm uncomfortable about accepting all the perks that come to me, stashing increasing amounts of disposable income in banks and investments, cheering for Claude Pepper and deciding in kingly fashion just how much largesse should be bestowed on children working hard to pay $500 per month for one-bedroom apartments. No, I won't be able to vote for the Party of the Young. I have interests to defend. Yet I wonder if we are being well served by Claude Pepper and other advocates of the status quo. Would not more help be available for the real poor—old and young—if so many perks and exemptions did not go to the affluent?

Senior Benefits

Bravo! It is a pleasure indeed to find a senior citizen like Joseph King who demonstrates some empathy for those of us who have not yet reached retirement age (My Turn, April 14). We do not share the perks of the elderly and are compelled to struggle with a system that places a heavy burden on middle-income working families.

CAROL WELLS
Carson City, Nevada

Joe King is still living in his ivory tower. Senior citizens from an affluent retirement community in California are not typical of the entire country, and he is naive to think he'll be able to exist comfortably for another 25 years with inflation. Wait until he's assessed $3,000 per month for a good nursing home.

HARRIETTE WETSEL
Akron, Ohio

While the aged are the primary beneficiaries of social security and Medicare, these social-insurance programs are intergenerational and *all* Americans benefit from their success. They help young and old, rich and poor alike. Thus, social security helps relieve children of the financial burden of caring for aging parents while providing parent independence and dignity in their retirement years; it also provides children with benefits when they survive the death of a contributing parent. Finally, because such support programs bind families together when health or economic security are threatened, if there is a backlash it will be one of young and old against Reaganomics, not young and old against each other as King fears.

CLAUDE PEPPER, *Chairman*
House Select Committee on Aging
Washington, DC

As I wax creative with rice and vegetables for my family of four the night before payday, it irks me to think that the FICA deduction from tomorrow's check might be going to a couple living in a $500,000 house a mile away. I'd begrudge my loss of that money less if I knew it was going to one of the thousands of single mothers living below poverty level.

CATHARINE BEECHER
Phoenix, Arizona

I have no pension. As a registered nurse, I came out of the war with battle scars and a husband who divorced me when I was 57. King lives in another world, cushioned and protected. I resent his generalizations about the affluent elderly.

DOROTHEA M. FASSETT
Southgate, Michigan

As a product of the Depression, I saved all my life for an independent retirement. I worked 41 years and when I retired, 18 years ago, I thought I'd saved enough to maintain my standard of living. Not so! My dollars are now worth around 30 cents and my standard of living has been going steadily downward.

FRED D. CROWTHER
Oxford, Maryland

Has King seriously considered the plight of those older people for whom an occasional movie at discount prices is probably the only affordable diversion? For most of them, a movie at regular prices would be unthinkable, let alone a concert or a show. A discount might make it possible to buy that can opener so

badly needed for arthritic hands, or to take that bus trip, or to buy necessary medication.

MARIANNE BRACHMAN
Westbury, Connecticut

King's statistics are deceiving. Most retired people live on fixed incomes that shrink when prices rise and interest rates drop. Furthermore, they spend a disproportionate share of their income on rapidly rising medical costs and supplemental health insurance.

JULES BRANDELL
Shorewood, Wisconsin

As a comfortable young retiree, Joe King fails to realize that poverty is prevalent among the very old. His life expectancy is another 20 years and he'd do well to stop flaunting his affluence and put some income back into his savings pool.

RICHARD L. MELA
Essex, Connecticut

Most senior benefits are derived from paid-in social-security taxes deposited over a very long period of time. The return of these funds that the government is paying out with one long hand is being taxed back with the other. As for "perks," King's choice of the word is unfortunate. What perk does a low subway fare provide? The incentive to become old?

GILBERT KIVENSON
Canoga Park, California

Health.   Early cross-sectional studies also suggested that health is likely to be adversely affected by retirement. Here again, however, these findings have been contradicted by more recent longitudinal studies. As discussed previously, poor health after retirement may well be caused by deteriorating health before retirement. Some workers exaggerate their health problems in order to have a more socially acceptable reason for seeking early retirement. And declines in health may be due simply to advancing age, rather than to retirement; ill health is one of the stressful life events that we are more likely to encounter as we grow older (Chapter 10). In actuality, retired people are no more likely to be sick than are people of the same age who are still working (Streib & Schneider, 1971; see also Ekerdt, Baden, Bossé, & Dibbs, 1983; Haynes, McMichael, & Tyroler, 1978).

There are individuals who do retire in reasonably good health, only to deteriorate thereafter. Yet such cases tend to be balanced by those wherein there is an *improvement* in health after retirement because the individual is no longer subjected to stressful, unhealthy, or dangerous working conditions. In fact, in one longitudinal study, some 38 percent of a sample of 263 men claimed that retirement had a positive effect on their health (Ekerdt, Bossé, & LoCastro, 1983; see also Minkler, 1981; Palmore, Fillenbaum, & George, 1984).

All in all, the evidence does *not* indicate that retirement exerts a significant negative effect on the physical and mental health of the retiree. In particular, there is no justification whatsoever for the stereotype of retirees who suffer severe psychological breakdowns, or even an early death, because they are no longer needed at a full-time job.

Marital Difficulties.   Another myth about retirement is expressed in the saying, "I married you for better or for worse, but not for lunch." That is, the extensive contact between husband and wife during retirement is believed by some to bring a substantial increase in marital tension and strife. For

Those who develop satisfying hobbies prior to retirement are more likely to enjoy their years away from work, as with this retiree's interest in Bonsai gardening. (John Maher/Stock, Boston)

Myths About Aging

Work and Retirement

Myth	*Best Available Evidence*
Most middle-aged and older adults are poor employment risks. Compared to young adults, they do inferior work, have poorer attitudes because they are more set in their ways ("you can't teach an old dog new tricks"), and more often become injured or ill.	There are some jobs where age-related decrements in performance are found, such as those requiring certain perceptual and memory tasks (Chapters 4 and 5). In general, however, there is no indication that older workers perform more poorly on most jobs, or that they are more likely to suffer from low morale. Older workers are *less* likely than young adults to be injured on the job, although they are more likely to become disabled and to take longer to recover when an injury or illness does occur.
A woman's primary role is to have children, so those who choose instead to pursue full-time careers will find their adult lives to be significantly less fulfilling.	Women who pursue full-time careers are no less (or more) happy with their adult years than are those who opt for motherhood.
Since work is so important to us, retirement is likely to cause severe psychological trauma or even an early death.	Most people adjust reasonably well to retirement, and do *not* experience serious psychological or physical trauma because they have left the world of full-time work.
Mandatory retirement policies cause widespread dissatisfaction, since many adults would work past age 65 or 70 if allowed to do so.	Very few workers are adversely affected by mandatory retirement policies. Most employees retire voluntarily, and more and more are opting for early retirement.
Most elderly retirees live in near-poverty, reside in drab apartments, and have great difficulty acquiring even the bare necessities of living.	Although there are important exceptions, the majority of retirees live in homes that are paid for and have enough money to enjoy themselves during retirement.
Because retirement causes husband and wife to spend so much more time together, it produces a substantial increase in marital strife.	There is no indication that retirement causes significantly more marital problems for most retired couples.
Most retirees relocate to such places as Florida and Arizona.	Only a small percentage of retirees change their residences because of retirement.
One major advantage of reaching retirement age is that all of one's health-care costs are paid for by the government.	The government pays only a portion of the health-care costs of the elderly. Some services, such as long-term care, are not covered at all until the individual uses up all resources and qualifies as being poor.

example, the director of a Florida mental health clinic concluded that marriages sometimes develop strains under the pressure of the enforced togetherness that retirement brings. "For the first time in their lives," he noted, they have to eyeball each other 24 hours a day" (*The Wall Street Journal*, March 2, 1983).

In many instances, however, the relationship between husband and wife improves after retirement. The spouses are now able to enjoy mutual recreational activities, and they have time for caring and communication that may not have existed during the working years. This appears to be more true for middle-class and upper-middle-class couples, where the wife is likely to welcome her husband's retirement and increased involvement in household tasks. But in working-class marriages, the wife is more likely to expect and to value exclusive control over the household. When her husband uses some of the extensive free time created by retirement to participate in household chores, she may well become irritated because her domain has been invaded (Kerckhoff, 1966).

Alternatively, preretirement factors may play a significant role. An increase in marital strife may occur after retirement only because the marriage was an unhappy one to begin with, and neither spouse enjoys the idea of having to spend more time with the other. In sum: There is no strong evidence that retirement has an adverse effect on the marriages of most elderly couples.

Changes in Residence.   Another common belief is that most adults change their residence soon after retirement. In actuality, migration rates decline substantially from age 25 onward and rise only slightly at retirement. Retirement meccas such as those in Florida and Arizona would seem to command a disproportionate amount of media attention, perhaps because of their extremely high densities of older adults. Yet only a very small proportion of retirees move to such communities; the overwhelming majority do *not* relocate (Atchley, 1985).

AFTERWORD

Some studies purport to show that retirement has a severe adverse effect on income, physical and mental health, life satisfaction, self-esteem, and marital harmony. However, these studies all too often overlook the possibility that the people in question had such problems even before they retired. More carefully controlled longitudinal studies indicate that the effects of retirement are considerably more positive. Retirement does bring a drop in income, but this often involves little or no change in the retiree's standard of living. Although there are exceptions, retirement does *not* in general cause ill physical or psychological health, feelings of uselessness and depression, dissatisfaction with life in general, declines in self-esteem, or increased marital strife. Some jobs are not intrinsically satisfying, and some employees do not mind retirement because they value the extrinsic aspects of work more highly. Or some employees who do enjoy the intrinsic aspects of their jobs may decide that 40 years of work is quite enough, and that it is time for a new life-style. While there are those who continue to work into their seventies and beyond, retirement has become a respected and desirable life event in our society. The majority of adults welcome it as an earned reward for their many years of work and retire voluntarily in order to pursue other activities.

The plight of those individuals who do suffer severe financial and emotional problems during retirement is a painful one, and their problems should not be underestimated. Future research in this area may profitably focus on identifying and assisting those who are likely to experience such difficulties. But the empirical evidence clearly indicates that the lot of most retirees has improved dramatically during the last three decades; few lead impoverished lives, either financially or socially. Retirement is most often a positive and welcome event, one that opens the way to a rewarding and busy twilight of the human life span.

The Economic Future of the Elderly: Can America Afford to Grow Old?

PROJECTED TRENDS

Although the majority of retirees are financially comfortable, there are troublesome signs regarding the economic future of the elderly in this country. We have noted some of these trends previously in this book.

First of all, the number and proportion of elderly persons are expected to increase dramatically during the next 50 years. (See Chapter 1.) This is particularly true for the very old (persons above the age of 85), many of whom will suffer from chronic health problems that require extensive and expensive health care.

A second trend involves the changing ratio between the number of persons in the work force and those who are not. As shown in Table 9.3, the ratio of nonworkers to workers is expected to increase substantially by

Table 9.3
Ratio of nonworkers to workers and dependency ratios, 1960–2030 (projected).

	1960	1970	1980	1990	2010	2030
Ratio of nonworkers to workers	1.26	1.14	.94	.85	.78	.92
Total age dependency ratio	.72	.67	.55	.56	.55	.70

Note: The ratio of nonworkers to workers is the ratio of all nonworkers in the population to all workers in the population, regardless of age. The total age dependency ratio is defined as the ratio of the population age 65 and older and below age 16 to the population between ages 16 and 64.

Source: Zedlewski et al. (1989).

Table 9.4
Projected real median income by marital status, age, and sex: 1990–2030.

	1990	2010	2030	Percentage Change 1990–2010	2010–2030
Married Couples	$15,530	$24,390	$36,660	+57	+50
Age: 65–69	17,260	28,180	40,100	+63	+42
70–79	14,956	23,920	36,830	+60	+54
80+	12,620	16,180	29,080	+28	+80
Unmarried Men	$7,200	$10,850	$16,860	+51	+55
Age: 65–69	8,360	14,680	18,240	+76	+24
70–79	7,600	11,750	17,880	+55	+52
80+	6,321	8,490	14,350	+34	+69
Unmarried Women	$6,000	$8,090	$12,900	+35	+59
Age: 65–69	6,320	10,070	14,950	+59	+48
70–79	6,200	8,440	13,740	+36	+63
80+	5,620	7,280	11,520	+30	+58

Source: Zedlewski et al. (1989).

the year 2030. At that time, there will be approximately one nonworker for every working person—a sizable group that will require some form of financial support.

To be sure, the gains in income among the elderly that have occurred during the last decade are expected to continue for the next 40 years. This is due in part to increased Social Security benefits, and to the greater availability of private pension funds. In fact, a recent study (Zedlewski et al., 1989) suggests that the income of adults age 65 and older will increase by approximately 50 percent between 1990 and 2030. (See Table 9.4.) But if much of this increase is to come from Social Security, the resources of this program may well be strained beyond the breaking point.

Taken together, then, these trends raise an important question: Will we be able to support the elderly in the style to which they have become accustomed? To answer this question, we must examine the major federal government support programs and how they work.

FEDERAL GOVERNMENT PROGRAMS

Social Security.   Currently, about 92 percent of all civilian workers must make Social Security payments. These workers are therefore eligible to receive benefits when they retire or if they become disabled before they retire.

The large majority of Social Security benefits are paid to retirees in the form of a monthly pension, or—in the case of health care—through Medicare. A retiree's exact monthly pension depends on many factors: the age when benefits begin, the number of eligible family members, and current earnings. In 1990, a retired married couple received an average of $10,800 per year.

Both employers and employees pay equal amounts into Social Security. In 1990, each paid 7.65 percent on the first $48,600 of the employee's income. Recent legislation has already slightly increased this rate, and it is likely to increase further in the years ahead. A large surplus of funds must be accumulated to support the large number of elderly persons who will become eligible for Social Security and to keep future workers from having to bear this entire burden (Quinn & Burkhauser, 1990). Yet as we observed earlier in this chapter, young adults may well object to having substantial contributions to Social Security deducted from their paychecks.

One way to reduce the amount needed by Social Security is to delay the age of retirement beyond 65, which is exactly what Congress did in the 1983 Social Security Amendments. Beginning in the year 2000 and continuing until 2022, the retirement age will increase by two months each year. Full Social Security benefits will therefore be delayed until age 67. However, it remains to be seen whether this strategy (along with increased payments) will resolve the problems that face Social Security.

Medicare. The second major expenditure of Social Security dollars is the Medicare program. In 1984, Medicare spent an average of $2,051 per person over the age of 65. (See Table 9.5.)

Medicare consists of two parts: Hospital Insurance (also called Part A), and Medical Insurance (Part B). (See Kane & Kane, 1990.) Medicare's Hospital Insurance *helps* pay for four basic health care services: inpatient

Table 9.5

Per capita personal health care expenditures for people 65 years of age and older, by source and type of service: 1984.

	Type of Service				
Source of Funds	Total Care	Hospital	Physician	Nursing Home	Other Care
Total per capita	$4,202	$1,900	$868	$880	$554
Private	1,379	216	344	457	362
Consumer	1,363	209	344	451	359
Out-of-pocket	1,059	59	227	441	332
Insurance	304	150	117	10	27
Other private	16	7	1	6	3
Government	2,823	1,684	524	423	192
Medicare	2,051	1,420	502	19	110
Medicaid	536	91	16	365	63
Other government	236	172	6	39	19

Source: U.S. Senate Special Committee on Aging (1987–1988).

hospital care, care in a skilled nursing facility, home health care, and hospice care (health care for the terminally ill). However, there are limits on the amounts that Hospital Insurance pays for each type of care. For example, care in a skilled nursing facility is provided for only a limited period of time after an individual is first hospitalized. In addition, the individual has to qualify as needing skilled nursing care rather than just custodial care. Medical Insurance helps pay for doctor's services (e.g., visiting a doctor's office for an illness), hospital outpatient services, and some additional services and supplies not covered by Part A.

The large majority of people are automatically enrolled in Medicare when they become eligible for Social Security benefits. All eligible individuals automatically receive Hospital Insurance coverage (Part A). To receive Medical Insurance coverage (Part B), however, individuals must pay a small monthly premium. Like most other health insurance plans, both parts of Medicare have deductibles and coinsurance—costs that must be either paid by the individual, or covered through a private supplemental insurance plan. Users of Medicare services will readily agree that dealing with this system is often complicated and frustrating.

In contrast to Social Security, predicting future Medicare outlays is very difficult. Because the number of beneficiaries and the use and cost of medical services have increased considerably, the growth in Medicare spending has been rapid: It increased by more than 11 percent per year from 1973 to 1984 (Aaron, Bosworth, & Burtless, 1989). To address the increasing costs of Medicare, Congress recently passed legislation that increased the taxes paid by workers into the hospital insurance fund, placed limits on the amounts paid to hospitals and doctors for services provided to the elderly, and increased the amount paid by elderly persons who use Medicare services. Yet here again, whether this action will resolve the problems facing Medicare remains to be seen.

Medicaid. Medicaid is a combined federal and state program that pays for health care for the poor. To be eligible for Medicaid, an individual must have *both* a low income *and* few assets that can be converted into income. Each state sets its own criteria of eligibility for Medicaid and determines what services will be covered under this program. Medicaid is designed to assist the poor regardless of age, but about 37 percent of its resources are spent on services for the elderly. Medicaid is the principal source of public financing for nursing home care.

Medicare pays very little for nursing home care, so disabled elderly persons who cannot live independently often must pay for years of such care out of their own pockets. Because one year in a nursing home costs an average of $25,000, even those elderly people who have considerable resources can quickly use up their life savings, as well as their pensions. Once this happens, and if their pension incomes are low enough, they finally become eligible for Medicaid.

Many policymakers object to a health care system that forces people to become paupers. To address this problem, some individuals have proposed private and government insurance plans that would pay for long-term health care for the elderly. Currently, however, few people are willing to spend private funds to pay for such a plan, and the government is very reluctant to institute yet another health care service that will become extremely expensive as the population ages. At present, therefore, this important and troublesome issue remains unresolved.

AFTERWORD

Ultimately, the economic well-being of the elderly is closely tied to the economic well-being of our nation as a whole. All of the projections presented in the preceding section are based on the assumption of continued economic growth and a reduction in the federal deficit. To the extent that we fail to achieve these goals, the elderly (along with everyone else) are likely to suffer economic hardships (Aaron, Bosworth, & Burtless, 1989).

Even if our economy remains relatively sound, the increasing number of elderly Americans may well place a severe strain on Social Security and other resources. Dealing with such problems will require insightful political leadership and quite possibly some sacrifices for all of us. As *Newsweek* put it (May 6, 1985): "If a society can be judged by the way it treats its elderly, then we are not without honor—so far. But as we all grow older, that honor will demand an even higher price."

Summary

WORK AND ADULT DEVELOPMENT

For most of us, work provides the income necessary to support ourselves and our families. Work may also be interesting for its own sake, contribute to our self-esteem and sense of identity, and provide important social rewards and punishments. Thus work exerts a significant effect on the quality of our lives and overall well-being in two major ways: intrinsically and extrinsically.

Aging appears to have little detrimental effect on job performance in some professional and artistic fields. For example, artists and musicians often do their best work late in life. Conversely, the most productive years for mathematicians and professional athletes occur during their twenties and thirties. However, the research evidence in this area is equivocal. The most justified conclusion appears to be that age often bears little or no relationship to job performance, but that some exceptions may be expected in certain jobs and professions.

There is some indication that young adults are more concerned with chances for advancement and for professional and personal development than are middle-aged and older workers. In general, however, the relationship between aging and job satisfaction is far from clear. Although the data are too equivocal to permit any firm conclusions, there is no convincing evidence that older workers tend to be less satisfied with their jobs than young adults.

Older workers are less likely than young adults to be injured on the job, or to be absent. But when they do sustain an injury, they are more likely to be disabled and to require more time to recover.

Even though many older adults are as competent and as satisfied as young employees, and even though federal legislation prohibits the denial of employment to those over 40 because of their age, severe age discrimination still exists in the workplace. This is due in part to negative stereotypes about older workers, who are more likely to be incorrectly perceived as resistant to change, slow to make decisions, and untrainable. Also, pensions and other fringe benefits for older workers are more costly to the employer.

Some theorists have argued that midlife career changes are becoming increasingly common, but there is little statistical evidence to support this conclusion. When such career changes do occur, they are most often caused by such external pressures as losing one's old job.

The study of work and aging is more problematical than might be expected. Job satisfaction and productivity are multidimensional variables, and chronological age provides only limited information about human capacities. Such age-related variables as job level and job complexity appear to be more closely related to job satisfaction and performance than age per se. To discriminate against employees over 40 solely because of age is not only illegal and harmful to the individual, but is also likely to cost the organization valuable and productive workers.

There are significantly more men than women in the labor force, but the percent of women has increased substantially during the last half century. Women have made considerable inroads into some occupations once dominated by men. They have not done nearly as well with regard to managerial and administrative positions, and their income has remained at only about 64 percent of what men receive.

Some theorists have argued that the difficulty of various jobs should be rated numerically, so that men and women can be assured of comparable pay for comparable work. Other theorists point out that although there is still sex discrimination in the workplace, women have hurt their own chances for advancement and higher pay by willingly discontinuing their work in order to bear and raise children. They conclude that the fairest course is to allow pay to fluctuate freely in accordance with supply and demand. With the difficulty of evaluating the demands made by different jobs, it appears unlikely that an effective system for determining comparable worth will be forthcoming in the near future.

Women who elect to pursue full-time careers are no less (or more) satisfied with their adult years than are women who opt for motherhood and raising a family. Married women who work enjoy better mental health than those who do not, but are also more likely to experience interrole conflicts. In the majority of couples, women still have primary responsibility for family matters, so those who elect to combine work and family roles may find it difficult to meet their obligations in both areas. Sex discrimination remains a significant problem in the world of work, but the influence of women has increased considerably during the past four decades and is likely to continue to do so in the future.

RETIREMENT

A retired person is one who is not employed at a full-time paying job *and* who receives at least some income from a pension earned through prior employment. The proportion of older people who retire has increased dramatically since the turn of the century. Although it is often assumed that mandatory retirement policies compel many people to leave work sooner than they would like, this belief is not supported by the empirical evidence. In fact, more and more people are opting for early retirement.

Most employees past age 45 who speculate about retirement view it as positive and desirable, and regard it as a reward that they deserve for having worked for so many years. Nor do most adults anticipate financial problems during retirement. Those who hold higher-level positions tend to regard retirement more favorably because their financial position is sound, but they are also more likely to postpone retiring because they find their work to be too enjoyable. Employees with low-level jobs are likely to favor retirement in theory, because their jobs tend to be dull and routine, but they often cannot afford to retire early because of their low income and poor pension plans. Thus middle-level employees are the ones most likely to opt for early retirement because they tend to have adequate retirement programs but don't enjoy their jobs enough to want to continue past working age. It is a common expectation of these workers that life will be more satisfying if they retire. Age discrimination, family and peer pressures, and health are also factors in the decision to retire early. However, the importance of health may well be exaggerated: To many employees, health is undoubtedly a more socially acceptable reason for retiring early than admitting that they just don't want to work anymore.

Some theorists have suggested that retirees tend to proceed through a series of distinct psychological and emotional stages, such as a honeymoon effect, disenchantment, rest and relaxation, reorientation, the retirement routine, and termination. However, the research evidence concerning this model is sparse and somewhat equivocal. Perhaps the most important conclusion is that some retirees ultimately experience strong and prolonged feelings of disenchantment, while many others do not. This appears to depend in large part on the individual's life style prior to retirement. Those who tended to have adequate finances, numerous satisfying hobbies and recreational activities, good health, and happy marriages prior to retiring are likely to find it considerably easier to adjust to retirement and to enjoy these years. Those with poor finances, few avocations, ill health, and unhappy marriages before retiring may well find that retirement is disenchanting and depressing.

In general, the majority of elderly adults find retirement to be a satisfying and busy period. The financial status of retirees has improved markedly during the last 30 years, and the stereotype of the elderly retiree who lives from hand to mouth on a meager income and who resides in a drab and dingy apartment must be rejected in the light of the available research evidence. Many retirees find that leaving the world of full-time work gives them time not previously available to pursue desired activities, although some find it necessary to accept low-level, part-time jobs in order to keep busy. There is no indication that retirement per se exerts a significant negative effect on the physical and mental health of the retiree, or that it has an adverse effect on the marriages of most couples.

The plight of those who do suffer severe financial and emotional problems during retirement should not be underestimated. But retirement is most often a positive and welcome event, one that opens the way to a rewarding and busy twilight of the human life span.

THE ECONOMIC FUTURE OF THE ELDERLY

Although the majority of retirees are financially comfortable, there are troublesome signs regarding the economic future of the elderly in this country. The number of elderly persons, particularly the very old, is expected to increase dramatically during the next 50 years. Furthermore, there will be about one nonworker for every working person by the year 2030. Whether Social Security, Medicare, and Medicaid can cope with so many older adults and nonworkers remains to be seen.

One currently unresolved problem involves nursing home care. Medicare pays very little for this, and one must be virtually poor in order to qualify for Medicaid. Yet new long-term health care plans for the elderly are unlikely to be approved, because they will become extremely expensive as the population ages.

If we fail to achieve continued economic growth and to reduce the federal deficit, the elderly (along with everyone else) are likely to suffer economic hardships. In any case, continuing to provide good support for the elderly is likely to become a major challenge in the years ahead.

Study Questions

1. What is the relationship between job satisfaction and satisfaction with life in general? Why might a person who is very satisfied with his or her job be dissatisfied with life in general? Why might a person who is satisfied

with life in general be very dissatisfied with his or her job? Are these likely possibilities? If so, can you give examples from your own life or from the life of someone you know? Clarify.

2. Although illegal, age and sex discrimination are still prevalent in the workplace. Why do employers continue to engage in these activities? What harm does this do? Other than litigation, can anything be done to reduce the amount of age and sex discrimination?

3. What can you do to make your retirement more satisfying (a) now? (b) on reaching middle age? (c) when you retire? What factors are likely to make retirement dissatisfying? Which is more common in this country, retirement that is satisfying or dissatisfying?

4. Is our current Social Security system unfair to young adults because they must contribute too much to support too many older adults who do not need financial aid? Is the Social Security system unfair to retirees? Or is the Social Security system generally fair to both young adults and retirees?

5. How will the increasing number of older adults in this country affect such federal programs as Social Security, Medicare, and Medicaid in this next decade? What changes in these programs are likely to be necessary?

Terms to Remember

Age discrimination

Early retirement

Extrinsic benefits of work

Intrinsic benefits of work

Job satisfaction

Medicaid

Medicare

Phases of retirement

Retired person

Retirement

Sex discrimination

Social Security

Work force

Part IV

Crises and Problems

Chapter 10
Stress and Coping

Mimi Forsyth/Monkmeyer Press Photo Service

A capable college student becomes so tense during an important examination that she cannot recall even the simplest facts and turns in a blank paper. A college football team needs to win its final game to earn a bowl invitation, trails by two points late in the game, and fights its way down to the opponent's goal line, only to have its normally reliable field goal specialist kick the ball so low that the defense blocks it easily. An employee who must deal every day with irascible customers and a demanding supervisor, but who cannot find another job or afford to quit, develops intense stomach pains.

Stories about the adverse effects of stress on human beings appear frequently in the news media. We hear about major traumatic events that result in serious physical or mental disorders; we read about certain types of work that are considered stressful enough to cause physical illnesses; we find that some athlete's performance was subpar because he or she experienced too much stress. However, stress is not always disadvantageous. A student who is too nonchalant about a forthcoming exam may fail to prepare adequately, and receive a poor grade. Or members of a top-rated football team may be so relaxed for a game with an inferior opponent that they suffer an ignominious defeat. Too much stress may well be injurious, but too little may result in lackluster and inferior performance.

Nevertheless, the debilitating effects of excessive stress are of primary concern in today's society. Numerous programs have been designed to teach people how to cope with stress. Many self-help books claim that heart attacks, depression, anxiety, hypertension, and other health problems can be avoided by changing our life-styles in ways that will reduce stress. And a thriving pharmaceutical industry dispenses vast quantities of anti-anxiety medications, such as Valium and Librium. Thus stress is widely regarded as a major disrupting force in the lives of individuals of all ages, and concern with this problem appears to have reached epidemic proportions.

What might this imply about the course of adult development? Conceivably, life may become more stressful with increasing age. Adults must typically contend with such new and demanding situations as work, marriage, raising children, divorce, the death of a loved one, and, eventually, retirement and old age. However, the opposite hypothesis is also a reasonable one. That is, we may well become more sure of ourselves as we grow older, and more established in work and family roles. The security provided by this firmer foundation in life, and increased maturity, may render us less vulnerable to those sources of stress that we encounter.

In this chapter, we examine empirical data dealing with stress and coping during adulthood. We begin with a brief historical tour of the development of scientific interest in stress research, which will illustrate the diverse approaches used by various theorists. We then define the concept of stress by presenting and discussing a general theoretical model. We conclude by examining the relationship between aging and stress, with emphasis on those sources of stress typically encountered during the adult life course and ways of coping with them.

The Scientific Study of Stress

HISTORICAL BACKGROUND

Fight or Flight.
The scientific study of stress is a relatively recent phenomenon. Early in the twentieth century, Walter Cannon observed that animals must respond quickly to life-threatening challenges in the environment in order to survive. Depending on the specific circumstances, the appropriate reaction might be to fight (as when faced with a weaker opponent) or to flee (if menaced by a superior enemy). Accordingly, Cannon characterized the standard response to danger as the **fight-or-flight reaction.** He showed that it is associated with the activation of specific aspects of the central nervous system, which results in increased cardiac output, heart rate, and arterial pressure (Cannon, 1929). Thus Cannon was among the first to investigate the effects of threatening external stimuli on an organism's behavior.

The General Adaptation Syndrome.
Undoubtedly the most prominent researcher in the field of stress and coping is Hans Selye. He dates the origin of the concept of stress to an experience he had in 1936, as a student of medicine at the University of Prague. Selye attended an introductory lecture on diagnosis presented by a famous hematologist, von Jaksch, who questioned five patients suffering from unrelated maladies. Without using any complicated instruments or chemical examinations, von Jaksch correctly diagnosed each of the patients. Selye was impressed by this demonstration, but he was also puzzled by the fact that von Jaksch

> [had not] said a word about all those signs and symptoms of disease which were perfectly obvious even to me, without previous knowledge of practical medicine. . . . All five patients, whatever their disease (one suffered from cancer of the stomach, another from tuberculosis, yet another from intense burns) had something in common: *they all looked and felt sick.* This may seem ridiculously childish and self-evident, but it was because I wondered about the obvious that the concept of *stress* was born. (Selye, 1983, p. 3)

Later, while attempting to discover a new sex hormone, Selye observed that laboratory rats given multiple doses of a crude ovarian extract developed such symptoms as gastric ulcers and enlargement of the adrenal gland. On investigating further, he found that crude extracts from other organs, extreme cold or heat, pain, and infectious agents all produced similar results. He therefore concluded that organisms exposed to a noxious stimulus of any kind exhibit the same pattern of responses. To Selye, this **General Adaptation Syndrome** consists of three stages:

1. *The Alarm Reaction.* When an organism is confronted with a stressful situation, the immediate reaction is alarm. This represents a general call to arms of the body's defenses and is accompanied by such typical symptoms of injury as excessively rapid heartbeat (tachycardia), loss of muscle tone, decreased temperature, and decreased blood pressure.

2. *The Stage of Resistance.* During this stage, the body tries to limit the effects of the stressful situation. The symptoms evidenced during the first stage diminish or disappear, and the organism is prepared for either fight or flight.

3. *The Stage of Exhaustion.* If the choice between fight or flight proves to be unsuccessful in reducing stress, the organism loses its ability to adapt to the situation and enters the stage of exhaustion. This can result in tissue break-down or even in death.

Each of these stages is accompanied by specific physiological changes. During the alarm reaction, for example, the cells of the adrenal cortex discharge secretory granules into the bloodstream. Conversely, during the stage of resistance, the cortex becomes rich in secretory granules. According to Selye, if these physiological changes do not occur, the organism is not experiencing stress.

In his later work, Selye (e.g., 1974) made two important additional contributions. He pointed out that not all stress is bad; in fact, too little stress can also have negative effects. Thus the moderate stress that may help a student or athlete to perform well must be distinguished from excessive stress, which is damaging because the organism cannot cope with the situation and enters the stage of exhaustion.

Selye also observed that stressful situations affect different individuals differently, depending on their biological makeup, age, training, dietary deficiencies, and other factors. For example, some athletes seem unusually able to rise to the occasion and perform well when the game hangs in the balance; others are more likely to "choke" under pressure and commit grave errors. Or a job that drives one employee to stomach ulcers may be handled with relative calm by another worker.

Although Selye's work represents a landmark in the study of stress, it does suffer from some significant shortcomings. (See, for example, Elliott & Eisdorfer, 1982; Stotland, 1984.) One of these concerns his definition of stress, which suffers from circularity: A stressful event is defined as whatever evokes the General Adaptation Syndrome, and the occurrence of this syndrome is what tells us that an event is stressful. In fact, arriving at an acceptable definition of stress is far from an easy task—as we will see in the following section.

THE PROBLEM OF DEFINING STRESS

As was the case with *intelligence* (Chapter 6) and *personality* (Chapter 7), no single definition of **stress** is widely accepted by researchers in this field.

Stimulus Definitions.   One possible way to define stress is in terms of the external situation: a difficult and all-important examination, a demanding supervisor, and so forth. Thus Cannon focused on those dangerous stimuli that disrupt the organism's normal internal processes, whereas Selye's early research defined stress in terms of the noxious stimulus that evokes the General Adaptation Syndrome.

Although this approach is appealingly simple, it fails to recognize the importance of the organism's behavior. A demanding supervisor may be regarded as a mere annoyance by one employee yet be perceived by a second worker as exerting enormous pressure. A forthcoming examination may cause one student considerable anxiety, while another student reacts with relative calm. Some people exhibit marked signs of stress when they travel by plane, but others do not. In each of these examples, the stimulus object or situation is the same, yet it is considerably more stressful for some individuals than for others. Therefore, some theorists prefer to conceptualize stress in other ways.

Response Definitions.   A second approach is to label the potentially stressful stimulus or situation as the **stressor** and to define stress in terms of the organism's **responses**. Thus Selye ultimately concluded that stress exists if and only if the General Adaptation Syndrome occurs, together with the expected physiological changes (which are supposedly the same for any and all noxious stimuli).

However, this approach has also been criticized as inadequate. There is some evidence that different stressful situations, such as public speaking and physical exercise, produce at least some bodily changes that are markedly different (Mason, 1974). It has also been suggested that an event can be stressful even if no physiological changes are immediately apparent. Furthermore, Selye's conception overlooks the importance of the individual's cognitions: How we interpret a given situation may have much more to do with the degree of stress that we experience than does objective reality. Some data indicate that if a stressor is not viewed as noxious or alarming, it produces physical responses that are negligible or even opposite to those predicted by Selye (Mason, 1971).

More Comprehensive Definitions.   In an effort to resolve these difficulties, some investigators have opted for a more comprehensive approach. They define stress in terms of the entire complex of stressors, responses (including physiological changes, cognitions, expectations, and perceptions), and related intervening variables, or **mediators**. (See, for example, Lazarus, 1966; 1971.)

As an illustration, suppose that you hear footsteps approaching from behind. This stimulus may or may not be a stressor, depending in part on your cognitions and expectations: Do you think that this is a mugger coming to attack you, or a friend or spouse planning to surprise you with a warm welcome? The degree of stress also depends on such mediators as the location and time of day: Are you safely in your home with only your spouse present or anxiously hurrying down a dark and deserted street at 3 A.M.?

As a second example, consider the stimulus of a failing grade on a college midterm examination. This event will be more stressful if the student appraises it as a disaster that cannot be overcome but less stressful if it is perceived as only a minor setback or as a challenge to do better in the future. Mediators that may increase the degree of stress include pressure from one's family to achieve straight A's, having goals that require an unusually high grade-point average (e.g., wishing to apply to medical school), or needing a passing grade in this course to avoid flunking out of school.

Afterword.   Each of the approaches discussed in the preceding section has been praised by some theorists and criticized by others. The inclusion of cognitions and mediators in the definition of stress appears to have distinct advantages, because it helps us to understand why different individuals react differently to the same stressor. Therefore, we will focus on the comprehensive definition in the pages that follow.

A GENERAL MODEL OF STRESS

The relationships among the various components of stress are shown in Figure 10.1. Notice that with one exception, these relationships are bidirectional. For example, stimuli may cause such responses as fight or flight, but

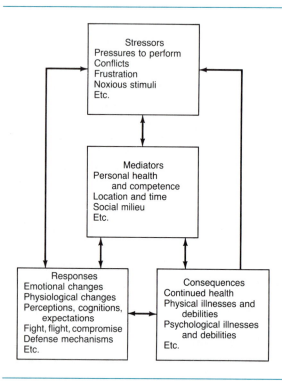

Figure 10.1
A general model of stress.   Source: Modified from Elliott & Eisdorfer (1982, p. 19).

some responses (e.g., cognitions) help to determine whether a stimulus is stressful. A stressor may ultimately lead to physical (or psychological) debilities, and a heart or stomach that has been weakened by stress can make one more vulnerable to subsequent external pressures. Thus stress operates in a circular and dynamic fashion, with each of the components continuously modifying and being modified by the other elements. (See Elliott & Eisdorfer, 1982.) For purposes of discussion, however, it is necessary to treat these components one at a time.

Stressors.   Some stimuli are much more likely to act as stressors than others. Few people would experience stress from a peaceful walk along a serene lake, with the sun shining and cool breezes blowing. Conversely, more than a few would find the following to be stressful.

External Pressures and Overstimulation. If you are required to achieve a level of performance that is very difficult for you or to behave in ways that run counter to your strongest convictions, you may well experience considerable stress. This is particularly true if the pressures continue for a substantial period of time. Common examples include an unusually demanding job, college course, parent, or Army drill sergeant. However, such pressures are not always from the outside. Some people create considerable stress for themselves by establishing goals that they think are reasonable, but which are actually far too demanding and perfectionistic.

Boredom and Understimulation. External pressures are among the best-known sources of stress. Although we all welcome some opportunity to relax and take life easy, having nothing to do for too long can also be stressful. Some people enjoy facing a challenge, improving their skills, and achieving difficult goals and cannot tolerate a succession of tasks that are too easy. Others welcome the excitement of risky vocations or avocations, such as tightrope walkers, test pilots, parachute jumpers, automobile racers, and those who like to take rides on roller coasters. Thus stress and frustration can be caused by external demands and pressures that are too low, as well as those that are too high.

Conflicts. Stress may result from having to make difficult and painful decisions. For example, young men during the 1960s who opposed the Vietnam War had to choose between two very unpalatable alternatives. They could submit to the draft and possibly risk their lives in what they regarded as a bad cause, in order to remain in good social standing; or they could avoid combat by going to prison. (Some sought to escape from this "avoidance-avoidance conflict" by emigrating to other countries, thereby incurring the pain of leaving their homes and loved ones.) Or a conflict may arise because the same object or goal has both positive and negative qualities (an "approach-avoidance conflict"). Thus a shy person may want to approach an attractive stranger and ask for a date, yet fear the possibility of rejection and ridicule. A military commander may have to send troops on a mission that is extremely important but likely to result in a very high casualty rate. Or a hungry laboratory rat may have to run through an electrified grid and receive a moderately painful shock in order to reach a food reward. Either approaching or avoiding the goal is both desirable and undesirable, so some discomfort is inevitable. The greater the strength of the conflicting alternatives, the greater the stress that is likely to result.

Frustration and Disappointment. Stress may also occur when our needs and wishes are frustrated, either by obstacles in the external world or by our own limitations. Examples include being turned down for a job or promotion because another applicant is superior, or because one lacks the necessary skills; losing a loved one or a valued possession; and suffering extended periods of hunger, which are far from uncommon in various parts of the world. The greater the disappointment, or the longer the period of deprivation, the more stress one is likely to experience.

Noxious Stimuli. Stress can also be caused by exposure to such noxious stimuli as cold, heat, pain, and infectious agents. Alternatively, a noxious stimulus may be psychological rather than physical. For example, in marked contrast to tightrope walkers and test pilots, some people break out in a cold sweat when standing on a balcony that is only a few stories high. The more intense the stimulus, the greater the probable stress.

"A Martyrdom of Pinpricks." Numerous minor stressors that occur during the same period of time may have a cumulative effect and produce considerable stress. An individual who accidentally rips a button off a shirt while hurrying to dress for work in the morning, finds an unexpected small dent in the family car, gets caught in moderate rush-hour traffic, and discovers that the coffee machine is out of order on arriving at work may react to this series of relatively trivial aggravations by becoming extremely upset. If one must deal with several *major* stressors at about the same time, such as losing one's job, the death of a loved one, and a serious illness, the effects may well be devastating.

Some of the more common stressors are summarized in Table 10.1. Once again, it is important to remember that these stimuli are only *potential* sources of stress. Their effect on a given individual depends in part on the other components of the model: responses, consequences, and mediators.

Responses.   The importance of such responses as fight or flight, cognitions and expectations, and physiological changes was discussed previously in this chapter. For example, you will probably experience less stress if

- You believe that you can handle a given situation without much difficulty.
- You appraise the situation as a challenge that will enable you to improve your skills or gain desired rewards, or as a welcome source of excitement, rather than as a threat of harm or loss.

- You are able to attack and overcome your opposition.
- You can escape from a threatening or unpleasant stimulus.

There is a third alternative to the fight-or-flight dichotomy posited by Cannon—namely, compromise or surrender. Rather than attacking or fleeing, you might agree that the best course is to obey the dictates of someone else. If you can do so without sacrificing important needs, or harming your self-esteem, you may well achieve a relatively stress-free solution.

Unfortunately, many stressful situations cannot be resolved so easily. Suppose once again that an employee who has an unpleasant job cannot afford to quit, dare not risk being fired by fighting with the boss, but also

Table 10.1
Stressors commonly used in animal and human research.

	Human Research	
Animal Research	Experimental Stimuli	Natural Events
Approach-approach conflicts (having to choose between two positive objects)	Approach-approach conflicts	Bereavement
	Approach-avoidance conflicts	Changes in status (e.g., job, salary, marriage)
	Avoidance-avoidance conflicts	
Approach-avoidance conflicts (being presented with an object that has both positive and negative qualities)	Electric shock	Conflicts
	Loss of prestige	Daily "hassles"
	Noise	Frustration
Avoidance-avoidance conflicts (having to choose between two negative objects)	Overstimulation	Migration
	Sleep deprivation	Physical illness (including surgery and hospitalization)
Competition	Threatening, unpleasant films	Pressure to perform or achieve
Electric shock	Uncontrollable situations	Retirement
Exposure to cold	Understimulation	Social isolation
Exposure to heat		Threats to self-esteem
Exposure to novel stimuli		Traumatic experiences
Food deprivation		
Handling		
Immersion in ice water		
Immobilization		
Maternal deprivation		
Prolonged, forced swimming		
Sensory deprivation		
Sleep deprivation		
Social crowding		
Social isolation		

Source: Modified from Elliott & Eisdorfer (1982, pp. 14, 16).

Major disasters are not the only causes of stress. Numerous minor stressors, such as one's car breaking down, may have a cumulative effect that results in considerable stress. (Nancy Bates/The Picture Cube)

cannot surrender to demands that seem excessive and unfair. As has been shown by Freud and others, we may well try to make such bad situations more tolerable by unconsciously or (less often) consciously adopting various psychological **defense mechanisms**. Thus, we may refuse to admit even to ourselves that a situation is far too stressful ("denial of reality") and blindly continue on a course that is damaging to our health. Or we may direct our anger at a safer target, such as a spouse or family pet, instead of the boss ("displacement"). There are many such defense mechanisms, all of which provide a temporary measure of emotional relief. (See Table 10.2; Ewen, 1988, pp. 32–38.)

Although we all use defense mechanisms from time to time, they may well make matters worse in the long run. Because they conceal the truth from oneself, they preclude an effective solution to the problem; and since their operation is usually unconscious, the user cannot readily discard them in favor of a better course of action. Thus, although our thoughts and expectations may make a situation more stressful, it is also possible to encounter stress without being consciously aware of it. That is, we may flee from stress psychologically as well as physically.

Consequences.   The responses evoked by stressors may have various long-term **consequences**. These include physical disorders, such as stomach ulcers, colitis, or headaches; psychological disorders, such as frequent anxiety or depression; or perhaps continued good health, if the level of stress is neither too high nor too low.

As elsewhere in this model, the relationship between responses and consequences is bidirectional. That is, consequences can also make certain responses

Table 10.2

Some common defense mechanisms

Defense Mechanism	Definition	Example
Denial of reality	Refusing to believe, or even to perceive, some threat in the external world	A person receives criticism that is clearly justified, but believes it is wholly erroneous and due to prejudice.
Displacement	Transferring feelings or behaviors, usually unconsciously, from one object to another that is less threatening	A person angry with the boss remains quiet at work, then releases this anger by shouting at his or her spouse.
Fantasy	Gratifying unfulfilled needs by imagining situations in which they are satisfied	A poor athlete pretends to be an All-American football player.
Identification	Reducing painful feelings of self-hate by becoming like illustrious objects or people	A socially unpopular or lonely person dresses like a famous rock music star.
Intellectualization	Unconsciously separating threatening emotions from the associated thoughts or events	A patient in psychotherapy discusses his or her painful problems in a dry voice, devoid of feeling.
Overcompensation	Unconsciously attempting to make up for a deficiency in one area by excelling in another, and carrying this to damaging extremes	A person who is very short, or who suffers from extreme self-hate, becomes a warmonger or dictator.
Projection	Unconsciously attributing one's own threatening impulses, emotions, or beliefs to other people or things	A person who is murderously angry, but finds this too threatening to accept consciously, believes that others are out to get him or her.
Rationalization	Using and believing superficially plausible explanations in order to justify illicit behavior and reduce feelings of guilt	People who cheat on their tax returns or school examinations justify themselves by arguing that "everyone does it."
Reaction formation	Unconsciously adopting the opposite of one's true (but highly threatening) beliefs, emotions, and impulses	A person who has homosexual desires, but finds this too threatening to face consciously, becomes an outspoken crusader against homosexuality.
Regression	Unconsciously adopting behaviors typical of an earlier, and safer, time in one's life	An adult faced with a traumatic life event, such as a painful divorce, becomes childishly dependent on his or her parents.
Repression	Unconsciously eliminating threatening material from one's mind and being unable to recall it on demand	Despite intense effort, an adult cannot remember the strong anger felt toward his or her parents during childhood.

more or less likely. Thus a physical or psychological debility may lead to more pronounced physiological changes when under stress, or to the greater use of defense mechanisms.

It is not always easy to distinguish between responses and consequences. The latter tend to occur some time after the stressor, whereas responses are more immediate. Also, consequences are more clearly identifiable as good or bad. Fight, flight, compromise, and even the defense mechanisms are not necessarily desirable or undesirable in and of themselves. Rather, it is the consequences of these responses that we typically assess as positive or negative. For example, fighting or confrontation may rectify a major social injustice or injure an innocent party or destroy a marriage. Running away may save the life of someone threatened by a wild animal in a forest or cost the lives of one's fellow soldiers in battle. Expecting to do well on a task may lead to better performance or to overconfidence and failure. Compromise and surrender may enable one to profit from the superior plans and ideas of someone else or lead to staggering violations of moral and ethical behavior. Thus the German soldiers who helped run concentration camps during World War II typically sought to excuse their heinous deeds and reduce stress by arguing that they were "only following orders."

Mediators.   As noted previously, mediators help us to understand why the same stressor has different effects on different people. Common mediators include one's personal competence, physical health, and ability to ward off illnesses and external threats; the physical setting, such as location and time of day; and the social milieu, as with the support or lack of support provided by one's immediate family.

An Illustrative Example: Environmental Demands and Personal Competence. As a further illustration of the general model, let us consider once again the potentially stressful effects of external pressures.

Some environments are more demanding than others and are more likely to evoke symptoms of stress. The relationship between this potential stressor and an individual's responses is mediated by **personal competence**: Some people are considerably more capable than others and are better able to deal with more extreme levels of pressure. Furthermore, people tend to be more competent in some respects than in others. Thus an athlete who can make quick and highly skilled physical movements, but who is not overly high in verbal or mathematical ability, may experience more stress during a classroom examination than on the football field. Personal competence is a multidimensional variable; it includes biological health, ego strength, cognitive skills, and sensorimotor functioning. To determine the likelihood that a given situation will be stressful, we must therefore consider the types of skills that are required and the individual's competence in these areas.

One interesting theoretical model that deals with these relationships is depicted in Figure 10.2. Consider first the individual whose life situation

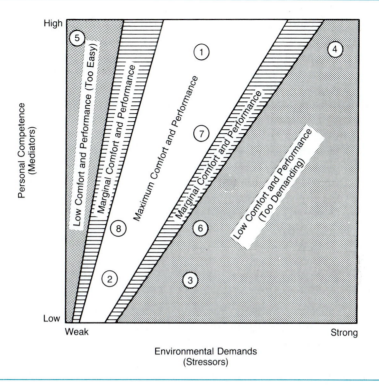

High
Low

Personal Competence
(Mediators)

Weak
Strong

Low Comfort and Performance (Too Easy)
Marginal Comfort and Performance
Maximum Comfort and Performance
Marginal Comfort and Performance
Low Comfort and Performance (Too Demanding)

Environmental Demands
(Stressors)

Figure 10.2

Environmental demands, personal competence, and stress.   Source: Modified from Lawton (1980, p. 12).

corresponds to position number 1 (high personal competence and moderate environmental stress). Suppose that this individual is a middle-aged man who lives in an area with a high crime rate. He is physically agile, however, and his self-confidence is very high. Because of these competencies, his response to his demanding environment is markedly positive: He goes about his business despite the risks and actually enjoys his self-image as a courageous individual who will not be cowed by the young toughs in his neighborhood (Lawton, 1980).

Person number 2 is much less competent than individual number 1. Yet both are equally free of emotional strain, and both perform up to the limit of their respective capabilities, because they are both well suited to their environments. That is, much fewer demands are made on person number 2. Placing the second individual in the environment of the first one would produce considerable stress, emotional disturbances, and a breakdown in performance (position number 3).

No matter how high your personal competence may be, there is always the possibility of encountering so much stress that your behavior will deteriorate markedly; everyone has a breaking point. Person number 4 is extremely competent, but is under so much pressure that she responds as adversely as individual number 3.

Person number 5 illustrates a point made previously in this chapter, namely that experiencing too little pressure for too long can also be stressful. This might be the case, for example, when fairly competent persons must reside in long-term care facilities that offer few opportunities to exercise their skills and abilities. The area of this section is considerably smaller than that of the section at the extreme right, however, indicating that people are more likely to suffer from too many environmental demands than from too few. For both persons number 4 and number 5, some of the possible consequences of experiencing so much stress include depression, social withdrawal, and/or the loss of self-respect and self-confidence.

How does this model concern aging? Suppose that as individual number 1 grows toward old age, his personal competence decreases to position number 6. (Research evidence indicates that this is more likely to be the exception than the rule, but it is true for some elderly adults. See, for example, Lawton, 1980.) His environment has not changed, but he no longer has sufficient competence to deal with it effectively, so he is likely to show symptoms of stress. He might therefore undergo training designed to improve his personal competence, possibly increasing it to a level that will once again make the environmental demands tolerable (position number 7). If his decline in competence is irreversible, or if he does not wish to undergo such training, he could instead move to a less stressful environment (position number 8). Other common ways of achieving a temporary reduction in environmental demands are simply sitting back and relaxing for a while or taking a much-needed vacation.

Although the model depicted in Figure 10.2 is logically appealing, further research is needed to evaluate its practical and predictive utility. After you develop ulcers, colitis, or a severe depression, it is easy to argue that your personal competence was poorly matched to the demands of your environment. But it is very difficult to predict in advance whether a given level of environmental demands, together with a particular level of personal competence, will or will not prove to be stressful. Nevertheless, the model does help to clarify the relationships between stress, environmental demands, and personal competence. It also illustrates once again that stress must be understood in terms of stressors, responses, mediators, and consequences.

Afterword.   In the preceding pages, we have seen that stress is not a simple phenomenon. Stressors may cause certain kinds of responses, or responses may cause certain stimuli to be more or less stressful. A response may lead to desirable or undesirable consequences, or a particular consequence may make certain responses more or less likely. Some people find a given stimulus to be quite stressful, while others do not. And some mediators affect the relationships among the other components of the model. Thus it is virtually impossible to make simple statements that are also accurate, like "situation X is always stressful" or "stressor A invariably leads to response B."

We cannot expect any one research study to deal with all (or even most) of this ever-changing, interrelated system. Of necessity, stress researchers typically simplify matters by studying one aspect of the model at a time. With this caveat in mind, let us now proceed to examine the evidence concerning the relationship between stress and aging.

Stress and Aging

THE EFFECTS OF MAJOR LIFE EVENTS

Methodological Issues. To reduce the study of stress to manageable proportions, some researchers prefer to focus on the effects of major life events. It is reasonable to hypothesize that events like marriage and divorce are at least somewhat stressful, even though different individuals may well respond in different ways, and that some of these events are more stressful than others. Accordingly, some investigators have sought to quantify the amount of stress caused by various life events (Holmes & Holmes, 1970; Holmes & Rahe, 1967; Rahe & Arthur, 1978).

Using this approach, the most stressful of all events, the death of a spouse, is arbitrarily assigned a rating of 100. The degree of stress associated with other events is then estimated relative to this standard, based on responses

Even joyful events, such as marriage, may be significant sources of stress. Some investigators regard marriage as more stressful than being fired from a job, although this is a complicated issue that also depends on such personal factors as age and competence. (Michael Siluk/The Image Works)

obtained from test populations. For example, divorce is accorded an intensity rating of 73; marriage, 50; and trouble with one's boss, 23. (See Table 10.3.) If you have been exposed in recent months to events that sum to 300 or more, it is estimated that the probability of your developing a major illness within the next two years is as high as .80.

The numerical scale shown in Table 10.3 is commonly cited in textbooks and articles. Yet it is controversial, and has been strongly attacked on methodological grounds. This scale implies that stressful life events, notably those

Table 10.3
Stressful life events: The social readjustment rating scale.

Life Event	Scale of Impact	Life Event	Scale of Impact
Death of spouse	100	Trouble with in-laws	29
Divorce	73	Outstanding personal achievement	28
Marital separation	65	Wife begins or stops work	26
Jail term	63	Beginning or ending school	26
Death of close family member	63	Change in living conditions	25
Personal injury or illness	53	Revision of personal habits	24
Marriage	50	Trouble with boss	23
Fired at work	47	Change in work hours or conditions	20
Marital reconciliation	45	Change in residence	20
Retirement	45	Change in schools	20
Change in health of family member	44	Change in recreation	19
Pregnancy	40	Change in church activities	19
Sex difficulties	39	Change in social activities	18
Gain of new family member	39	Small mortgage or loan	17
Business readjustment	39	Change in sleeping habits	16
Change in financial state	38	Change in number of family get-togethers	15
Death of close friend	37	Change in eating habits	15
Change to different line of work	36	Vacation	13
Change in number of arguments with spouse	35	Christmas	12
High mortgage	31	Minor violations of the law	11
Foreclosure of mortgage or loan	30		
Change in responsibilities at work	29		
Son or daughter leaving home	29		

Source: Holmes and Rahe (1967).

with high intensity ratings, *cause* such undesirable consequences as major illnesses. However, some of these life events may well *result from* existing disorders. (Recall once again that in the general model of stress, the relationships between potential stressors, responses, consequences, and mediators are primarily bidirectional.) Having sexual difficulties or more arguments with one's spouse, or being fired at work, could be due to an underlying psychological or physical illness. If this disorder then becomes more evident in subsequent months, it is clearly erroneous to conclude that an otherwise healthy individual was laid low by stress. (See Elliott & Eisdorfer, 1982; Siegler, 1980.)

This scale also focuses on events that require us to make significant readjustments in our lives: learning to live without a spouse, moving to a new location or a new school, changing jobs, and so on. Yet stress can be caused by chronic conditions that do not necessitate personal change. For example, an employee may face a consistent overload or underload at work. No daily or monthly readjustment is involved, since the situation remains essentially the same, yet considerable stress may result. Or apparently minor daily hassles can accumulate to produce serious effects, as we have seen. These important sources of stress are not tapped by the readjustment scale.

Furthermore, this scale contains an overabundance of events that are more likely to befall young adults. The elderly are much less likely to get married or divorced, take out a mortgage, change their schools, be confined to jail, or switch to a different line of work. Suppose, then, that researchers find that these life events occur much less frequently with increasing age. While this might mean that the elderly lead relatively stress-free lives, it more probably reflects the youth-oriented emphasis of this particular set of events (Goldberg & Comstock, 1980; Kasl, 1983; Rabkin & Struening, 1976). Some researchers have tried to resolve this problem by developing scales based on life events that are more appropriate for middle-aged and elderly adults (e.g., Kiyak, Liang, & Kahana, 1976; Plomin et al., 1990), one example of which is shown in Table 10.4.

Finally, the social readjustment rating scale may well sacrifice accuracy in order to gain simplicity. For example, the degree of stress caused by trouble with your boss is influenced by various mediators. If your skills are in great demand, and you have many possible job opportunities, this life event will probably be much less stressful than if you cannot afford to quit or be fired. Or pregnancy, and the gain of a new family member, may be much more stressful to an unmarried teenager than to a happily married 30-year-old woman. Therefore, expecting these potential stressors to have intensities of 23 and 39 in all instances may well be a serious oversimplification.

One possible alternative is to collapse the various life events into four major categories: changes in personal relationships, changes in financial resources, changes in environment and location, and changes in health. Then, separate scores may be obtained for each category (Wilson & Schulz, 1983; see also Schulz, 1985). Conceivably, we might find that changes within each category are more extreme for the elderly. For example, a relationship

Table 10.4
Stressful life events appropriate for middle-aged and elderly adults.

Life Event	Mean Rated Importance (3=great importance, 1=little importance)	Percent of Subjects in This Study Who Experienced This Event
Death of spouse	2.96	15.6
Death of child	2.96	5.1
Nursing home care for spouse	2.91	2.3
Serious illness of child	2.88	8.9
Divorce	2.85	12.3
Serious conflicts with child	2.83	6.4
Mental illness of spouse	2.81	3.2
Deterioration in married life	2.80	10.6
Mental illness of self	2.79	3.3
Home care for spouse	2.78	5.9
Can't manage to look after self	2.77	2.6
Getting married	2.76	92.7
Death of siblings or friends	2.75	28.4
Improvement in married life	2.67	16.8
Changes in relations with grandchildren	2.67	6.5
Home care for self	2.64	8.8
Forced change in residence with reduced contacts	2.59	5.6
Somatic illness of spouse	2.56	23.6
Somatic illness of self	2.41	29.0
Making a new acquaintance	2.22	38.9
Major improvement in financial status	2.20	36.1
Retirement	2.19	40.7
Major deterioration in financial status	2.13	18.9
Loss of sexual ability or interest	2.10	19.0
Paying fine for minor violation of law	1.93	13.2

Note: Mean age of sample=58.6 years.

Source: Plomin et al., "Genetic Influence of Life Events During Last Half of Life Span" (1990), *Journal of Psychology and Aging, 5*, pp. 24–30. Copyright 1990 by the American Psychological Association. Reprinted by permission.

change for a young adult might involve breaking up with a boy- or girl-friend, whereas an aged individual might more often have to face the death of a loved one. Or we might hypothesize that the elderly are more likely to experience threats from several categories, such as suffering financial losses and having to relocate to a nursing home.

Another intriguing alternative is to focus on those frustrating daily hassles that we all must contend with. (Recall our previous discussion of "a martyr-dom of pinpricks.") A scale to measure this stressor has been developed by Richard Lazarus and his associates (Delongis et al., 1982). They found that daily hassles predicted the outbreak of psychosomatic diseases significantly better than did life events scores, possibly because they occurred closer in time to these consequences. High levels of daily stress have also been found to often precede the occurrence of migraine headaches (Köhler & Haimerl, 1990).

Despite the controversy that surrounds the use of numerical scales, both life events and daily hassles can be useful tools for assessing stress. Consider, for example, the death of a spouse from cancer or an automobile accident. Here, it is not very likely that some response or consequence of the surviving spouse caused this unfortunate event. Rather, it is more logical to assume that the stressful event caused various undesirable consequences. We may therefore ask: Does the likelihood that we will encounter stressful life events and daily hassles change markedly as we grow older?

Life Events and Aging.   Growing old is widely believed to be quite stressful. Events such as retirement, widowhood, having all of one's children leave home, and failing health are more likely to occur during the second half of life. On the other hand, numerous other stressful life events are more likely to befall young adults (as we have seen). If the elderly expect certain events to be a natural aspect of old age (e.g., ill health), they may suffer relatively little stress. Also, as we grow older, increased experience in living may make it easier to deal with stress.

What has empirical research evidence to say about this issue? In one study, young newlyweds showed *more* emotional stress than adults age 50 and 60 (Lowenthal et al., 1975). Another study reported a relatively low incidence of stressful life events for 375 subjects, whose ages ranged from 45 to 70: in an eight-year period, 80 percent had not retired, 75 percent had no major illnesses, 94 percent had not been widowed, and 85 percent did not experience the last child leaving home (Palmore et al., 1979; see also Shanan & Jacobowitz, 1982). No comparison data were obtained from young adults, however.

Various research findings have associated changes in residence with negative consequences among the aged. In one study, patients were matched on such factors as age, sex, race, health, length of hospitalization, and ability to ambulate. Those transferred from one California institution to another had a significantly higher death rate than a control group that was not relocated (Killian, 1970). When patients who relocated from their homes to an institution were compared with patients transferred from another institution, the former group lived for an average of about one month less, presumably because they experienced a more severe environmental change (Schulz & Aderman, 1974; see also Schulz, 1978). Here again, however, a life event like relocation may instead be caused by an existing physical or psychological illness—hence the need to control for level of health when trying to ascertain the effects of stress.

The relationship between expectations and stressfulness is supported once again by the research evidence in this area. As we observed in Chapter 8, life events are more likely to be stressful if they are temporally non-normative (i.e., if they occur at an atypical age). Not surprisingly, mortality rates for the widowed are significantly higher than for married controls matched on age and sex. However, there is a markedly lower rate of illnesses and death when widowhood occurs at older ages. This event is more easily anticipated when one is old, and may therefore be less stressful. An elderly widow is also more likely to have at least some friends who are widows, and who are willing and able to provide needed emotional support. Conversely, young widows tend to find themselves in so atypical a position that their friends do not know how to provide effective help. (See Kraus & Lilienfeld, 1959; Morgan, 1976; Stroebe et al., 1982.)

In contrast to widowhood, divorce is *less* common among the elderly. Therefore, when the aged do have to go through a divorce, they typically experience more extreme suffering and illnesses than do young adults (Chiriboga, 1982). In fact, one extensive study of the widowed found that older men suffered much more following a divorce or separation than did those who lost a spouse through death (Hyman, 1983). Thus the stressfulness of a life event is significantly influenced by its temporal normativity.

Age-related differences have also been observed with regard to daily hassles. Middle-aged men tend to worry more about economic problems, such as rising prices and taxes, whereas young adults express more concern with social and academic difficulties (Delongis et al., 1982).

In sum: Certain stressful life events are more likely to occur at different ages. (See Table 10.5.) Also, a life event is likely to cause considerably more stress if it occurs at an atypical age. Thus, the relationship between aging and stress is not a simple one. Potential stressors like widowhood, ill health, and having to care for a disabled relative are *more intense* when they occur at younger ages but are *more common* at older ages. Conversely, such potential stressors as divorce and one's first job are *more common* at younger ages and *more intense* at older ages.

Table 10.5

Aging and the likelihood of specific stressful life events.

Some Events More Likely to Occur During the First Half of Life	Some Events More Likely to Occur During the Second Half of Life
Beginning or ending school	Having to care for a disabled relative
Beginning to work (first job)	Ill health
Divorce	Last child leaving home
Jail term	Relocation to a nursing home
Marriage	Retirement
Pregnancy	Widowhood and the death of friends
Taking out a mortgage	Birth of a grandchild

Positive Life Events and Stress. Stress is not due only to negative life events, such as widowhood and divorce. As indicated in Table 10.3, such happy occasions as marriage, pregnancy, and a good new job are also common sources of stress. This has been attributed to the resulting dramatic changes in one's self-image and style of living:

Stressed by Success

Mrs. J. was most embarrassed to be seeking the help of her university counselor. In the past few months, everything in her life had gone beautifully. She had just finished her doctoral dissertation, which her advisor regarded as outstanding. She had received an award as the best teacher-scholar at her university, and had lined up a publisher for the book she was writing. Though jobs were scarce, she had secured a position at an excellent Eastern university. Yet she felt very strange, like everything was unreal. She questioned whether she deserved this success, and wondered if she would wake up one day to find that it had all disappeared.

   The counselor helped Mrs. J. to understand the reasons for her stress. Because of her new job, she would soon be moving to a new area, thereby losing the respect and support she received in her present community. Her previous self-image as "just a nice, average person" had been greatly exceeded by her successes, and it was frightening to abandon this old, comfortable, and predictable view of herself. Her success also meant a change in the relationship with her husband: previously she had moved because of his job changes, but now he was going to have to move because of hers. When she realized that her grief and anxiety about losing her familiar roles was natural and understandable, she was able to face her new situation with considerable pleasure. (Schneider, 1984. See also Berglas, 1986)

STRESS AND LONGEVITY

Suppose that adults who experience considerable stress are more likely to die at a fairly young age. Studies of the elderly will fail to reveal an abnormal number of negative consequences, because many of the adults who would show such symptoms have been weeded out by death. That is, the aged may represent a relatively select, stress-resistant group. Therefore, it is important to determine whether high levels of stress are associated with a shorter life span.

Stress and Heart Disease. Medical, psychological, and sociological researchers have found a significant relationship between stress and heart disease, with sudden cardiac death often preceded by several months of increased stress. There is some indication that such potential stressors as rejection by a loved one, a setback or continued emotional strain at work, or a loss of prestige increase the likelihood of coronary diseases. (See, for example, Jenkins, 1971; Russek, 1962; 1965; Sales, 1969; House, 1975.) As noted above, relocation has been linked with higher death rates among the elderly. Also, stressful life events have been related to the occurrence of suicide attempts (Dohrenwend & Dohrenwend, 1974).

Type A and Type B Individuals.   It has long been believed that individual behavioral styles mediate the levels of stress that we experience. The so-called **Type A individual** is characterized by intense ambition, competitiveness, aggressiveness, restlessness, and perfectionism in many areas. These are the people who make business calls while waiting in the dentist's office, rather than waste a single moment of time; frequently battle against self-imposed deadlines; are perceived by their spouses as driving themselves much too hard; prefer respect to affection; and treat life as a deadly serious game which they are out to win. **Type B individuals** may be equally serious, and just as successful. But these people are more easygoing, are seldom impatient, do not feel compelled by time pressures, are less competitive and preoccupied with achievement, and tend to do one thing well. (See Wright, 1988.)

Although type theories may well oversimplify the human personality (Chapter 7), behavioral scientists have taken considerable interest in the Type A–Type B distinction. The early research in this area indicated that the incidence of coronary heart disease was two to three times greater among Type A individuals and as much as six times greater for Type A men between the ages of 39 and 49 (Friedman & Rosenberg, 1959; 1974; Jenkins, 1974; 1975; Suinn, 1977). As a result, stern warnings against following the Type A behavior pattern were often found in both the professional literature and the popular media.

More recent research has painted a somewhat different picture. First of all, the relationship between Type A behavior and coronary heart disease appears to be much weaker than the early evidence suggested (Booth-Kewley & Friedman, 1987). Second, Type A behavior may be an important precipitating factor only for a person's first heart attack (Matthews, 1988). Third, only some aspects of Type A behavior may be related to the increased probability of heart disease. To date, the best evidence suggests that hostility may be the culprit: People who are generally more hostile and display anger more frequently are more likely to have heart attacks (Friedman & Booth-Kewley, 1987; Matthews, 1988). Thus it may well be anger (rather than the overall behavior pattern) that makes Type A individuals more vulnerable to potential stressors and more likely to suffer such negative consequences as heart disease and an early death.

Until future research clarifies these important issues, probably the most advisable course is to follow this caution recommended by Wright (1988): Type A individuals are notorious for denying that they behave in this way, at least until they suffer their first heart attack. They (and all of us) would do better to run the race of life like a marathon, rather than as a series of intense 100-yard dashes.

Afterword.   The best available evidence indicates that stress is associated with decreased life expectancy, particularly for middle-aged men who fit at least some aspects of the Type A description. Therefore, the selective attrition caused by death may be another reason why the consequences of stress have not been found to be more severe among the aged.

Myths About Aging

Stress and Coping

Myth	*Best Available Evidence*
Stress is always disadvantageous and debilitating and should be avoided whenever possible.	Extreme stress can have debilitating effects. But too little stress can inhibit your motivation and lead to lackluster and inferior performance. Some people enjoy facing a challenge, improving their skills, and achieving difficult goals; some willingly seek out risky and stressful vocations or avocations. Stress may also facilitate personal growth and development, as when one learns to deal with disappointment and frustration.
The intensity of a stressor can be assessed by assigning it a single score that applies in all instances. For example, the death of a spouse is always more stressful than divorce.	A life event is likely to be more stressful if it is temporally non-normative. For example, the elderly are likely to find divorce even more painful than widowhood. Thus the intensity of a given stressor may well vary as a function of the age at which it occurs.
You will experience much more stress during the second half of your life than during the first half.	There is some truth to this idea, because some extremely stressful life events are more likely to occur during old age (e.g., widowhood, terminal illnesses). But the relationship between aging and stress is more complicated than this. Some traumatic life events are more common at older ages, but are more intense when they occur at younger ages. Other potential stressors are more common at younger ages and more intense at older ages.
As you grow older, your ability to cope with those stressful life events that you do face decreases markedly.	If your health, economic resources, and social resources decline as you grow toward old age, your ability to cope with stress may be compromised. But if these capacities remain more or less intact, there is no reason to expect your ability to cope with stressful life events to decline with increasing age.

COPING WITH STRESS

Coping with stress refers to a particular class of responses: those thoughts (conscious and unconscious) and/or actions that we use to eliminate or alleviate the demands made by a stressor.

Aging and Coping Ability.

Does our ability to cope with stress decline as we grow older? If so, we should expect to find that negative consequences often occur for the first time at relatively advanced ages. However, this does not appear to be the case. For relatively normal older adults (i.e., those who do not have a history of serious physical or physiological disorders), stressful but temporally normative life events have *not* been found to cause significant personality changes or increases in maladjustment (Chiriboga, 1981; Costa & McCrae, 1980; Maas & Kuypers, 1974; Palmore et al., 1979).

For those older adults who suffer from ill health or from a significant decline in economic and social resources, the ability to cope with stress may be compromised. But there is no indication that more normal elderly individuals suffer any appreciable decrement in their ability to cope with stress.

Aging and Coping Processes.

When you are faced with a stressful life event, one possible course is to take action designed to resolve the troublesome situation (**problem-focused coping**). For example, if you discover that you have the symptoms of a potentially serious illness, you might seek out expert medical advice. If, instead, you must contend with a demanding parent or boss, you might choose among such task-oriented tactics as fight, flight, or compromise. That is, you may regard the stressful situation as a problem that can be solved by appropriate action.

Relaxation and distraction are effective ways of dealing with some stressors. (Guy Gillette/Photo Researchers, Inc.)

Alternatively, you might try to achieve an emotional acceptance of the existing situation (**emotion-focused coping**). Faced with the possibility of a major illness, you might concentrate on maintaining a positive and optimistic attitude. Or you might prefer to put this issue out of your mind, perhaps with the aid of one or more defense mechanisms. The differences between the problem-focused and emotion-focused methods for coping with stress are further illustrated by the following self-report items and statements (Folkman & Lazarus, 1980; Schmitz-Scherzer & Thomae, 1983):

Problem-Focused Coping	*Emotion-Focused Coping*
"I got the person responsible to change his or her mind."	"I looked for the 'silver lining.'"
"I made a plan of action and followed it."	"I accepted sympathy and understanding from another person."
"I stood my ground and fought for what I wanted."	"I tried to forget the whole thing."
	"Well, maybe I am not too well off, but what can you expect for someone my age?"
	"Even if I am bad off, there are many whose health is worse."

Is there a relationship between aging and the choice of coping strategy? Early research in this area found that older adults are more likely to use emotion-focused coping, primarily because they more often must deal with life events that cannot be successfully resolved by problem-focused coping. For example, there is no way to eliminate the pain caused by certain arthritic conditions or incurable illnesses by direct action on the environment. So older adults opt instead to regulate their emotions, as by developing greater tolerance and acceptance of their situation. Thus it is the nature of the problems encountered by the elderly, rather than aging per se, that causes the preference for emotion-focused coping (Schulz et al., 1991; see also Folkman & Lazarus, 1980; Folkman et al., 1987; Koenig, George, & Siegler, 1988).

Additional evidence supporting this conclusion has been reported by Schmitz-Scherzer and Thomae (1983). They conducted a longitudinal study of some 222 German men and women, primarily from what was formerly West Germany. The older cohort was born between 1890 and 1895, and the younger cohort was born between 1900 and 1905. The subjects were assessed on six separate occasions between 1965 and 1977, so the ages at the times of assessment varied from 60 to over 80. Among other measures, subjects were asked the extent to which they perceived various problem areas to be stressful. Over the 12-year period, health problems became considerably more

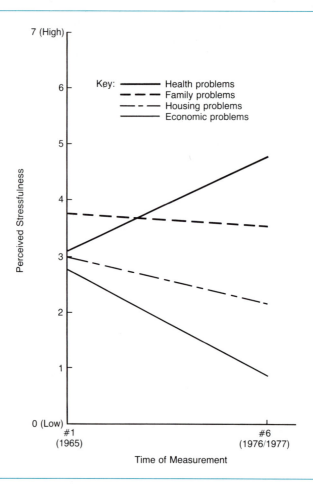

Figure 10.3
Stress caused by various problem areas for a sample of German adults. Source: Modified from Schmitz-Scherzer & Thomae (1983, p. 211).

prominent with increasing age; family, economic, and housing problems either remained at about the same level or declined markedly. (See Figure 10.3.) The younger adults in this study were also more likely to use problem-focused coping (finding the best doctor or treatment; getting the most out of their health insurance), whereas the older adults relied more on emotion-focused coping (learning to accept their disabilities; revising their expectations of life accordingly).

More recent research has produced similar findings. Folkman et al. (1987) found that younger adults were more likely to identify their problems as falling in the areas of finances and work, and to rely on problem-focused coping. Conversely, older adults more often identified their problems as involving health and home issues, and preferred to use emotion-focused coping. In a cross-sectional study of 890 adults age 34 to 63, Brandtstadter and Renner (1990) found a gradual increase in the use of emotion-focused coping with increasing age. Felton and Revenson (1987) controlled for diagnosis, physical limitations caused by an illness, and perceived seriousness of an illness, and they still found a small but significant relationship: Older people were less likely to use problem-focused coping.

In sum: Both problem-focused and emotion-focused coping are commonly used to deal with stress, and both can effectively improve life satisfaction and reduce depression. However, emotion-focused coping is more common among the elderly. This is an adaptive and sensible solution in view of the kinds of stressors that they most often face.

AFTERWORD

Stress is a significant problem in our society. It is experienced by adults of all ages, and it is associated with higher illness and mortality rates.

The relationship between aging and stress is a complicated one, and it involves various important issues. What potential stressors are most likely to be salient during young adulthood, middle age, and old age? What mediators cause different people to respond to stressors in different ways? How do adults of different ages cope with stress? How can we best deal with potential stressors, so as to minimize the probability of negative consequences?

As we have seen throughout this chapter, gerontological researchers and social scientists have discovered many important answer to these questions. Given the current interest in the scientific study of stress, we may expect further valuable findings to be forthcoming within the next decade.

Summary

THE SCIENTIFIC STUDY OF STRESS

Walter Cannon was among the first to investigate the effects of threatening external stimuli on an organism's behavior. He characterized the standard response to danger as the fight-or-flight reaction. Modern investigators have added a third alternative to Cannon's dichotomy, namely compromise or surrender.

Undoubtedly the most prominent name in the field of stress research is that of Hans Selye. He concluded that organisms exposed to noxious stimuli of any kind exhibit a three-stage pattern of responses, which he called the General Adaptation Syndrome. He also argued that stress occurs if and only if each stage is accompanied by specific physiological changes, a contention that has been challenged by modern researchers. Selye pointed out that too little stress can also have negative effects, and that individual differences play an important role in the response to stressful situations.

Selye's definition of stress suffers from circularity: A stressful event is whatever evokes the General Adaptation Syndrome, and the occurrence of this syndrome is what tells us that an event is stressful. However, it is not easy to arrive at an acceptable definition of stress. Some theorists have defined stress solely in terms of the external situation, or solely in terms of the organism's responses, but these approaches overlook important considerations. Accordingly, some investigators prefer to define stress in terms of the entire complex of stressors, responses, mediators, and consequences. This approach more readily enables us to understand why different individuals react differently to the same stressor. It also emphasizes that the relationships among the various components of stress are primarily bidirectional: Stress operates in a circular and dynamic fashion, with each of the components continuously modifying and being modified by the other elements.

Among the more common stressors are external pressures and overstimulation, boredom and understimulation, conflicts, frustration and disappointment, and noxious physical and psychological stimuli. Important responses include physiological changes, emotional changes, expectations, cognitions, perceptions, fight, flight, compromise, and the psychological defense mechanisms. The possible negative consequences of stress include such physical and psychological disorders as anxiety, depression, stomach ulcers, colitis, headaches, and coronary diseases. Or, if the level of stress is neither too high nor too low, good health and performance may result. Common mediators include personal competence, physical and psychological health, the physical setting, and the social milieu. For example, personal competence mediates the relationship between the stressfulness of one's environment, responses, and consequences.

Stress is not a simple phenomenon. It is virtually impossible to make simple statements that are also accurate, like "situation X is always stressful" or "stressor A invariably leads to response B." Of necessity, therefore, stress researchers typically simplify matters by studying one aspect of this phenomenon at a time.

STRESS AND AGING

It is reasonable to hypothesize that certain life events are stressful to varying degrees, even though different individuals may well respond in different ways. Some investigators have sought to quantify the amount of stress caused by various life events, but such scales have been strongly attacked on methodological grounds. The relationship between aging and stress is complicated, and is affected by the temporal normativity of the life event. Some stressful events are more common at advanced ages but more intense when they occur at younger ages; others are more common at younger ages and more intense at older ages.

Stress is associated with coronary and other diseases, and with a decreased life expectancy. The likelihood of suffering a stress-related illness that leads to death is greater for middle-aged men who fit at least some characteristics of the Type A description. Thus the selective attrition caused by death may be another reason why the consequences of stress have not been found to be more severe among the aged.

For those adults whose health, economic resources, and social resources remain reasonably intact, there is no indication that the ability to cope with stress declines with increasing age. Both problem-focused coping and emotion-focused coping are typically used in stressful situations. The elderly rely more on emotion-focused coping, because they must more often contend with situations that are not amenable to the problem-focused approach (e.g., incurable illnesses or injuries).

Gerontological researchers have investigated various important issues: determining those stressors most likely to be salient at different ages, identifying important mediators, and ascertaining how adults of different ages cope with stress. The scientific study of stress has produced much valuable information in these areas, and is likely to continue to do so in the future.

Study Questions

1. What are some of the harmful consequences of too much stress? What are some of the harmful consequences of too little stress? Why can it be difficult to determine how much stress is the right amount (that is, neither too much nor too little)? *Hint:* Why must we consider mediators such as personal competence when deciding how much stress a person is encountering?
2. In the general model of stress presented in this chapter, why is the relationship between stressors and responses treated as bidirectional? Why is the relationship between responses and consequences treated as bidirectional? What does this imply about the definition of "stress"? Why is (only) the relationship between consequences and stressors treated as unidirectional?
3. How do the various psychological defense mechanisms help to reduce stress? Have you ever used any of these defense mechanisms? Why is the use of defense mechanisms likely to make matters worse in the long run? Why is it difficult to abandon defense mechanisms, even when their effects are harmful to the person using them?
4. Why are the stressful life events listed in Table 10.4 (p. 334) more suitable for use with middle-aged and elderly adults than the stressful life events listed in Table 10.3 (p. 332)? What does this imply about the different kinds of stressors that are typically encountered by older and younger adults?

5. In what situations would you use problem-focused coping to reduce stress? In what situations might you prefer emotion-focused coping? Or does the choice depend more on personal preferences than on situational factors?

Terms to Remember

Consequences of stress	*Personal competence*
Coping with stress	*Problem-focused coping*
Defense mechanism	*Responses to stress*
Emotion-focused coping	*Stress*
Fight-or-flight reaction	*Stressor*
General Adaptation Syndrome	*Type A individual*
Mediator	*Type B individual*

Chapter 11

Adult Psychopathology

David M. Grossman/Photo Researchers, Inc.

A 68-year-old writer, once celebrated for his ability to remember complicated details, cannot sustain a simple thought or find basic words with which to express himself. A former supervisor cannot recall the plot of a television program she watched ten minutes ago. A woman who has led a pleasant life becomes obsessed with the idea that she is a failure and that only her suicide will enable her family to draw closer together. An elderly man experiences attacks of apprehension, fear, and even terror for no apparent reason.

Throughout this book, we have seen that the probability of contracting certain physical illnesses and injuries increases with increasing age. Yet these are by no means the only health problems that afflict older adults; as the preceding examples indicate, much pain and anguish can also be caused by mental disorders. In this chapter, we examine the empirical evidence dealing with adult psychopathology. Among the issues that we discuss are the forms of psychopathology most common among older adults, including Alzheimer's disease, depression, and anxiety disorders; how mental health professionals diagnose and assess these disorders; how likely you are to suffer such disorders as you grow through adulthood; and appropriate methods of treatment.

Substantive and Methodological Issues

DEFINING MENTAL HEALTH AND PSYCHOPATHOLOGY

Before we can examine the various types of psychopathology that afflict middle-aged and elderly adults, we must first ask an important question: What defines a mentally healthy individual? That is, how do we distinguish between mental health and psychopathology? As elsewhere in this book (e.g., the sections on intelligence, personality, stress), arriving at a satisfactory definition is far from an easy task.

Situational Factors.   Whether behavior is pathological often depends on the specific situation. For example, suppose that an older man spends much of each day crying, feeling sad, and refusing to leave the house to go to the movies or enjoy any other form of recreation. Your first thought might be that he is suffering from one form of psychopathology, namely depression. But suppose you are informed that his spouse died suddenly a few days ago. Now you would surely conclude that he is going through the normal process of bereavement and is not suffering from any psychological disorder at all!

As this example illustrates, we cannot judge whether an adult is pathological based solely on his or her behavior; the behavior must be evaluated in the context in which it occurs. As Williams (1972) observes:

There is a danger in confusing the mental disorders with suffering, and mental health with happiness. A person who is clinically depressed is unhappy and suffers. But one can be unhappy and suffer without being clinically depressed, and, indeed, without any impairment in the capacity to act within the confines of one's natural abilities. (p. 4)

The death of a parent, spouse, or friend becomes temporally normative as we grow old (as we have seen); and the pain of bereavement is a natural emotion, one that may or may not result in such forms of psychopathology as clinical depression.

Other Factors.   Behavior that is readily accepted in one culture may be regarded as pathological in another part of the world. For example, the concept of feminine equality is anathema in certain Middle Eastern countries, and any woman who dares to walk alongside a man (rather than discreetly behind) will experience severe disapproval. Similarly, a female Navy lieutenant serving in Saudi Arabia during the 1990–1991 crisis in Iraq was berated and prodded with a stick by a native for daring to appear in public without veiling her face (*Time*, January 21, 1991). "Judgments cannot be made about mental health without taking into account the cultural background and current environment of the individual" (Birren & Renner, 1980, p. 6). Age may also be a factor: Talking in nonsense syllables is normal for a baby, but likely to indicate pathology for an adult.

Definition of Mental Health.   In spite of these difficulties, clinicians and researchers have identified some of the key components that distinguish mental health from psychopathology. **Mental health** reflects the ability of an individual to deal with the issues of life in an effective way. It involves the capacity to achieve a reasonably satisfactory integration of one's instinctual drives with goals, achievements, and interpersonal relationships in ways that are socially acceptable, personally satisfying, and appropriately flexible. In contrast, psychopathology (or mental illness) refers to the failure to achieve a satisfactory integration of one's self into one's usual social milieu. (See Birren & Renner, 1980; Busse, 1987.)

DIAGNOSIS AND ASSESSMENT

Causes of Psychopathology.   During the nineteenth century, such pioneering clinical investigators as Sigmund Freud attributed psychopathology entirely to experiences during childhood, most often involving the parents. Examples include a lack of physical affection, excessive indulgence or frustration of the child's needs, overly severe parental standards, observing the parents' sexual intercourse, being seduced by an adult, or (in the case of the boy) being threatened with castration. Subsequent theorists rejected Freud's emphasis on sexuality while maintaining the focus on parental pathogenic behaviors, such as pampering, neglect, domination, overprotectiveness, over-permissiveness, ridicule and derision, perfectionism, blind adoration, partiality to other siblings, physical abuse, excessive anxiety, a lack of love and tenderness, inconsistent punishment, and dissuading the child from fulfilling his or her true innate potentials. (See Ewen, 1988.)

Modern clinicians agree that childhood causes of psychopathology are extremely important, but they have identified numerous others as well. (See Tables 11.1 and 11.2.) For example, such biological factors as endocrine disorders, infections, metabolic disorders, and even dietary deficiencies can contribute to depression and other forms of psychopathology. Insofar as psychosocial factors are concerned, exposure to a variety of stressors during adulthood has been linked to psychopathology (as we observed in the preceding chapter). Conversely, regular religious participation and being married are associated with a lower occurrence of psychiatric illness.

A detailed discussion of these causes of psychopathology is beyond the scope of this book; the interested reader is referred to the most recent edition of any of the major textbooks on abnormal psychology. The important point for our purposes is that because there are so many possible causes of psychopathology, diagnosing the disorder that afflicts a particular adult (and selecting an appropriate treatment) is an extremely difficult task. This is par-

Early clinical investigators such as Sigmund Freud felt that most psychopathologies had their roots in early childhood experiences. (Kathy Sloane/Photo Researchers, Inc.)

Table 11.1

Psychosocial risk factors associated with psychiatric illness.

General Category	Specific Examples	Research Findings
Demographic variables	Age	Lower prevalence of psychiatric disorders among older adults
	Sex	Affective and somatic disorders are more prevalent among women. Alcohol and substance abuse disorders are more common among men.
	Race/ethnicity	Increased rates of alcohol and drug abuse among non-whites
Early events and achievements	Education	Low education increases risk of psychiatric illness. Some types of illness (e.g., major depression) may be more common among the highly educated.
	Childhood traumas	Increased risk of psychiatric illness
Later events and achievements	Occupation/income	Low socioeconomic status related to increased psychiatric illness
	Marital status	Married people are slightly less likely to have psychiatric illness.
Social integration	Personal attachments to social organizations (e.g., religious groups, community)	Religious participation and attendance is associated with fewer psychiatric illnesses.
	Environmental contexts	Higher rates of psychiatric symptoms among urban residents (as compared with rural residents)
Vulnerabilty and protective factors	Job stress, chronic financial strain, chronic physical illness, caregiving stress	All of these stressors are related to higher rates of psychiatric illness.
	Social support	High levels of social support are related to less psychiatric illness.
Provoking agents and coping efforts	Life events	Negative life events are related to increased illness, especially depression, alcohol abuse, and anxiety.
	Coping strategies	Effectiveness varies with type of stressor.

Source: Based on George (1989).

ticularly true for elderly adults, who are more likely to suffer from a variety of medical conditions (and take medications) that may contribute (directly or indirectly) to a psychological disorder. As a result, the diagnosis and assessment of older adults typically involves professionals from several disciplines (e.g., biomedical areas, psychology, psychiatry, social work, nursing), a variety of measures, and a formal classification system.

Classifying Mental Disorders: DSM-III-R. Classification is an important aspect of any science, including psychology. Before we can arrive at meaningful explanations of human behavior, we must first organize what would otherwise be an overwhelming amount of data into a convenient framework.

One popular system for classifying the various forms of psychopathology is **DSM-III-R**, the 1987 revision of the *Diagnostic and Statistical Manual of Mental Disorders* prepared by the American Psychiatric Association. DSM-III-R is a revision of a system first used by the U.S. Army during World War II.

Earlier versions of DSM had to be revised for several reasons. Most importantly, too many patients had symptoms that did *not* fall within one specific category. For example, obsessive-compulsive behavior is characterized by persistent thoughts and/or actions that a person cannot seem to stop. Thus, the individual may feel compelled to check the alarm clock 15 or 20 times at night to be sure that it is set properly. In contrast, anxiety involves extremely unpleasant feelings that are similar to intense nervousness. In the second version of DSM, obsessive-compulsive neurosis and anxiety neurosis were separate and distinct categories. Yet many patients were found to suffer from both obsessive-compulsive symptoms and anxiety, making it difficult to use this classification system. In DSM-III-R, however, obsessive-compulsive disorder is classified as one of the anxiety disorders, making it clear that these symptoms often occur together.

DSM-III-R evaluates people on five dimensions, or axes, including specific maladaptive or psychiatric symptoms (Axis I), any long-standing personality or developmental problems (Axis II), and any medical or physical disorders

Table 11.2

Biological factors associated with psychiatric illness.

General Category	Specific Examples	Possible Effects
Heredity		May be related to some types of dementia and schizophrenia
Drugs and medication	Alcohol, amphetamines, sedatives	May cause depression, treatable dementia, anxiety disorder
Endocrine disorders	Hyper- and hypothyroidism	May cause depression, treatable dementia
Infections	Encephalitis, neurosyphilis	May cause depression, dementia
Malignant disease	Metastases, tumors	May cause depression, dementia, treatable dementia
Metabolic disorders	Electrolyte imbalance, uremia	May cause depression, treatable dementia
Trauma	Postconcussion, subdural	May cause depression, dementia, treatable dementia
Nutritional disorders	Vitamin B12 deficiency, folate deficiency, caffeine	May cause treatable dementia, anxiety disorder

Source: Based on Jenike (1989).

Table 11.3
A synopsis of DSM-III-R, Axis I.

1. *Organic Mental Disorders:* Disorders that have a known physical cause, such as an injury to or pathology of the brain.

   A. Dementias Arising in the Senium and Presenium. Degenerative change in brain tissue occurring before age 65 (presenile) or after age 65 (senile).
   (a) Primary Degenerative Dementia of the Alzheimer Type. Involves a multifaceted loss of intellectual abilities, such as memory, judgment, and abstract thought, and changes in personality and behavior. Generally progressive, with onset either before (presenile) or after (senile) age 65.
   (b) Multi-infarct Dementia. Stepwise deterioration in intellectual functioning that occurs when localized areas of brain tissue are destroyed because of an inadequate supply of blood.

   B. Psychoactive Substance-Induced Organic Mental Disorders. Organic brain damage caused by the use of a specific substance, such as alcohol or drugs.

2. *Schizophrenia:* Characterized by a gross distortion of reality; disorganization and fragmentation of thought, perception, and emotion.

3. *Delusional (Paranoid) Disorders:* Characterized by delusions of persecution and/or grandeur, jealousy, rigidity.

4. *Mood Disorders:* Characterized by disturbances of emotion and mood. Includes bipolar disorder, major depression.

5. *Anxiety Disorders:* Characterized by unusually high anxiety and efforts to defend against it. Includes phobic disorder, anxiety states, obsessive-compulsive disorder.

6. *Dissociative Disorders:* Characterized by escaping from one's own personality and identity. Includes psychogenic amnesia, multiple personality.

7. *Somatoform Disorders:* Characterized by complaints of bodily symptoms for which there are no physical causes. Includes conversion disorder, hypochondriasis.

8. *Psychosexual Disorders:* Characterized by problems associated with sexual behavior, such as failure to attain an erection (male erectile disorder), inhibited orgasm, vaginismus, or premature ejaculation.

9. *Psychoactive Substance Use Disorders:* Disorders caused by the abuse of or addiction to a specific substance, such as alcohol, tobacco, or drugs (including barbiturates, cocaine, amphetamines, hallucinogens, and others).

10. *Disorders Usually First Evident in Infancy, Childhood, and Adolescence:* The lengthy category includes such disorders as mental retardation, anorexia nervosa, bulimia, attention disorders, and conduct disorders.

Note: For purposes of convenience, this table presents primarily the major categories of Axis I delineated by DSM-III-R. Categories not relevant to the present chapter have been deemphasized, and many subcategories have been omitted.

Source: *Diagnostic and Statistical Manual of Mental Disorders (Third Edition, Revised).* Washington, D.C.: American Psychiatric Association, 1987.

that may also be present (Axis III). DSM-III-R entirely omits the popular term *neurosis*, on the grounds that it has been used in so many different ways that it has lost its meaning. (Not all psychologists and psychiatrists agree with this decision, however, and "neurosis" continues to enjoy widespread usage.) A synopsis of Axis I is shown in Table 11.3.

DSM-III-R includes 16 major categories in all, each containing anywhere from 4 to 40 or more subcategories. Just as earlier versions of DSM proved to be fallible, we may reasonably expect that new discoveries will someday cause DSM-III-R to become outdated; these categories are not etched in stone, and DSM is constantly being revised. The interested reader is referred once again to any of the major textbooks on abnormal psychology.

Diagnosis and Assessment: I. Interviews.   Even with the aid of DSM-III-R, it is no simple task to decide which classification applies to a given adult. To answer this important question, clinicians typically rely on such formal **assessment** techniques as the interview.

You have undoubtedly encountered the interview at some point in your life, as when you applied for a job or for admission to college. The clinical interviewer pays close attention not only to *what* the respondent says, but also to *how* he or she answers. In particular, the emotions that accompany the interviewee's statements often provide the clinician with valuable clues regarding any mental disorders that may be present.

The specific information elicited during a clinical interview depends in part on the theoretical orientation of the interviewer. Some clinicians prefer to devote many of their questions to childhood causes, whereas others stress current behaviors and problems. Also, some clinicians like to operate from vague outlines and compose specific questions as the interview proceeds; others are more comfortable with a structured format that lists all of the questions to be asked.

An example of a structured procedure for conducting clinical interviews with older adults is outlined in Table 11.4. The first step is to obtain information about the patient's present symptoms (when they began, how long they have lasted, if they have become more severe over time), and about any previous occurrences of these or other symptoms. The interviewer must be careful not to accept the patient's reassurances at face value (e.g., "I guess I'm just getting old, and most people slow down when they get to be my age"), lest a treatable psychiatric disorder be overlooked. Common symptoms that should be investigated carefully include excessive weakness or lethargy, a depressed mood or "the blues," memory problems, difficulty in concentrating, feelings of helplessness and hopelessness, suspicion of other people, anxiety and agitation, sleep problems, and appetite problems (Blazer, 1989). Any psychiatric symptoms and illnesses within the family should also be ascertained; for example, dementia sufferers often have a family history of this disorder.

As would be expected from our previous discussion, the interviewer also inquires about biological and psychosocial factors that may contribute to the patient's mental disorder. These include medical problems (assessed by a physical examination), medications that may produce or exacerbate psychological symptoms, and such potential stressors as the patient's family. Thus the interviewer tries to ascertain how the family interacts with the patient,

Table 11.4

One procedure for conducting psychiatric interviews with geriatric patients.

I. History

1. Symptoms

2. Present episode, including onset, duration, and change in symptoms over time

3. Past history of medical and psychiatric disorders

4. Family history of depression, alcohol abuse/dependence, psychoses, and suicide

II. Physical Examination

1. Evaluation of neurologic deficits, possible endocrine disorders, occult malignancy, cardiac dysfunction, and occult infections

III. Mental Status Examination

1. Disturbance of consciousness

2. Disturbance of mood and affect

3. Disturbance of motor behavior

4. Disturbance of perception (hallucinations, illusions)

5. Disturbance of cognition (delusions)

6. Disturbance of self-esteem and guilt

7. Suicidal ideation

8. Disturbance of memory and intelligence (memory, abstraction, calculation, aphasia, and knowledge)

Source: Blazer (1989), "The Psychiatric Interview of the Geriatric Patient," *Geriatric Psychiatry*, p. 264. Edited by E. W. Busse and D. G. Blazer. Copyright 1989, American Psychiatric Press, Inc.

the type and amount of support given to the patient by the family, and how family members are coping with the stress caused by the patient's illness. Finally, the interviewer may learn about the specific nature of the patient's disorder by directly observing the presence of specific symptoms, such as delusions, hallucinations, and suicidal wishes. (See Blazer, 1989.)

Whatever the specific format may be, interviewing older adults requires considerable skill and sensitivity. Psychological assessment procedures may be frightening to the elderly, who are more likely to regard any illnesses they may have as incurable. Thus the interviewer must be careful to avoid such behaviors as irritability, impatience, and boredom, which are likely to increase the patient's fears and feelings of rejection. (See Gurland, 1982.) The pace of the interview should be unhurried, even if the patient takes considerable time to respond. The interviewer should be sensitive to such problems as hearing and vision impairments, by speaking slowly and clearly in a low-pitched voice and bringing up important points more than once. The interviewer should *not* shy away from such potentially sensitive areas as suicidal feelings, sexual problems, and feelings about growing old and dying, lest vital information be overlooked; but distressing topics should be avoided at the close of the interview, and a clear statement of the next step in the assessment process should be given, so that the patient leaves with reduced anxiety.

Diagnosis and Assessment: II. Psychometric Instruments. A second important assessment procedure is the psychometric approach, which includes standardized questionnaires, tests, and projective devices. Such well-known measures of personality as the MMPI, Rorschach, and TAT, discussed in Chapter 7, are commonly used for diagnostic purposes.

One problem with these measures (and with interviews) is that they are time-consuming. Suppose that a clinician wishes to determine if an older adult enjoys reasonable mental health or needs treatment. What is needed here is not a lengthy measure that probes deeply into the patient's personality, but rather a quickly administered screening test that will indicate if a problem is likely to exist. If the subject scores well (healthy), no further action is taken, and considerable time is saved. If, instead, the subject scores relatively poorly (pathological), the clinician knows that longer and more detailed assessment procedures are needed. No diagnoses are made from the screening test, which provides only a rough indication of mental health.

One screening test that helps to detect cognitive dysfunction and dementia is the Mini-Mental State Examination (Folstein et al., 1975; see Figure 11.1). This instrument requires only 5 to 10 minutes to administer; it assesses recall, attention and calculation, language, and orientation. Seven to 12 errors suggest mild to moderate cognitive impairment; 13 or more errors suggest severe impairment.

A screening test widely used to help detect depression is the Center for Epidemiologic Studies Depression Scale, or CES-D (Radloff, 1977). Twenty questions are read to the subject, dealing with his or her feelings during the preceding week. (See Table 11.5.) The maximum possible score on each item (most depressed) is 3, and a total score of 16 or higher suggests that the person is at risk for clinical depression. An earlier brief measure of depression, the Zung Self-Rating Depression Scale, uses somewhat similar items (e.g., "I am more irritable than usual," "My life is pretty full," "I'd do better if I felt better," "I feel downhearted, blue, and sad," "I feel that others would be better off if I am dead," "I don't have much to look forward to"). (See Zung, 1965; 1967; Okimoto et al., 1982.) However, the popularity of this instrument has declined in recent years because of a lack of normative data (Blazer, 1989).

Afterword. When DSM-III-R is used in combination with appropriate assessment procedures, it is possible to arrive at very detailed diagnoses. Yet because of the aforementioned methodological and substantive problems, such diagnoses are not always as accurate as one would wish.

Furthermore, this practice is far from universal. A quite different picture is evidenced by actual doctors' notes concerning elderly patients in long-term care institutions who suffer primarily from physical problems. These patients are frequently diagnosed in such simple terms as "depressed" or

Table 11.5
The Center for Epidemiologic Studies Depression Scale (CES-D).

The following questions are read to the subject:

In the *last week*, how often would you say you

1. were bothered by things that usually don't bother you?
2. did not feel like eating; your appetite was poor?
3. felt that you could not shake off the blues even with help from your family or friends?
4. felt that you were just as good as other people?
5. had trouble keeping your mind on what you were doing?
6. felt depressed?
7. felt that everything you did was an effort?
8. felt hopeful about the future?
9. thought your life had been a failure?
10. felt fearful?
11. found that your sleep was restless?
12. were happy?
13. talked less than usual?
14. felt lonely?
15. thought people were unfriendly?
16. enjoyed life?
17. had crying spells?
18. felt sad?
19. felt that people disliked you?
20. could not get "going"?

The subject is given a card with these responses to choose from:

0=Rarely or none of the time (less than one day in the last week)

1=Some or a little of the time (1 or 2 days in the last week)

2=Occasionally or a moderate amount of the time (3 or 4 days in the last week)

3=Most or all of the time (5–7 days in the last week)

Note: The instructions read to the subject state, "The next few questions are about your feelings and attitudes. I am going to read a list of statements. For each statement, please tell me the category which best describes how often you felt or behaved this way. You can use this card to tell me your answers." Questions 4, 8, 12, and 16 are scored in the reverse direction ("rarely or none of the time"=3, and so on). Thus the maximum possible score (most depressed) is 60 (3×20).
Source: Radloff (1977).

"senile," with no indication as to the procedure used to arrive at this conclusion. More often than not, these diagnoses seem to have been made casually during the course of a physical examination. Thus the problem of diagnosis and assessment may be exacerbated by the failure to use the best available procedures.

1 I would like to ask you a few questions dealing with concentration and memory. Some are a little bit more difficult than others.

	correct	error	not attempted refused	Record answers in error:
a. What is the year?	1	0	9	year: _____
b. What season of the year is it?	1	0	9	season: _____
c. What is the date?	1	0	9	date: _____
d. What is the day of the week?	1	0	9	day: _____
e. What is the month?	1	0	9	month: _____
f. What state are we in?	1	0	9	state: _____
g. What county are we in?	1	0	9	county: _____
h. What (city/town) are we in?	1	0	9	city: _____
i. What floor of the building are we on?	1	0	9	floor: _____
j. What is this address? (If institutionalized: What is the name of this place?)	1	0	9	address/name: _____

2 I am going to name 3 objects. After I have said them, I want you to repeat them. Remember what they are because I am going to ask you to name them again in a few minutes:
APPLE TABLE PENNY
Could you repeat the 3 items for me?

Do not repeat the items for the participant until after the first trial. The participant may give the items in any order. If there are errors on the first trial, repeat the items up to six times until they are learned.

first trial only

	correct	error	not attempted refused
a. apple	1	0	9
b. table	1	0	9
c. penny	1	0	9

3 Can you subtract 7 from 100, and then subtract 7 from the answer you get and keep subtracting 7 until I tell you to stop? Please do the subtraction out loud.

Count only 1 error if participant makes subtraction error, but subsequent answers are 7 less than the error.

Record Response:	correct	error	can't do	not attempted refused
a. 93 _____	1	0	7	9
b. 86 _____	1	0	7	9
c. 79 _____	1	0	7	9
d. 72 _____	1	0	7	9
e. 65 _____	1	0	7	9

4 I am going to spell a word forwards and I want you to spell it backwards. The word is *world*. W-O-R-L-D. Spell *world* backwards.

Repeat spelling if necessary.

Record Response:	correct	error	can't do	not attempted refused
a. D _____	1	0	7	9
b. L _____	1	0	7	9
c. R _____	1	0	7	9
d. O _____	1	0	7	9
e. W _____	1	0	7	9

5 Now what were the 3 objects I asked you to remember?

Objects may be repeated in any order.

	correct	error	not attempted refused
a. apple	1	0	9
b. table	1	0	9
c. penny	1	0	9

6 (Show wrist watch.) What is this called? 1 0 9

7 (Show pencil.) What is this called? 1 0 9

8 I'd like you to repeat a phrase after me: No if's, and's, or but's.

Allow only 1 trial. Code 1—Correct required an accurately articulated repetition.   correct 1 error 0 refused 9

9 Read the words on this card and then do what it says.

Hand card 11. Code 1—Correct required the participant to close his or her eyes. Card says: Close your eyes   correct 1 error 0 refused 9

10 *Read the full statement below and then hand participant a blank piece of paper. Do not repeat instructions or coach.*

I am going to give you a piece of paper. When I do, take the paper in your right hand, fold the paper in half with both hands, and put the paper down on your lap.

	correct	error	refused
a. takes paper in right	1	0	9
b. folds paper in half	1	0	9
c. puts paper down on lap	1	0	9

11 Write any complete sentence on that piece of paper for me.   1 0 9

Must have a subject and verb and make sense. Spelling and grammatical errors are OK. Repeat the instructions, if necessary.

12 Here's a drawing. Please copy the drawing on the same paper.   1 0 9

Hand participant card 12. Correct if 2 convex 5-sided figures and intersection makes a 4-sided figure.

Drawing

Figure 11.1
Items from the Mini–Mental State Examination.   Source: Folstein et al. (1975).

Epidemiology and Treatment of Adult Psychopathology

INTRODUCTION

Now that we have established *what* the various kinds of psychopathology are, we must ascertain *how often* and *where* these disorders occur. The greater the frequency of a particular illness, the more people will benefit if we diagnose and treat it correctly. The study of the distribution of illnesses in time and place, and of the factors that influence this distribution, is known as **epidemiology.**

Methods of Study. One way to obtain epidemiological data is by examining hospital records or **case registers** and counting how often each disorder occurs. Unfortunately, this straightforward procedure may well produce misleading results. Many individuals who suffer from certain disorders, such as depression, never go to a hospital or visit a psychotherapist. Using this method, therefore, allows numerous cases of pathology to remain undetected.

Instead, the epidemiologist may resort to a potentially more accurate method: assessing the mental health of every person in a specified geographical area, either directly or indirectly. However, such **field surveys** are expensive and difficult to conduct. They are most feasible in geographically isolated communities (e.g., islands such as Iceland), where the number of people to be assessed is relatively small and there is little movement of the population to other areas. To date, the majority of field surveys have been conducted in northern Europe and Japan (Kay & Bergmann, 1982).

Incidence and Prevalence Rates. Whatever the method, the results of epidemiological studies are typically expressed in two different ways. **Incidence rates** refer to the number of *new* cases of disease that occur within a specified period of time among a specified population. This includes those who contract the given illness for the first time and those who suffer a recurrent episode after having experienced a period of health:

$$\text{Incidence Rate} = \frac{\text{Number of New Cases}}{\text{Population at Risk}}$$

The denominator of this fraction, the **population at risk,** consists of all adults in the specified geographical area who might conceivably contract this illness. (Appropriate census or other demographical data may be used to determine this figure.) For example, suppose that 50 new cases of depression occur each day among those age 65 and over in Baltimore, Maryland. Since there are approximately 100,000 people age 65 and above in Baltimore, the daily incidence rate would be 50/100,000, or .0005 (or .05 percent). Alternatively, incidence rates may be based on a monthly or yearly period.

In contrast, **prevalence rates** refer to the *total number* of people in a given community who suffer from the illness in question:

$$\text{Prevalence Rate} = \frac{\text{Total Number of Cases}}{\text{Population at Risk}}$$

This figure may be based on a single point in time ("point prevalence"), or on a specified period of time ("period prevalence"). Thus a 7 percent point prevalence rate of depression among adults in Baltimore would mean that at the specified point in time, 7 percent of the adults in this city were found to suffer from depression. Prevalence rates may instead be reported as rates per thousand; in the preceding example, this would be expressed as 70 per 1,000.

When the frequency of an illness changes markedly at different ages, or when we are primarily interested in the relationship between aging and psychopathology, epidemiological results are best reported in terms of age-specific incidence and prevalence rates. To illustrate, we might find that the incidence rate for depression in Baltimore is 35 per 1,000 for people age 60 to 69 but only 10 per 1,000 for those age 50 to 59. Or, we might discover that the incidence rate for this disorder remains much the same throughout adulthood.

Afterword.   Age-specific incidence and prevalence rates help us to ascertain which disorders first occur in middle and old age. If a mental disorder that originates in childhood or adolescence persists into old age, we will find high prevalence rates and low incidence rates among the elderly. If, instead, a disorder typically occurs for the first time at an advanced age, the incidence rates will be markedly higher at older ages.

Age-specific incidence and prevalence rates are readily available for most major mental disorders. Before we turn to these findings, however, a note of caution must be sounded. As previously mentioned, field surveys and case registers may well yield significantly different figures for the same disorder. There is also some question as to the reliability of psychiatric diagnosis with elderly patients, even when attempts are made to be detailed and precise (e.g., Klerman, 1983). Various investigators have used different methods of diagnosis and assessment, making it difficult to compare the results of different studies. Thus the data to be discussed in the following sections should be taken as a general indication of the extent of these disorders, rather than as a mathematically exact determination.

ALZHEIMER'S DISEASE AND OTHER DEMENTIAS

Definition of Dementia.   The term **dementia** (or **dementing illness**) refers to a disease that leads initially to the loss of cognitive functioning and, in later stages, to the loss of motor and physical functioning. In particular, the symptoms of dementia include the following (Biegel, Sales, & Schulz, 1991):

A decline in intellectual ability severe enough to interfere with the sufferer's work and social life

Impairments in memory, judgment, and abstract thinking

Language problems due to brain damage (aphasia)

An inability to carry out a requested action, even though the sufferer understands the request and is physically able to perform it (apraxia)

A failure to recognize or identify familiar objects despite good vision and sense of touch (agnosia)

Several different types of dementia are classified by DSM-III-R under the category of organic mental disorders. As a group, these are the most prevalent psychiatric disorders of later life. The criteria used by clinicians to diagnose dementia are shown in Table 11.6.

More than 70 different conditions can cause dementia. Of these, the two most common among elderly persons are Alzheimer's disease and Multi-infarct dementia.

Incidence and Prevalence of Alzheimer's Disease.

Considerable attention is currently being devoted to **Alzheimer's disease**, which has been singled out as a "disease of catastrophic proportions" by the U.S. Department of Health and Human Services. It has been estimated that the prevalence of mild dementia among adults age 65 and over is approximately 12 percent and that the prevalence of moderate to severe dementia is about 6 percent (Mortimer, 1988); the majority of these dementias are thought to be caused by Alzheimer's disease. However, a recent study suggests that the prevalence of dementia and Alzheimer's disease may be much higher. These findings indicated that 10.3 percent of subjects over the age of 65 had probable Alzheimer's disease, and a startling 47.2 percent of those over age 85 had probable Alzheimer's disease (Evans, Funkenstein, & Albert, 1989). If these percentages are converted into head counts, the implications are indeed alarming: There are approximately 2.5 to 3 million cases of probable Alzheimer's disease in the United States.

Incidence rates for Alzheimer's disease are more difficult to obtain, partly because few large-scale population studies have been carried out. One longitudinal study found an incidence rate of .083 percent at age 60, .333 percent at age 70, 1.337 percent at age 80, and 5.371 at age 90 (Sayetta, 1986). According to this study, you are 16 times more likely to contract Alzheimer's disease at age 80 than at age 60, and 65 times more likely to do so at age 90 than at age 60. A similar pattern of increasing rates with increasing age has been reported by other investigators, although the specific numerical values vary considerably (e.g., Akesson, 1969; Hagnell et al., 1983). Although more accurate incidence rates are needed, the available data do indicate that the likelihood of contracting Alzheimer's disease for the first time increases sharply as an adult grows from age 60 to age 90.

Table 11.6
Diagnostic criteria for dementia.

A. Demonstrable evidence of impairment in short- and long-term memory. Impairment in short-term memory (inability to learn new information) may be indicated by inability to remember three objects after five minutes. Long-term memory impairment (inability to remember information that was known in the past) may be indicated by inability to remember past personal information (e.g., what happened yesterday, birthplace, occupation) or facts of common knowledge (e.g., past presidents, well-known dates).

B. At least one of the following:
    (1) impairment in abstract thinking, as indicated by inability to find similarities and differences between related words, difficulty in defining words and concepts, and other similar tasks
    (2) impaired judgment, as indicated by inability to make reasonable plans to deal with interpersonal, family, and job-related problems and issues
    (3) other disturbances of higher cortical function, such as aphasia (disorder of language), apraxia (inability to carry out motor activities despite intact comprehension and motor function), agnosia (failure to recognize or identify objects despite intact sensory function), and "constructional difficulty" (e.g., inability to copy three-dimensional figures, assemble blocks, or arrange sticks in specific designs)
    (4) personality change (i.e., alteration or accentuation of premorbid traits)

C. The disturbance in A and B significantly interferes with work or usual social activities or relationships with others.

D. Not occurring exclusively during the course of delirium.

E. Either (1) or (2):
    (1) there is evidence from the history, physical examination, or laboratory tests of a specific organic factor (or factors) judged to be etiologically related to the disturbance
    (2) in the absence of such evidence, an etiologic organic factor can be presumed if the disturbance cannot be accounted for by any nonorganic mental disorder (e.g., major depression accounting for cognitive impairment)

Criteria for severity of dementia:
　Mild: Although work or social activities are significantly impaired, the capacity for independent living remains, with adequate personal hygiene and relatively intact judgment.
　Moderate: Independent living is hazardous and some degree of supervision is necessary.
　Severe: Activities of daily living are so impaired that continual supervision is required (e.g., unable to maintain minimal personal hygiene, largely incoherent or mute).

Reprinted with permission from the *Diagnostic and Statistical Manual of Mental Disorders, third edition, revised.* Copyright 1987. American Psychiatric Association.

Causes of Alzheimer's Disease.

The causes of Alzheimer's disease are not yet known. Some researchers believe that the cholinergic system of the brain may be responsible, because the brains of Alzheimer's victims exhibit a significant decrease in an enzyme called choline acetyltransferase (Davies & Maloney, 1976; Perry et al., 1977; Perry et al., 1978). Other researchers contend that the brains of Alzheimer's victims possess relatively high amounts of trace metals such as aluminum, although here the evidence is equivocal (e.g., Crapper, Kirshnan, & Quittkat, 1976; McDermott et al., 1977). A third area of investigation concerns the possibility of genetic determinants. The risk of senile dementia, Down's syndrome, leukemia, and Hodgkin's disease has been found to be significantly higher among relatives of patients suffering from Alzheimer's disease than that in the general population (Heston & Mastri, 1977; Larson, Sjogren, & Jacobsen, 1963).

Whatever the causes, Alzheimer's disease is associated with various physiological changes in the brain. These include a loss of neurons, widened fissures, narrower and flatter ridges, senile plaques scattered throughout the cortex, and the replacement of normal nerve cells in the basal ganglia with tangled threadlike structures.

Onset and Course of Alzheimer's Disease.

The age of onset for Alzheimer's disease can be either early (ages 40 to 65) or late (age 66 and over). The onset of Alzheimer's disease is deceptively mild, and its course is one of steady deterioration. In the first stage, patients may exhibit minor symptoms and mood changes. They may also have less energy and drive, be less spontaneous, be slower to learn to react, and forget some basic words. Patients may also lose their temper more easily than they did before. Because these symptoms are so subtle, they often go undetected or are regarded as temporary and unimportant changes in the individual.

In the second stage, patients may still be able to perform familiar activities, but they are likely to need help with complicated tasks. The ability to speak and to understand are noticeably impaired, and patients may be insensitive to the feelings of others.

The third stage is characterized by profound memory losses, particularly of the recent past. Patients may forget the time, the date, the season, and where they are, and they may fail to recognize familiar people. Psychotic symptoms may occur, including delusions, hallucinations, paranoid thoughts, and severe agitation.

Memory continues to deteriorate in the fourth stage, and patients are likely to need help with all of their activities. They are often completely disoriented and unable to recognize loved ones and close friends, and they often lose control of bowel and bladder. Patients may become completely mute and inattentive and be totally unable to care for themselves. The process of deterioration ultimately leads to the final stage, death, although this may take anywhere from one to ten years; there is currently no cure for Alzheimer's disease, nor can its course be slowed or reversed. (See Biegel, Sales, & Schulz, 1991.)

Alzheimer's has been called the cruelest of all diseases because it kills its victims twice. First there is the living death of being unable to remember the simplest fact or perform the most basic daily function; then the body gradually sinks into coma and death. The ravages of Alzheimer's disease are graphically illustrated by the following case histories:

Case 1. A Former Writer

He had been a successful writer for more than 40 years, celebrated for his ability to remember the details of a complex and important story virtually without using notes. But soon after his retirement at age 68, he began to experience difficulty in finding the right words to express himself, and he frequently appeared to lose the thread of his thoughts. Within months, he couldn't remember his schedule for the day. In a few years he could not remember if he had just eaten.

It became necessary to give the man sedatives and sleeping pills, otherwise he would wander around the entire night. When not sedated, he became irritable and sometimes violent. Eventually, he had to be placed in a nursing home, where he continued to decline until he was unable to perform even the simplest functions for himself. He could not remember the names of those close to him. (Fischman, 1984, p. 27)

Case 2. A 46-Year-Old Supervisor

She immediately forgets the plot of the last television show she watched, and she has trouble reading newspaper articles because she loses the gist of the story after two or three sentences. She has long since forgotten the names and phone numbers of relatives, and no longer cooks or drives because she can't remember how. "Can you imagine the embarrassment of an educated woman not knowing who the president is, or having to ask where the bathroom is in your own house?" she asks in frustration. (*Newsweek*, December 3, 1984, p. 60)

Case 3. A Harvard Graduate

This 57-year old was diagnosed as having Alzheimer's disease three years ago. Now he stays home, while his wife holds down a part-time job. She must leave handwritten notes around the house so that he will remember to turn off the gas, or not go out until she comes back. He often speaks in cryptic, broken sentences. He sometimes can't remember the names of his stepchildren, or even his wife. One night he brought her a can of beer, and she reminded him that she prefers it in a glass. He went back and forth to the kitchen four or five times, always forgetting to bring the glass. She yelled at him, then felt guilty. Yet despite the stress, she clings to every moment because she knows her time with him is limited. (*Newsweek*, December 3, 1984, pp. 58–59)

Case 4. A Noted Actress

Toward the end of her life, every move had to be plotted out for her, as if life had become a script she couldn't learn. "We are going to the dining-room table, we are going to have lunch," the nurses would say. And when she had to negotiate the tiny step to the bathroom: "Now we are coming to the step, lift up your left foot." Sometimes she missed it on the first try. "But quite often," her daughter reported, "she'll be able to do it."

This was not a towering achievement for the woman who had once effortlessly swirled across movie dance floors, matching Fred Astaire step for dazzling step. But it did represent a last, faint flicker of awareness. Three years later, bedridden and speechless, Rita Hayworth died. (*Newsweek*, December 18, 1989, p. 54)

An overview of Alzheimer's disease from a neurologist's perspective is shown in the feature box on pages 365 to 367.

Broken Connections, Missing Memories

Chicago neurologist Jacob Fox sifts through the intricacies of the brain to separate the symptoms of Alzheimer's disease from spells of ordinary forgetfulness

By J. Madeleine Nash

Q. Many older people, noticing they have trouble remembering things, are petrified that they may be developing Alzheimer's. Are their fears warranted?

A. One of about every 20 patients I see at Rush-Presbyterian-St. Luke's Medical Center could be described as an Alzheimer's-phobic. My rule of thumb is that the person who thinks he or she has Alzheimer's doesn't. Almost invariably, the Alzheimer's patient is brought in by a family member. Either the patient is not aware of the problem or just can't get it together to make an appointment with a doctor.

Q. But why do so many older people seem to have trouble with memory lapses?

A. There's something known as age-associated memory impairment. It sometimes takes the form of absentmindedness, like misplacing things. The typical story is, you come into the house, you put your briefcase down, and you're distracted by something. Maybe the kids are having a fight. So you go break up the fight, and then you can't remember where you put your briefcase. Another common difficulty is thinking of names, particularly proper names. I myself have always had difficulty with names, and I've always been slightly absentminded. So when a person comes in with complaints about memory, I can say with a great deal of honesty that we both have the same problem, only I have it worse.

Q. Have you ever tried to train yourself to have a better memory?

A. Most memory tricks have to do with connecting words to visual images. When I've tried it, I couldn't remember the visual image I was supposed to recall!

Q. What is usually the first symptom of Alzheimer's disease?

A. The typical patient starts with memory problems and then deteriorates into more general confusion. A truck driver may keep delivering things to the wrong place, or a bookkeeper may not be keeping the books right anymore. Motor skills are usually retained longer, although certain patients will have difficulty early on with tasks like using a screwdriver or tying shoelaces.

Q. Why is memory the first to go?

A. In Alzheimer's disease one of the most profoundly affected areas of the brain is the hippocampus. Memories may not actually be stored in the hippocampus. Instead the area may act as a retrieval mechanism for reaching those memories.

Q. Why then do Alzheimer's patients often retain vivid memories of childhood events?

A. There is reason to believe that recently learned information is not dealt with in the same way as information learned a long time ago. So, even though the hippocampus may be involved in learning something initially, as time goes on, that information may be stored or processed in other areas of the brain. This may, in fact, be the explanation for why Alzheimer's patients initially have problems learning and remembering new things, but are better at remembering old things.

Q. What exactly does Alzheimer's disease do to the brain?

A. People argue about this. There are billions and billions of cells that make up the brain, like the bricks that make up a house, and for years it was thought that Alzheimer's disease was caused by a loss of these cells. Some recent studies suggest, however, that what is important may not be a loss of cells so much as a shrinkage. Each brain cell has a central body, attached to which are the axons and dendrites. The simplest way to think about it is that the dendrite is the part of the cell that receives information, and the axon is the part that sends information out. Maybe it's these axons and dendrites that shrink.

Q. The axons and dendrites connect one brain cell to another. Is this why they are central to memory?

A. When you learn something and retain it, something must change in the brain. Most people now believe that what happens is that certain connections between brain cells and groups of brain cells become enhanced. So it's reasonable to believe that in an illness like Alzheimer's these connections may be the first things to be disrupted.

Q. What distinguishes an Alzheimer's brain from a normal brain?

A. There are two pathological hallmarks of Alzheimer's: plaques and tangles. A plaque appears to be a conglomeration of deteriorating nerve-cell terminals. A tangle, on the other hand, is a conglomeration of deteriorating neurofilaments, little tubes that traverse the central body of the brain cell. Sometimes the cell dies, and all that's left is the tangle. The question is, Which abnormality is key?

Perhaps the answer is neither. If you just looked at heart tissue after a heart attack, you would see scarring. You wouldn't realize that what caused the heart attack was the fact that a blood vessel got blocked. So in Alzheimer's

disease maybe we are seeing only the second or third or fourth steps; maybe we have yet to locate where the real action is. In other words, the plaques and tangles may just be the graves of brain cells and may not speak to what caused their deaths.

Q. Do you have any favorite theory about what causes Alzheimer's?

A. I can honestly say that when it comes to the cause of Alzheimer's, I'm an agnostic. I'm waiting to find out. One theory is that if we all lived to 120, we'd all get Alzheimer's disease. I think if you told people they would get Alzheimer's when they were 120 years old, they wouldn't be terribly upset. The real question, then, is, Why do some people get Alzheimer's at age 50, 60, 70, 80?

Q. Is Alzheimer's disease really as frighteningly common as it appears?

A. A diagnosis of Alzheimer's used to be reserved for younger people who became prematurely senile. Senility in older people was believed to be due to something else, like hardening of the arteries. But now we know that the difference between senile old people and normal old people is that one group generally has Alzheimer's and the other doesn't. We also know that Alzheimer's becomes more common as people grow older, and since the population of this country is aging, we are seeing more patients with Alzheimer's. A colleague of mine estimates that 10 percent of people over 65 have Alzheimer's, and past the age of 85 the number may approach 50 percent. So sometime in the next century, when we have 80 million people in this country above the age of 65, we might have 8 million Alzheimer's patients.

Q. Last year a woman diagnosed with Alzheimer's killed herself with the help of a "suicide machine." What was your reaction?

A. That incident was unfortunate because it focused attention on death in mildly affected patients, whereas the biggest problem for those of us who care for Alzheimer's patients is the prolongation of life in advanced stages of disease. The question for us is, When patients inevitably lose the ability to swallow, should we advise their families to put in a stomach tube to feed them? My own personal advice is that they shouldn't. If these patients could come out of their state for a moment, knowing they would return to a state of absolutely no comprehension and no hope, would they want to be kept alive? Would I want to be kept alive like that? It's not being kept alive as a human being, but as a shell, and that seems inappropriate to me. The truth is, the person is gone and doesn't really care.

Q. What's hardest for families who are trying to cope with an Alzheimer's patient?

A. The realization that the person is different. For all of us, our definition of personhood to some extent involves thinking and understanding. I'm not saying that the person with Alzheimer's is no longer a human being. But it's not like losing a leg. When you lose a leg you're still the same person you were before. Here, as the brain fails, the person becomes like a shadow, like a reflection in the pool that is very, very blurry.

Q. What advice do you have for families struggling with an Alzheimer's patient?

A. People frequently use their children as a model for dealing with an Alzheimer's patient. But to treat patients as you would a child, to try to teach them and train them, is absolutely counterproductive. I tell families not to be bothered by what the Alzheimer's patient does if it's just a bother in theory. The best example of this is the patient who paces or talks to the television set, or who does a task over and over again. Maybe they'll keep folding or unfolding laundry, or maybe they like to wash the same dish 20 or 30 times. Family members tell me it's driving them crazy. My answer is, What are you going to have this person do instead of folding and unfolding laundry? Are they going to read Plato? Are they going to go to a play by Shakespeare? What's the big deal?

Q. Is there anything an early-stage Alzheimer's patient should not be allowed to do?

A. The one thing I'm adamant about is driving. We've done a study where approximately a third of our patients, if we look six months back, have either been involved in an accident or have had a moving violation. So generally we advise that Alzheimer's patients shouldn't drive. Sometimes, if this upsets the patient, I tell the family, Put the car away and say it's been stolen. Disconnect the battery and say the car is not working. Steal the keys, if you have to.

This is what I call creative lying, and again, the wrong model is child rearing. If young children do things you don't like, you don't lie to them about the reasons, because, after all, you are trying to teach them the correct way to behave. But an Alzheimer's patient is not learning anymore, and so the issue for the family is not training or teaching, but surviving. I don't see the harm in little white lies, or even not-so-little white lies, if they maintain a certain degree of peace in the family unit.

Q. How hopeful are you that ways of treating Alzheimer's disease will be found?

A. Currently we have no proven treatment. I really don't know, but I think that in the next few years we could begin to have reasonable palliative treatments, meaning medicines that improve the symptoms of the patients and make them function better. But there's no good reason to believe that treating the symptoms will prevent progression of the disease. If people are in pain from cancer, they're clearly better off if you treat the pain. But they still have the cancer.

Rita Hayworth was one noted victim of Alzheimer's disease, currently regarded as a disease of catastrophic proportions by the United States Department of Health and Human Services. (UPI/Bettmann Newsphotos)

Coping with Alzheimer's Disease. Receiving a diagnosis of Alzheimer's disease has been likened to receiving a death sentence. Patients respond with a variety of strong emotions, including shock, anger, fear, despair, and disbelief; some deny or refuse to acknowledge their condition altogether. Most want to talk about it, however, and wish to be included in family plans regarding their future. Yet they are sad and fearful because they know that as the dementia progresses, they will be unable to relate to their family with dignity and respect. Perhaps the most distressing aspect of Alzheimer's disease is the awareness of having profound cognitive deficits that will only get worse. Observing the unraveling of a self-identity that one has spent a lifetime creating is a load that virtually no one can bear with equanimity. (See Biegel, Sales, & Schulz, 1991; Cohen & Eisdorfer, 1986.)

As the number of individuals suffering from Alzheimer's disease has increased, so too has the quantity and diversity of available services. Diagnostic and treatment centers, located at many major universities throughout the United States, carry out research on Alzheimer's disease and offer experimental treatments as they become available. Formal support groups provide emotional aid to patients in the early stages of the disease. Adult day-care centers offer a safe and caring environment for patients in the middle stages. And for those in the later stages of Alzheimer's disease, some long-term care facilities provide special low-stimulus environments (Biegel, Sales, & Schulz, 1991). There are drawbacks, however. Such services are relatively few compared to the need, can be expensive, and may refuse to accept "difficult" patients who must be constantly watched or restrained (*Newsweek*, December 18, 1989).

It has been said that each case of Alzheimer's disease claims not one but two victims, because caregiving involves considerable emotional and physical stress. Approximately 70 percent of Alzheimer's patients remain at home and are cared for by a family member. One man, whose wife is in her tenth year of Alzheimer's and cannot speak or recognize anyone, put it this way: "You go through episodes of wanting to be relieved of it, the horror that goes on day after day, night after night. You often feel a desire that the person die—and then you feel like a monster for entertaining such thoughts." (See *Newsweek*, December 18, 1989, p. 55.)

A number of national organizations have responded to the extreme challenge associated with caring for an Alzheimer's patient at home. Foremost among these is the Alzheimer's Disease and Related Disorders Association (ADRDA), which coordinates a national network of support groups for caregivers and supports research on Alzheimer's disease. Some state units have also developed services for caregivers of Alzheimer's patients, such as respite programs that provide temporary relief from the burden of caregiving. (See Pfeiffer et al., 1989; Biegel, Sales, & Schulz, 1991.) Although formal evaluations of programs such as these are rarely carried out, the fact that people use them can be construed as evidence of their value.

Multi-infarct Dementia. A second form of dementia common among the elderly is **Multi-infarct dementia.** It is important to distinguish between this disorder and Alzheimer's disease in order to provide appropriate treatment, although differentiation is difficult without special training and the use of sophisticated equipment.

Multi-infarct dementia has an abrupt onset, progresses in stages, and is more prevalent among men. It is caused by an inadequate flow of blood to the brain, which results in the destruction of localized areas of brain tissue ("infarcts"). The symptoms of Multi-infarct dementia include impairments in memory, judgment, abstract thinking, and impulse control. There may also be a significant change in personality, depending on the location of the infarcts. Multi-infarct dementia follows a stepwise course with clearly differentiated levels of severity at different times, whereas the development of Alzheimer's disease is more gradual and progressive. Physical impairments are more common with Multi-infarct dementia. (See Table 11.7.)

Afterword. Our discussion of dementia and Alzheimer's disease has been far from pleasant. The symptoms are extremely painful, both for patient and

Table 11.7
A comparison of Alzheimer's disease and Multi-infarct dementia.

Characteristic	Alzheimer's Disease	Multi-infarct Dementia
Typical age of onset	60s–80s	50s–70s
Sex most affected	Probably women	Men
Course of disease	Progressive	Stepwise
Physical impairments	Few, appear late in life	Frequent

caregiver. It has been suggested that almost half of those over age 85 have probable Alzheimer's disease. Dementia is currently the fourth leading cause of death in the United States, accounting for 100,000 to 120,000 deaths annually. And the prevalence rates are increasing; it is estimated that by the year 2050, the number of Alzheimer's patients may reach 14 million (*Newsweek*, December 18, 1989). Thus the cost of this disorder, in both suffering and dollars, is likely to increase substantially in the years to come. This will prove to be a major challenge to our already burdened lawgivers and economic system, and to all of us.

Most forms of adult psychopathology do not follow this pattern. The incidence and prevalence rates for most psychological disorders decline with increasing age, so it would *not* be correct to conclude that the likelihood of contracting any psychological disorder increases in middle and old age; in fact, the reverse is true (see Table 11.1). Dementias such as Alzheimer's disease are the exception to the rule—unfortunately, a most painful and troublesome exception.

DEPRESSION

Definition.   Most of us experience periods of **depression** from time to time, but this is not necessarily indicative of psychopathology. Clinical depression is characterized by negative changes in mood that are powerful and pervasive: The sufferer experiences unusually strong and frequent feelings of dejection, worthlessness, gloom and dismay about the past, hopelessness about the future, and often apprehension. (See Table 11.8.) For example:

Case 5.   A 64-Year-Old Retired Travel Agent

Mrs. H. and her husband have two sons who live in another section of the country; she hears from them only when they need financial assistance. She has led a pleasant and even exciting life, including extensive travel and active participation in community affairs. She believes that she has been a failure in life, however, and that she has not treated her husband or her sons properly. She has also become obsessed with the idea that if she were to kill herself, this drastic act would enable her family to draw closer together. Her physical health is excellent, and she is not subjected to unusual life stresses; yet she has a strong tendency for negative thinking about herself. (Gallagher & Thompson, 1983, pp. 27–28)

Case 6. A 73-Year-Old Widower

Three years ago neighbors found Mr. B., a widower for 10 years, collapsed in his apartment. He was unkempt, unshaven, confused, and disoriented as to place and time. His only response to questions was, "I just want to die." The little food in his apartment apparently had not been touched for days. There was no evidence of alcohol or drug use, but lab tests did reveal a kidney infection and dehydration. He refused to eat, and complained that he was miserable. He viewed treatment as worthless because it was "only" extending his life. His speech and thinking were markedly slowed, his emotions were dulled, and he saw no hope for the future. (Gallagher & Thompson, 1983, p. 25)

Table 11.8
Diagnostic criteria for major depressive episode.

Note: A "major depressive syndrome" is defined as criterion A below.
A. At least five of the following symptoms have been present during the same two-week period and represent a change from previous functioning; at least one of the symptoms is either (1) depressed mood, or (2) loss of interest or pleasure. (Do not include symptoms that are clearly due to a physical condition, mood-incongruent delusions or hallucinations, incoherence, or marked loosening of associations.)

  (1) depressed mood (or can be irritable mood in children and adolescents) most of the day, nearly every day, as indicated either by subjective account or observation by others
  (2) markedly diminished interest or pleasure in all, or almost all, activities most of the day, nearly every day (as indicated either by subjective account or observations by others of apathy most of the time)
  (3) significant weight loss or weight gain when not dieting (e.g., more than 5 percent of body weight in a month), or decrease or increase in appetite nearly every day (in children, consider failure to make expected weight gains)
  (4) insomnia or hypersomnia nearly every day
  (5) psychomotor agitation or retardation nearly every day (observable by others, not merely subjective feelings of restlessness or being slowed down)
  (6) fatigue or loss of energy nearly every day
  (7) feelings of worthlessness or excessive or inappropriate guilt (which may be delusional) nearly every day (not merely self-reproach or guilt about being sick)
  (8) diminished ability to think or concentrate, or indecisiveness, nearly every day (either by subjective account or as observed by others)
  (9) recurrent thoughts of death (not just fear of dying), recurrent suicidal ideation without a specific plan, or a suicide attempt or a specific plan for committing suicide
B. (1) It cannot be established that an organic factor initiated and maintained the disturbance.
  (2) The disturbance is not a normal reaction to the death of a loved one (uncomplicated bereavement).
     Note: Morbid preoccupation with worthlessness, suicidal ideation, marked functional impairment or psychomotor retardation, or prolonged duration suggest bereavement complicated by major depression.
C. At no time during the disturbance have there been delusions or hallucinations for as long as two weeks in the absence of prominent mood symptoms (i.e., before the mood symptoms developed or after they have remitted).
D. Not superimposed on schizophrenia, schizophreniform disorder, delusional disorder, or psychotic disorder NOS.

Somatic symptoms and physiological changes are also common aspects of depression, and distorted perceptions and thoughts may occur in some instances.

It is not easy to distinguish depression from the dementias. Approximately 50 percent of all depressed patients demonstrate some degree of cognitive impairment, with 15 percent exhibiting severe, dementia-like symptoms. Conversely, about 25 percent of all patients suffering from dementia are also depressed. Thus it is not surprising that some curable cases of depression have been mistaken for Alzheimer's disease (Wolinsky, 1983). One way to differentiate true dementia from the dementia syndrome caused by depression is that the latter is reversible, whereas the former is not. (See Boller et al., 1984.)

Some theorists distinguish between depression and related functional disorders, such as the demoralization that results from membership in a low status group or from the loss of health and power. In contrast to depression, demoralization is *not* accompanied either by physiological symptoms or by perceptual and thought distortions (Gurland, 1982; Gurland & Toner, 1982).

Incidence and Prevalence Rates.   Although it is not uncommon to find elderly persons who have symptoms of depression, these symptoms are seldom severe enough to warrant a diagnosis of psychopathology. As shown in Table 11.9, about 15 percent of the elderly have psychiatric symptoms of depression. But as Table 11.10 indicates, only 0.5 to 1.6 percent actually suffer from major depression (Blazer, 1989).

For adults of all ages, those who are seriously ill tend to be more depressed. This is due primarily to being helpless and highly dependent on other people, however, rather than to being ill per se. Cancer patients capable of normal activity have been found to be significantly less depressed than bedridden diabetics, even though the former illness is at least as severe. Some data also indicate that when the level of physical disability is statistically controlled, the relationship between illness and depression disappears.

Table 11.9

Prevalence of psychiatric symptoms in community populations of older adults.

Site	Number of Cases	Age	Assessment Strategy	Disorder/ Symptoms	Prevalence (percent)
Durham County	997	65+	Depression scale	Depression	15
New Haven	2,811	65+	CES-D	Depression	15
Iowa	3,217	65+	Selected questions	Trouble falling asleep	14

Source: Blazer (1989, p. 245).

Table 11.10

Prevalence of selected psychiatric symptoms in community populations of older adults.

New Haven Epidemiologic Catchment Area	3,058	65+	Interview	Major depression	male female	= 0.5 = 1.6
				Alcohol abuse	male female	= 3.0 = 0
				Schizophrenia	male female	= 0 = 0.9
England	297	65+	Interview	Anxiety disorder		5–10
North Carolina	1,297	65+	Interview	Anxiety disorder		5.5

Source: Blazer (1989, p. 246).

(See, for example, Cassileth et al., 1984; Gurland et al., 1983; Larson, 1978; Linn et al., 1980.) Furthermore, the relationship between physical disability and depression appears to be more prominent among the middle-aged than the elderly. One reason for this (as we observed in Chapter 7) is that the elderly are more likely to conceptualize ill health as normal for their age, so they tend to face their illnesses with relative calm and equanimity.

Treatment.   In marked contrast to the dementias, the anguish of depression can be eased by appropriate treatment. Currently popular methods include drug therapy, electroconvulsive therapy, cognitive therapy, behavior therapy, and family therapy.

   Drug therapy is widely used to treat elderly patients suffering from depression, and the drugs most often used are **antidepressants**. Of the various antidepressants, tricyclics (nortriptyline, desipramine, doxepin) are typically used with older adults; they tend to be effective yet relatively free of side effects (Blazer, 1989). If tricyclics prove ineffective, other antidepressants may be tried (e.g., trazodone), although they may have such undesirable side effects as excessive daytime sedation.

   The use of **electroconvulsive therapy (ECT)** (or "shock therapy") has declined in recent years. This is due partly to advances in drug therapy, and perhaps also to negative media coverage about the side effects of ECT. Nevertheless, the induction of a seizure can reverse a major depression (Blazer, 1989). Many therapists now prefer to administer the electric shocks to only one side of the brain, rather than to both cerebral hemispheres (as in the earlier days of ECT); this appears to be equally effective, and tends to lessen distressing side effects (such as confusion and memory losses). The overall success rate of ECT with patients who failed to respond to drug therapy is about 80 percent (Blazer, 1989). These improvements end in relapses as often as 50 percent of the time, however, and memory losses do occur even when only one cerebral hemisphere receives shocks, so ECT should be prescribed only when other methods have proved ineffective. Yet in such instances, especially when the patient engages in self-destructive behavior (suicide attempts, refusing to eat), ECT may well be the treatment of choice.

Cognitive therapy differs from drug therapy and ECT in virtually every respect. It is based on the assumption that in many instances, people behave in self-defeating and pathological ways because they are not aware of their true motives, beliefs, and feelings. Thus, the goal of cognitive therapy is to help patients understand the causes and dynamics of their disorders and to change their self-defeating modes of thought. This is done by means of verbal communication, and by giving various assignments (e.g., keeping a daily or weekly log of behaviors and thoughts), rather than such physical methods as drugs or electric shocks. Although some theorists (including Freud and others) contend that patients over the age of 45 are too inflexible to profit from cognitive therapy (Gotestam, 1982), it is being used successfully with older adults suffering from depression. The case of Mrs. H. is a good example:

The Treatment of Mrs. H. (Case Number 5)

Because of Mrs. H.'s strong tendency to think negatively about herself, cognitive therapy was selected as the treatment of choice. . . . Mrs. H. was asked to keep a daily record of her negative thoughts, and to bring this to each therapy session for discussion. For example, she became unreasonably angry when her husband forgot to pick

Although controversial, electroconvulsive shock therapy may be the treatment of choice in some instances. (Will McIntyre/Photo Researchers, Inc.)

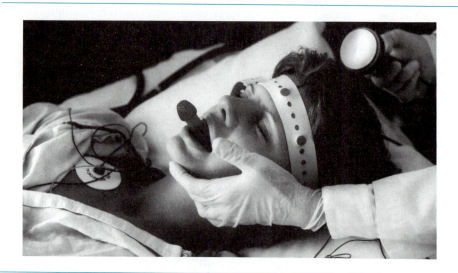

up some clothes from the cleaners, and grew intensely sad at night when she thought about her sons. Her view of life reflected an "all-or-none" philosophy: "either I'm a great success and completely happy, or a total failure and miserably unhappy." And she dwelt on the past in such terms as "if only I had . . ." and "I can't be happy unless things are the way they used to be."

With the aid of the therapist, Mrs. H. soon realized that such thoughts served to fuel her depression. She learned to recognize them as distorted and fallacious, and to reassess her situation from a more realistic perspective. Thus she learned that she could find new sources of happiness to replace the pleasures which she had enjoyed in the past, but which were no longer possible: "things change in life all the time, and this can open new paths to satisfaction." She also traced the roots of her negative thinking to her guilt about having been a working mother long before this was socially acceptable, and to the corresponding belief that she had seriously neglected her husband and children in order to pursue her own career. By learning to monitor her thoughts, and to replace her overly negative cognitions with more realistic appraisals, Mrs. H. was able to achieve a marked decrease in depression. (Gallagher & Thompson, 1983, pp. 27–29)

In contrast to cognitive therapy, **behavior therapy** does not strive to promote understanding on the part of the client. The goal is to change pathological behaviors and alleviate troublesome symptoms, using the principles and procedures devised by experimental psychologists in their study of normal behavior. Thus the behavior therapist may provide training in relaxation or assertiveness, model desired behavior, role-play troublesome situations with the client in order to help the client discover more effective behaviors, or use a variety of other techniques.

The Treatment of Mr. B. (Case Number 6)

Mr. B. first received a series of 10 ECT treatments over a six-week period, and was released from the hospital as markedly improved. He functioned reasonably well for about eight weeks, when he again began to experience severe mood shifts.

Unlike Mrs. H., Mr. B. had few negative thoughts about himself. He was intensely lonely, however, and had had no meaningful interpersonal relationships since the death of his wife ten years ago. He also found few activities to be pleasant, and many to be unpleasant. Accordingly, behavior therapy was selected as the treatment of choice.

Relaxation training helped to decrease the aversiveness of Mr. B.'s interpersonal encounters, while role-playing and other techniques enabled him to improve his communication skills and develop more positive interactions with other people. He was encouraged to leave his apartment to have lunch, and then visit the park or his neighbors, so as to use his newly developed skills. Eventually he started to take the initiative to plan social activities, such as attending the local senior center and joining a card club. By the end of therapy, Mr. B. had significantly increased his social relationships. His depression was markedly reduced, and remained so during a one-year follow-up period. (Gallagher & Thompson, 1983, pp. 25–26)

Family support can help a depressed patient achieve a successful outcome, but family stress and dysfunction can exacerbate the depressive symptoms. Therefore, some clinicians prefer to meet with both the depressed patient and family members at the same time, a procedure known as **family therapy**. With the permission of the patient, the family is instructed as to the nature of the depressive disorder and the potential risks that may occur late in life (especially suicide). Family members can help advise the therapist about important changes in the patient's behavior, such as increased withdrawal from people or a preoccupation with medication or weapons, and they can remove potential suicide implements if necessary. The family can also be taught how to respond effectively to the patient's expressions of low self-esteem and pessimism, as by paraphrasing what the patient says and expressing understanding without trying to intervene (e.g., "I hear what you are saying, and I understand"). Finally, if the symptoms of depression become severe enough to require hospitalization, the clinician can explain this to the family and secure their cooperation. (See Blazer, 1989.)

Afterword.   The preceding discussion supports a point made previously in this chapter: Most psychological disorders do *not* become more prevalent with increasing age. Clinical depression afflicts only a small percentage of older adults, and treatment methods are available for those who do contract this disorder. In sum: The normal course of aging is not necessarily, or even usually, accompanied by increases in depression.

Myths About Aging

Adult Psychopathology

Myth	*Best Available Evidence*
If you live into your eighties or beyond, you are very likely to suffer such severe mental deterioration that you become mindless or "senile."	Dementias do afflict a significant proportion of the elderly and are more likely to occur with increasing age. But even if you live to be 80 or older, the chances of your contracting a dementia are less than 50-50.
You are likely to become more depressed as you grow toward old age.	The incidence and prevalence of clinical depression do *not* increase with increasing age.
You are more likely to contract a serious mental illness as you grow older.	Although Alzheimer's disease is an important and troublesome exception, the incidence rates for most forms of psychopathology decline with increasing age.
Middle-aged and elderly adults are not amenable to treatment by cognitive and behavior therapy.	Successful cognitive and behavior therapy has been and is being done with the middle-aged and elderly.

ANXIETY DISORDERS

Definition.   One of Freud's most valuable contributions was his discovery that psychological pain can be just as troublesome as physical pain, if not more so. He called such psychic pain **anxiety**, which is a highly unpleasant emotion similar to intense nervousness. (See, for example, Freud, 1926/1959.)

All of us experience anxiety at one time or another, and this is in no way indicative of psychopathology. When anxiety becomes so pervasive and intense as to cause serious interference with an individual's normal functioning, however, professional intervention is warranted.

There are several varieties of **anxiety disorder**. In *generalized anxiety*, severe anxiety occurs without any apparent cause. *Phobic disorders* involve an intense but irrational fear of a specific object or situation that is actually not dangerous, as with agoraphobia (the fear of being in public places from which escape might be difficult) and claustrophobia (the fear of closed places). In *obsessive-compulsive disorders*, thoughts or actions are repeatedly performed for no apparent reason except to reduce anxiety. For example, the sufferer may feel compelled to check that the front door is locked not once, but ten or fifteen times, before leaving the house. Anxiety disorders are typically accompanied by physical changes, including perspiring, dizziness, nausea, dry mouth, and an upset stomach. (See Table 11.11.)

Incidence and Prevalence Rates.   Anxiety disorders occur among adults of all ages. The prevalence among older adults is fairly high, and has been estimated at approximately 5 to 10 percent (Blazer, 1989; see Table 11.10). Older adults may become anxious for various reasons, including failing health, the loss of loved ones and friends, intellectual declines, feelings of helplessness and worthlessness, and loss of control over the immediate environment. Phobic anxiety may be difficult to diagnose among the elderly, however, because they may well be embarrassed by these symptoms and conceal them behind protestations of physical illness (Jenike, 1989). As is true of most forms of psychopathology, incidence rates for anxiety disorders decline with increasing age (Brickman & Eisdorfer, 1989); you are less likely to contract such a disorder for the first time as you grow through adulthood.

Treatment.   Various forms of psychotherapy are used to treat anxiety disorders. These include psychoanalysis, cognitive therapy, and behavior therapy, the last of which has become increasingly popular. In *systematic desensitization*, for example, phobic anxiety is reduced by having the client list the feared stimuli in hierarchical order (e.g., "being in a public place," "approaching the public place," and ending with "thinking of going outside"). The client then imagines being in these situations, starting with the lowest one in the hierarchy (least anxiety-provoking), while practicing previously taught techniques of muscular relaxation. In some instances, the client may be

Table 11.11
Diagnostic criteria for generalized anxiety disorder.

A. Unrealistic or excessive anxiety and worry (apprehensive expectation) about two or more life circumstances, e.g., worry about possible misfortune to one's child (who is in no danger) and worry about finances (for no good reason), for a period of six months or longer, during which the person has been bothered more days than not by these concerns. In children and adolescents, this may take the form of anxiety and worry about academic, athletic, and social performance.

B. If another Axis I disorder is present, the focus of the anxiety and worry in A is unrelated to it, e.g., the anxiety or worry is not about having a panic attack (as in panic disorder), being embarrassed in public (as in social phobia), being contaminated (as in obsessive-compulsive disorder), or gaining weight (as in anorexia nervosa).

C. The disturbance does not occur only during the course of a mood disorder or a psychotic disorder.

D. At least 6 of the following 18 symptoms are often present when anxious (do not include symptoms present only during panic attacks):

Motor tension
(1) trembling, twitching, or feeling shaky
(2) muscle tension, aches, or soreness
(3) restlessness
(4) easy fatigability

Autonomic hyperactivity
(5) shortness of breath or smothering sensations
(6) palpitations or accelerated heart rate (tachycardia)
(7) sweating, or cold clammy hands
(8) dry mouth
(9) dizziness or lightheadedness
(10) nausea, diarrhea, or other abdominal distress
(11) flushes (not flashes) or chills
(12) frequent urination
(13) trouble swallowing or "lump in throat"

Vigilance and scanning
(14) feeling keyed up or on edge
(15) exaggerated startle response
(16) difficulty concentrating or "mind going blank" because of anxiety
(17) trouble falling or staying asleep
(18) irritability

E. It cannot be established that an organic factor initiated and maintained the disturbance, e.g,., hyperthyroidism, caffeine intoxication.

Reprinted with permission from the *Diagnostic and Statistical Manual of Mental Disorders, third edition, revised.* Copyright 1987. American Psychiatric Association.

asked to use the relaxation techniques while actually in the anxiety-provoking situation. Relaxation procedures have also been found to be effective in helping clients learn to control feelings of anxiety before they get out of hand.

Many older adults respond favorably to behavior therapy and psychotherapy, which are preferable to medication whenever a choice exists (Jenike, 1989). If these methods prove to be ineffective, however, the next step is drug therapy. Among the drugs used to treat anxiety disorders are the benzo-diazepines (e.g., Valium, Librium, Serax). Alternatively, drug therapy may be used in combination with psychotherapy.

AFTERWORD

Our review of adult psychopathology has been both disturbing and reassuring. We have seen that Alzheimer's disease is extremely painful, incurable, and increasing in prevalence. The torment undergone by these patients, and by those who must care for them, can only be imagined by those of us fortunate enough to avoid this experience. This is truly a disease of catastrophic proportions, and it is a problem that is likely to become even worse in the next few decades.

Yet we have also observed that the incidence and prevalence of most forms of psychopathology decline with increasing age. (Thus we have chosen not to discuss certain disorders, such as schizophrenia and some forms of what used to be called neurosis. Though important, these disorders often originate in childhood or young adulthood; they are less likely to occur for the first time during late adulthood and are less common among older adults.) We have also seen that there are useful forms of treatment for older adults who do become clinically depressed or suffer from an anxiety disorder. The quality of differential diagnosis is improving, when one wishes to take the necessary time and effort, and an increasing number of therapeutic procedures are being offered for various geriatric disorders.

Although many effective treatment methods are currently available, many elderly persons are not receiving needed treatment for their disorders. There is a shortage of properly trained personnel; some professionals are biased against treating the elderly; and some elderly individuals are reluctant to seek treatment from mental health services. These are problems that must be resolved, so that more people can make the latter part of their lives more meaningful and fulfilling.

Summary

SUBSTANTIVE AND METHODOLOGICAL ISSUES

It is not always easy to distinguish between mental health and psychopathology. Whether or not behavior is pathological may depend on the specific situation, cultural factors, and the age of the individual. In general, mental health reflects the ability to deal with the issues of life in an effective way, as by satisfying instinctual drives in ways that are socially acceptable and appropriately flexible.

Psychopathology may be caused by various factors. Such pioneering clinical investigators as Sigmund Freud attributed psychopathology entirely to experiences during childhood, notably those involving the parents. Modern clinicians agree that childhood causes are important but have identified numerous other factors related to psychopathology, some of which are psychosocial (e.g., age, sex, race, education, income, marital status, religious participation, stress) and some biological (such as medication, endocrine disorders, infections, tumors, metabolic disorders, concussions, and nutrition disorders).

Because there are so many possible causes of psychopathology, diagnosis and assessment can be a difficult task. One popular system for classifying the various forms of psychopathology is DSM-III-R, the 1987 revision of the *Diagnostic and Statistical Manual* prepared by the American Psychiatric Association. Among the common assessment procedures are clinical interviews and psychometric instruments. The latter include measures that probe deeply into the patient's personality and rough, quickly administered screening tests.

EPIDEMIOLOGY AND TREATMENT OF ADULT PSYCHOPATHOLOGY

The greater the frequency of a particular disorder, the more people who will benefit if we diagnose and treat it correctly. Field surveys and the case register method are commonly used to obtain epidemiological data, which are typically expressed in terms of incidence rates and prevalence rates.

Dementias lead initially to the loss of cognitive functioning and in later stages to the loss of motor and physical functioning. Of the more than 70 different conditions that can cause dementia, the two most common among elderly persons are Alzheimer's disease and Multi-infarct dementia. Alzheimer's has become a disease of catastrophic proportions; it may afflict as many as 10 percent of adults over age 65, and 47 percent of adults over 85. Alzheimer's disease is incurable, and its course cannot be slowed or reversed. It has been called the cruelest of all diseases because it kills its victims twice: First there is the living death of being unable to remember the simplest fact, perform the most basic daily function, or even recognize loved ones and recall one's own identity; then, the body gradually sinks into coma and death. The course of Alzheimer's disease is gradual and progressive. The causes of the disease are not yet known. Various services exist to help Alzheimer's patients and their caregivers, who also experience considerable emotional and physical stress. In contrast to Alzheimer's disease, Multi-infarct dementia has an abrupt onset, progresses in stages, is more prevalent among men, more often involves physical impairments, and is caused by an inadequate flow of blood to the brain. The symptoms of Multi-infarct dementia include impairments in memory, judgment, abstract thinking, and impulse control and possible changes in personality.

Clinical depression is characterized by negative changes in mood that are powerful and pervasive. The sufferer experiences unusually strong and frequent feelings of dejection, apprehension, worthlessness, gloom and dismay about the past, and hopelessness about the future. Depression may well be mistaken for a dementia because it often involves some degree of cognitive impairment. Although it is not uncommon to find elderly persons who have symptoms of depression, these are rarely severe enough to warrant a diagnosis of psychopathology; the prevalence of clinical depression among older adults is low, and the incidence declines with increasing age. Various forms of treatment are available to those who do contract clinical depression, including chemotherapy (usually with antidepressants), electroconvulsive therapy, cognitive therapy, behavior therapy, and family therapy.

Anxiety is a universal experience and is considered pathological only when it becomes so pervasive and intense as to seriously interfere with an individual's normal functioning. Varieties of anxiety disorder include generalized anxiety, phobic disorders, and obsessive-compulsive disorders. The prevalence of anxiety disorders among older adults is fairly high, but various forms of psychotherapy and (if necessary) chemotherapy have proved effective in treating this disorder.

Although many effective treatment methods are currently available, many elderly persons are not receiving needed treatment for their disorders. This problem must be resolved, so that more people can make the latter part of their lives more meaningful and fulfilling.

Study Questions

1. What are the most important causes of adult psychopathology? What does the variety of causes imply about our ability to diagnose the disorder that afflicts a particular individual?
2. Why is it important to classify the various kinds of mental disorders? Why has it proved necessary to revise the standard classification system several times? What does this imply about our ability to diagnose the disorder that afflicts a particular individual?
3. Why has Alzheimer's disease been called the cruelest of all diseases?
4. Of the disorders discussed in this chapter, which are you significantly more likely to contract as you grow past middle age? What does this imply about the general level of mental health among older adults?
5. How do methods for treating depression differ from methods for treating anxiety disorders? Have these methods proved successful with older adults, or is their effectiveness limited to young adults?

Terms to Remember

Alzheimer's disease

Antidepressant

Anxiety

Anxiety disorder

Assessment

Behavior therapy

Case register method

Cognitive therapy

Dementia (dementing illness)

Depression

Drug therapy

DSM-III-R

Electroconvulsive therapy (ECT)

Epidemiology

Family therapy

Field survey

Incidence rate

Mental health

Multi-infarct dementia

Organic mental disorder

Population at risk

Prevalence rate

Psychopathology

Psychotherapy

Chapter 12
Death and Dying

Rameshwar Das/Monkmeyer Press Photo Service

In Chapter 1, we observed that many more of us are living to old age than ever before. There has also been a significant change in our manner of dying: Illnesses that are of long duration (**chronic**) have replaced those that are brief and severe (**acute**) as the major causes of death. This means that dying will be a fairly drawn-out process for many of us (Schulz & Schlarb, 1987–88). Furthermore, this process is likely to place considerable demands on those family members and friends who are with us during this difficult time. As a result, death and dying has become an important aspect of adult development and aging.

Partly for this reason, recent years have seen a remarkable crescendo of discussion about death and dying. Library shelves are now filled with volumes concerning the philosophical, religious, sociological, anthropological, psychological, and medical views of death. It is not unusual for more than 700 books to be published on these topics in a single year. Entire journals are now devoted to the inspection, dissection, and analysis of every imaginable aspect of death and dying.

This fascination with death is hardly new. Noted philosophers from Epicurus to Bertrand Russell, playwrights, poets, novelists, and many others have written incisively about death for more than two thousand years. During the past two decades, however, our quest for knowledge has taken a significant turn: For the first time, investigators in a variety of disciplines have sought to collect systematic empirical data about death and dying. Much of this data-gathering has been stimulated and carried out by psychologists; but sociologists, anthropologists, and physicians have participated as well. This area is also prone to methodological problems, and some researchers have drawn intriguing but overly speculative conclusions that go far beyond the actual evidence. Yet we can now answer some important questions about death and dying, and make educated guesses in various areas where firm conclusions are not yet possible.

This chapter addresses four major issues. First we examine the demography of death, including leading causes and mortality rates. Next we survey the evidence dealing with the fear of death, which some psychologists and philosophers believe to be a major determinant of human behavior. Our third topic concerns the experiences of the terminally ill and the effects on their families and friends. For example, do all of the dying proceed through a series of similar psychological stages? Or are their experiences with the specter of death primarily different? Part four deals with the grief and bereavement that result from the death of someone close to us and describes how these intense and painful feelings may be alleviated.

The Demography of Death

Although the course of human history has been highlighted by astonishing scientific advances, methods for preventing death exist only in the realm of

TYPE/PRINT IN PERMANENT BLACK INK FOR INSTRUCTIONS

SEE OTHER SIDE AND HANDBOOK

U.S. STANDARD
CERTIFICATE OF DEATH

LOCAL FILE NUMBER — STATE FILE NUMBER

DECEDENT

1. DECEDENT'S NAME *(First, Middle, Last)*
2. SEX
3. DATE OF DEATH *(Month, Day, Year)*
4. SOCIAL SECURITY NUMBER
5a. AGE—Last Birthday *(Years)*
5b. UNDER 1 YEAR — Months / Days
5c. UNDER 1 DAY — Hours / Minutes
6. DATE OF BIRTH *(Month, Day, Year)*
7. BIRTHPLACE *(City and State or Foreign Country)*
8. WAS DECEDENT EVER IN U.S. ARMED FORCES? *(Yes or no)*
9a. PLACE OF DEATH *(Check only one; see instructions on other side)*
HOSPITAL: ☐ Inpatient ☐ ER/Outpatient ☐ DOA — OTHER: ☐ Nursing Home ☐ Residence ☐ Other *(Specify)*
9b. FACILITY NAME *(If not institution, give street and number)*
9c. CITY, TOWN, OR LOCATION OF DEATH
9d. COUNTY OF DEATH
10. MARITAL STATUS—Married, Never Married, Widowed, Divorced *(Specify)*
11. SURVIVING SPOUSE *(If wife, give maiden name)*
12a. DECEDENT'S USUAL OCCUPATION *(Give kind of work done during most of working life. Do not use retired.)*
12b. KIND OF BUSINESS/INDUSTRY

SEE INSTRUCTIONS ON OTHER SIDE →

13a. RESIDENCE—STATE
13b. COUNTY
13c. CITY, TOWN, OR LOCATION
13d. STREET AND NUMBER
13e. INSIDE CITY LIMITS? *(Yes or no)*
13f. ZIP CODE
14. WAS DECEDENT OF HISPANIC ORIGIN? (Specify No or Yes—If yes, specify Cuban, Mexican, Puerto Rican, etc.) ☐ No ☐ Yes *Specify:*
15. RACE—American Indian, Black, White, etc. *(Specify)*
16. DECEDENT'S EDUCATION *(Specify only highest grade completed)* Elementary/Secondary (0-12) / College (1-4 or 5+)

NAME OF DECEDENT: ______ For use by physician or institution

PARENTS

17. FATHER'S NAME *(First, Middle, Last)*
18. MOTHER'S NAME *(First, Middle, Maiden Surname)*

INFORMANT

19a. INFORMANT'S NAME *(Type/Print)*
19b. MAILING ADDRESS *(Street and Number or Rural Route Number, City or Town, State, Zip Code)*

DISPOSITION

20a. METHOD OF DISPOSITION ☐ Burial ☐ Cremation ☐ Removal from State ☐ Donation ☐ Other *(Specify)* ______
20b. PLACE OF DISPOSITION *(Name of cemetery, crematory, or other place)*
20c. LOCATION—City or Town, State
21a. SIGNATURE OF FUNERAL SERVICE LICENSEE OR PERSON ACTING AS SUCH ▶
21b. LICENSE NUMBER *(of Licensee)*
22. NAME AND ADDRESS OF FACILITY

SEE DEFINITION ON OTHER SIDE

PRONOUNCING PHYSICIAN ONLY

Complete items 23a-c only when certifying physician is not available at time of death to certify cause of death.
23a. **To the best of my knowledge, death occurred at the time, date, and place stated.** *Signature and Title* ▶
23b. LICENSE NUMBER
23c. DATE SIGNED *(Month, Day, Year)*

ITEMS 24-26 MUST BE COMPLETED BY PERSON WHO PRONOUNCES DEATH →

24. TIME OF DEATH M
25. DATE PRONOUNCED DEAD *(Month, Day, Year)*
26. WAS CASE REFERRED TO MEDICAL EXAMINER/CORONER? *(Yes or no)*

CAUSE OF DEATH

SEE INSTRUCTIONS ON OTHER SIDE

27. PART I. Enter the diseases, injuries, or complications that caused the death. Do not enter the mode of dying, such as cardiac or respiratory arrest, shock, or heart failure. List only one cause on each line.

Approximate Interval Between Onset and Death

IMMEDIATE CAUSE (Final disease or condition resulting in death) → a. ______
DUE TO (OR AS A CONSEQUENCE OF):
b. ______
DUE TO (OR AS A CONSEQUENCE OF):
c. ______
DUE TO (OR AS A CONSEQUENCE OF):
d. ______

Sequentially list conditions, if any, leading to immediate cause. Enter **UNDERLYING CAUSE** (Disease or injury that initiated events resulting in death) **LAST**

PART II. Other significant conditions contributing to death but not resulting in the underlying cause given in Part I.
28a. WAS AN AUTOPSY PERFORMED? *(Yes or no)*
28b. WERE AUTOPSY FINDINGS AVAILABLE PRIOR TO COMPLETION OF CAUSE OF DEATH? *(Yes or no)*
29. MANNER OF DEATH ☐ Natural ☐ Accident ☐ Suicide ☐ Homicide ☐ Pending Investigation ☐ Could not be Determined
30a. DATE OF INJURY *(Month, Day, Year)*
30b. TIME OF INJURY M
30c. INJURY AT WORK? *(Yes or no)*
30d. DESCRIBE HOW INJURY OCCURRED
30e. PLACE OF INJURY—At home, farm, street, factory, office building, etc. *(Specify)*
30f. LOCATION (Street and Number or Rural Route Number, City or Town, State)

SEE DEFINITION ON OTHER SIDE

CERTIFIER

31a. CERTIFIER *(Check only one)*
☐ CERTIFYING PHYSICIAN *(Physician certifying cause of death when another physician has pronounced death and completed Item 23)*
To the best of my knowledge, death occurred due to the cause(s) and manner as stated.
☐ PRONOUNCING AND CERTIFYING PHYSICIAN *(Physician both pronouncing death and certifying to cause of death)*
To the best of my knowledge, death occurred at the time, date, and place, and due to the cause(s) and manner as stated.
☐ MEDICAL EXAMINER/CORONER
On the basis of examination and/or investigation, in my opinion, death occurred at the time, date, and place, and due to the cause(s) and manner as stated.
31b. SIGNATURE AND TITLE OF CERTIFIER ▶
31c. LICENSE NUMBER
31d. DATE SIGNED *(Month, Day, Year)*
32. NAME AND ADDRESS OF PERSON WHO COMPLETED CAUSE OF DEATH (ITEM 27) *(Type/Print)*

REGISTRAR

33. REGISTRAR'S SIGNATURE ▶
34. DATE FILED *(Month, Day, Year)*

DEPARTMENT OF HEALTH AND HUMAN SERVICES — PUBLIC HEALTH SERVICE — NATIONAL CENTER FOR HEALTH STATISTICS — 1989 REVISION

PHS-T-003
REV. 1/89

Figure 12.1
A typical death certificate. Source: Courtesy Indiana State Board of Health.

science fiction. In 1988, for example, the number of deaths in the United States totaled 2,167,999 (National Center for Health Statistics, 1990). However, important changes have occurred in the most common causes and places of death.

CAUSES OF DEATH

In the preceding chapter, we observed that classification is an important aspect of any science. This also applies to the study of mortality rates: Causes of death are classified according to formal criteria established by the World Health Organization, aided by such standardized instruments as the death certificate. This useful form records such information as immediate and other causes of death; whether death was due to an accident, suicide, or homicide; the time and place of death; and biographical data, such as the deceased's name, sex, age, birthplace, and immediate family. (See Figure 12.1.)

Table 12.1

Mortality rates for the United States (1988), including age-adjusted rates by sex and race.

Rank	Cause of Death	Percent of Total Deaths*	Ratio of Males to Females	Ratio of Blacks to Whites
1	Heart diseases	35.3	1.87	1.40
2	Malignant neoplasms (including tumors, cancers)	22.4	1.46	1.32
3	Cerebrovascular diseases (including strokes)	6.9	1.17	1.87
4	Accidents†	4.5	2.70	1.28
5	Chronic obstructive pulmonary diseases	3.8	1.96	0.84
6	Pneumonia and influenza	3.6	1.72	1.44
7	Diabetes mellitus	1.9	1.07	2.36
8	Suicide	1.4	3.98	0.56
9	Chronic liver disease and cirrhosis	1.2	2.30	1.73
10	Nephritis, nephrotic syndrome, and nephrosis (kidney disease)	1.0	1.50	2.83
11	Atherosclerosis	1.0	1.33	1.12
12	Homicide and legal intervention	1.0	3.31	6.43
13	Septicemia	1.0	1.27	2.60
14	Certain conditions originating in the perinatal period	0.8	1.26	2.69
15	Human immunodeficiency virus infection	0.8	8.57	3.38
—	All other causes	13.4	——	——

*Not age adjusted
†Approximately half of all accident fatalities involve motor vehicles.
Source: National Center for Health Statistics (1990, pp. 5, 7).

Leading Causes of Death.   As noted at the outset of this chapter, deaths in our society are more often due to chronic than to acute illnesses. Deaths from communicable diseases have decreased markedly since 1900; for example, pneumonia and influenza caused only 4 percent of all deaths in 1988. Conversely, more than half of all current deaths are caused by such degenerative diseases as heart ailments, cancer, and strokes. (See Table 12.1.)

As noted in Chapter 3, we have become more knowledgeable about the dangers of cigarette smoking, high blood pressure, high blood levels of LDL cholesterol, obesity, physical inactivity, and stress. Partly for this reason, there has been a decline in deaths from heart disease and strokes since 1950. (See Figure 12.2.) In addition, the number of accidental deaths declined from 105,312 in 1979 to 94,500 in 1989. And the age-adjusted death rate for cancer decreased slightly between 1987 and 1988, the third

Figure 12.2
Age-adjusted death rates for five leading causes of death, United States, 1950–1988.   Source: National Center for Health Statistics (1990, p. 6).

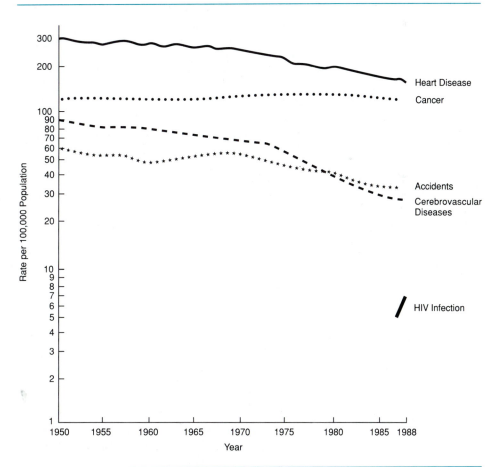

consecutive year that this has happened. Unfortunately, however, a new killer is looming on the horizon: human immunodeficiency virus infection. HIV infection was the fifteenth leading cause of death in 1988, producing 16,602 fatalities. And it is likely to rank considerably higher in the near future, because the World Health Organization has predicted that there will be as many as 30 million AIDS cases throughout the world by the year 2000. (See American Public Health Association, 1991; National Center for Health Statistics, 1990.)

The frequency of the leading causes of death varies as a function of gender and race. As of 1988, males were almost nine times as likely as females to die from HIV infection, four times as likely to commit suicide, and 3.3 times as likely to die from homicide and legal intervention. Blacks were more than six times as likely as whites to die from homicide and legal intervention, and more than three times as likely to die from HIV infection. (See Table 12.1.)

The Demographics of Suicide.   Suicide is of some interest to geriatricians because of its relationship to depression, one of the most common adult disorders (Chapter 11), and because suicide rates vary as a function of age (as well as race and sex). Suicide is most common among white males, especially those over 65. This is the group that most often achieves the dominant positions in our society and suffers the greatest losses in status and financial rewards with retirement and old age. Conversely, suicide rates for females tend to remain fairly constant with increasing age. For non-whites, there is a slight tendency for suicide rates to peak at about age 20 and again at about age 80, but the rates remain significantly lower at all ages than the corresponding figures for whites. (See Figures 12.3 and 12.4.)

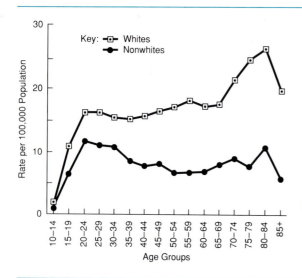

Figure 12.3
Suicide by age and race, United States, 1985.   Source: McIntosh (1988–1989), "Official U.S. elderly suicide data bases: Levels, availab ility, omissions." *Omega: Journal of Death and Dying, 19,* pp. 337–350.

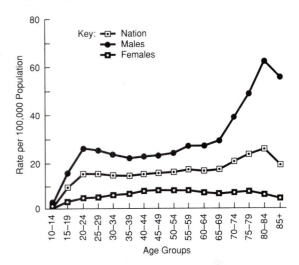

Figure 12.4
Suicide by age and sex, United States, 1985.   Source:
McIntosh (1988–1989), "Official U.S. elderly suicide
data bases: Levels, availability, omissions." *Omega:
Journal of Death and Dying, 19,* pp. 337–350.

PLACES OF DEATH

Relatively little research attention has been paid to the locations where
Americans are most likely to die, even though this information can be readily obtained from death certificates. From 1949 to 1979, deaths were much
more common in institutional settings. (See Table 12.2.) However, more recent data obtained from studies examining the impact of hospice programs

Table 12.2
Percent of deaths in and out of institutions in the United States, 1949 and 1958.

	Percent of Deaths		
Location	1949	1958	1979*
Not in an institution	50.5	39.1	15
In an institution	49.5	60.9	85
General hospitals	(39.5)	(46.6)	
Convalescent and nursing homes, homes for the aged, etc.	(1.6)	(6.0)	
Nervous and mental hospitals	(3.2)	(3.5)	
Chronic disease and other special hospitals	(0.9)	(1.5)	
Tuberculosis hospitals	(0.9)	(0.6)	
Maternity hospitals	(0.2)	(0.1)	
Other	(3.2)	(2.6)	

*Cancer deaths only.
Source: Adapted from Lerner (1976, p. 140); Mor & Hiris (1983).

suggest a reversal of this trend (Mor & Hiris, 1983; Morris et al., 1984). These researchers report that when patients are given a choice, they prefer to die at home. Furthermore, dying at home may occur in as many as 50 percent of the cases if the patient is enrolled in a hospice program. This is possible because many of the health and social services typically delivered in an institutional setting are provided in the patient's home.

Regardless of whether one dies at home or in an institution, various medical personnel will play an important role in the process of dying. Many terminal patients come to rely on these professionals not only for medical care, but also for social and emotional support. This is likely to cause problems for both the staff and the patient, as we will see in a subsequent section.

The Fear of Death

Some theorists believe that the **fear of death (death anxiety)**, conscious and unconscious, is the prime mover for all human behavior.[1] In his Pulitzer Prize–winning book, *The Denial of Death*, Ernest Becker (1973) argues that

> *Of all things that move man, one of the principal ones is his terror of death.* . . . The idea of death, the fear of it, haunts the human animal like nothing else; it is a mainspring of human activity—activity designed largely to avoid the fatality of death, to overcome it by denying in some way that it is the final destiny for man.

The overriding importance of death anxiety as a motivator is characteristic of the school known as existential psychology, typified by Rollo May:

> To grasp what it means to exist, one needs to grasp the fact that he might not exist, that he treads at every moment on the sharp edge of possible annihilation and can never escape the fact that death will arrive at some unknown moment in the future. . . . Without this awareness of nonbeing. . . . existence is vapid [and] unreal. . . . [But] with the confrontation of nonbeing, existence takes on vitality and immediacy, and the individual experiences a heightened consciousness of himself, his world, and others around him. . . . [Thus] the confronting of death gives the most positive reality to life itself. (May 1958/1967, pp. 47–49)

As these theorists suggest, the fear of death can be both a destructive and a creative force. This universal fear may lead to neurosis, or even to psychosis; but it is also responsible for the pleasures of existence, and for many of humanity's most outstanding achievements. Because of death anxiety, some people are motivated to transcend their physical mortality through their productions: Artists and writers may hope that their works will live forever, scientists may seek major discoveries that will have lasting benefits for all of humankind, politicians may strive to have their accomplishments

---

[1] Some writers use the term *fear* when the cause is known and readily available to consciousness, and reserve the term *anxiety* for causes that are vague or unconscious. Others use the two terms more or less interchangeably, as will we in this book.

permanently recorded on the pages of history, and so on. Or, for many people, having children may be a form of immortality.

Although existentialist theory is important and provocative, it is by no means universally accepted. Others have argued that most of us experience little anxiety over the prospect of dying because it looms far in the future (e.g., Schulz, 1978). In fact, many different conceptions of death have been proposed by philosophers, religious leaders, psychologists, and others, some of which date back to ancient Greece. Nevertheless, there does appear to be general agreement on at least one point: Death is an experience that few people eagerly seek out. What is it about death that makes it so undesirable to most of us?

REASONS FOR FEARING DEATH

There are two general reasons why death is unattractive: It involves physical suffering and psychological suffering. These two categories are not mutually exclusive; neither one exists in isolation, and each can intensify the other.

The Fear of Physical Suffering. As noted previously, deaths from chronic degenerative diseases (e.g., cancer) have increased significantly since 1900. We are all aware that patients with terminal cancer may experience months or even years of pain, undergo forms of therapy that have distressing side effects, or suffer the removal of limbs or breasts. To many people, the possibility of such extreme pain, deterioration, and sometimes disfigurement is frightening indeed. So, too, are the dependency and loss of control that may accompany physical deterioration.

The Fear of Isolation and Loneliness. Being identified as a dying person often results in profound life changes. The terminal patient is often isolated and may well be treated differently by family, friends, and health professionals, who are likely to consider death a taboo subject. Thus, the prospect of a lingering terminal illness may evoke fears of being lonely, or of being unable to talk about the issues that are most important to the patient.

The Fear of Nonbeing. Human beings are the only creatures on earth who must live with the constant awareness that they will someday cease to exist. As we have seen, this knowledge of our ultimate nonbeing can arouse intense anxiety.

The Fear of Cowardice and Humiliation. We may also fear that we will become cowards in the face of death, either because of the accompanying physical pain or because we dread the thought of not existing. Thus the aforementioned sources of death anxiety may well create the "fear of fear itself."

The Fear of Failing to Achieve Important Goals. Some people define the length of their lives in terms of accomplishments, rather than years. If a university professor were asked how long he or she wanted to live, the reply might well be: "Long enough to write two more books." Or an elderly person may express the desire to survive until an important birthday or anniversary, or an offspring's wedding. We may therefore fear death because it will deprive us of cherished goals and experiences.

The Fear of the Impact of Death on One's Survivors.

Yet another source of death anxiety is the probable impact on one's survivors. Where finances permit, life insurance and trust funds can help parents alleviate the economic impact on their children. But finding some way to relieve the psychological and emotional impact is quite another matter.

The Fear of Punishment or of the Unknown.

Some religions preach that transgressors are doomed to dire fates, such as consignment to Hell. Believers may become profoundly afraid of what they will experience after they die. However, it is also possible that religion will have precisely the opposite effect. That is, those who believe in more supportive religions may find that their faith significantly reduces their fear of death.

The Fear of the Death of Others.

Death anxiety is not limited to our own demise. We may also fear losing someone close to us and having to experience their physical and psychological suffering. Each of the fears already listed can also be experienced vicariously, in relation to the death of a loved one.

In theory, then, there are numerous reasons why the fear of death might dominate our lives. But does it? To answer this important question, let us now turn to an examination of the relevant research evidence.

RESEARCH ON DEATH ANXIETY

Conceptual and Methodological Issues.

Most often, death anxiety has been assessed by written questionnaires. A typical example of these **direct measures** is Templer's (1970) Death Anxiety Scale, which consists of fifteen true-false items:

1. I am very much afraid to die.
2. The thought of death seldom enters my mind.
3. It doesn't make me nervous when people talk about death.
4. I dread to think about having to have an operation.
5. I am not at all afraid to die.
6. I am not particularly afraid of getting cancer.
7. The thought of death never bothers me.
8. I am often distressed by the way time flies so very rapidly.
9. I fear dying a painful death.
10. The subject of life after death troubles me greatly.
11. I am really scared of having a heart attack.
12. I often think about how short life really is.
13. I shudder when I hear people talking about a World War III.
14. The sight of a dead body is horrifying to me.
15. I feel that the future holds nothing for me to fear.

The responses to these items are mathematically combined into a single death-anxiety score. Various comparable questionnaires have been devised by other researchers (e.g., Boyar, 1964; Collett & Lester, 1969; Lester, 1967; Sarnoff & Corwin, 1959; Tolor & Reznikoff, 1967).

How psychometrically sound are these instruments? On the positive side, there is some support for their validity. For example, psychiatric patients who were rated high in anxiety by a clinician scored significantly higher on Templer's scale than did a control group. Subjects who viewed a movie depicting gruesome automobile accidents showed significantly greater death anxiety on Boyar's scale than did subjects who watched an innocuous movie. Intercorrelations between various death anxiety questionnaires have been found to vary from +.41 to +.72, indicating a fairly high degree of agreement (Durlak, 1972; Handal et al., 1984–85).

Unfortunately, these questionnaires suffer from serious conceptual flaws. First of all, they assess only the *public and conscious* aspects of death anxiety. Our *conscious but private* feelings may well be quite different, but too sensitive and intimate to share with other people. If subjects believe that such fears are a sign of serious personal weakness, or that these fears are no one else's business, they may deliberately falsify their answers in order to appear more courageous. Some studies do indicate that when subjects are identified by name, they report less fear of death than when the questionnaires are administered anonymously (Jones & Sigall, 1971; Schulz, Aderman, & Manko, 1976).

Furthermore, the fear of death is typically assumed to be partly or primarily *unconscious*. Because this repressed aspect is hidden even from ourselves, it cannot be assessed by instruments that depend entirely on conscious self-reports, even if subjects are trying their best to be honest and accurate. For this reason, attempts have been made to tap the less-conscious aspects of death anxiety by using various **indirect measures**. These include the following:

- *The Word Association Test:* The experimenter states a single word, and the subject must reply with the first word that comes to mind (Jung, 1905; 1910). Subjects with greater death anxiety will presumably respond more slowly to death-related words (e.g., *cemetery*), or will give more unusual responses, than is the case with neutral words.
- *The Color Word Interference Test:* The subject is asked to state the color in which a word is printed, disregarding its meaning. Here again, subjects with greater death anxiety will presumably respond more slowly to death-related words than to equally common but more neutral words.
- *The Death Anxiety Slideshow Measure:* Subjects are shown a series of slides. Some are death oriented, such as a slide of the word *graveyard* followed by a picture of a graveyard; others are neutral, as with the word *greenness* followed by a picture of a backyard lawn scene. During this presentation, a physiological measure of anxiety is obtained by monitoring the subjects' heart rates. Subjects who fear death more will

presumably show more pronounced changes in heart rate to the death-oriented slides than to the neutral ones.

In theory, if much of our death anxiety is beyond our awareness, we should show considerably more fear on these indirect measures than on direct questionnaires. Some studies do find this to be the case, indicating that a significant part of death anxiety is unconscious (e.g., Feifel, 1974; Feifel & Branscomb, 1973; Feifel, Freilich, & Hermann, 1973; Feifel & Nagy, 1980). However, the evidence in this area is equivocal. Other investigators have reached precisely the opposite conclusion: They report that subjects obtain similar scores on direct and indirect measures, which implies that we do *not* repress our fear of death (e.g., Littlefield & Fleming, 1984–85). It has also been argued that the indirect measures of death anxiety are of questionable validity. One study found little or no relationship among these measures, indicating that they do *not* assess the same concept (Handal et al., 1984–85).

Another problem with most direct questionnaires is that they treat death anxiety as a unidimensional concept. That is, they yield only a single score for each subject. Although this assumption is appealingly simple, it is almost certainly erroneous. We have seen that death anxiety has aspects that are conscious and public, conscious and private, and (very possibly) unconscious. We have also noted various reasons why we may fear death, and it is quite possible to suffer from some of these anxieties but not from others. Thus an unmarried person may fear the physical suffering associated with dying, but have no survivors to worry about. A devoted parent may be extremely concerned with the impact of his or her death on the children, but much less anxious about the possibility of physical pain. Or, dedicated scientists and artists may fear the interruption of their work far more than any other aspect of dying.

Here, the empirical data are more clear-cut. Even Templer's straightforward scale has been found to include several distinct factors: the fear of the unknown aspects of death, the fear of suffering, the fear of loneliness at the time of death, and the fear of personal extinction (Conte et al., 1982). There is one questionnaire that does distinguish among four sources of death anxiety, though all are public and conscious: death of self, death of others, dying of self, and dying of others (Collett & Lester, 1969). These investigators obtained low intercorrelations among the four subscales, indicating once again that death anxiety is multidimensional. And still other researchers have drawn a similar conclusion (e.g., Feifel, 1990; Florian & Har-Even, 1983–84; Kastenbaum & Costa, 1977; Littlefield & Fleming, 1984–85).

How many dimensions does this variable have? As yet, the answer is far from certain. If we consider the conscious and unconscious aspects of death anxiety together with the various reasons for fearing death, numerous possible varieties may be identified. In Table 12.3, for example, cell number 1 refers to the death-related fears of physical suffering that you are willing to reveal publicly. Cell number 2 concerns the physical fears that you are aware of, but may not wish to share with other people. Cell number 3 deals with those physical fears that you will not admit even to yourself. Cells number 4

Table 12.3

The multidimensional nature of death anxiety: 21 possible varieties.

Reasons for Fearing One's Own Death	Psychological Level		
	Public and Conscious	Private and Conscious	Unconscious
Physical suffering (and bodily deterioration)	1	2	3
Nonbeing	4	5	6
Cowardice and humiliation	7	8	9
Interruption of goals	10	11	12
Impact on survivors: psychological and emotional suffering	13	14	15
Impact on survivors: economic hardship	16	17	18
Punishment	19	20	21

Note: These varieties are purely hypothetical, and are presented only for purposes of discussion and illustration; they have *not* been confirmed by empirical research. Also, all of the fears listed above can be experienced vicariously, in relation to the death of a loved one.

through number 6 involve your fears of nonbeing, so prominent in existential theory; and so on. Not all of the varieties listed in Table 12.3 may be important, or even truly different from one another. But it does seem clear that death anxiety is far too complicated a concept to be summarized by a single score, or perhaps even by just two or three scores.

In sum: Research on death anxiety has all too often relied on simple unidimensional scores, based solely on the public and conscious level. It is only recently that investigators have begun to tap the true richness and complexity of this variable, including its multidimensionality and possible unconscious aspects.

Substantive Findings.   Death anxiety has been studied in relation to various aspects of adult behavior. As might be expected from the preceding discussion, relatively few clear and consistent patterns have emerged from the available data. In this section, we will explore some of the more interesting questions posed by researchers in this area.

Does our fear of death become stronger as we grow older? More recent studies have *not* found pronounced increases in death anxiety during the first half of adulthood, at least at a conscious level. In fact, some studies of young adults have yielded small but statistically significant negative correlations between age and direct measures of death anxiety. This weak, inverse relationship has been observed for junior college students (mean age 27 years) and for members of such death-related professions as funeral personnel and firemen. However, the same studies also obtained mostly nonsignificant correlations when indirect measures were used to assess death anxiety, and for subjects in such professions as secretarial work and teaching (Handal et al., 1984–85; Lattaner &

Hayslip, 1984–85). Similar nonsignificant results were reported in an earlier large-scale study, wherein the Death Anxiety Scale was administered to more than 2,000 subjects of various ages (Templer, Ruff, & Franks, 1971).

The relationship between aging and the fear of death does appear to be moderated by physical health. Adults who suffer from serious illnesses, especially acute disorders, tend to show greater death anxiety than do healthy adults (Viney, 1984–85). These patients are likely to express considerable concern with such fears as physical suffering, nonbeing, and cowardice and humiliation (e.g., "I worry about whether I'll have the strength to die with dignity"). Because ill health is more likely to occur at advanced ages, a corresponding age-related increase in death anxiety may be expected. However, the failure to verbalize such fears does *not* necessarily mean that death anxiety is absent. As we have seen, our conscious and private feelings may differ from those that are conscious and public. Furthermore, the tendency to repress our death anxiety may well increase as we pass middle age and death becomes a more immediate threat. It has been found that adults past the age of 50 are more likely to deny their fears of death, yet their unconscious death anxiety is just as high as that of younger adults (Corey, 1961; Feifel & Branscomb, 1973). As was the case with young adults, however, the evidence does *not* indicate that healthy men and women become more afraid of death (at least at a conscious level) as they grow from middle to old age.

Are such personal characteristics as sex and religious beliefs related to death anxiety? As noted previously in this chapter, it is conceivable that religious beliefs might either intensify or alleviate the fear of death. A recent review of 36 studies dealing with this issue found that in 24 of them, or two-thirds, increased faith was significantly related to decreased anxiety. That is, those who were more religious were less afraid of death than those who were not as religious. Seven studies failed to detect any significant relationship, and only three studies found that greater faith was related to greater fears of death (Spilka, Hood, & Gorsuch, 1985; see also DaSilva & Schork, 1984–85; Florian and Har-Even, 1983–84).

The evidence concerning gender and death anxiety is more inconsistent. Some researchers have found that women show higher anxiety on direct measures, and are less likely to repress their fears of death. If this pattern were reliable, it could be argued that men are more reluctant to admit their death anxiety because they regard such fears as unmasculine. However, various other studies have not obtained significant differences in death anxiety between the sexes. (See, for example, DaSilva & Schork, 1984–85; Lester, 1984–85; Pollak, 1979–80.) All too many researchers in this area have based their conclusions solely on unidimensional death anxiety scores, so further research of a multidimensional nature is needed before firm conclusions can be drawn.

Is death anxiety higher among the mentally ill? The data in this area are also equivocal, and consist primarily of unidimensional studies. Some of these suggest that the mentally ill score unusually high on direct questionnaires, but others report no significant differences between psychiatric patients and more normal subjects (Templer, 1971; Templer & Ruff, 1971; Feifel & Hermann, 1973). However, those who actually attempt suicide appear to have less conscious fear of death than does the general population (Lester, 1967; Tarter, Templer, & Perley, 1974).

Does death anxiety influence the likelihood of participating in life-threatening activities? People who are high in death anxiety might seem less likely to engage in risky, life-threatening professions and avocations. To test this hypothesis, Feifel and Nagy (1980) obtained samples of such risk-takers as alcoholics, drug addicts, and inmates serving prison sentences for committing violent crimes. Also included were a sample of deputy sheriffs, who engage in life-threatening behaviors that are socially acceptable; and a control group of federal government employees, who were not involved in such risky behaviors. The results did *not* support the hypothesis; the various risk-taking groups were not significantly lower (or higher) in conscious or unconscious death anxiety than the control group.

Do dreams provide any evidence about unconscious fears of death? Most psychologists agree that dreams provide important clues about our unconscious wishes, feelings, beliefs, and motives, although dream interpretation can be a difficult and controversial affair. (See, for example, Foulkes, 1966; Freud, 1900/1965a; Fromm, 1951; Hall, 1966; Jung, 1964.) In one study, subjects who scored either high or low on direct measures of death anxiety had a significantly higher proportion of death-related dreams than did subjects with moderate scores (Handal & Rychlak, 1971). This curvilinear relationship suggests once again that some people who have relatively little death anxiety at the conscious level, public and private, may well be considerably more afraid at an unconscious level.

Afterword.   The evidence reviewed fails to support the existentialist belief as to the overwhelming importance of death anxiety. However, it could be argued that the negative findings are due partly or largely to methodological difficulties. Hypotheses involving the unconscious aspects of death anxiety remain controversial, but a number of studies do suggest that a significant part of these fears is indeed beyond our awareness. More data, and more valid indirect measures, are needed in order to determine the extent to which death anxiety influences human behavior.

With the available evidence, there is no reason to expect that you will become increasingly preoccupied with the prospect of your own death as you grow through adulthood. However, serious physical illnesses represent an important exception. When such disorders make the prospect of death more imminent and real, anxiety is likely to increase markedly; these fears may take various forms, since death anxiety is not unidimensional. As a result, helping terminally ill patients to deal with their anxieties is far from an easy task—as we will see in the following pages.

The Process of Dying: The Terminal Stages of Life

A **terminal illness** is one from which the patient has no reasonable hope of ever recovering, although there may be periods of remission and apparent health. Terminality has been defined in various ways; according to the U.S. Department of Health and Human Services, an illness is terminal if a physician certifies that the individual has a life expectancy of six months or less (Schulz & Schlarb, 1987–88).

The **terminal phase of life** is the last decline in health from which there is *no* major remission and which ends in death. This phase is a time of steady and rapid deterioration, especially of the central nervous system, and it may well be evidenced by sudden sharp declines in scores on mental and psychomotor tests. (Recall the discussion of terminal drop in Chapter 6.)

Interest in these terminal stages of life is currently at an all-time high, and for good reason. As we observed at the outset of this chapter, deaths in our society are much more often due to prolonged chronic diseases than to quickly terminating acute illnesses. This is particularly true for the aged, among whom 80 percent of all deaths occur. Therefore, virtually all of us will eventually have to deal with the *process* of dying—as a patient, as a concerned family member or friend, or perhaps in some professional capacity. Yet there is, at present, relatively little empirical information about such important issues as the typical duration of terminal illnesses; the magnitude of the accompanying disabilities, physical pain, and psychological distress; coping strategies used by terminal patients; or even the number of patients who are aware that their illnesses are terminal.

THE MEDICAL STAFF AND THE DYING

For health care professionals, the terminal prognosis implies a dramatic shift in treatment strategy. That is, instead of doing everything possible to bring about a recovery, the medical staff must concentrate instead on managing the patient's last days. This can cause significant social, emotional, and psychological problems for all concerned.

Attitudes and Behaviors of Physicians and Nurses.
Numerous studies indicate that physicians and nurses have difficulty dealing with terminal illnesses. To cope with this stressful situation, they may well resort to such psychological defense mechanisms as denial of reality and intellectualization (Chapter 10). Thus physicians and nurses may avoid the patient who is in the process of dying, or even fail to make eye contact during those meetings that do take place. They may seek to have minimal contact with the patient's family. Or they may refer to the patient in distant and unemotional terms, as by using bed location or type of illness rather than the patient's name. (See, for example, Buckingham et al., 1976; Kastenbaum & Aisenberg, 1971; Kübler-Ross, 1969; Marie, 1978; Pearlman et al., 1969.)

Responses to stress Reactions to stressors that are more immediate than consequences, and are not in and of themselves desirable or undesirable. Includes fight, flight, or compromise; cognitions, expectations, and perceptions; physiological changes; and the defense mechanisms.

Retention Occurs when information is stored for later use; the second process in the act of remembering. Some theorists prefer to characterize this stage in terms of encoding (q.v.).

Retina Part of the eye that transforms incoming light energy into impulses that can be communicated to the brain. Includes the cones, rods, and fovea.

Retinal detachment A form of retinal disorder consisting of a separation between the inner and outer layers of the retina.

Retinal disorders The most common causes of blindness in the United States. Varieties include diabetic retinopathy, retinal detachment, and senile macular degeneration.

Retired person An individual who is *not* working full time *and* who receives at least some income from a pension earned through prior employment.

Retirement Leaving the world of full-time work and beginning to collect one's pension or related benefits.

Retrieval Occurs when certain information is distinguished from everything else in memory and is brought back to awareness for current use; the third process in the act of remembering. Material may be retrieved through recognition or recall.

Ribonucleic acid (RNA) A molecule that transfers genetic information from the DNA molecules to the location in the cell where proteins are assembled.

Right to die The right to insist that life-sustaining procedures *not* be used if the only effect will be to artificially prolong the dying process.

Rigidity A trait characterized by an inability to shift from one form of behavior to another, even though such a shift might well be advantageous to the individual.

Rods Photoreceptor cells in the retina that respond to low levels of illumination and are responsible for night vision. Most plentiful in the periphery of the retina, and completely absent from the fovea.

Sample Any subgroup of cases drawn from a clearly specified population. In a *random sample,* each element in the population has an equal chance of being included in the sample.

Secondary memory (1) In structural theory, the separate and distinct memory system that has an enormous capacity and retains information for periods from one or two minutes to many years. (2) Memories that last from one or two minutes to many years, but whose duration is best explained in terms of process theory.

Selective attrition   Occurs when subjects who drop out during the course of a longitudinal study are *not* representative of the group as a whole. This results in a sample that is atypical in at least some respects, and may well bias measurements taken during the latter part of the study.

Self-disclosure   Revealing information about oneself that one would normally keep secret. An important aspect of both close friendships and loving relationships.

Semantic   Pertaining to the meaning of a word.

Semantic memory   In Tulving's theory, a form of memory that consists of general knowledge, meanings, and abstract relationships.

Senile macular degeneration   A form of retinal disorder wherein a specialized part of the retina that is responsible for sharp central and reading vision loses its ability to function effectively.

Sensory memory   A form of memory that holds incoming visual or auditory information for periods from one-quarter of a second to a few seconds after the stimulus is withdrawn.

Sequential research   Research strategies designed to eliminate the confounding that occurs in cross-sectional research (between aging effects and cohort effects) and in longitudinal research (between aging effects and time of measurement effects).

Serial learning   A form of learning wherein the subject must repeat back a list of items (e.g., common words, nonsense syllables) in the exact order in which they were presented.

Sex discrimination   Denying an individual a job, a promotion, more pay, or other desired work benefit solely because of his or her gender; most often used to refer to the unfair treatment of women at work. Although illegal, sex discrimination is still a significant problem in the world of work.

Short-term memory   A synonym for primary memory.

Social comparison theory   Posits that we all possess a basic drive to evaluate our abilities and opinions. If we cannot obtain appropriate objective data, we perform these self-evaluations by comparing ourselves with other people.

Somesthesis   Sensations that arise from stimulation of the skin, viscera, and kinesthetic receptors.

Stage   A period in one's life, usually consisting of several years, during which most or all people of the same age supposedly encounter much the same experiences and problems.

Static visual acuity The ability to identify a stationary object, or features thereof, by sight. Usually refers to situations where the observer is also stationary.

Statistic A numerical quantity that summarizes some characteristic of a sample.

Statistically non-normative life event A major event in one's life that happens to few other people in that culture. In this country, examples include suffering a stroke or winning a state lottery.

Statistically normative life event A major event in one's life that also happens to the majority of people in that culture. In this country, examples include getting married or retiring from work.

Stress A complicated phenomenon that involves the interrelationships among stressors, responses, consequences, and mediators. Typically, there is some threat or demand that affects one's inner stability.

Stressor A stimulus that is likely to impose some demands, or some degree of threat, on an individual.

Stroke An illness characterized by brain damage and by the often severe physical, cognitive, and social disabilities that result. Most often caused by the occlusion of a cerebral artery, which blocks the flow of blood to the cerebral hemispheres, or by a blood vessel that ruptures and produces a brain hemorrhage.

Structural theory A theory that focuses on separate and distinct memory systems that store information in the human brain.

Study phase The period during which subjects in an experiment practice and try to learn the material in question.

Temporally non-normative life event A major event in one's life that occurs at an age which is atypical for people in that culture. In this country, examples include getting married for the first time at age 45 or becoming a widow at age 25.

Temporally normative life event A major event in one's life that occurs at an age that is typical for people in that culture. In this country, examples include getting married for the first time in one's twenties or becoming a widow at age 65.

Terminal drop A sudden, severe drop in WAIS scores that indicates the existence of physical illness and serves as a warning of imminent death.

Terminal illness An illness from which there is no reasonable hope of ever recovering, although there may be periods of remission and apparent health.

Terminal phase of life   The last decline in health from which there is no major remission and which ends in death. A time of steady and rapid deterioration, especially of the central nervous system.

Test phase   The period during which subjects in an experiment are examined for their ability to remember the material in question.

Time of measurement effect   Occurs when behavior or personality is influenced in some way by the time periods in which these characteristics are measured.

Trait   A specific aspect of personality that initiates and guides consistent forms of behavior, such as shyness, friendliness, ambitiousness, cleanliness, and literally thousands of others.

Type   A pattern of personality and behavior that supposedly applies to numerous individuals.

Type A individual   A person characterized by intense ambition, competitiveness, aggressiveness, and perfectionism.

Type B individual   A person who is relatively easygoing, seldom impatient, and not compelled by the need to compete or achieve.

Variable   Any characteristic that can take on different values.

Verbal scales   Six subtests of the Wechsler Adult Intelligence Scale that require the use of words and are for the most part *not* highly speeded: information, comprehension, arithmetic, similarities, digit span, and vocabulary.

Verbal subtests   A synonym for verbal scales.

Visual acuity   The ability to distinguish one object from another by sight.

WAIS   The Wechsler Adult Intelligence Scale.

Wechsler Adult Intelligence Scale   The most commonly used measure of adult intelligence, consisting of six verbal scales (which require the use of words) and five performance scales (which do not).

Wisdom   A desirable personal characteristic that involves intelligence, good reasoning ability, good judgment, the realization that one may err, the ability to learn from past mistakes, the ability to solve one's own problems and give good advice to others, and an understanding of self and others. More likely to be found among older adults because it is related to experience.

Work force   All those adults who are currently employed, plus all those who are currently seeking employment.

Working memory   A synonym for primary memory, which emphasizes both the limited storage capacity of this memory and the selection or manipulation of the information that it contains.

References

Aaron, H. J., Bosworth, B. P., & Burtless, G. (1989). *Can America afford to grow old?* Washington, DC: The Brookings Institution.

Achte, K. A., & Vauhkonen, M. L. (1971). Cancer and the psyche. *Omega: Journal of Death and Dying, 2,* 45–46.

Adams, B. (1979). Mate selection in the United States: A theoretical summarization. In W. Burr, R. Hill, I. Nye & R. Reiss (Eds.), *Contemporary theories about the family. Vol 1: Research-based theories.* New York: Free Press.

Adams, O., & Lefebvre, L. (1981). Retirement and mortality. *Aging and Work, 4,* 115–120.

Akesson, H. O. (1969). A population study of senile and arteriosclerotic psychoses. *Human Heredity, 19,* 546–566.

Allport, G. W. (1937). *Personality: A psychological interpretation.* New York: Holt.

Allport, G. W. (1955). *Becoming: Basic considerations for a psychology of personality.* New Haven: Yale University Press.

Allport, G. W. (1961). *Pattern and growth in personality.* New York: Holt, Rinehart and Winston.

Allport, G. W. (1968). *The person in psychology: Selected essays.* Boston: Beacon Press.

Alpaugh, P. K., & Birren, J. E. (1977). Variables affecting creative contributions across the adult life span. *Human Development, 20,* 240–248.

Altman, I., & Taylor, D. A. (1973). *Social penetration: the development of interpersonal relationships.* New York: Holt, Rinehart and Winston.

Amberson, J. I., Atkeson, B. M., Pollack, R. H., & Malatesta, V. J. (1979). Age differences in dark-interval threshold across the life span. *Experimental Aging Research, 5,* 423–433.

American Cancer Society. (1987). *Cancer facts and figures.* New York: American Cancer Society.

American Heart Association. (1988). *1988 heart facts.* Dallas: American Heart Association National Center.

American Psychiatric Association. (1987). *Diagnostic and statistical manual of mental disorders (3rd ed., rev.).* Washington, DC: American Psychiatric Association.

American Public Health Association. (1991, January,. 1980s saw record U.S. progress in cutting accidental deaths. *The Nation's Health,* p. 1.

Anastasi, A. (1976) *Psychological testing* (4th ed.). New York: Macmillan.

Anders, T. R., Fozard, J. L., & Lillyquist, T. D. (1972). Effects of age upon retrieval from short-term memory. *Developmental Psychology, 6,* 214–217.

Anderson, Y. W., & Rochard, C. (1979). Cold snaps, snowfall, and sudden death from ischemic heart disease. *Canadian Medical Association Journal, 121,* 1580–1583.

Angleitner, A. (1976). Changes in personality observed in questionnaire data from the Riegel questionnaire on rigidity, dogmatism, and attitude toward life. In H. Thomae (Ed.), *Patterns of aging.* Basel–New York: Karger.

Anthony, J. (1974). Children at risk from divorce: A review. In J. Anthony & C. Koupernic (Eds.), *The child in his family: Children at psychiatric risk.* New York: Wiley.

Antonoff, S. R., & Spilka, B. (1984–85). Patterning of facial expressions among terminal cancer patients. *Omega: Journal of Death and Dying, 15,* 101–108.

Antonucci, T. C. (1984). Personal characteristics, social support, and social behavior. In E. Shanas & R. H. Binstock (Eds.), *Handbook of aging and the social sciences* (2nd ed.). New York: Van Nostrand Reinhold.

Arenberg, D. (1967). Regression analyses of verbal learning on adult age differences at two anticipation intervals. *Journal of Gerontology, 22,* 411–414.

Arenberg, D. (1968). Input modality in short-term retention of old and young adults. *Journal of Gerontology, 23,* 462–465.

Arenberg, D. (1976). The effects of input condition on free recall in young and old adults. *Journal of Gerontology, 31,* 551–555.

Arenberg, D., & Robertson-Tchabo, E. A. (1977). Learning and aging. In J. E. Birren & K. W. Schaie (Eds.), *Handbook of the psychology of aging.* New York: Van Nostrand Reinhold.

Assmann, G., & Schulte, H. (1986). PROCAM-trial: Prospective cardiovascular Munster trial. Zurich: Panscientia Verlag, 8–9, 12.

Arkin, A. M. Emotional care of the bereaved (1981). In O. S. Margolis, H. C. Raether, A. H. Kutscher, J. B. Powers, I. B. Seeland, R. DeBellis & D. J. Cherico (Eds.), *Acute grief: Counseling the bereaved.* New York: Columbia University Press.

Arking, G. (1976). The elderly widow and her family, neighbors, and friends. *Journal of Marriage and the Family, 38,* 757–768.

Ash, P. (1966). Pre-retirement counseling. *The Gerontologist, 6,* 97–99, 127–128.

Atchley, R. C. (1976). *The sociology of retirement.* New York: Halsted.

Atchley, R. C. (1977). *Social forces of later life* (2nd ed.). Belmont, CA: Wadsworth.

Atchley, R. C. (1982). Retirement: Leaving the world of work. *Annals of the American Academy of Political and Social Science, 464,* 120–131.

Atchley, R. C. (1985). *Social forces and aging: An introduction to social gerontology.* Belmont, CA: Wadsworth.

Atchley, R. C., & Miller, S. J. (1980). Older people and their families. In C. Eisdorfer (Ed.), *Annual review of gerontology and geriatrics (Vol. 1).* New York: Springer.

Atchley, R. C., & Robinson, J. L. (1982). Attitudes toward retirement and distance from the event. *Research on Aging, 4,* 299–313.

Ausman, L. M., & Russell, R. M. (1990). Nutrition and aging. In E. L. Schneider & J. W. Rowe (Eds.), *Handbook of the biology of aging* (3rd ed.). New York: Academic Press.

Babchuck, N. (1978–79). Aging and primary relations. *International Journal of Aging and Human Development, 9,* 137–151.

Backman, C. W., & Secord, P. F., (1959). The effect of perceived liking on interpersonal attraction. *Human Relations, 12,* 379–384.

Baddeley, A. D. (1970). Estimating the short-term component in free recall. *British Journal of Psychology, 61,* 13–15.

Baddeley, A.D. (1981). The concept of working memory: A view of its current state and probable future direction. *Cognition, 10,* 17–23.

Bahr, S. J., & Peterson, E. T. (Eds.). (1989). *Aging and the family.* Lexington, MA: Lexington, 1989.

Bailey, R. C., Finney, P., & Heim, B. (1975). Self-concept support and friendship duration. *Journal of Social Psychology, 96(2),* 234–237.

Ball, K., & Sekuler, R. (1986). Improving visual perception in older observers. *Journal of Gerontology, 41,* 176–182.

Baltes, P. B., & Baltes, M. M. (1990). Psychological perspectives on successful aging: The model of selective optimization with compensation. In P. B. Baltes & M. M. Baltes (Eds.), *Successful aging: Perspectives from the behavioral sciences.* New York: Cambridge University Press.

Baltes, P. B., Cornelius, S. W., Spiro, A., Nesselrode, J. R., & Willis, S. L. (1980). Integration versus differentiation of fluid/crystallized intelligence in old age. *Developmental Psychology, 16,* 625–635.

Baltes P. B., & Labouvie, G. V (1973). Adult development of intellectual performance: Description, explanation, and modification. In C. Eisdorfer & M. P. Lawton (Eds.), *The psychology of adult development and aging.* Washington, DC: American Psychological Association.

Baltes, P. B., Nesselrode, J.R., Schaie, K. W., & Labouvie, E. W. (1972). On the dilemma of regression effects in examining ability-level-related differentials in ontogenic patterns of intelligence. *Developmental Psychology, 6,* 78–84.

Baltes, P. B., Reese, H. W., & Nesselrode, J. R. (1977). *Life-span developmental psychology: Introduction to research methods.* Monterey, CA: Brooks/Cole.

Barber, C. E. (1989).Transition to the empty nest. In S. J. Bahr & E. T. Peterson (Eds.), *Aging and the family.* Lexington, MA: Lexington.

Barrett, C. J. (1978). Effectiveness of widows' groups in facilitating change. *Journal of Consulting and Clinical Psychology, 46,* 20–31.

Barton, D., Crowder, M. K., & Flexner, J. M. (1979–80). Teaching about dying and death in a multidisciplinary student group. *Omega: Journal of Death and Dying, 10,* 265–270.

Bartoshuk, L. M., Rifkin, L. M., Marks, L. E., & Bars, P. (1986). Taste and aging. *Journal of Gerontology, 41,* 51–57.

Bartoshuk, L. M., & Weiffenbach, J. M. (1990). Chemical senses and aging. In E. L. Schneider & J. W. Rowe (Eds.), *Handbook of the biology of aging* (3rd ed.). New York: Academic Press.

Baruch, G. K., & Barnett, R. C. (1980). On the well-being of adult women. In L. A. Bond & J. C. Rosen (Eds.), *Competence and coping during adulthood.* Hanover, NH: University Press of New England.

Bashore, T. R. (1989). Age, physical fitness, and mental processing speed. In M. P. Lawton (Ed.), *Annual review of gerontology and geriatrics (Vol. 9)* pp. 120–144. New York: Springer.

Bass, D. M. (1985). The hospice ideology and success of hospice care. *Research on Aging, 7,* 307–327.

Bayley, N., & Oden, M. H. (1955). The maintenance of intellectual ability in gifted adults. *Journal of Gerontology, 10,* 91–107.

Beck, S. H. (1982). Adjustment to and satisfaction with retirement. *Journal of Gerontology, 37,* 616–624.

Beck, S. H. (1984). Retirement preparation programs: Differentials in opportunity and use. *Journal of Gerontology, 39,* 596–602.

Becker, E. (1973). *The denial of death.* New York: Free Press.

Bee, H. L. (1987). *The journey of adulthood.* New York: Macmillan.

Beisecker, A. E. (1988). Aging and the desire for information and input in medical decisions: Patient consumerism in medical encounters. *Gerontologist, 28,* 330–345.

Bem, D. J., & Allen, A. (1974). On predicting some of the people some of the time: The search for cross-situational consistencies in behavior. *Psychological Review, 81,* 506–520.

Bengtson, V. L., & Robertson, J. F. (Eds.). (1985). *Grandparenthood.* Beverly Hills, CA: Sage Publications.

Bennett, T. S. (1984). Divorce. In R. J. Corsini (Ed.), *Encyclopedia of Psychology.* New York: Wiley.

Benoliel, J. Q. (1979). Dying is a family affair. In E. R. Prichard et al. (Eds.), *Home care: Living with dying.* New York: Columbia University Press.

Berglas, S. (1986). *The success syndrome.* New York: Plenum.

Bergman, M. (1980). *Aging and the perception of speech.* Baltimore, MD: University of Baltimore Press.

Bergman, M., Blumenfeld, V. G., Cascardo, D., Dash, B., Levitt, H., & Margulios, M. K. (1976). Age-related decrements in hearing for speech: Sampling and longitudinal studies. *Journal of Gerontology, 31,* 533–538.

Berkman, L. F., & Syme, S. L. (1979). Social networks, host resistance, and mortality: A nine year follow-up study of Alameda County residents. *American Journal of Epidemiology, 109,* 186–204.

Berscheid, E., & Walster, E. (1974). Physical attractiveness. In L. Berkowitz (Ed.), *Advances in experimental social psychology (Vol 7).* New York: Academic Press.

Berscheid, E., & Walster, E. (1978). *Interpersonal attraction* (2nd ed.). Reading, MA: Addison-Wesley.

Biegel, D. E., Sales, E., & Schulz, R. (1991). *Family caregiving in chronic illness.* Newbury Park, CA: Sage Publications.

Binet, A., & Simon, T. (1905). Methods nouvelles pour le diagnostic du niveau intellectuel des anormaux. *Année Psychologique, 11,* 191–244.

Birhill, W. R., & Schaie, K. W. (1975). The effect of differential reinforcement of cautiousness in intellectual performance among the elderly. *Journal of Gerontology, 30,* 578–583.

Birren, J. E. (1964). *The psychology of aging.* Englewood Cliffs, N. J.: Prentice-Hall.

Birren, J. E. (1974). Translations in gerontology—from lab to life: Psychophysiology and speed of response. *American Psychologist, 29,* 808–815.

Birren, J. E., & Fisher, L. M. (1990). The elements of wisdom: Overview and integration. In R. J. Sternberg (Ed.), *Wisdom: Its nature, origins, and development* (pp. 317–332). Cambridge: Cambridge University Press.

Birren, J. E., & Renner, J. (1980). Concepts and issues of mental health and aging. In J. E. Birren & R. B. Sloane (Eds.), *Handbook of mental health and aging.* Englewood Cliffs, NJ: Prentice-Hall.

Bjorksten, J. (1968). The cross-linkage theory of aging. *Journal of the American Geriatric Society, 16,* 408–427.

Blanchard-Fields, F. (1986). Reasoning on social dilemmas varying in emotional saliency: An adult-developmental study. *Psychology and Aging, 1,* 325–333.

Blau, Z. S. (1981). *Aging in a changing society* (2nd ed.). New York: Franklin Watts.

Blazer, D. (1982). Social support and mortality in an elderly community sample. *American Journal of Epidemiology, 115,* 684–694.

Blazer, D. (1989a). Affective disorders in late life. In E. W. Busse & D. G. Blazer (Eds.), *Geriatric psychiatry.* Washington, DC: American Psychiatric Press.

Blazer, D. (1989b). The epidemiology of psychiatric disorders in late life. In E. W. Busse & D. G. Blazer (Eds.), *Geriatric psychiatry.* Washington, DC: American Psychiatric Press.

Blazer, D. (1989c). The psychiatric interview of the geriatric patient. In E. W. Busse & D. G. Blazer (Eds.), *Geriatric psychiatry.* Washington, DC: American Psychiatric Press.

Blood, R. O., & Wolfe, D. M. (1960). *Husbands and wives.* New York: Free Press.

Blum, J. E., & Jarvik, L. F. (1974). Intellectual performance of octogenarians as a function of education and initial ability. *Human Development, 17,* 364–375.

Blumenfeld, N., Levy, N. B., & Kaufman, D. (1978–79). The wish to be informed of a fatal illness. *Omega: Journal of Death and Dying, 9,* 323–327.

Boller, F., Goldstein, G., Dorr, C., Kim, Y., Moossy, J., Richey, E., Wagener, D., & Wolfson, S. K., Jr. (1984). Alzheimer and related dementias: A review of current knowledge. In G. Goldstein (Ed.), *Advances in clinical neurophysiology (Vol. 1).* New York: Plenum.

Booth, A. (1972). Sex and social participation. *American Sociological Review, 37(2),* 183–192.

Booth-Kewley, S., & Friedman, H. S. (1987). Psychological predictors of heart disease: A quantitative review. *Psychological Bulletin, 101,* 343–362.

Botwinick, J. (1967). *Cognitive processes in maturity and old age.* New York: Springer.

Botwinick, J. (1977). Intellectual abilities. In J. E. Birren & K. W. Schaie (Eds.), *Handbook of the psychology of aging.* New York: Van Nostrand Reinhold.

Botwinick, J., & Birren, J. E. (1963). Cognitive processes: Mental abilities and psycho-motor responses in healthy aged men. In J. E. Birren, R. N. Butler, S. W. Greenhouse, L. Solkoff & M. R. Yarrow (Eds.), *Human aging.* Public Health Service Publication No. 896. Washington, DC: United States Government Printing Office.

Botwinick, J., & Storandt, M. (1974). *Memory, related functions and age.* Springfield, IL: Charles C. Thomas.

Botwinick, J., West, R., & Storandt, M. (1978). Predicting death from behavioral test performance. *Journal of Gerontology, 33,* 755–762.

Bourne, L. E., Dominowski, R. L., & Loftus, E. F. (1979). *Cognitive processes.* Englewood Cliffs, NJ: Prentice-Hall.

Bower, G. H. (1970). Analysis of a mnemonic device. *American Scientist, 58,* 496–510.

Bowers, I. C. H., & Bahr, J. (1989). Remarriage among the elderly. In S. J. Bahr & E. T. Peterson (Eds.), *Aging and the family.* Lexington, MA: Lexington.

Boyar, J. I. (1964). *The construction and partial validation of a scale for the measurement of fear of death.* Unpublished doctoral dissertation, University of Rochester, Rochester, NY.

Bradley, R. H., & Webb, R. (1976). Age-related differences in locus of control orientation in three behavioral domains. *Human Development, 19,* 49–56.

Branch, L. & Jette, A. (1983). Elders' use of informal long-term care assistance. *The Gerontologist, 23,* 51–56.

Brandtstadter, J. (1984). Personal and social control over development: Some implications of an action perspective in life-span developmental psychology. In P. B. Baltes & O. G. Brim (Eds.), *Life-span development and behavior (Vol. 6),* (pp. 1–32). Orlando, FL: Academic Press.

Brandstadter, J. (1989). Personal self-regulation of development: Cross-sequential analyses of development-related control beliefs and emotions. *Developmental Psychology, 25,* 96–108.

Brandstadter, J. & Renner, G. (1990). Tenacious goal pursuit and flexible goal adjustment: Explication and age-related analysis of assimilative and accommodative strategies of coping. *Psychology and Aging, 5,* 58–67.

Bransford, J. D., Stein, B. S., Shelton, T. S., & Owings, R. A. (1980). Cognition and adaptation: The importance of learning to learn. In J. Harvey (Ed.), *Cognition, social behavior, and the environment.* Hillsdale, NJ: Erlbaum.

Breaugh, J. A., & DiMarco, N. (1979). *Age differences in the rated desirability of job outcomes.* Paper presented at the annual meeting of the American Psychological Association, New York, NY.

Brenton, M. (1974). *Friendship.* New York: Stein & Day.

Breytspraak, L. M. (1984). *The development of self in later life.* Boston: Little, Brown & Co.

Brickman, A. L., & Eisdorfer, C. (1989). Anxiety in the elderly. In E. W. Busse & D. G. Blazer (Eds.), *Geriatric psychiatry.* Washington, DC: American Psychiatric Press.

Brock, D. B., Guralnik, J. M., & Brody, J. A. (1990). Demography and epidemiology of aging in the United States. In E. L. Schneider & J. W. Rowe (Eds.), *Handbook of the biology of aging* (3rd ed.). New York: Academic Press.

Brody, E. (1978). The aging family. *Annals of the American Academy of Political and Social Science, 438,* 13–27.

Brody, E. (1981). Women in the middle and family help to older people. *The Gerontologist, 21,* 471–480.

Brody, E., Johnson, P., Fulcomer, M., & Lang, A. (1983). Women's changing roles and help to elderly parents: Attitudes of three generations of women. *Journal of Gerontology, 38,* 597–607.

Brotman, H. (1980). *Every ninth American.* Washington, DC: Developments in Aging, United States Senate Special Committee on Aging.

Brown, B. B. (1981). A life-span approach to friendship: Age-related dimensions of an ageless relationship. In H. Lopata & D. Maines (Eds.), *Research on the interweave of social roles: Vol. 2. Friendship.* Greenwich, CT: JAI Press.

Brown, J. A. (1958). Some tests of the decay theory of immediate memory. *Quarterly Journal of Experimental Psychology, 10,* 12–21.

Bruckner, R. (1967). Longitudinal research on the eye. *Gerontologia Clinica, 9,* 87–95.

Buckingham, R. W., Lack, S. A., Mount, B. M., MacLean, L. D., & Collins, J. T. (1976). Living with the dying: Use of the technique of participant observation. *Canadian Medical Association Journal, 115,* 1211–1215.

Bugelski, B. R., Kidd, E., & Segmen, J. (1968). Image as a mediator in one-trial paired-associate learning. *Journal of Experimental Psychology, 76,* 69–73.

Buhler, C. (1968). Fulfillment and failure of life. In C. Buhler & F. Massarik (Eds.), *The course of human life.* New York: Springer.

Burg, A. (1966). Visual acuity as measured by dynamic and static tests: A comparative evaluation. *Journal of Applied Psychology, 50,* 460–466.

Burgess, A. W., & Holmstrum, L. L. (1978). Recovery from rape and prior life stress. *Research in Nursing and Health, 1,* 165–174.

Burish, T., & Lyles, J. Coping with the adverse effects of cancer treatments. In T. Burish & Bradley (Eds.), *Coping with chronic illness* (pp. 159–189). Residence Press.

Burnside, I. M. (1975). Sexuality and the older adult: Implications for nursing. In I. M. Burnside (Ed.), *Sexuality and aging.* Los Angeles: University of Southern California Press.

Burt, J. J., & Meeks, L. B. (1985). *Education for sexuality: Concepts and programs for teaching (3rd ed.).* Philadelphia: Saunders College Publishers.

Busse, E. W. (1987). Mental health. In G. L. Maddox (Ed.), *The encyclopedia of aging.* New York: Springer.

Busse, E. W., & Blazer, D. G. (Eds.). (1980). *Handbook of geriatric psychiatry.* New York: Van Nostrand Reinhold.

Butler, R. N., & Lewis, M. (1976). *Aging and mental health.* St. Louis: C. V. Mosby.

Byrd, E., & Gertman, S. (1959). Taste sensitivity in aging persons. *Geriatrics, 14,* 381–384.

Caldwell, D., & Mishara, B. L. (1972). Research on attitudes of medical doctors toward the dying patient: A methodological problem. *Omega: Journal of Death and Dying, 3,* 341–346.

Campbell, A., Converse, P. E., & Rodgers, W. L. (1976). *The quality of American life: Perceptions, evaluation, and satisfaction.* New York: Russell Sage Foundation.

Campbell, T. W. (1980). Death anxiety in a coronary care unit. *Psychosomatics, 21,* 127–136.

Campbell, T. W., Abernethy, V., & Waterhouse, G. J. (1983–84). Do death attitudes of nurses and physicians differ? *Omega: Journal of Death and Dying, 14(1),* 43–49.

Candy, S. (1977). *A comparative analysis of friendship functions in six age groups of men and women.* Unpublished doctoral dissertation, Wayne State University.

Canestrari, R. E., Jr. (1963). Paced and self-paced learning in young and elderly adults. *Journal of Gerontology, 18,* 165–168.

Canestrari, R. E., Jr. (1966). The effect of commonality on paired-associate learning in two age groups. *Journal of Genetic Psychology, 108,* 3–7.

Canestrari, R. E., Jr. (1968). Age changes in acquisition. In G. A. Talland (Ed.), *Human aging and behavior*. New York: Academic Press.

Cannon, W. G. (1929). *Bodily changes in pain, hunger, fear and rage: An account of recent researches into the function of emotional excitement* (2nd ed.). New York: Appleton.

Cantor, M. H. (1980). The informal support system: Its relevance in the lives of the elderly. In E. Borgatta & N. McCluskey (Eds.), *Aging and society*. Beverly Hills, CA: Sage Publications.

Cantor, M. H. (1983). Strain among caregivers: A study of experience in the United States. *The Gerontologist, 23,* 597–604.

Carpenter, D. G. (1965). Diffusion theory of aging. *Journal of Gerontology, 20,* 191–195.

Cash, T. F., & Derlega, V. J. (1978). The matching hypothesis: Physical attractiveness among same-sexed friends. *Personality and Social Psychology Bulletin, 4,* 240–243.

Cassem, N. H., & Hackett, T. P. (1975). Stress on the nurses and therapist in the intensive care unit and the coronary care unit. *Heart and Lung, 4,* 252–259.

Cassileth, B. R., Lusk, E. J., Strouse, T. B., Miller, D. S., Brown, L. L., Cross, P. A., & Tenaglia, A. N. (1984). Psychosocial status in chronic illness: A comparative analysis of six diagnostic groups. *New England Journal of Medicine, 311,* 506–511.

Castelli, W. P. (1978). CHD risk factors. In W. Reichel (Ed.), *The geriatric patient*. New York: H.P. Publishing Co.

Cattell, R. B. (1940). A culture-free intelligence test. *Journal of Educational Psychology, 31,* 161–179.

Cattell, R. B. (1963). Theory of fluid and crystallized intelligence: A critical experiment. *Journal of Educational Psychology, 54,* 1–22.

Cattell, R. B. (1965). *The scientific analysis of personality*. London: Penguin.

Cattell, R. B. (1973). *Personality and mood by questionnaire*. San Francisco: Jossey-Bass.

Cattell, R. B. (1979). *Personality and learning theory: Vol. I. The structure of personality in its environment*. New York: Springer.

Cattell, R. B. (1980). *Personality and learning theory: Vol. 2. A systems theory of maturation and structured learning*. New York: Springer.

Cattell, R. B., Eber, H. W., & Tatsuoka, M. M. (1970). *Handbook for the Sixteen Personality Factor Questionnaire*. Champaign, IL: Institute for Personality and Ability Testing.

Cavanaugh, J. C. (1990). *Adult development and aging*. New York: Wadsworth.

Cavanaugh, J. C., & Poon, L. W. (1989). Metamemorial predictors of memory performance in young and old adults. *Psychology and Aging, 4,* 365–370.

Cerella, J. (1985). Information processing rates in the elderly. *Psychological Bulletin, 98,* 67–83.

Cerella, J. (1990). Aging and information-processing rate. In J. E. Birren & K. W. Schaie (Eds.), *Handbook of the psychology of aging* (3rd ed.) (pp. 201–221). New York: Academic Press.

Cherlin, A., & Furstenberg, F. F. (1985). Styles and strategies of grandparenthood. In V. L. Bengtson & J. F. Robertson (Eds.), *Grandparenthood*. Beverly Hills, CA: Sage Publications.

Chiriboga, D. A. (1979, November). *Marital separation in early and late life: A comparison*. Paper presented at the meeting of the Gerontological Society, Dallas.

Chiriboga, D. A. (1981). *Consistency in adult personality: The influence of social stress.* Paper presented at the 12th International Conference of Gerontology, Hamburg.

Chiriboga, D. A. (1982). Adaptation to marital separation in later and earlier life. *Journal of Gerontology, 37,* 109–114.

Chown, S. (1961). Age and the rigidities. *Journal of Gerontology, 16,* 353–362.

Christenson, C., & Gagnon, J. (1965). Sexual behavior in a group of older women. *Journal of Gerontology, 20,* 351–356.

Christenson, C., & Johnson, A. B. (1973). Sexual patterns in a group of older never-married women. *Journal of Geriatric Psychiatry, 6,* 80–98.

Cicirelli, V. G. (1981). *Helping elderly parents: The role of adult children.* Boston: Auburn House.

Ciocco, A. (1940). On mortality in husbands and wives. *Human Biology, 12,* 508.

Clayton, P. J. (1973). The clinical morbidity of the first year of bereavement: A review. *Comprehensive Psychiatry, 14(2),* 151–157.

Clayton, V. P., & Birren, J. E. (1980). The development of wisdom across the life span: A reexamination of an ancient topic. In P. B. Baltes & O. G. Brim, Jr. (Eds.), *Life-span development and behavior (Vol. 3).* New York: Academic Press.

Clayton, V. P., & Overton, W. F. (1973). *The role of formal operational thought in the aging process.* Paper presented at the annual meeting of the Gerontological Society of America, Miami, FL.

Cleek, M. D., & Pearson, T. A. (1985). Perceived causes of divorce: An analysis of inter-relationships. *Journal of Marriage and the Family, 47,* 179–191.

Clopton, W. (1973). Personality and career change. *Industrial Gerontology, 17,* 9–17.

Cobb, S., & Kasl, S. V. (1977). *Termination: The consequences of job loss.* NIOSH Publication No. 77–224. Cincinnati, OH: United States Department of Health, Education, and Welfare.

Cohen, D., & Eisdorfer, C. (1986). *The loss of self: A family resource for the care of Alzheimer's disease and related disorders.* New York: Norton.

Cohen, G. (1979). Language comprehension in old age. *Cognitive Psychology, 11,* 412–429.

Cohen, J. (1965). Some statistical issues in psychological research. In B. B. Wolman (Ed.), *Handbook of clinical psychology.* New York: McGraw-Hill.

Cohen, K. P. (1979). *Hospice: Prescription for terminal care.* Germantown, MD: Aspen Systems Corp.

Collett, L., & Lester, D. (1969). Fear of death and fear of dying. *Journal of Psychology, 72,* 179–181.

Collins, K. J., Dore, C., Exton-Smith, A. N., Fox, R. H., MacDonald, E. C., & Woodward, P. M. (1977). Accidental hypothermia and impaired temperature homeostasis in the elderly. *British Medical Journal, 278,* 353–356.

Comfort, A. (1964). *Aging: The biology of senescence.* New York: Holt, Rinehart and Winston.

Comfort, A. (1974). Sexuality in old age. *Journal of the American Geriatrics Society, 22,* 440–442.

Comptroller General of the United States. (1979). *Report to Congress: Hospice care—a growing concept in the United States.* Washington, DC: General Accounting Office.

Conte, H. R., Weiner, M. B., & Plutchik, R. (1982). Measuring death anxiety: Conceptual, psychometric, and factor analytic aspects. *Journal of Personality and Social Psychology, 43*, 775–785.

Cook, T. D., & Campbell, D. T. (1979). *Quasi-experimentation: Design and analysis issues for field settings.* Chicago: Rand McNally.

Cooper, R. M. Bilash, I., & Zubek, J. P. (1959). The effect of age on taste sensitivity. *Journal of Gerontology, 14*, 56–58.

Coren, S. Porac, C., & Ward, L. M. (1978). *Sensation and perception.* New York: Academic Press.

Corey, L. G. (1961). An analogue of resistance to death awareness. *Journal of Gerontology, 16*, 59–60.

Cornelius, S. W., & Caspi, A. (1987). Everyday problem solving in adulthood and old age. *Psychology and Aging, 2*, 144–153.

Corso, J. F. (1987). Sensory-perceptual processes and aging. In K. W. Schaie & C. Eisdorfer (Eds.), *Annual review of gerontology and geriatrics (Vol. 7)* (pp. 29–55). New York: Springer.

Costa, P. T., Jr. & McCrae, R. R. (1976). Age differences in personality structure: A cluster analytic approach. *Journal of Gerontology, 31*, 564–570.

Costa, P. T., Jr. & McCrae, R. R. (1978). Objective personality assessment. In M. Storandt, I.C. Siegler & M. F. Elias (Eds.), *The clinical psychology of aging.* New York: Plenum.

Costa, P.T ., Jr., & McCrae, R. R. (1980). Still stable after all these years: Personality as a key to some issues in adulthood and old age. In P. B. Baltes & O. G. Brim, Jr. (Eds.), *Life-span development and behavior (Vol. 3).* New York: Academic Press.

Costa, P. T., Jr., Zonderman, A. B., & McCrae, R. R. (1983).*Longitudinal course of social support in the Baltimore Longitudinal Study of Aging.* Paper presented at the NATO Advanced Workshop: Social Support Theory, Research, and Application, Chateau de Bonas, France.

Cotman, C. W. (1990). Synaptic plasticity, neurotrophic factors, and transplantation in aged brain. In E. L. Schneider & J.W. Rowe (Eds.), *Handbook of the biology of aging* (3rd ed.). New York: Academic Press.

Cox, P. R., & Ford, J. R. (1970). The mortality of widows shortly after widowhood. In T. Ford & G. F. DeJong (Eds.), *Social demography.* Englewood Cliffs, NJ: Prentice-Hall.

Craik, F. I. M. (1968a). Short-term memory and the aging process. In G. A. Talland (Ed.), *Human aging and behavior.* New York: Academic Press.

Craik, F. I. M. (1968b). Two components in free recall. *Journal of Verbal Learning and Verbal Behavior, 7*, 996–1004.

Craik, F. I. M. (1971). Primary memory. *British Medical Bulletin, 27*, 232–236.

Craik, F. I. M. (1977) Age differences in human memory. In J. E. Birren & K. W. Schaie (Eds.), *Handbook of the psychology of aging.* New York: Van Nostrand Reinhold.

Craik, F. I. M., & Byrd, M. (1982). Aging and cognitive deficits: The role of attentional resources. In F. I. M. Craik & S. E. Trehub (Eds.), *Aging and cognitive processes.* New York: Plenum.

Craik, F. I. M, & Lockhart, R. S. (1972). Levels of processing: A framework for memory research. *Journal of Verbal Learning and Verbal Behavior, 11*, 671–684.

Craik, F. I. M. & Masani, P. A. (1967). Age differences in the temporal integration of language. *British Journal of Psychology, 58*, 291–299.

Craik, F. I. M., Morris, R. G., & Gick, M. L. (1989). Adult age differences in working memory. In G. Vallas & T. Shallice (Eds.), *Neuropsychological impairments of short-term memory.* New York: Cambridge University Press.

Craik, F. I. M., & Rabinowitz, J. C. (1985). The effects of presentation rate and encoding task on age-related memory deficits. *Journal of Gerontology, 40*, 309–315.

Craik, F. I. M., & Simon, E. (1980). Age differences in memory: The roles of attention and depth of processing. In L. W. Poon, J. L. Fozard, L. S. Cermak, D. Arenberg & L. W. Thompson (Eds.), *New directions in memory and aging: Proceedings of the George Talland Memorial Conference.* Hillsdale, NJ: Erlbaum.

Craik, F. I. M., & Tulving, E. (1975). Depth of processing and the retention of words in episodic memory. *Journal of Experimental Psychology: General, 104*, 268–294.

Crapper, D. R., Kirshnan, S. S., & Quittkat, S. (1976). Aluminum, neurofibrillary degeneration, and Alzheimer's disease. *Brain, 99*, 67–80.

Crowder, R. G. (1980). Echoic memory and the study of aging memory systems. In L. W. Poon, J. L. Fozard, L. S. Cermak, D. Arenberg & L. W. Thompson (Eds.), *New directions in memory and aging.* Hillsdale, NJ; Erlbaum.

Crowder, R. G., & Morton, J. (1969). Precategorical acoustic storage (PAS). *Perception and Psychophysics, 5*, 365–373.

Crowder, R. G., & Prussin, H. A. (1971). Experiments with the stimulus suffix effect. *Journal of Experimental Psychology Monographs, 91*, 169–190.

Crowder, R. G., & Raeburn, U. P. (1970). The stimulus suffix effect with reversed speech. *Journal of Verbal Learning and Verbal Behavior, 9*, 342–345.

Cumming, E., & Henry, W. E. (1961). *Growing old.* New York: Basic Books.

Cunningham, W. R. (1987). Intellectual abilities and age. In K. W. Schaie & C. Eisdorfer (Eds.), *Annual review of gerontology and geriatrics (Vol. 7)* (pp. 117–134). New York: Springer.

Cunningham, W. R., Clayton, V., & Overton, W. Fluid and crystallized intelligence in young adulthood and old age. *Journal of Gerontology, 30*, 53–55.

Curtis, H. J. (1966). *Biological mechanisms of aging.* Springfield, IL: Charles C. Thomas.

Darley, J. M. Glucksberg, S., Kamin, L. J., & Kinchla, R. A. (1981). *Psychology.* Englewood Cliffs, NJ: Prentice-Hall.

Darwin, C. J., Turvey, M. T., & Crowder, R. G. (1972). Auditory analogue of the Sperling partial report procedure: Evidence for brief auditory storage. *Cognitive Psychology, 3*, 255–267.

DaSilva, A., & Schork, M. (1984–85). Gender differences in attitudes to death among a group of public health students. *Omega: Journal of Death and Dying, 15*, 77–84.

Davies, P., & Maloney, A. J. F. (1976). Selective loss of central cholinergic neurons in Alzheimer's disease. *Lancet, 2*, 1403.

Dawson, D., Hendershot, G., & Fulton, J. (1987). Aging in the eighties: Functional limitations of individuals 65 and over. *Advance Data Number 133,* National Center for Health Statistics.

Delongis, A., Coyne, J. C., Dakof, B., Folkman, S., & Lazarus, R. S. (1982). Relationship of daily hassles, uplifts, and major life events to health status. *Health Psychology, 1,* 119–136.

Demming, J. A., & Pressey, S. L. (1957). Tests "indigenous" to the adult and older years. *Journal of Counseling Psychology, 2,* 144–148.

Denny, M. R. (1984). Age differences. In R. J. Corsini (Ed.), *Encyclopedia of psychology.* New York: Wiley.

The Denver Post. How women age. (1982, September 26).

Department of Health, Education, and Welfare. (1977). Monocular visual acuity of persons 4–74 years. *Vital Health Statistics,* Series 11, No. 201.

Dickinson, G.E., & Pearson, A. A. (1979). Differences in attitudes toward terminal patients among selected medical specialties of physicians. *Medical Care, 17,* 682–685.

Dickinson, G. E., & Pearson, A. A. (1980–81). Death education and the physicians' attitudes toward dying patients. *Omega: Journal of Death and Dying, 11,* 167–174.

Diener, E., Larsen, R. J., & Emmons, R. A. (1984). Person situation interactions: Choice of situation and congruence response models. *Journal of Personality and Social Psychology, 47,* 580–592.

Dion, K. K., Berscheid, E., & Walster, E. (1972). What is beautiful is good. *Journal of Personality and Social Psychology, 24,* 285–290.

Doering, M., Rhodes, S. R., & Schuster, M. (1983). *The aging worker: Research and recommendations.* Beverly Hills, CA; Sage.

Dohrenwend, B. S., & Dohrenwend, B. P. (1974). *Stressful life events: Their nature and effects.* New York: Wiley.

Doppelt, J. E., & Wallace, W. L. (1955). Standardization of the Wechsler Adult Intelligence Scale for older persons. *Journal of Abnormal and Social Psychology, 51,* 312–330.

Doty, R. L., Deems, D. A., & Stellar, S. (1988). Olfactory dysfunction in Parkinsonism: A general deficit unrelated to neurologic signs, disease stage, or disease duration. *Neurology, 38,* 1237–1244.

Douglas, K., & Arenberg, D. (1978). Age changes, cohort differences, and cultural change on the Guilford-Zimmerman Temperament Survey. *Journal of Gerontology, 33,* 737–747.

Douvan, E. (1979). Differing views on marriage 1957 to 1976. *Newsletter, Center for Continuing Education of Women* (University of Michigan), *12,* 1–2.

Dowd, J. (1975). Aging as exchange: A preface to theory. *Journal of Gerontology, 30,* 584–594.

Drachman, D. A., & Leavitt, J. (1972). Memory impairment in the aged: Storage versus retrieval deficit. *Journal of Experimental Psychology, 93,* 302–308.

Dublin, L. I. (1951). *The facts of life—from birth to death.* New York: Macmillan.

Dublin, L. I., Lotka, A. J., & Spiegelman, M. (1949). *Length of life table.* New York: Ronald.

Durlak, J. (1972). Measurement of the fear of death: An examination of some existing scales. *Journal of Clinical Psychology, 28,* 545–547.

Eichorn, D. (1973). The Institute of Human Development Studies: Berkeley and Oakland. In L. F. Jarvik, C. Eisdorfer, & J. E. Blum (Eds.), *Intellectual functioning in adults: Psychological and biological influences.* New York: Springer.

Eisdorfer, C. (1962). Changes in cognitive functioning in relation to intellectual level in senescence. In C. Tibbits & W. Donahue (Eds.), *Social and psychological aspects of aging.* New York: Columbia University Press.

Eisdorfer, C. (1977). Stress, disease, and cognitive change in the aged. In C. Eisdorfer & R. O. Friedel (Eds.), *Cognitive and emotional disturbance in the elderly.* Chicago: Yearbook Medical Publishers.

Eisdorfer, C., & Service, C. (1967). Verbal rote learning and superior intelligence in the aged. *Journal of Gerontology, 22,* 158–161.

Eisdorfer, C., & Wilkie, F. (1973). Intellectual changes with advancing age. In L. F. Jarvik, C. Eisdorfer, & J. E. Blum (Eds.), *Intellectual functioning in adults.* New York: Springer.

Eisner, D.A. (1972). Developmental relationships between field independence and fixity-mobility. *Perceptual and Motor Skills, 34,* 767–770.

Ekblom, B. (1963). Significance of psychological factors with regard to risk of death among elderly persons. *Acta Psychiatrica Scandinavica, 39,* 627–633.

Ekerdt, D. J., Baden, L., Bosse, R., & Dibbs, E. (1983). The effect of retirement on physical health. *American Journal of Public Health, 73,* 779–783.

Ekerdt, D. J., Bosse, R., & Levkoff, S. (1985). An empirical test for phases of retirement: Findings from the normative aging study. *Journal of Gerontology, 40,* 96–101.

Ekerdt, D. J., Bosse, R., & LoCastro, J, S. (1983). Claims that retirement improves health. *Journal of Gerontology, 38,* 231–236.

Elias, C. S., & Hirasuna, N. (1976). Age and semantic and phonological encoding. *Developmental Psychology, 12,* 497–503.

Elliott, G. R., & Eisdorfer, C. (Eds.) (1982). *Stress and human health.* New York: Springer.

Engen, T. (1977). Taste and smell. In J. E. Birren & K. W. Schaie (Eds.), *Handbook of the psychology of aging.* New York: Van Nostrand Reinhold.

Erber, J. T. (1974). Age differences in recognition memory. *Journal of Gerontology, 29,* 177–181.

Eriksen, C. W., & Collins, J. F. (1967). Some temporal characteristics of visual pattern perception. *Journal of Experimental Psychology, 89,* 659–667.

Eriksen, E. H. (1963). *Childhood and society* (2nd ed.). New York: Norton.

Eriksen, E. H. (1968). *Identity: Youth and crisis.* New York: Norton.

Esquire. The aging body. (1982, May).

Evans, D. A., Funkenstein, H. H., & Albert, M. S. (1989). Prevalence of Alzheimer's disease in a community population of older persons. *Journal of the American Medical Association, 262,* 2551–2556.

Evans, G. W., Brennan, P. L., Skorpanich, M. A., & Held, D. (1984). Cognitive mapping and elderly adults: Verbal and location memory for urban landmarks. *Journal of Gerontology, 39,* 452–457.

Evans, P. A. L., & Bartolome, F. (1980). The relationship between professional life and private life. In C. B. Derr (Ed.), *Work, family, and the career: New frontiers in theory and research.* New York: Praeger.

Evans, R. I. (1970). *Gordon Allport: The man and his ideas.* New York: E. P. Dutton.

Ewen, R. B. (1984). Personality theories. In R. J. Corsini (Ed.), *The encyclopedia of psychology.* New York: Wiley.

Ewen, R. B. (1988). *An introduction to theories of personality* (3rd ed.). Hillsdale, NJ: Lawrence Erlbaum Associates.

Eysenck, H. J. (1967) *The biological basis of personality.* Springfield, IL: Charles C. Thomas.

Eysenck, H. J. & Eysenck, S. B. G. (1969). *Personality structure and measurement.* London: Routledge & Kegan.

Eysenck, M. W. (1974). Age differences in incidental learning. *Developmental Psychology, 10,* 936–941.

Farrell, M. P., & Rosenberg, S. D. (1981). *Men at midlife.* Boston: Auburn House.

Feifel, H. (1974). Religious conviction and fear of death among the healthy and the terminally ill. *Journal for the Scientific Study of Religion, 13,* 353–360.

Feifel, H. (1990). Psychology and death: Meaningful rediscovery. *American Psychologist, 45,* 537–543.

Feifel, H., & Branscomb, A. (1973). Who's afraid of death? *Journal of Abnormal Psychology, 81,* 282–288.

Feifel, H. Freilich, J., & Hermann, L. (1973). Death fear in dying heart and cancer patients. *Journal of Psychosomatic Research, 17,* 161–166.

Feifel, H., Hanson, S., Jones, R., & Edwards, L. (1967). Physicians consider death. *Proceedings of the 75th Annual Convention of the American Psychological Association, 2,* 201–202.

Feifel, H., & Heller, J. (1960). Normalcy, illness, and death. In *Proceedings of the Third World Congress of Psychiatry.* Toronto: University of Toronto Press.

Feifel, H., & Hermann, L.. (1973). Fear of death in the mentally ill. *Psychological Reports, 33,* 931–938.

Feifel, H., & Nagy, V. T. (1980). Death orientation and life-threatening behavior. *Journal of Abnormal Psychology, 89,* 38–45.

Feinleib, M. (1984, February 2). Presentation before the subcommittee on health and long-term care of the Select Committee on Aging of the United States House of Representatives. Washington, DC.

Felton, B., & Kahana, E. (1974). Adjustment and situationally-bound locus of control among institutionalized aged. *Journal of Gerontology, 29,* 295–301.

Felton, B., & Revenson, T. A. (1987). Age differences in coping with chronic illness. *Psychology and Aging, 2,* 164–170.

Festinger, L. (1954). A theory of social comparison process. *Human Relations, 1,* 117–140.

Fillenbaum, G. G., George, L. K., & Palmore, E. B. (1985). Determinants and consequences of retirement among men of different races and economic levels. *Journal of Gerontology, 40,* 85–94.

Finch, C. E. (1977). Neuroendocrine and anatomic aspects of aging. In C. E. Finch & L. Hayflick (Eds.), *Handbook of the biology of aging.* New York: Van Nostrand Reinhold.

Finch, C. E., & Landfield, P. W. (1985). Neuroendocrine and autonomic functions in aging mammals. In C. E. Finch & E. L. Schneider (Eds.), *Handbook of the biology of aging* (2nd ed.). New York: Van Nostrand Reinhold.

Finkle, T. J., & Walsh, D. A. (1979, September). *Sentence and discourse comprehension in young and old adults.* Paper presented at the 87th meeting of the American Psychological Association, New York.

Fischer, C. S. (1982). *To dwell among friends*. Chicago, IL: University of Chicago Press.

Fischer, C. S., Jackson, R. M., Stueve, C. A., Gerson, K., Jones, L. M., & Baldassare, M. (1977). *Networks and places: Social relations in the urban setting*. New York: Free Press.

Fischman, J. (1984). The mystery of Alzheimer's. *Psychology Today, 18(1)*, 27.

Fisseni, H. (1985). Perceived unchangeability of life and some biographical correlates. In J. M. A. Munnichs, P. Mussen, E. Olbrich & P. G. Coleman (Eds.), *Life-span and change in gerontological perspective* (pp. 103–131). Orlando, FL: Academic Press.

Fleg, J. L., & Lakatta, E. G. (1988). Role of muscle loss in the age-associated reduction in VO_2 max. *Journal of Applied Psychology, 65*, 1147–1151.

Florian, V., & Har-Even, D. (1983–84). Fear of personal death: The effects of sex and religious belief. *Omega: Journal of Death and Dying, 14*, 83–91.

Fobair, P., & Cortoba, C. (1982). Scope and magnitude of the cancer problem in psychosocial research. In J. Cohen et al. (Eds.), *Psychosocial aspects of cancer* (pp. 9–15). New York: Raven Press.

Folkman, S., & Lazarus, R. S. (1980). An analysis of coping in a middle-aged community sample. *Journal of Health and Social Behavior, 21*, 219–239.

Folkman, S., Lazarus, R. S., Pimley, S., & Novacek, J. (1987). Age differences in stress and coping processes. *Psychology and Aging, 2*, 171–184.

Folstein, M. F., Folstein, S. E., & McHugh, P. R. (1975). "Mini-mental state:" A practical method for grading the cognitive state of patients for the clinician. *Journal of Psychiatric Research, 12*, 189–198.

Foulkes, D. (1966). *The psychology of sleep*. New York: Scribners.

Fozard, J. L. (1990). Vision and hearing. In J. E. Birren & K. W. Schaie (Eds.), *Handbook of the psychology of aging* (3rd ed.) (pp. 150–170). New York: Academic Press.

Franklin, P. A. (1984, August). *Psychological services for the terminally ill in hospice programs*. Paper presented at the 92nd Annual Convention of the American Psychological Association, Toronto.

Fredrick, J. F. (1971). Physiological reactions induced by grief. *Omega: Journal of Death and Dying, 2*, 71–75.

Fredrick, J. F., (1981). The biochemistry of acute grief with regard to neoplasia. In O.S. Margolis, H. C. Raether, A. H. Kutscher, J. B. Powers, I. B. Seeland, R. DeBellis, & D. J. Cherico (Eds.), *Acute grief: Counseling the bereaved*. New York: Columbia University Press.

Freese, A. S., (1980). *Stroke: The new hope and the new help*. New York: Random House.

Freud, S. (1959). *Inhibitions, symptoms, and anxiety*. (Original publication: 1926). Paperback reprint, New York: Norton.

Freud, S. (1963). *Mourning and melancholia*. (Original publication: 1917). Paperback reprint: *General psychological theory*. New York: Collier.

Freud, S. (1965a). *Three essays on the theory of sexuality*. (Original publication: 1905). Standard edition: London: Hogarth Press, Vol. 7. Paperback reprint: New York: Avon Books.

Freud, S. (1965b). *New introductory lectures on psychoanalysis*. (Original publication: 1933). Standard edition: London, Hogarth Press, Vol. 22. Paperback reprint: New York: Norton.

Freud, S. (1965c). *The interpretation of dreams.* (Original publication: 1900). Paperback reprint: New York: Avon Books.

Freud, S. (1966). *Introductory lectures on psychoanalysis* (rev. ed.). (Original publication: 1916–1917). Standard edition: London: Hogarth Press, Vol. 15–16. Paperback reprint: New York: Norton.

Frick, M. H., Elo, O., Haapa, K., et al. (1987). Helsinki heart study: Primary-prevention trial with gemfibrozil in middle-aged men with dyslipidemia: Safety of treatment, changes in risk factors, and incidence of coronary heart disease. *New England Journal of Medicine, 317,* 1237–1245.

Friedman, H. S., & Booth-Kewley, S. (1988). Validity of Type A construct: A reprise. *Psychological Bulletin, 104,* 318–384.

Friedman, M., & Rosen, R. (1959). Association of specific overt behavior pattern with blood and cardiovascular findings. *Journal of the American Medical Association, 169,* 1286.

Friedman, M., & Rosen, R. (1974). *Type A behavior and your heart.* New York: Knopf.

Fries, J. F. (1983). The compression of morbidity. *Milbank Memorial Fund Quarterly, 61,* 397–419.

Fries, J.F. & Crapo, L.M. (1981). *Vitality and aging.* New York: W. H. Freeman.

Frisancho, A. R. (1984). New standards of weight and body composition by frame size and height for assessment of nutritional status of adults and the elderly. *American Journal of Clinical Nutrition, 84,* 808–819.

Fromm, E. (1941). *Escape from freedom.* New York: Holt, Rinehart & Winston.

Fromm, E. (1947). *Man for himself: Inquiry into the psychology of ethics.* New York: Holt, Rinehart & Winston.

Fromm, E. (1951). *The forgotten language: An introduction to the understanding of dreams, fairy tales, and myths.* New York: Holt, Rinehart & Winston.

Fromm, E. (1974). *The art of loving.* (New York: Harper & Row, 1956) Paperback reprint: New York: Perennial.

Frontera, W. R., Meredith, C. N., O'Reilly, K. P., Knuttgen, H. G., & Evans, W. J. (1988). Strength conditioning in older men: Skeletal muscle hypertrophy and improved function. *Journal of Applied Psychology, 64,* 1038–1044.

Furry, C. A., & Baltes, P. B. (1973). The effect of age differences in ability-extraneous performance variables on the assessment of intelligence in children, adults, and the elderly. *Journal of Gerontology, 28,* 73–80.

Gallagher, D., & Thompson, L. W. (1983). Depression. In P. M. Lewinsohn & L. Teri (Eds.), *Clinical geropsychology: New directions in assessment and treatment.* New York: Pergamon Press.

Gallagher, D., & Thompson, L. W. (1989). Bereavement and adjustment disorders. In E. W. Busse & D. G. Blazer (Eds.), *Geriatric psychiatry* (pp. 459–473). Washington, DC: American Psychiatric Press.

Gardner, E. F., & Monge, R. H. (1977). Adult age differences in cognitive abilities and educational background. *Experimental Aging Research, 3,* 337–383.

Gardner, H., (1983). *Frames of mind.* New York: Basic Books.

Garland, C., Barrett-Connor, E., Suarez, L., Criqui, M. H., & Mingard, D. L. (1985). Effects of passive smoking on ishemic heart disease mortality of nonsmokers: A prospective study. *American Journal of Epidemiology, 121,* 645–650.

Garraway, W. M., Whisnant, J. P., & Drury, L. (1983). The continuing decline in the incidence of stroke. *Mayo Clinic Proceedings, 58,* 520–523.

Garraway, W. M., Whisnant, J. P., Kurland, L. T., & O'Fallon, W. M. (1979). Changing pattern of cerebral infarction, 1945-1974. *Stroke, 10,* 657–663.

Garstecki, D. (1981). Aural rehabilitation for the aging adult. In D. Beasley & G. A. Davis (Eds.), *Aging: Communication processes and disorders.* New York: Grune & Stratton.

Gatz, M., & Siegler, I. C. (1981, August). *Locus of control: A retrospective.* Paper presented at the American Psychological Association Meetings, Los Angeles.

George, L. K. (1989). Social and economic factors. In E. W. Busse & D. G. Blazer (Eds.), *Geriatric psychiatry.* Washington, DC: American Psychiatric Press.

George, L. K., & Weiler, S. J. (1981). Sexuality in middle and late life. *Archives of General Psychiatry, 38,* 919–923.

Gladis, M., & Braun, H. (1958). Age differences in transfer and retroaction as a function of intertask response similarity. *Journal of Experimental Psychology, 55,* 25–30.

Gleitman, H. (1983). *Basic psychology.* New York: Norton.

Glick, I. O., Weiss, R. S., & Parkes, C. M. (1974). *The first year of bereavement.* New York: Wiley.

Glick, P. C. (1979). Future American families. *Washington Cofo Memo, 11(3),* 2–5.

Goff, G. B., Rosner, B. S., Detre, T., & Kennard, D. (1965). Vibration perception in normal man and medical patients. *Journal of Neurological and Neurosurgical Psychiatry, 28,* 503.

Goldberg, E. L., & Comstock, G. W. (1980). Epidemiology of life events: Frequency in general populations. *American Journal of Epidemiology, 111,* 736–752.

Golde, P., & Kogan, N. (1959). A sentence completion procedure for assessing attitudes toward old people. *Journal of Gerontology, 14,* 355–363.

Goode, W. J. (1963). *World revolution and family patterns,* New York: The Free Press.

Goodwin, J. S. (1981). *Suppressor cells in human disease.* New York: Marcel Dekker.

Gordon, S. K., & Clark, W. C. (1974). Application of signal detection theory to prose recall and recognition in elderly and young adults. *Journal of Gerontology, 29,* 64–72.

Gore, S., & Mangione, T. W. (1983). Social roles, sex roles, and psychological distress: Additive and interactive models of sex differences. *Journal of Health and Social Behavior, 24,* 300–312.

Gotestam, K. G. (1982). Behavioral and dynamic psychotherapy with the elderly. In J. E. Birren & R. B. Sloane (Eds.), *Handbook of mental health and aging.* Englewood Cliffs, NJ: Prentice-Hall.

Goudy, W. J. (1981). Changing work expectations: Findings from the Retirement History Study. *The Gerontologist, 21,* 644–649.

Gould, R. (1972). The phases of adult life: A study in developmental psychology. *American Journal of Psychiatry, 129,* 521–531.

Gould, R. (1978). *Transformations: Growth and change in adult life.* New York: Simon & Schuster.

Graney, M. J. (1975). Happiness and social participation in aging. *Journal of Gerontology, 30,* 701–706.

Granick, S., Kleben, M. H., & Weiss, A. D. (1976). Relationships between hearing loss and cognition in normally hearing aged persons. *Journal of Gerontology, 4,* 434–440.

Graves, J. P., Dalton, G. W., & Thompson, P. H. (1980). Career stages: In organizations. In C. B. Derr (Ed.), *Work, family, and the career: New frontiers in theory and research*. New York: Praeger.

Greer, D., & Mor, V. (1983). *A preliminary final report of the National Hospice Study.* Providence, RI: Brown University.

Griffitt, W. (1974). Attitude similarity and attraction. In T. L. Huston (Ed.), *Foundations of interpersonal attraction*. New York: Academic Press.

Gross, A. E., & Crofton, C. (1977). What is good is beautiful. *Sociometry, 40,* 85–90.

Guilford, J. P. (1967). *The nature of human intelligence*. New York: McGraw-Hill.

Guilford, J. P. (1980). Fluid and crystallized intelligences: Two fanciful concepts. *Psychological Bulletin, 88,* 406–412.

Guilford, J. P. (1984). Human intelligence. In R. J. Corsini (Ed.), *Encyclopedia of psychology*. New York: Wiley.

Gurland, B. J. (1982). The assessment of the mental health status of older adults. In J. E. Birren & R. B. Sloane (Eds.), *Handbook of mental health and aging*. Englewood Cliffs, NJ: Prentice-Hall.

Gurland, B. J., Copeland, J., Kuriansky, J., Kelleger, M., Sharpe, L., & Dean, L. (1983). *The mind and mood of aging*. New York: Haworth Press.

Gurland, B. J., & Toner, J. A. (1982). Depression in the elderly: A review of recently published studies. In C. Eisdorfer (Ed.), *Annual review of gerontology and geriatrics (Vol. 3)*. New York: Springer.

Gutmann, D. L. (1975). Parenthood: Key to comparative study of the life cycle? In N. Datan & L. Ginsberg (Eds.), *Life-span developmental psychology: Normative life crises*. New York: Academic Press.

Guttentag, R. E. (1985). Memory and aging: Implications for theories of memory development during childhood. *Developmental Review, 5,* 56–82.

Haber, R. N., & Nathanson, L. S. (1968). Post-retinal iconic storage? Some further observations on Park's camel as seen through the eye of a needle. *Perception and Psychophysics, 3,* 349–355.

Haber, R. N., & Standing, L. (1969). Direct measures of short-term visual storage. *Quarterly Journal of Experimental Psychology, 21,* 43–54.

Haber, R. N., & Standing, L. (1970). Direct estimates of apparent duration of a flash followed by visual noise. *Canadian Journal of Psychology, 24,* 216–229.

Hagestad, G. (1978). *Patterns of communication and influence between grandparents and grandchildren in a changing society*. Paper presented at the World Congress of Sociology, Sweden.

Hagestad, G. (1980). *Role change and socialization in adulthood: The transition to the empty nest*. Unpublished manuscript. State College, PA: The Pennsylvania State University.

Hagestad, G. (1985). Continuity and connectedness. In V. L. Bengtson & J. F. Robertson (Eds.), *Grandparenthood*. Beverly Hills, CA: Sage Publications.

Hagnell, O., Lanke, J., Rorsman, B., Ohman, R., & Ojesjio. (1983). Current trends in the incidence of senile and multi-infarct dementia: A prospective study of a total population followed over 25 years. The Lundby study. *ARCHIV fur Psychiatrie und Nervenbrankheiten, 233,* 423–438.

Hall, C. S. (1966). *The meaning of dreams.* New York: McGraw-Hill.

Hall, D. T. (1975). Pressures from work, self, and home in the life stages of married women. *Journal of Vocational Behavior, 6,* 121–132.

Handal, P. J., Peal, R. L., Napoli, J. G., & Austrin, H. R. (1984–85). The relationship between direct and indirect measures of death anxiety. *Omega: Journal of Death and Dying, 15,* 245–262.

Handal, P. J., & Rychlak, J. F. (1971). Curvilinearity between dream content and death anxiety and the relationship of death anxiety to repression-sensitization. *Journal of Abnormal Psychology, 77,* 11–16.

Hanley-Dunn, P., & McIntosh, J. L. (1984). Meaningfulness and recall of names by young and old adults. *Journal of Gerontology, 39,* 583–585.

Harkins, S. W., Price, D. D., & Martelli, M. (1986). Effects of age in pain perception: Thermonociception. *Journal of Gerontology, 41,* 58–63.

Harman, D. (1968). Free radical theory of aging: Effect of free radical reaction inhibitors on the mortality rate of male LAF_1 mice. *Journal of Gerontology, 23,* 476–482.

Harman, D. (1981). The aging process. *Proceedings of the National Academy of Sciences, 78,* 7124–7128.

Harre, R., & Lamb, R. (1984). *The encyclopedic dictionary of psychology.* Cambridge, MA: The MIT Press.

Harris, J. E., & Morris, P. E. (1984). *Everyday memory: Actions and absentmindedness.* New York: Academic Press.

Harris, L., & Associates (1975). *The myth and reality of aging.* Washington, DC: National Council on the Aging.

Harris, L. & Associates. (1981). *Aging in the eighties: America in transition.* Washington, DC: National Council on the Aging.

Harrison, D. E. (1985). Cell tissue transplantation: A means of studying the aging process. In C. E. Finch & E. L. Schneider (Eds.), *Handbook of the biology of aging* (2nd ed.). New York: Van Nostrand Reinhold.

Hartley, J. T., Harker, J. O., & Walsh, D. A. (1980). Contemporary issues and new directions in adult development of learning and memory. In L. W. Poon (Ed.), *Aging in the 1980s.* Washington, DC: American Psychological Association.

Harvard Medical School. (1979). A look at high blood pressure, Part II. *Harvard Medical School Newsletter, 4(9),* 1–2, 5.

Hatfield, C. B., Hatfield, R. E., Geggie, P. H. S., Taylor, J., Soti, K. Winthers, L., Harris, A., & Greenley, N. (1983–84). Attitudes about death, dying, and terminal care: Differences among groups at a university teaching hospital. *Omega: Journal of Death and Dying, 14,* 51–63.

Hayflick, L. (1965). The limited *in vitro* lifetime of human diploid cell strains. *Experimental Cell Research, 37,* 614–636.

Hayflick, L. (1973). The biology of human aging. *American Journal of Medical Science, 265(1),* 432–445.

Hayflick, L. (1980). Cell aging. In C. Eisdorfer (Ed.), *Annual review of gerontology and geriatrics (Vol. 1).* New York: Springer.

Hayflick, L. (1986). The cell biology of human aging. *Scientific American, 242,* 58–65.

Haynes, S. G., McMichael, A. J., & Tyroler, H. A. (1978). Survival after early and normal retirement. *Journal of Gerontology, 33,* 269–278.

Hayslip, B., Jr, & Sterns, H. L. (1979). Age differences in relationships between crystallized and fluid intelligence in problem solving. *Journal of Gerontology, 34,* 404–414.

Hazzard, W. R., & Bierman, E. L. (1978). Old age. In D. W. Smith, E. L. Bierman, & N. M. Robinson (Eds.), *The biologic ages of man.* Philadelphia: W. B. Saunders.

Hebb, D. O. (1978). On watching myself get old. *Psychology Today, 12(11),* 15–23.

Hegeler, S. (1976). *Sexual behavior in elderly Danish males.* Paper presented at the International Symposium on Sex Education and Therapy, Stockholm, Sweden.

Heglin, H. (1956). Problem solving set in different age groups. *Journal of Gerontology, 11,* 310–317.

Hellerstein, H. K., & Friedman, E. H. (1970). Sexual activity and the post-coronary patient. *Archives of International Medicine, 125,* 987–999.

Heron, A., & Chown, S. (1967). *Age and function.* London: Churchill.

Hertzog, C., Dixon, R. A., & Hultsch, D. F. (1990). Relationship between metamemory, memory predictions, and memory task performance in adults. *Psychology and Aging, 5,* 215–227.

Hertzog, C., Schaie, K. W., & Gribben, K. (1978). Cardiovascular changes in intellectual functioning from middle to old age. *Journal of Gerontology, 33,* 872–883.

Hess, B. (1972). Friendship. In M. Riley, M. Johnson, & A. Foner (Eds.), *Aging and society: Vol. 3. A sociology of age stratification.* New York: Russell Sage Foundation.

Heston, L. L., & Mastri, A. R. (1977). The genetics of Alzheimer's disease: Associations with hematologic malignancy and Down's syndrome. *Archives of General Psychiatry, 34,* 976–981.

Hetherington, B. M. (1972). Effects of father absence on personality development in adolescent daughters. *Developmental Psychology, 7,* 313–386.

Hetherington, B. M., Cox, M., & Cox, R. (1976). Divorced fathers. *Family Coordinator, 25(4),* 417–428.

Hetherington, B. M., Cox, M., & Cox, R. (1977). The aftermath of divorce. In J. H. Stevens, Jr., & M. Mathews (Eds.), *Mother-child, father-child relations.* Washington, DC: National Association for the Education of Young Children.

Hetherington, B. M., & Duer, J. The effects of father absence on child development. In W. W. Hartup (Ed.), *The young child: Review of research. (Vol 2).* Washington, DC: National Association for the Education of Young Children.

Heyman, D. K., & Gianturco, D. J. (1973). Long-term adaptation by the elderly to bereavement. *Journal of Gerontology, 3,* 359–362.

Hills, B. L. (1980). Vision, visibility, and perception in driving. *Perception, 9,* 183–216.

Hirsch, B. J. (1981). Social networks and the coping process: Creating personal communities. In B. H. Gottleib (Ed.), *Social networks and social support.* Beverly Hills, CA: Sage.

Hochschild, A. R. (1976). Disengagement theory: A logical, empirical and phenomenological critique. In J. F. Gubrium (Ed.), *Times, roles, and self in old age.* New York: Human Sciences Press.

Hoenders, H. J., & Bloemendal, H. (1983). Lens proteins and aging. *Journal of Gerontology, 38,* 278–286.

Hoerr, S. O. (1963). Thoughts on what to tell the patient with cancer. *Cleveland Clinic Quarterly, 30,* 11–16.

Hoffmann, L. W., & Manis, J. (1978). Influences of children on marital interaction and parental satisfaction and dissatisfaction. In R. Lerner & G. Spanier (Eds.), *Child influences on marital and family interaction.* New York: Academic Press.

Holahan, C. K., & Gilbert, L. A. (1979a). Conflict between major life roles: Women and men in dual career couples. *Human Relations, 32,* 451–467.

Holahan, C. K., & Gilbert, L. A. (1979b). Interrole conflict for working women: Career versus jobs. *Journal of Applied Psychology, 64,* 86–90.

Holden, C. (1976). Hospices: For the dying, relief from pain and fear. *Science, 193,* 389–391.

Holmes, H. H., & Rahe, R. H. (1967). The social readjustment rating scale. *Journal of Psychosomatic Research, 11(2),* 213–218.

Holmes, T. S., & Holmes, H. H. (1970). Short-term intrusions into the life style routine. *Journal of Psychosomatic Research, 14(2),* 121–132.

Holt, R. R. (1982), Occupational stress. In L. Goldberger & S. Breznitz (Eds.), *Handbook of stress.* New York: Free Press.

Hooper, F. H., Hooper, J. O., & Colbert, K. C. (1984). *Personality and memory correlates of intellectual functioning.* Basel: Karger.

Horn, J. (1974). Regriefing: A way to end pathological mourning. *Psychology Today, 1(2),* 184.

Horn, J. L. (1970). Organization of data on life-span development of human abilities. In L. R. Goulet & P. B. Baltes (Eds.), *Life-span developmental psychology. (Vol. 1).* New York: Academic Press.

Horn, J. L. (1978). Human ability systems. In P. B. Baltes (Ed.), *Life-span development and behavior (Vol. 1).* New York: Academic Press.

Horn, J. L., & Cattell, R. B. (1967). Age differences in fluid and crystallized intelligence. *Acta Psychologica, 26,* 107–129.

Horn, J. L., & Donaldson, G. (1980). Cognitive development II: Adulthood development of human abilities. In O. G. Brim, Jr., & Kagan (Eds.) *Constancy and change in human development: A volume of review essays.* Cambridge, MA: Harvard University Press.

Horvath, T. B., & Davis, K. L. (1990). Central nervous system disorders in aging. In E. L. Schneider & J. W. Rowe (Eds.), *Handbook of the biology of aging* (3rd ed.) (pp. 306–329). New York: Academic Press.

House, J. S. (1975). Occupational stress as a precursor to coronary disease. In W. D. Gentry & R. B. Williams, Jr. (Eds.), *Psychological aspects of myocardial infarction and coronary care.* St. Louis: Mosby.

House, J. S., Robbins, C., & Metzner, H. L. (1982). The association of social relationships and activities with mortality: Prospective evidence from the Tecumseh Community Health Study. *American Journal of Epidemiology, 116,* 123–140.

Howell, D. S., Sapolsky, A. S., Pita, J. C., & Woessner, J. F.(1976). The pathogenesis of osteoarthritis. *Seminars in Arthritis and Rheumatism, 5(4),* 365–383.

Hugin, F., Norris, A., & Schock, N. (1960). Skin reflex and voluntary reaction time in young and old males. *Journal of Gerontology, 15,* 388–391.

Hulicka, I. M. (1966). Age differences in Wechsler Memory Scale Scores. *Journal of Genetic Psychology, 109,* 134–145.

Hulicka, I. M. (1967) Age differences in retention as a function of interference. *Journal of Gerontology, 22,* 180–184.

Hulicka, I. M., & Weiss, R. L. (1965). Age differences in retention as a function of learning. *Journal of Consulting Psychology. 29,* 125–129.

Hulin, C. L., & Smith, P. C. (1965). A linear model of job satisfaction. *Journal of Applied Psychology, 49,* 209–216.

Hultsch, D. F. (1971). Adult age differences in free classification and free recall. *Developmental Psychology, 4,* 338–342.

Hultsch, D. F. (1974). Learning to learn in adulthood. *Journal of Gerontology, 29,* 302–308.

Hultsch, D. F. (1975). Adult age differences in retrieval: Trace-dependent and cue-dependent forgetting. *Developmental Psychology, 11,* 197–201.

Hultsch, D. F., & Craig, E. R. (1976). Adult age differences in the inhibition of recall as a function of retrieval cues. *Developmental Psychology, 12,* 83–84.

Hultsch, D. F., & Dixon, R. A. (1990). Learning and memory in aging. In J. E. Birren & K. W. Schaie (Eds.), *Handbook of the psychology of aging* (3rd ed.) (pp. 259–274). New York: Academic Press.

Hunt, E. (1978). Mechanics of verbal ability. *Psychological Review, 85,* 109–130.

Hunt, E. (1980). Intelligence as an information-processing concept. *British Journal of Psychology, 71,* 449–474.

Hunt, E. & Hertzog, C. (1981). *Age-related changes in cognition during the working years.* Arlington, VA: Office of Naval Research.

Hunt, M. (1974). *Sexual behavior in the 1970's.* Chicago: Playboy Press.

Hyman, G. A. (1969). Medical needs of the bereaved family. In A. H. Kutscher (Ed.), *But not to lose.* New York: Frederick Fell.

Hyman, H. H. (1983). *Of time and widowhood.* Durham, NC: Duke University Press Policy Studies.

Idler, E. L., & Angel, R. J. (1990). Self-rated health and mortality in the NHANES-I epidemiologic follow-up study. *American Journal of Public Health, 80,* 446–452.

Idler, E. L., Kasl, S. V., & Lemke, J. H. (1990). Self-evaluated health and mortality among the elderly in New Haven, Connecticut, and Iowa and Washington counties, Iowa, 1982–1986. *American Journal of Epidemiology, 131,* 91–103.

Jalavisto, E., Orma, E., & Tawast, M. (1951). Aging and relation between stimulus intensity and duration in corneal sensibility. *Acta Physiologica Scandinavica, 23,* 224–233.

Jarvik, L. F., & Falek, A. (1963). Intellectual stability and survival in the aged. *Journal of Gerontology, 18,* 173–176.

Jenike, M. A. (1989). *Geriatric psychiatry and psychopharmacology.* Chicago: Year Book Medical Publishers.

Jenkins, C. D. (1971). Psychologic and social precursors of coronary disease. *New England Journal of Medicine, 284,* 244–255; 307–317.

Jenkins, C. D. (1974, June 22). Behavior that triggers heart attacks. *Science News, 105(25),* 402.

Jenkins, C. D. (1975). The coronary-prone personality. In W. D. Gentry & R. B. Williams (Eds.), *Psychological aspects of myocardial infarction and coronary care.* St. Louis: Mosby.

Jones, E. E., & Sigall, H. (1971). The bogus pipeline: A new paradigm for measuring affect and attitude. *Psychological Bulletin, 76,* 349–364.

Jones, H. E. (1959). Intelligence and problem-solving. In J. E. Birren (Ed.), *Handbook of aging and the individual.* Chicago: University of Chicago Press.

Joyce, C. (1984). A time for grieving. *Psychology Today, 18(11),* 42–46.

Jung, C. G. (1984) *Psychoanalysis and association experiments.* (Original publication: 1905). Standard edition: Princeton, NJ: Princeton University Press, Vol. 2.

Jung, C. G. (1910). *The association method.* (Original publication). Standard edition: Princeton, NJ: Princeton University Press, Vol. 2.

Jung, C. G. (1931). *The aims of psychotherapy.* (Original publication). Standard edition: Princeton, NJ: Princeton University Press, Vol. 16.

Jung, C. G. (1933). *Modern man in search of a soul.* New York: Harcourt, Brace & World.

Jung, C. G. (1964). *Man and his symbols.* London: Aldus Books.

Jung, C. G. (1971). *The stages of life.* (Original publication: 1930–1931). Paperback reprint: *The portable Jung.* New York: Viking.

Jung, C. G. (1972). *Two essays on analytical psychology.* (Original publication: 1917, 1928). Paperback reprint: Princeton, NJ: Princeton University Press.

Jung, C. G. (1976). *Psychological types.* (Original publication: 1921). Paperback reprint: Princeton, NJ: Princeton University Press.

Kahana, B. (1976). Social and psychological aspects of sexual behavior among the aged. In E. S. E. Hafez (Ed.), *Aging and reproductive physiology (Vol. 2).* Ann Arbor, MI: Ann Arbor Science.

Kahn, R. L. (1981). *Work and health.* New York: Wiley.

Kalish, R. A. (1981). *Death, grief, and caring relationships.* Monterey, CA: Brooks/Cole.

Kandel, D. B. (1978). Similarity in real-life adolescent friendship pairs. *Journal of Personality and Social Psychology, 36,* 306–312.

Kane, R. L., & Kane, R. A. (1990). Health care for older people: Organizational and policy issues. In R. H. Binstock & L. K. George (Eds.), *Aging and the social sciences* (3rd ed.) (pp. 415–437). New York: Academic Press.

Kaplan, M. F., & Anderson, N. H. (1973). Information integration theory and reinforcement theory as approaches to interpersonal attraction. *Journal of Personality and Social Psychology, 28,* 301–312.

Kasl, S. (1983). Pursuing the link between stressful life experiences and disease: A time for reappraisal. In C. L. Cooper (Ed.), *Stress research: Issues for the Eighties.* New York: Wiley.

Kasl, S., & Berkman, L. F. (1981). Some psychosocial influences on the health status of the elderly: The perspective of social epidemiology. In J. L. McGaugh & S. B. Kiesler (Eds.), *Aging: Biology and behavior.* New York: Academic Press.

Kastenbaum, R., & Aisenberg, R. (1972). *The psychology of death.* New York: Springer.

Kastenbaum, R., & Costa, P. T. (1977). Psychological perspectives on death. *Annual Review of Psychology, 28,* 225–241.

Kastenbaum, R., & Weisman, A. D. (1972). The psychological autopsy as a research procedure in gerontology. In D. P. Dent, R. Kastenbaum & S. Sherwood (Eds.), *Research planning and action for the elderly.* New York: Behavioral Publications.

Kausler, D. H. (1982). *Experimental psychology and human aging.* New York: Wiley.

Kausler, D. H., & Lair, C. V. (1966). Associative strength and paired-associate learning in elderly subjects. *Journal of Gerontology, 21,* 278–280.

Kausler, D. H., & Puckett, J. M. (1980). Frequency judgments and correlated cognitive abilities in young and elderly adults. *Journal of Gerontology, 35,* 376–382.

Kay, D. W. K., & Bergmann, K. (1982). Epidemiology of mental disorders among the aged in the community. In J. E. Birren & R. B. Sloane (Eds.), *Handbook of mental health and aging.* Englewood Cliffs, NJ: Prentice-Hall.

Kay, H. (1954). The effects of position in a display upon problem solving. *Quarterly Journal of Experimental Psychology, 6,* 155–169.

Kay, H. (1955). Some experiments on adult learning. In *Old age in the modern world.* Edinburgh, Scotland: Livingstone.

Keller, M. L., Leventhal, H. Prohaska, T. R., & Leventhal, E. A. (1989). Beliefs about aging and illness in a community sample. *Research in Nursing and Health, 12,* 247–255.

Kelly, J. (1977). The aging male homosexual. *The Gerontologist, 17,* 328–332.

Kelly, J. B., & Wallerstein, J. S. (1976). The effects of parental divorce: Experiences of child in early latency. *American Journal of Orthopsychiatry, 46,* 20–32.

Kenshalo, D. R. (1977). Age changes in touch, vibration, temperature, kinesthesis, and pain sensitivity. In J. E. Birren & K. W. Schaie (Eds.), *Handbook of the psychology of aging.* New York: Van Nostrand Reinhold.

Kerckhoff, A. C. (1966). Husband-wife expectations and reactions to retirement. In I. H. Simpson & J. C. McKinney (Eds.), *Social aspects of aging.* Durham, NC: Duke University Press.

Kerson, T. S. (1985). Heart disease. In T. S. Kerson & W. L. Kerson (Eds.), *Understanding chronic illness: The medical and psychosocial dimension of nine diseases,* (pp. 149–186). New York: Free Press.

Kiesler, R. C., & McCrae, J. A. (1981). Trends in the relationship between sex and psychological distress. *American Sociological Review, 46,* 443–452.

Killian, E. C. (1970). Effect of geriatric transfers on mortality rates. *Social Work, 15,* 19–26.

Kimbrell, G. McA., & Furchgott, E. (1963). The effect of aging on olfactory threshold. *Journal of Gerontology, 18,* 364–365.

Kimmel, D. C. (1977). Patterns of aging among gay men. *Christopher Street, 2,* 28–31.

Kimmel, D. C. (1980). *Adulthood and aging: An interdisciplinary developmental view* (2nd ed.). New York: Wiley.

King, H. F. (1955). An age analysis of some agricultural accidents. *Occupational Psychology, 29,* 245–255.

Kinsey, A. C., Pomeroy, W. B., & Martin, C. E. (1948). *Sexual behavior in the human male.* Philadelphia: W. B. Saunders.

Kinsey, A. C., Pomeroy, W. B., Martin, C. E., & Gebhard, P. H., (1953). *Sexual behavior in the human female.* Philadelphia: W. B. Saunders.

Kirkwood, T. B. L. (1985). Comparative and evolutionary aspects of longevity. In C. E. Finch & E. L. Schneider (Eds.), *Handbook of the biology of aging* (2nd ed.). New York: Van Nostrand Reinhold.

Kivnick, H. Q. (1982). Grandparenthood: An overview of meaning and mental health. *The Gerontologist, 22,* 59–66.

Kiyak, A., Liang, J., & Kahana, E. (1976, August). *Methodological inquiry into the schedule of recent life events.* Paper presented at an annual meeting of the American Psychological Association, Washington, DC.

Kleegman, S. (1959). Frigidity in women. *Quarterly Review of Surgery, Obstetrics, and Gynecology, 16,* 243–248.

Kleemeier, R. W. (1962). Intellectual change in the senium. *Proceedings of the Social Statistics Section of the American Statistical Association, 1,* 290–295.

Klerman, G. L. (1983). Problems in the definition and diagnosis of depression. In L. D. Breslau & M. R. Haug (Eds.), *Depression and aging: Causes, care, and consequences.* New York: Springer.

Kliegl, R., & Baltes, P. B. (1987). Theory-guided analysis of mechanisms of development and aging through testing-the-limits and research on expertise. In C. Schooler & K. W. Schaie (Eds.), *Cognitive functioning and social structure over the life course* (pp. 95–119). Norwood, NJ: Ablex.

Kligman, A. M., Grove, A. L., & Balin, A. K. (1985). Aging of human skin. In C. E. Finch & E. L. Schneider (Eds.), *Handbook of the biology of aging* (2nd ed.). New York: Van Nostrand Reinhold.

Kline, D. W., & Baffa, G. (1976). Differences in the sequential integration of form as a function of age and interstimulus interval. *Experimental Aging Research, 2,* 333–343.

Kline, D. W., & Orme-Rogers, C. (1978). Examination of stimulus persistence as the basis for superior visual identification performance among older adults. *Journal of Gerontology, 33,* 76–81.

Kline, D. W., & Schieber, F. (1981). What are the age differences in visual sensory memory? *Journal of Gerontology, 36,* 86–89.

Kline, D. W., & Schieber, F. (1985). Vision and aging. In J. E. Birren & K. W. Schaie (Eds.), *Handbook of the psychology of aging* (2nd ed.). New York: Van Nostrand Reinhold.

Kline, D. W. & Szafran, J. (1975). Age differences in backward monoptic visual noise making. *Journal of Gerontology, 30* 307–311.

Klodin, V. M. (1976). The relationship of scoring treatment and age in perceptual-integrative performance. *Experimental Aging Research, 2,* 303–313.

Kobrin, F. E. (1976). The primary individual and the family: Changes in living arrangements in the U. S. since 1940. *Journal of Marriage and the Family, 38,* 233–239.

Koenig, H. G., George, L. K., & Siegler, I. C. (1988). The use of religion and other emotion-regulating coping strategies among older adults. *The Gerontologist, 28,* 303–310.

Kogan, N. (1973). Creativity and cognitive style: A life-span perspective. In P. B. Baltes & K. W. Schaie (Eds.), *Life-span developmental psychology: Personality and socialization.* New York: Academic Press.

Kohler, T., & Haimerl, C. (1990). Daily stress as a trigger of migraine attacks: Results of thirteen single subject studies. *Journal of Consulting and Clinical Psychology, 58,* 870–872.

Kolodny, A. L., & Klipper, A. (1978). Bone and joint diseases. In W. Reichel (Ed.), *The geriatric patient.* New York: H. P. Publishing Co.

Kolodny, R. C., Masters, W. H., & Johnson, V. E. (1979). *Textbook of sexual medicine.* Boston: Little, Brown.

Kosnik, W., Winslow, L., Kline, D., Rasinski, K., & Sekuler, R. (1988). Visual changes in daily life. *Journal of Gerontology, 43,* 863–870.

Krag, C. L., & Kountz, W. B. (1950). Stability of body functions in the aged: I. Effect of exposure of the body to cold. *Journal of Gerontology, 5,* 227–235.

Kraus, A. S., & Lilienfeld, A. N. (1959). Some epidemiological aspects of the high mortality rate in the young widowed group. *Journal of Chronic Diseases, 10,* 207–217.

Kriauciunas, R. (1968). The relationship of age and retention interval activity in short term memory. *Journal of Gerontology, 23,* 169–173.

Kryter, K. (1970). *The effects of noise on man.* New York: Academic Press.

Kübler-Ross, E. (1969). *On death and dying.* New York: Macmillan.

Kübler-Ross, E. (1975). *Death: The final stage of growth.* Englewood Cliffs, NJ: Prentice-Hall.

Labby, D. H. (1984). Sexuality. In C. K. Cassel & J. R. Walsh (Eds.), *Geriatric medicine. Volume II: Fundamentals of geriatric care.* New York: Springer-Verlag.

Labouvie-Vief, G., DeVoe, M., & Bulka, D. (1989). Speaking about feelings: Conceptions of emotion across the life span. *Psychology and Aging, 4,* 425–437.

Labouvie-Vief, G., Hakim-Larson, J., & Hobart, C. J. (1987). Age, ego level, and the life-span development of coping and defense processes. *Psychology and Aging, 2,* 286–293.

Lachman, M. E. (1983). Perceptions of intellectual aging: Antecedent or consequence of intellectual functioning? *Developmental Psychology, 19,* 482–498.

Lachman, M. E. (1985). Personal efficacy in middle and old age: Differential and normative patterns of change. In G. H. Elder, Jr. (Ed.), *Life-course dynamics: Trajectories and transitions, 1968–1980.* Ithaca, NY: Cornell University Press.

Lachman, M. E. (1986). Locus of control in aging research: A case for multidimensional and domain-specific assessment. *Journal of Psychology and Aging, 1,* 34–40

Lachman, M. E., & Leff, R. (1989). Perceived control and intellectual functioning in the elderly: A 5-year longitudinal study. *Developmental Psychology, 25,* 722–728.

Lakatta, E. G. (1990). Heart and circulation. In E. L. Schneider & J. W. Rowe (Eds.), *Handbook of the biology of aging* (3rd ed.) (pp. 181–216). New York: Academic Press.

Larson, R. (1978). Thirty years of reasearch on the subjective well-being of older Americans. *Journal of Gerontology, 33,* 109–125.

Larson, T., Sjogren, T., & Jacobson, G. (1963). Senile dementia: A clinical, sociomedical and genetic study. *Acta Psychiatrica Scandinavica, 39, (supplement 167),* 1–259.

Lasagna, L. (1969). The doctor and the dying patient. *Journal of Chronic Disease, 22,* 65–68.

Latham, K. R., & Johnson, L. K. (1979). Aging at the cellular level. In I. Rossman (Ed.), *Clinical geriatrics* (2nd ed.). Philadelphia: Lippincott.

Lattaner, B. A., & Hayslip, B., Jr. (1984-85). Occupation-related differences in levels of death anxiety. *Omega: Journal of Death and Dying, 15,* 53–66.

Lauer, J., & Lauer, R. (1985). Marriages made to last. *Psychology Today, 19,* 22–26.

Laurence, M. W. (1966). Age differences in performance and subjective organization in the free recall of pictorial material. *Canadian Journal of Psychiatry, 20,* 388–399.

Laurence, M. W. (1967a). Memory loss with age: A test of two strategies for its retardation. *Psychonomic Science, 9,* 209–210.

Laurence, M. W. (1967b). A developmental look at the usefulness of list categorization as an aid to free recall. *Canadian Journal of Psychology, 21,* 153–165.

Lawton, M. P. (1980). *Environment and aging.* Monterey, CA: Brooks/Cole.

Lawton, M. P., Whelihan, W. M., & Belsky, J. K. (1980). Personality tests and their uses with older adults. In J. E. Birren & R. B. Sloane (Eds.), *Handbook of mental health and aging.* Englewood Cliffs, NJ: Prentice-Hall.

Lazarus, R. S. (1966). *Psychological stress and the coping process.* New York: McGraw-Hill.

Lazarus, R. S. (1971). The concepts of stress and disease. In L. Levi (Ed.), *Society, stress, and disease: The psychosocial environment and psychosomatic diseases (Vol. 1).* London: Oxford University Press.

Lee, G. R. (1985). Kinship and social support of the elderly: The case of the United States. *Aging and Society, 5,* 19–38.

Lee, J. A., & Pollack, R. H. (1978). The effect of age on perceptual problem-solving strategies. *Experimental Aging Research, 4,* 37–54.

Lefcourt, H. M. (1976). *Locus of control: Current trends in theory and research.* Hillsdale, NJ: Erlbaum.

Lehman, H. C. (1942). The creative years: Oil paintings, etchings, and architectural works. *Psychological Review, 49,* 19–42.

Lehman, H. C. (1953). *Age and achievement.* Princeton, NJ: Princeton University Press.

Lehman, H. C. (1956). Reply to Dennis' critique of *Age and achievement. Journal of Gerontology, 11,* 333–337.

Lehman, H. C. (1958). The influence of longevity upon curves showing man's creative production rate at successive age levels. *Journal of Gerontology, 13,* 187–191.

Lehman, H. C. (1960). The age decrement in outstanding scientific creativity. *American Psychologist, 15,* 128–134.

Leif, H. I., & Fox, R. C. (1963). Training for detached concern in medical students. In H. I. Lief & N. R. Lief (Eds.), *The psychological basis of medical practice,* New York: Harper & Row.

Lemon, B. W., Bengtson, V. L., & Peterson, J. A. (1972). An exploration of the activity theory of aging: Activity and life satisfaction among inmovers to a retirement community. *Journal of Gerontology, 27,* 511–523.

Leon, G. R., Gillum, B., Gillum, R., & Gouze, M. (1979). Personality stability and change over a 30-year period—middle age to old age. *Journal of Consulting and Clinical Psychology, 47,* 517–524.

Lerman, S. (1983). An experimental and clinical evaluation of lens transparency and aging. *Journal of Gerontology, 38,* 293–301.

Lerner, M. (1976). When, why, and where people die. In E. S. Schneidman (Ed.), *Death: Current perspectives.* Palo Alto, CA: Mayfield.

Lester, D. (1967). Fear of death of suicide persons. *Psychological Reports, 20,* 1077–1078.

Lester, D. (1984-85). The fear of death, sex and androgyny: A brief note. *Omega: Journal of Death and Dying, 15,* 271–274.

Levenson, H. (1974). Activism and powerful others: Distinctions within the concept of internal-external control. *Journal of Personality Assessment, 38,* 377–383.

Levinger, G. (1974). A three-level approach to attraction: Toward an understanding of pair relatedness. In T. L. Huston (Ed.), *Foundations of interpersonal attraction.* New York: Academic Press.

Levinger, G. (1978, August). *Models of close relationships: Some new directions.* Invited address presented at the annual meeting of the American Psychological Association, Toronto.

Levinson, D. J. (1978). *The seasons of a man's life.* New York: Knopf.

Levinson, D. J. (1986). A conception of adult development. *American Psychologist, 41,* 3–13.

Levinson, D. J., Darrow, C. M., Klein, E. B., Levinson, M. H., & McKee, B. (1974). The psychosocial development of men in early adulthood and midlife transition. In D. F. Ricks, A. Thomas, & M. Roff (Eds.), *Life history research in psychopathology.* Minneapolis: University of Minnesota Press.

Lieberman, M. A. (1965). Psychological correlates of impending death: Some preliminary observations. *Journal of Gerontology, 20,* 181–190.

Lieberman, M. A. (1982). The effects of social supports on response to stress. In L. Goldberger & S. Breznitz (Eds.), *Handbook of stress.* New York: Free Press.

Liegner, L. M. (1975). St. Christopher's hospice, 1974: Care of the dying patient. *Journal of the American Medical Association, 234(10),* 1047–1048.

Light, L. L. (1990). Interactions between memory and language in old age. In J. E. Birren & K. W. Schaie (Eds.), *Handbook of the psychology of aging* (3rd ed.) (pp. 275–290). New York: Academic Press.

Lindemann, E. (1944). Symptomatology and management of acute grief. *American Journal of Psychiatry, 101,* 141–148.

Lindsay, P. H., & Norman, D. A. (1977). *Human information processing.* (2nd ed.) New York: Academic Press.

Linn, M. W., Hunter, K., & Harris, R. (1980). Symptoms of depression and recent life events in community elderly. *Journal of Clinical Psychology, 36,* 675–682.

Lirette, W. L., Palmer, R. L., Ibarra, I. D., Kroenig, P. M., & Gaines, R. K. (1969). Management of patients with terminal cancer. *Postgraduate Medicine, 46,* 145–149.

Littlefield, C., & Fleming, S. (1984–85). Measuring fear of death: A multidimensional approach. *Omega: Journal of Death and Dying, 15,* 131–138.

Loevinger, J. (1976). *Ego development.* San Francisco: Jossey-Bass.

Logan, R. D. (1986). A reconceptualization of Erikson's theory: The repetition of existential and instrumental themes. *Human Development, 29,* 125–136.

Lowenthal, M., & Haven, C. (1968). Interaction and adaptation: Intimacy as a critical variable. *American Sociological Review, 33,* 20–30.

Lowenthal, M., Thurnher, M., & Chiriboga, D. (1975). *Four stages of life.* San Francisco: Jossey-Bass.

Lyons, J. (1968). Chronological age, professional age, and eminence in psychology. *American Psychologist, 23,* 371–373.

Maas, H. J., & Kuypers, J. A. (1974). *From thirty to seventy.* San Francisco: Jossey-Bass.

Macht, M. L., & Buschke, H. (1984). Speed of recall in aging. *Journal of Gerontology, 39,* 439–443.

Makinodan, T. (1974). Cellular basis of immunosenescence. In *Molecular and cellular mechanisms of aging.* Paris: INSERM, Coll. Inst. Nat. Sante Rec. Med., Vol. 27.

Mandler, G. (1967). Organization and memory. In K. W. Spence & J. T. Spence (Eds.), *The psychology of learning and motivation: Advances in research and theory (Vol. 1).* New York: Academic Press.

Manton, K. G., Siegler, I. C., & Woodbury, M. A. (1986). Patterns of intellectual development in later life. *Journal of Gerontology, 41,* 486–499.

Margolis, O. S., Raether, H. C., Kutscher, A. H., Powers, J. B., Seeland, I. B., DeBellis, R., & Cherico, D. J. (1981). *Acute grief: Counseling the bereaved.* New York: Columbia University Press.

Marie, H. (1978). Reorienting staff attitudes toward the dying. *Hospital Progress, 59,* 74–76.

Markus, E. J. (1971). Perceptual field dependence among aged persons. *Perceptual and Motor Skills, 33,* 175–178.

Martin, G. M. (1977). Genotropic theories of aging: An overview. In C. E. Finch & L. Hayflick (Eds.), *Handbook of the biology of aging.* New York: Van Nostrand Reinhold.

Martin, L. R. (1982). Overview of the psychosocial aspects of cancer. In J. Cohen, et al. (Eds.), *Psychosocial aspects of cancer.* (pp. 1–8). New York: Raven.

Maslow, A. H. (1968). *Toward a psychology of being* (2nd ed.). New York: Van Nostrand Reinhold.

Maslow, A. H. (1970). *Motivation and personality* (2nd ed.). New York: Harper & Row.

Mason, J. W. (1971). A reevaluation of the concept of non-specificity in stress theory. *Journal of Psychiatric Research, 8,* 323–333.

Mason, J. W. (1974). Specificity in the organization of neuroendocrine response profiles. In P. Seeman & G. Brown (Eds.), *Frontiers in neurology and neuroscience research.* Toronto: University of Toronto Press.

Mason, S. E. & Smith, A. D. (1977). Imagery in the aged. *Experimental Aging Research, 3,* 17–32.

Massaro, D. W. (1972). Perceptual images, processing time and perceptual units in auditory perception. *Psychological Review, 79,* 124–145.

Masters, W. H., & Johnson, V. E. (1966). *Human sexual response.* Boston: Little, Brown.

Masters, W. H., & Johnson, V. E. (1970). *Human sexual inadequacy.* Boston: Little, Brown.

Mathison, J. (1970). A cross-cultural view of widowhood. *Omega: Journal of Death and Dying, 1,* 201–218.

Matlin, M. W. (1984). Perceptual development. In R. J. Corsini (Ed.), *Encyclopedia of psychology.* New York: Wiley.

Matthews, K. A. (1988). Coronary heart disease and Type A behaviors: Update on and alternative to the Booth-Kewley and Friedman (1987) quantitative review. *Psychological Bulletin, 104,* 373–380.

Matthews, S. H. (1986). *Friendships through the life course.* Newbury Park, CA: Sage.

May, R. (1967). Contributions of existential psychotherapy. In R. May, E. Angel, & H. F. Ellenberger (Eds.), *Existence: A new dimension in psychiatry and psychology.* (New York: Basic Books, 1958). Paperback reprint: New York: Touchstone Books.

May, R. (1969). *Love and will*. New York: Norton.

McCall's. (1976, September). Divorcees: The new poor, pp. 103, 120, 122, 124, 152.

McCary, J. L. (1978). *Human sexuality* (3rd ed.). New York: Van Nostrand Reinhold.

McCloskey, M., & Watkins, M. J. (1978). The seeing-more-than-is-there phenomenon: Implications for the locus of iconic storage. *Journal of Experimental Psychology: Human Perception and Performance, 4*, 553–564.

McConnel, E., & Deljavan, F. (1982). Aged deaths: The nursing home and community differential. *The Gerontologist, 22*, 318–323.

McCormick, K. (1982). *An exploration of the functions of friends and best friends*. Unpublished doctoral dissertation, Rutgers University of New Jersey.

McCrae, R. R., & Costa, P. T., Jr. (1984). *Emerging lives, enduring dispositions*. Boston: Little, Brown.

McDermott, J. R., Smith, A. I., Iqbal, K., & Wisnieski, M. (1977). Aluminum and Alzheimer's disease. *Lancet, 2*, 710–711.

McFarland, R. A., & Doherty, B. M. (1959). Work and occupational skills. In J. E. Birren (Ed.), *Handbook of aging and the individual*. Chicago: University of Chicago Press.

McFarland, R. A., Domey, R. G., Warren, A. B., & Ward, D. C. (1960). Dark adaptation as a function of age: I. A statistical analysis. *Journal of Gerontology, 15*, 149–154.

McIntosh, J. L. (1988–89). Official U.S. elderly suicide data bases: Levels, availability, omissions. *Omega: Journal of Death and Dying, 19*, 337–350.

McKinlay, J. B. (1981). Social network influences on morbid episodes and the career of help seeking. In L. Eisenberg & A. Kleinman (Eds.), *The relevance of social science for medicine*. Dordrecht, Holland: D. Reidel.

Medvedev, Zh. A (1964). The nucleic acids in development and aging. In B. L. Strehler (Ed.), *Advances in gerontological research (Vol. 1)*. New York: Academic Press.

Medvedev, Zh. A (1974). Caucasus and Altay longevity: A biological or social problem? *The Gerontologist, 14*, 381–387.

Meier, D. E. (1984). The cell biology of aging. In C. K. Cassel & J. R. Walsh (Eds.), *Geriatric medicine (Vol. 1)*. New York: Springer-Verlag.

Meier, D. E. (1988). Skeletal aging. In B. Kent & R. Butler (Eds.), *Human aging research: Concepts and techniques*. (pp. 221–244). New York: Raven.

Meister, K. A. (1984). The 80s search for the fountain of youth comes up very dry. *American Council on Science and Health News & Views, (9/10)*, 8–11.

Merton, R. K. (1957). *Social theory and social structure* (rev. ed.). New York: Free Press.

Meyer, B. J. F., Rice, G. E., Knight, C. C., & Jessen, J. L. (1979a, summer). *Differences in the type of information remembered from prose by young, middle, and old adults*. (Research Report No. 5, Prose Learning Series.) Tempe, AZ: Arizona State University, Department of Educational Psychology, College of Education.

Meyer, B. J. F., Rice, G. E., Knight, C. C., & Jessen, J. L. (1979b, summer). *Effects of comparative and descriptive discourse types on the reading performance of young, middle, and old adults*. (Research Report No. 7, Prose Learning Series.) Tempe, AZ: Arizona State University, Department of Educational Psychology, College of Education.

The Miami Herald. (1984, December 14). Sense of smell fades with age, study finds, pp. 1, 16.

Michael, R. T., Fuchs, V. R., & Scott, S. R. (1980). Changes in the propensity to live alone: 1950–1976. *Demography, 17,* 39–56.

Mihal, W. L., & Barrett, G. V. (1976). Individual differences in perceptual information processing and their relation to automobile accident involvements. *Journal of Applied Psychology, 61,* 229–233.

Miller, G. A., Galanter, E., & Pribram, K. H. (1960). *Plans and the structure of behavior.* New York: Holt, Rinehart & Winston.

Minkler, M. (1981). Research on the health effects of retirement: An uncertain legacy. *Journal of Health and Social Behavior, 22,* 117–130.

Mischel, W. (1968). *Personality and assessment.* New York: Wiley.

Mischel, W. (1973). Toward a cognitive social learning reconceptualization of personality *Psychological Review, 80,* 252–283.

Mischel, W. (1977). The interaction of person and situation. In D. Magnusson & N. S. Endler (Eds.), *Personality at the crossroads: Current issues in interactional psychology.* Hillsdale, NJ: Erlbaum.

Mistler-Lachman, J. L. (1977). Spontaneous shift in encoding dimensions among elderly subjects. *Journal of Gerontology, 32,* 68–72.

Mitchell, R. E., & Trickett, E. J. (1980). Social network research and psychosocial adaptation: Implications for community mental health practice. In P. Insel (Ed.), *Environmental variables and the prevention of mental illness.* Lexington, MA: D. C. Heath.

Monge, R. H. (1971). Studies of verbal learning from the college years through middle age. *Journal of Gerontology, 26,* 324–329.

Monge, R. H., & Hultsch, D. F. (1971). Paired-associate learning as a function of adult age and the length of the anticipation and inspection intervals. *Journal of Gerontology, 26,* 157–162.

Moon, M. (1983). The role of the family in the economic well-being of the elderly. *The Gerontologist, 23,* 45–50.

Mor, V., & Hiris, J. (1983). Determinants of site of death among hospice cancer patients. *Journal of Health and Social Behavior, 24,* 375–385.

Morgan, D. G., & May, P. C. (1990). Age-related changes in synaptic neurochemistry. In E. L. Schneider & J. W. Rowe (Eds.), *Handbook of the biology of aging* (3rd ed.). New York: Academic Press.

Morgan, L. A. (1976). A re-examination of widowhood and morale. *Journal of Gerontology, 31,* 687–695.

Morrell, R. W., Park, D. C., & Poon, L. W. (1990). Effects of labeling techniques on memory and comprehension of prescription information in young and old adults. *Journal of Gerontology, 45,* 166–172.

Morris, J. N., Mor, V., Hiris, J., & Sherwood, S. (1984). *Satisfaction with the site of death.* Paper presented at the Annual Meeting of the Gerontological Society of America, San Antonio, TX.

Morris, J. N. & Sherwood, S. (1984). Informal support sources for vulnerable elderly persons: Can they be counted on, why do they work? *International Journal of Aging and Human Development, 18,* 81–98.

Morse, N. C. (1953). *Satisfactions in the white-collar job.* Ann Arbor: University of Michigan Survey Research Center.

Mortimer, J. A. (1988). The epidemiology of dementia: International comparisons. In J. A. Brody & G. L. Maddox (Eds.), *Epidemology and aging* (pp. 150–167). New York: Springer.

Murdock, B. B., Jr. (1967). Recent developments in short-term memory. *British Journal of Psychology, 58,* 421–433.

Murphy, C. (1983). Age-related effects on the threshold, psychophysical function, and pleasantness of menthol. *Journal of Gerontology, 38,* 217–222.

Murphy, C. (1985). Cognitive and chemosensory influences on age-related changes in the ability to identify blended foods. *Journal of Gerontology, 40,* 47–52.

Murray, H. A., et al. (1938). *Explorations in personality.* New York: Oxford University Press.

Murstein, B. I., & Christy, P. (1976). Physical attractiveness and marriage adjustment in middle-aged couples. *Journal of Personality and Social Psychology, 34,* 537–542.

Mussen, P. H., Conger, J., Kagan, J., & Geiwitz, J. (1979). *Psychological development: A life-span approach.* New York: Harper & Row.

Myers, G. C., & Manton, K. G. (1984a). Compression of mortality: Myth or reality. *The Gerontologist, 24,* 345–353.

Myers, G. C., & Manton, K. G. (1984b) Recent changes in the U. S. age at death distribution: Further observations. *The Gerontologist, 24,* 572–575.

Naeim, F., & Walford, R. L. (1985). Aging and cell membrane complexes: The lipid bilayer, integral proteins, and cytoskeleton. In C. E. Finch & E. L. Schneider (Eds.), *Handbook of the biology of aging* (2nd ed.). New York: Van Nostrand Reinhold.

National Center for Health Statistics. (1984). *Health United States.* Washington, DC: U.S. Government Printing Office.

National Center for Health Statistics. (1986). *National Health Interview Survey, advance data from vital and health statisitics,* No. 125, DHHS Publ. No. PHS 86-1250.

National Center for Health Statistics. (1990). Advance report of final mortality statistics, 1988. *Monthly vital statistics report,* Vol. 39, No. 7 supp. Hyattsville, MD: Public Health Service.

National Geographic. (1973). Every day is a gift when you are over 100, pp. 143.

National Institute on Aging. (1983a). *Age page: Aging and your eyes.* Bethesda, MD: U. S. Department of Health and Human Services.

National Institute on Aging. (1983b). *Age page: Hearing and the elderly.* Bethesda, MD: U. S. Department of Health and Human Services.

National Institute on Aging. (1984). *Age page: Can life be extended?* Bethesda, MD: U. S. Department of Health and Human Services.

National Institute on Aging. (1989a). *Accidents and the elderly.* Bethesda, MD: U. S. Department of Health and Human Services.

National Institute on Aging. (1989b). *Aging and alcohol abuse.* Bethesda, MD: U. S. Department of Health and Human Services.

National Institute on Aging. (1989c). *Can life be extended?* Bethesda, MD: U. S. Department of Health and Human Services.

National Institute on Aging. (1989d). *Dietary supplements: More is not always better.* Bethesda, MD: U. S. Department of Health and Human Services.

National Institute on Aging. (1989e). *Don't take it easy—exercise!* Bethesda, MD: U. S. Department of Health and Human Services.

National Institute on Aging. (1989f). *High blood pressure: A common but controllable disorder.* Bethesda, MD: U. S. Department of Health and Human Services.

National Institute on Aging. (1989g). *Smoking: It's never too late to stop.* Bethesda, MD: U. S. Department of Health and Human Services.

Neisser, U. (1967). *Cognitive psychology.* New York: Appleton-Century-Crofts.

Neisser, U. (1978). Memory: What are the important questions? In M. M. Gruneberg, P. E. Morris, & R. N. Sykes (Eds.), *Practical aspects of memory.* London: Academic Press.

Neisser, U. (1982). *Memory observed.* San Francisco: Freeman.

Nesselroade, J. R., & Labouvie, E. W. (1985) Experimental design in research on aging. In J. E. Birren & K. W. Schaie (Eds.), *Handbook of the psychology of aging* (2nd ed.). New York: Van Nostrand Reinhold.

Neubeck, G. (1972). The myriad motives for sex. *Sexual Behavior, 2,* 50–56.

Neugarten, B. L. (1977). Personality and aging. In J. E. Birren & K. W. Schaie (Eds.), *Handbook of the psychology of aging.* New York: Van Nostrand Reinhold.

Neugarten, B. L., & Associates. (Eds.). (1964). *Personality in middle and late life.* New York: Atherton.

Neugarten, B. L. , Crotty, J., & Tobin, S. S. (1964). Personality types in an aged population. In B. L. Neugarten & Associates (Eds.), *Personality in middle and later life.* New York: Atherton.

Neugarten, B. L., & Gutmann, D. L. (1958). Age-sex roles and personality in middle age: A thematic apperception study. *Psychological Monographs: General and Applied, 17,* Whole No. 470.

Neugarten, B. L., Havighurst, R. J., & Tobin, S. S. (1968). Personality and pattern of aging. In B. L. Neugarten (Ed.), *Middle age and aging.* Chicago: University of Chicago Press.

Neugarten, B. L., & Weinstein, K. (1964). The changing American grandparent. *Journal of Marriage and the Family. 26,* 199–204.

Newman, G., & Nichols, C. R. (1960). Sexual activities and attitudes in older persons. *Journal of the American Medical Association, 173,* 33–35.

Newsweek. (1984, December 3) A slow death of the mind, pp. 56–62.

Newsweek. (1985, April 22). The myths of comparable worth.

Newsweek. (1985, May 6). Who's taking care of our parents? 61–68.

Newsweek. (1986, March 17). Running for your life: A Harvard study links exercise with longevity, p. 70.

Newsweek. (1989, December 18). The brain killer, 54–56.

Newsweek. (1990, June 18). The doctor's suicide van, pp. 46–49.

Newsweek. (1990, July 19). Trading places, pp. 48–54.

Newton, P. A., (1984). Chronic pain. In C. K. Cassel & J. R. Walsh (Eds.), *Geriatric medicine (Vol. 2).* New York: Springer-Verlag.

Nichols, R. V. (1981). Sudden death, acute grief, and ultimate recovery. In O. S. Margolis, H. C. Raether, A. H. Kutscher, J. B. Powers, I. B. Seeland, R. DeBellis, & D. J. Cherico (Eds.), *Acute grief: Counseling the bereaved.* New York: Columbia University Press.

Northhouse, L. (1988). Social support in patient's and husband's adjustment to breast cancer. *Nursing Research, 2,* 91–95.

Noyes, R., Jr. (1971). The art of dying. *Perspectives in Biology and Medicine, 14,* 432–447.

Nystrom, E. P. (1974). Activity patterns and leisure concepts among the elderly. *American Journal of Occupational Therapy, 28,* 337–345.

Ohrloff, C., & Hockwin, O. (1983). Lens metabolism and aging: Enzyme activities and enzyme alterations in lenses of different species during the process of aging. *Journal of Gerontology, 38,* 271–277.

Ohta, R. J., & Kirasic, K. C. (1983). The investigation of environmental learning in the elderly. In G. D. Rowles & R. J. Ohta (Eds.), *Aging and milieu.* New York: Academic Press.

Okimoto, J. T., Barnes, R. F., Veith, R. C., Raskind, M. A., Inui, T. S., & Carter, W. B. (1982). Screening for depression in geriatric mental patients. *Journal of Psychiatry, 139,* 799–802.

Okun, M. A. (1976). Adult age and cautiousness in decision: A review of the literature. *Human Development, 19,* 220–233.

Okun, M. A., & Elias, C. S. (1977). Cautiousness in adulthood as a function of age and payoff structure. *Journal of Gerontology, 32,* 451–455.

Okun, M. A., Siegler, I. C., & George, L. K. (1978). Cautiousness and verbal learning in adulthood. *Journal of Gerontology, 33,* 94–97.

Okun, M. A., Stock, W. A., & Ceurvorst, R. W. (1980). Risk taking through the adult life span. *Experimental Aging Research, 6,* 463–474.

Oppenheimer, R. (1956). Analogy in science. *American Psychologist, 11,* 127–135.

Osterweis, M., Solomon, F., & Green. D. (Eds.). (1984). *Bereavement: Reactions, consequences, and care.* Washington, DC: National Academy Press.

Owens, W. A., Jr. (1966). Age and mental ability: A second follow-up. *Journal of Educational Psychology, 57,* 311–325.

Paivio, A. (1971). *Imagery and verbal processes.* New York: Holt, Rinehart & Winston.

Palmore, E. (1970). The effects of aging on activities and attitudes. In E. Palmore (Ed.), *Normal aging (Vol. 1).* Durham, NC: Duke University Press.

Palmore, E. (1981). *Social patterns in normal aging: Findings from the Duke longitudinal study.* Durham, NC: Duke University Press.

Palmore, E., & Cleveland, W. (1976). Aging, terminal decline and terminal drop. *Journal of Gerontology, 31,* 76–81.

Palmore, E., Cleveland, W., Nowlin, J. B., Ramm, D., & Siegler, I. C. (1979). Stress and adaptation in late life. *Journal of Gerontology, 34,* 841–851.

Palmore, E., Fillenbaum, G. G., & George, L. K. (1984). Consequences of retirement. *Journal of Gerontology, 39,* 109–116.

Palmore, E., George, L. K., & Fillenbaum, G. G. (1982). Predictors of retirement. *Journal of Gerontology, 37,* 733–742.

Palmore, E., & Luikart, C. (1972). Health and social factors related to life satisfaction. *Journal of Health and Social Behavior, 13,* 68–80.

Panek, P. E., Barrett, G. V., Sterns, G. V., & Alexander, R. A. (1978). Age differences in perceptual style, selective attention, and perceptual-motor reaction time. *Experimental Aging Research, 4,* 377–387.

Parkes, C. M. (1964). Effects of bereavement on physical mental health—a study of medical records of widows. *British Journal of Medicine, 2,* 274–279.

Parkes, C. M. (1972). *Bereavement: Studies of grief in adult life.* New York: International Universities Press.

Parkes, C. M. (1981a). Emotional involvement of the family during the period preceding death. In O. S. Margolis et al. (Eds.), *Acute grief: Counseling the bereaved.* New York: Columbia University Press.

Parkes, C. M. (1981b). Psychosocial care of the family after the patient's death. In O. S. Margolis et al. (Eds.), *Acute grief: Counseling the bereaved.* New York: Columbia University Press.

Parkes, C. M., Benjamin, B., & Fitzgerald, R. G. (1969). Broken heart: A statistical study of increased mortality among widowers. *British Medical Journal, 1,* 740–743.

Parkinson, S. R., & Perey, A. (1980). Aging, digit span, and the stimulus suffix effect. *Journal of Gerontology, 35,* 736–742.

Parnes, H. S., & Nestel, G. (1981). The retirement experience. In H. S. Parnes (Ed.), *Work and retirement: A longitudinal study of men.* Cambridge, MA: MIT Press.

Passamani, E., Frommer, P., & Levy, R. (1984). Coronary heart disease: An overview. In N. Wenger & H. Hellerstein (Eds.), *Rehabilitation of coronary patients* (pp. 1–15). New York: Wiley.

Paulhus, D. (1983). Sphere-specific measures of perceived control. *Journal of Personality and Social Psychology, 44,* 1253–1265.

Pearlman, J., Stotsky, B. A., & Dominick, J. R. (1969). Attitudes toward death among nursing home personnel. *Journal of Genetic Psychology, 114,* 63–75.

Perlmutter, M. (1980). An apparent paradox about memory aging. In L. W. Poon, J. L. Fozard, L. S. Cermak, D. Arenberg & L. W. Thompson (Eds.), *New directions in memory and aging: Proceedings of the George A. Talland memorial conference.* Hillsdale, NJ: Erlbaum.

Perlmutter, M., Adams, C., Berry, J., Kaplan, M., Person, D., & Verdonik, F. (1987). Aging and memory. In K. W. Schaie & C. Eisdorfer (Eds.), *Annual review of gerontology and geriatrics (Vol. 7)* (pp. 57–92). New York: Springer.

Perlmutter, M., Metzger, R., Nezworski, T., & Miller, K. (1981). Spatial and temporal memory in 20- and 60-year-olds. *Journal of Gerontology, 36,* 59–65.

Perret, E., & Regli, F. (1970). Age and the perceptual threshold for vibratory stimuli. *European Neurology, 4,* 65–76.

Perry, E. K., Perry, R. H., Blessed, G., & Tomlinson, B. E. (1977). Necropsy evidence of central cholinergic deficits in senile dementia. *Lancet, 3,* 1981.

Perry, E. K., Tomlinson, B. E., Blessed, G., Bergmann, K., Gibson, P. H., & Perry, R. H. (1978). Correlation of cholinergic abnormalities with senile plagues and mental test scores in senile dementia. *British Medical Journal, 2,* 1457–1459.

Peterson, E. T., (1989). Grandparenting. In S. J. Bahr & E. T. Peterson (Eds.), *Aging and the family* (pp. 157–174). Lexington, MA: Lexington.

Peterson, L. R., & Peterson, M. J. (1959). Short-term retention of individual verbal items. *Journal of Experimental Psychology, 58,* 193–198.

Pfeiffer, E. (1974). Sexuality in the aging individual. *Journal of the American Geriatrics Society, 22,* 481–484.

Pfeiffer, E., Cairl, R., Middleton, L., Alexander, L., Kleine, E., & Elbare, J. (1989). *Alzheimer's disease: Caregiver practices, programs, and community-based strategies*. Tampa: Suncoast Gerontology Center, University of South Florida.

Pfeiffer, E., & Davis, G. C. (1972). Determinants of sexual behavior in middle and old age. *Journal of the American Geriatrics Society, 20*, 151–158.

Pfeiffer, E., Verwoerdt, A., & Davis, G. C. (1972). Sexual behavior in middle life. *American Journal of Psychiatry, 128*, 1262–1267.

Pfieffer, E., Verwoerdt, A., & Davis, G. C. (1974). Sexual behavior in middle life. In P. Erdman (Ed.), *Normal aging II: Reports from the Duke longitudinal studies, 1970–1973*. Durham, NC: Duke University Press.

Pfeiffer, E., Verwoerdt, A., & Wang, H. S. (1968) Sexual behavior in aged men and women. I. Observations on 254 community volunteers. *Archives of General Psychiatry, 19*, 753–758.

Pfeiffer, E., Verwoerdt, A., & Wang, H. S. (1969). The natural history of sexual behavior in a biologically advantaged group of aged individuals. *Journal of Gerontology, 24*, 193–198.

Pitcher, B. L., & Larson, D. C. (1989). Elderly widowhood. In S. J. Bahr & E. T. Peterson (Eds.), *Aging and the family* (pp. 59–82). Lexington, MA: Lexington.

Pleck, J. (1977). The work-family role system. *Social Problems, 24*, 417–427.

Plemons, J. K., Willis, S. L., & Baltes, P. B. (1978). Modifiability of fluid intelligence in aging: A short-term longitudinal training approach. *Journal of Gerontology, 33*, 224–231.

Plomin, R., Lichtenstein, P., Pederson, N. L., McClearn, G. E., & Nesselroade, J. R. (1990). Genetic influence on life events during the last half of the life span. *Psychology and Aging, 5*, 25–30.

Plude, D. J., & Hoyer, W. J. (1985). Attention and performance: Identifying and localizing age deficits. In N. Charness (Ed.), *Aging and human performance*. London: Wiley.

Plude, D. J., & Hoyer, W. J. (1986). Age and the selectivity of visual information processing. *Journal of Psychology and Aging, 1*, 4–10.

Pocs, O., Godrow, A., Tolone, W. L., & Walsh, R. H. (1977). Is there sex after 40? *Psychology Today, 11(6)*.

Pollak, J. M. (1979–80). Correlates of death anxiety. *Omega: Journal of Death and Dying, 10*, 97–121.

Pollis, C. (1969). Dating involvement and patterns of idealization: A test of Waller's hypothesis. *Journal of Marriage and the Family, 31(4)*, 765–771.

Poon, L. W. (1985). Differences in human memory with aging: Nature, causes, and clinical implications. In J. E. Birren & K. W. Schaie (Eds.), *Handbook of the psychology of aging* (2nd ed.). New York: Van Nostrand Reinhold.

Poon, L. W., Walsh-Sweeney, L., & Fozard, J. L. (1980). Memory skill training for the elderly: Salient issues on the use of imagery mnemonics. In L. W. Poon, J. L. Fozard, L. S. Cermak, D. Arenberg, & L. W. Thompson (Eds.), *New directions in memory and aging: Proceedings of the George A. Talland memorial conference*. Hillsdale, NJ: Erlbaum.

Prentis, R. S. (1980). White-collar working women's perception of retirement. *The Gerontologist, 20*, 90–95.

President's Commission on Mental Health. (1978). *Report*. Washington, DC: U. S. Government Printing Office.

Puglisi, J. T. (1980). Semantic encoding in older adults as evidenced by release from proactive inhibition. *Journal of Gerontology, 35*, 743–745.

Quinn, J. F., & Burkhauser, R. V. (1990). Work and retirement. In R. H. Binstock & L. K. George (Eds.), *Aging and the social sciences* (3rd ed.) (pp. 308–327). New York: Academic Press.

Quint, J. C. (1967). *The nurse and the dying patient.* Chicago: Aldine.

Quirk, D. A., & Skinner, J. H. (1973). Physical capacity, age, and employment. *Industrial Gerontology, 19*, 49–62.

Rabbitt, P. (1965). An age-decrement in the ability to ignore irrelevant information. *Journal of Gerontology, 18*, 375–378.

Rabbitt, P. (1968). Age and the use of structure in transmitted information. In G. A. Talland (Ed.), *Human aging and behavior.* New York: Academic Press.

Rabbitt, P. (1977). Changes in problem-solving ability in old age. In J. E. Birren & K. W. Schaie (Eds.), *Handbook of the psychology of aging.* New York: Van Nostrand Reinhold.

Rabbitt, P. (1979). Some experiments and a model of changes in attentional selectivity with old age. In F. Hoffmeister & C. Mueller (Eds.), *Brain functions in old age: Evaluation of changes and disorders.* Berlin: Springer.

Rabinowitz, J. C., Craik, F. I. M., & Ackerman, B. P. (1982). A processing resource account of age differences in recall. *Canadian Journal of Psychology, 36*, 325–344.

Rabkin, J. G., & Struening, E. L. (1976). Life events, stress, and illness. *Science, 194*, 1013–1020.

Radloff, L. S. (1977). The CES-D scale: A self-report depression scale for research in the general population. *Applied Psychological Measurement, 1*, 385–401.

Rahe, R. H., & Arthur, R. J. (1978). Life change and illness studies: Past history and future directions. *Journal of Human Stress, 4*, 3–15.

Rappaport, B. Z. (1984). Audiology. In C. K. Cassel & J. R. Walsh (Eds.), *Geriatric medicine: Volume I. Medical, psychiatric, and pharmacological topics.* New York: Springer-Verlag.

Raskind, M. A. (1989). Organic mental disorders. In E. W. Busse & D. G. Blazer (Eds.), *Geriatric psychiatry.* Washington, DC: American Psychiatric Press.

Raush, H., Barry, W., Hertel, R., & Swain, M. (1974). *Communication, conflict, and marriage.* San Francisco: Jossey-Bass.

Raymond, B. J. (1971). Free recall among the aged. *Psychological Reports, 29*, 1179–1182.

Rea, M. P., Greenspoon, S., & Spilka, B. (1975). Physicians and the terminal: Some selected attitudes and behavior. *Omega: Journal of Death and Dying, 6*, 291–301.

Reedy, M. N. (1983). Personality and aging. In D. S. Woodruff & J. E. Birren (Eds.), *Aging: Scientific perspectives and social issues* (2nd ed.). Monterey, CA: Brooks/Cole.

Reff, M. E. (1985). RNA and protein metabolism. In C. E. Finch & E. L. Schneider (Eds.), *Handbook of the biology of aging* (2nd ed.). New York: Van Nostrand Reinhold.

Reichard, S., Livson, S., & Petersen, P. (1962). *Aging and personality.* New York: Wiley.

Reid, D. W., Haas, G., & Hawkings, D. (1977). Locus of desired control and positive self-concept of the elderly. *Journal of Gerontology, 32*, 441–450.

Reimanis, G., & Green, R. F. (1987). Imminence of death and intellectual decrement in the aging. *Development Psychology, 5*, 270–272.

Reker, G. T., Peacock, E. J., & Wong, P. T. (1987). Meaning and purpose in life and well-being: A life-span perspective. *Journal of Gerontology, 42,* 44–49.

Reno, V. P. (1971). Why men stop working at or before age 65. *Social Security Bulletin, 34,* 3–17.

Reno, V. P. (1972). Compulsory retirement among newly entitled workers: A survey of new beneficiaries. *Social Security Bulletin, 35,* 3–15.

Rice, R. W. (1984). Organizational work and the overall quality of life. In S. Oskamp (Ed.), *Applied social psychology annual (Vol. 5).* Beverly Hills, CA: Sage.

Riegel, K. F. (1959). Personality theory and aging. In J. E. Birren (Ed.), *Handbook of aging and the individual.* Chicago: University of Chicago Press.

Riegel, K. F., & Riegel, R. M. (1960). A study of changes of attitudes and interest during later years of life. *Vita Humana, 3,* 177–206.

Riegel, K. F., & Riegel, R. M. (1972). Development, drop, and death. *Developmental Psychology, 6,* 306–319.

Reigel, K. F., Riegel, R. M., & Meyer, G. (1967). Sociopsychological factors of aging: A cohort sequential analysis. *Human Development, 10,* 27–56.

Robbins, S. (1978). Stroke in the geriatric patient. In W. Reichel (Ed.), *The geriatric patient.* New York: H. P. Publishing Co.

Robins, M., & Baum, H. M. (1981). The national survey of stroke incidence. *Stroke, 12 (Pt. 2, Suppl. 1),* 1-45–1-47.

Rockstein, M., & Sussman, M. (1979). *Biology of aging.* Belmont, CA: Wadsworth.

Rohles, R. H. (1969). Preference for the thermal environment by the elderly. *Human Factors, 11,* 37–41.

Rorschach, H. (1942). *Psychodiagnostics: A diagnostic test based on perception.* (Original publication: 1921). Berne: Huber.

Rosen, B., & Jerdee, T. H. (1976a). The nature of job-related stereotypes. *Journal of Applied Psychology, 61,* 180–183.

Rosen, B., & Jerdee, T. H. (1976b). The influence of age stereotypes on managerial decisions. *Journal of Applied Psychology, 61,* 428–432.

Rosenfeld, M., & Owens, W. A., Jr. (1965, April). *The intrinsic-extrinsic aspects of work and their demographic correlates.* Paper presented at the Midwestern Psychological Association, Chicago.

Rotter, J. B. (1966). Generalized expectancies for internal versus external control of reinforcement. *Psychological Monographs, 80,* (1, Whole No. 609).

Rous, J. (1969). Effect of age on the functional state of the olfactory analyser. *Ceskoslovenska Otolaryngologie, 18,* 248–256.

Routh, D. A., & Mayes, J. T. (1974). On consolidation and the potency of delayed stimulus suffixes. *Quarterly Journal of Experimental Psychology, 26,* 1–74, 472–479.

Rowlatt, C., & Franks, L. M. (1978). Aging in tissues and cells. In J. C. Brocklehurst (Ed.), *Geriatric medicine and gerontology* (2nd ed.). New York: Churchill Livingstone.

Rubenstein, E., & Federman, D. D. (Eds.). (1982). *Scientific American medicine.* New York: Scientific American, Inc.

Rubin, Z. (1970). Measurement of romantic love. *Journal of Personality and Social Psychology, 16,* 267–268.

Rumelhart, D. E. (1977). *Introduction to human memory processing.* New York: Wiley.

Russek, H. I. (1962). Emotional stress and coronary heart disease in American physicians, dentists, and lawyers. *American Journal of Medical Science, 243,* 716.

Russek, H. I. (1965). Stress, tobacco, and coronary disease in North American professional groups. *Journal of the American Medical Association, 192,* 189–194.

Rutter, M. (1979). Protective factors in children's responses to stress and disadvantage. In M. W. Kent & J. E. Rolf (Eds.), *Primary prevention of pathology: Volume III. Social competence in children.* Hanover, NH: University Press of New England.

Ryff, C., & Baltes, P. B. (1976). Value transition and adult development in women: The instrumentality-terminality sequence hypothesis. *Developmental Psychology, 12,* 567–568.

Sales, S. M. (1969). Organizational role as a risk factor in coronary disease. *Administrative Science Quarterly, 14,* 324–336.

Salthouse, T. A. (1976). Age and tachistoscopic perception. *Experimental Aging Research, 2,* 91–103.

Salthouse, T. A. (1980). Age and memory: Strategies for localizing the loss. In L. W. Poon, L. S. Cermak, D. Arenberg & L. W. Thompson (Eds.), *New directions in memory and aging.* Hillsdale, NJ: Erlbaum.

Salthouse, T. A. (1982). *Adult cognition: An experimental psychology of human aging.* New York: Springer-Verlag.

Salthouse, T. A. (1990). Cognitive competence and expertise in aging. In J. E. Birren & K. W. Schaie (Eds.), *Handbook of the psychology of aging* (3rd ed.) (pp. 311–319). New York: Academic Press.

Sands, L. P., Terry, H., & Meredith, W. (1989). Change and stability in adult intellectual functioning assessed by Wechsler item responses. *Psychology and Aging, 4,* 79–87.

Sarason, S. B. (1977). *Work, aging, and social change: Professionals and the one life–one career imperative.* New York: Free Press.

Sarnoff, I., & Corwin, S. M. (1959). Castration anxiety and the fear of death. *Journal of Personality, 27,* 374–385.

Saunders, C. (1965). The last stages of life. *American Journal of Nursing, 65(3),* 70–75.

Sayetta, R. B. (1986). Rates of senile dementia—Alzheimer's type in the Baltimore Longitudinal Study. *Journal of Chronic Diseases, 39,* 271–286.

Schaefer, C., Coyne, J., & Lazarus, R. (1981). The health-related functions of social support. *Journal of Behavioral Medicine, 4,* 381–406.

Schaie, K. W. (1958). Rigidity-flexibility and intelligence: A cross-sectional study of the adult life span from 20 to 70 years. *Psychological Monographs, 72 (Whole No. 462),* 1–26.

Schaie, K. W. (1965). A general model for the study of developmental problems. *Psychological Bulletin, 64,* 92–107.

Schaie, K. W. (1973). Methodological problems in descriptive developmental research on adulthood and aging. In J. R. Nesselroade & H. W. Reese (Eds.), *Life-span developmental psychology: Methodological issues.* New York: Academic Press.

Schaie, K. W. (1977). Quasi-experimental designs in the psychology of aging. In J. E. Birren & K. W. Schaie (Eds.), *Handbook of the psychology of aging,* New York: Van Nostrand Reinhold.

Schaie, K. W. (1978). External validity in the assessment of intellectual development in adulthood. *Journal of Gerontology, 33,* 696–701.

Schaie, K. W. (Ed.) (1983). *Longitudinal studies of adult psychological development.* New York: Guilford Press.

Schaie, K. W. (1988). Ageism in psychological research. *American Psychologist, 43,* 179–183.

Schaie, K. W. (1990). Intellectual development in adulthood. In J. E. Birren & K. W. Schaie (Eds.), *Handbook of the psychology of aging* (3rd ed.) (pp. 291–310). New York: Academic Press.

Schaie, K. W., & Baltes, P. B. (1975). On sequential strategies in developmental research: Description or explanation. *Human Development, 18,* 384–390.

Schaie, K. W., & Hertzog, C. (1983). Fourteen-year cohort-sequential analysis of adult intellectual development. *Developmental Psychology, 19,* 531–543.

Schaie, K. W., Labouvie, G. V., & Buech, B. U. (1973). Generational and cohort-specific differences in adult cognitive functioning. *Developmental Psychology, 9,* 151–166.

Schaie, K. W., & Labouvie-Vief, G. (1974). Generational versus ontogenic components of change in adult cognitive behavior: A fourteen-year cross-sequential study. *Developmental Psychology, 10,* 305–320.

Schaie, K. W., & Parham, I. A. (1976). Stability of adult personality: Fact or fable? *Journal of Personality and Social Psychology, 34,* 146–158.

Schaie, K. W., & Parham, I. A. (1977). Cohort-sequential analyses of adult intellectual development. *Developmental Psychology, 13,* 649–653.

Scheidt, R. J., & Schaie, K. W. (1978). A taxonomy of situations for an elderly population: Generating situational criteria. *Journal of Gerontology, 33,* 848–857.

Schiffman, S. (1977). Food recognition of the elderly. *Journal of Gerontology, 32,* 586–592.

Schiffman, S., & Pasternak, M. (1979). Decreased discrimination of food odors in the elderly. *Journal of Gerontology, 34,* 73–79.

Schlessinger, B., & Miller, G. A. (1973). Sexuality and the aged. *Medical Aspects of Human Sexuality, 3,* 46–52.

Schludermann, E. H., Schludermann, S. M., Merryman, P. W., & Brown, B. W. (1983). Halstead's studies in the neuropsychology of aging. *Archives of Gerontology and Geriatrics, 2,* 49–172.

Schmitz-Scherzer, R., & Thomae, H. (1983). Constancy and change of behavior in old age: Findings from the Bonn longitudinal study on aging. In K. W. Schaie (Ed.), *Longitudinal studies of adult psychological development.* New York: Guilford Press.

Schneider, E. L., & Reed, J. D. (1985). Modulations of aging processes. In C. E. Finch & E. L. Schneider (Eds.), *Handbook of the biology of aging* (2nd ed.). New York: Van Nostrand Reinhold.

Schneider, J. (1984). *Stress, loss, and grief.* Baltimore: University Park Press.

Schneider, W., & Shiffrin, R. M. (1977). Controlled and automatic human information processing: I. Detection, search, and attention. *Psychological Review, 84,* 1–66.

Schoenbach, V. J., Kaplan, B. H., Fredman, L., & Kleinbaum, D. G. (1986). Social ties and mortality in Evans County, Georgia. *American Journal of Epidemiology, 123,* 577–591.

Schofield, J. D., & Davies, I. (1978). Theories of aging. In J. C. Brocklehurst (Ed.), *Geriatric medicine and gerontology* (2nd ed.). New York: Churchill Livingstone.

Schultz, N. R., Elias, M. F., Robbins, M. A., Streeten, D., & Blakeman, N. (1986). A longitudinal comparison of hypertensives and normotensives on the WAIS. *Journal of Gerontology, 41,* 169–175.

Schulz, J. H. (1974). The economics of mandatory retirement. *Industrial Gerontology, 1,* 1–10.

Schulz, J. H. (1988). The economics of aging (4th ed.). Dover, MA: Auburn House Publishing Co.

Schulz, R. (1976). Effects of control and predictability on the physical and psychological well-being of the institutionalized aged. *Journal of Personality and Social Psychology, 33,* 563–573.

Schulz, R. (1978). *The psychology of death, dying, and bereavement.* Reading, MA: Addison-Wesley.

Schulz, R. (1982). Emotionality and aging: A theoretical and empirical integration. *Journal of Gerontology, 37,* 42–52.

Schulz, R. (1985). Emotions and affect. In J. E. Birren & K. W. Schaie (Eds.), *Handbook of the psychology of aging* (2nd ed.). New York: Van Nostrand Reinhold.

Schulz, R., & Aderman, D. (1974). Clinical research and the stages of dying. *Omega: Journal of Death and Dying, 5,* 137–143.

Schulz, R., Aderman, D., & Manko, G. (1976, April). *Attitudes toward death: The effects of different methods of questionnaire administration.* Paper presented at the meeting of the Eastern Psychological Association, New York.

Schulz, R., & Curnow, C. (1988). Peak performance and age among superathletes: Track and field, swimming, baseball, tennis, and golf. *Journal of Gerontology: Psychological Sciences, 43,* 1113–1120.

Schulz, R., & Decker, S. (1983, August). *Long-term adjustment to physical disability: The role of social comparison processes, social support, and perceived control.* Paper presented at the annual meeting of the American Psychological Association, Anaheim, CA.

Schulz, R., Heckhausen, J., & Locher, J. L. (1991). Adult development, control, and adaptive functioning. *Journal of Social Issues, 47,* 177–196.

Schulz, R. & Manson, S. (1984). Social perspectives on aging. In C. Cassel & J. R. Walsh (Eds.), *Geriatric medicine: Principles and practice (Vol. 2).* New York: Springer.

Schulz, R., & Rau, M. T. (1985). Social support through the life course. In S. Cohen & L. Syme (Eds.), *Social support and health.* New York: Academic Press.

Schulz, R., & Schlarb, J. (1987–88). Two decades of research on dying: What do we know about the patient? *Omega: Journal of Death and Dying, 18,* 299–317.

Schulz, R., & Tompkins, C. A. (1990). Life events and changes in social relationships: Examples, mechanisms, and measurement. *Journal of Social and Clinical Psychology, 9,* 69–78.

Schulz, R., Tompkins, C. A., & Rau, M. T. (1988). A longitudinal study of the psychosocial impact of stroke on primary support persons. *Psychology and Aging, 3,* 131–141.

Schulz, R., Tompkins, C. A., & Wood, D. (1987). The social psychology of caregiving: Physical and psychological costs of providing support to the disabled. *Journal of Applied Social Psychology, 17,* 401–428.

Schulz, R., Visintainer, P., & Williamson, G. M. (1990). Psychiatric and physical morbidity effects of caregiving. *Journal of Gerontology: Psychological Sciences, 45,* 181–191.

Schulz, R., Williamson, G., Morycz, R. & Biegel, D. (in press). Perspectives on caregiving. In S. Zarit & L. Pearlin (Eds.), *Social structure and caregiving: Family and cross-national perspectives*. Hillsdale, NJ: Lawrence Erlbaum Associates.

Scoggins, C. H. (1981). The cellular basis of aging. *Western Journal of Medicine, 135*, 521–525.

Scott, R. B., & Mitchell, M. C. (1988). Aging, alcohol, and the liver. *Journal of the American Geriatrics Society, 36*, 255–265.

The Seattle Times. (1982, January 29). The case of the missing memory: Special treatment aids the frustrated victims, p. B1.

Sechrest, L. (1976). Personality. *Annual Review of Psychology, 27*, 1–27.

Segerberg, O., Jr. (1974). *The immortality factor*. New York: E. P. Dutton.

Sekaran, U. (1983). How husbands and wives in dual-career families perceive their family and work worlds. *Journal of Vocational Behavior, 22*, 288–302.

Selye, H. (1974). *Stress without distress*. Philadelphia: Lippincott.

Selye, H. (1983). The stress concept: Past, present, and future. In C. L. Cooper (Ed.), *Stress research: Issues for the Eighties*. New York: Wiley.

Shanan, J., & Jacobowitz, J. (1982). Personality and aging. In C. Eisdorfer (Ed.), *Annual review of gerontology and geriatrics (Vol. 3)*. New York: Springer.

Shanas, E. (1979). Social myth as hypothesis: The case of the family relations of old people. *The Gerontologist, 19*, 3–9.

Shanas, E. (1980). Older people and their families: The new pioneers. *Journal of Marriage and the Family, 42*, 9–15.

Shanas, E., Townsend, P., Wedderburn, D., Friis, H., Milhhj, P. & Stehouver, J. (1968). *Older people in three industrial societies*. New York: Atherton Press.

Shanteau, J., & Nagy, G. F. (1979). Probability of acceptance in dating choice. *Journal of Personality and Social Psychology, 37*, 522–533.

Sheehy, G. (1976). *Passages*. New York: E. P. Dutton.

Shneidman, E. S. (1973). *Deaths of man*. New York: Quadrangle/N.Y. Times.

Shneidman, E. S. (Ed.) (1976). *Death: Current perspectives*. Palo Alto, CA: Mayfield.

Shock, N. W. (1974). Physiological theories of aging. In M. Rockstein, M. L. Sussman, & J. Chesky (Eds.), *Theoretical aspects of aging*. New York: Academic Press.

Shock, N. W. (1977). Biological theories of aging. In J. E. Birren & K. W. Schaie (Eds.), *Handbook of the psychology of aging*. New York: Van Nostrand Reinhold.

Shock, N. W. (1985). Longitudinal studies of aging in humans. In C. E. Finch & E. L. Schneider (Eds.), *Handbook of the biology of aging* (2nd ed.). New York: Van Nostrand Reinhold.

Shock, N. W., & Norris, A. H. (1970). Neuromuscular coordination as a factor in age changes in muscular exercise. In D. Brunner & E. Jokl (Eds.), *Medicine and sport (Vol. 4)* Basel: Karger.

Siegler, I. C. (1975). The terminal drop hypothesis: Fact or artifact? *Experimental Aging Research, 1*, 169–185.

Siegler, I. C. (1980). The psychology of adult development and aging. In E. W. Busse & D. G. Blazer (Eds.), *Handbook of geriatric psychiatry*. New York: Van Nostrand Reinhold.

Siegler, I. C. (1983). Psychological aspects of the Duke longitudinal studies. In K. W. Schaie (Ed.), *Longitudinal studies of adult psychological development.* New York: Guilford Press.

Siegler, I. C., & Botwinick, J. (1979). A long-term longitudinal study of intellectual ability of older adults: The matter of selective subject attrition. *Journal of Gerontology, 34,* 242–245.

Siegler, I. C., & Edelman, C. D. (1977, April). *Age discrimination in employment: The implications for psychologists.* Paper presented at the meeting of the Western Psychological Association, San Francisco.

Siegler, I. C., & Gatz, M. (1985). Age patterns in locus of control. In E. Palmore, E. Busse, G. Maddox, J. Nowlin, & I. E. Siegler (Eds.), *Normal aging III.* Durham, NC: Duke University Press.

Sigall, H., & Landy, D. (1973). Radiating beauty: The effects of having a physically attractive partner on person perception. *Journal of Personality and Social Psychology, 28,* 218 –244.

Silverstone, F. A., Brandfonbrener, M., Shock, N. W., & Yiengst, M. J. (1957). Age differences in the intravenous glucose tolerance tests and the response to insulin. *Journal of Clinical Investigation, 36,* 504–514.

Silverstone, G., & Wynter, L. (1975). The effects of introducing a heterosexual living space. *The Gerontologist, 15,* 83–87.

Simonton, D. K. (1988). *Scientific genius: A psychology of science.* Cambridge: Cambridge University Press.

Simonton, D. K. (1990). Creativity and wisdom in aging. In J. E. Birren & K. W. Schaie (Eds.), *Handbook of the psychology of aging* (3rd ed.) (pp. 320–329). New York: Academic Press.

Simonton, D. K. (1991). Creative productivity through the adult years. *Generations, 15,* 13–16.

Sivak, M., Olson, P. L., & Pastalan, E. A. (1981). Effect of driver's age on nighttime legibility of highway signs. *Human Factors, 23,* 59–64.

Skinner, B. F. (1983). Intellectual self-management in old age. *American Psychologist, 38,* 239–244.

Skinner, B. F., & Vaughan, M. E. (1983). *Enjoy old age: A program of self-management.* New York: Norton.

Skinner, E. A., & Connell, J. P. (1986). Control understanding: Suggestions for a developmental framework. In M. M. Baltes & P. B. Baltes (Eds.), *The psychology of control and aging* (pp. 35–71). Hillsdale, NJ: Lawrence Erlbaum Associates.

Smith, A. D. (1975). Aging and interference with memory. *Journal of Gerontology, 30,* 319–325.

Smith, A. D. (1977). Adult age differences in cued recall. *Developmental Psychology, 13,* 326–331.

Smith, A. D. (1980). Age differences in encoding, storage, and retrieval. In L. W. Poon, J. L. Fozard, L. S. Cermak, D. Arenberg & L. W. Thompson (Eds.), *New directions in memory and aging.* Hillsdale, NJ: Erlbaum.

Smith, A. D., & Fullerton, A. M. (1981). Age differences in episodic and semantic memory: Implications for language and cognition. In S. Beasley & L. Davis (Eds.), *Communication processes and disorders.* New York: Grune & Stratton.

Smith, D. S. (1979). Life course, norms, and the family system of older Americans in 1900. *Journal of Family History, 4,* 285–298.

Smith, D. W., Bierman, E. L., & Robinson, N. M. (Eds.). (1978). *The biologic ages of man.* Philadelphia: W. B. Saunders.

Smith, P. C., Kendall, L. M., & Hulin, C. L. (1969). *The measurement of satisfaction in work and retirement: A strategy for the study of attitudes.* Chicago: Rand-McNally.

Smith, R. P., Woodward, N. J., Wallston, B. S., Wallston, K. A., et al. (1988). Health care implications of desire and expectancy for control in elderly adults. *Journal of Gerontology, 43,* 1–7.

Smythe, H. (1975). Nonsteroidal therapy in inflammatory joint disease. *Hospital Practice, 10(9),* 51–56.

Soldo, B. J. (1979). The housing and characteristics of independent elderly: A demographic overview. *Occasional Papers in Housing and Urban Development, No. 1.* Washington, DC: United States Department of Housing and Urban Development.

Soldo, B. J., Sharma, M., & Campbell, R. T. (1984). Determinants of the community living arrangements of older unmarried women. *Journal of Gerontology, 39.*

Solnick, R. E., & Corby, N. (1983). Human sexuality and aging. In D. S. Woodruff & J. E. Birren (Eds.), *Aging: Scientific perspectives and social issues* (2nd ed.). Monterey, CA: Brooks/Cole.

Solomon, S., & Saxe, L. (1977). What is intelligent, as well as attractive, is good. *Personality and Social Psychology Bulletin, 3,* 670–673.

Soltero, I., Liu, K., Cooper, R., Stamler, J., & Garside D. (1978). Trends in mortality from cerebrovascular disease in the United States, 1960–1975. *Stroke, 9,* 549–555.

Sorensen, R. C. (1973). *Adolescent sexuality in contemporary America.* New York: Abrams.

Spakes, P. R. (1979). Family, friendship, and community interaction as related to life satisfaction of the elderly. *Journal of Gerontological Social Work, 1,* 279–294.

Spearman, C. E. (1904). "General intelligence," objectively determined and measured. *American Journal of Psychology, 15,* 201–292.

Sperling, G. (1960). The information available in brief visual presentations. *Psychological Monographs, 74 (11, Whole No. 498).*

Spilka, B., Hood, R., & Gorsuch, R. (1985). *The psychology of religion: An empirical approach.* Englewood Cliffs, NJ: Prentice Hall.

Spirduso, T., & MacRae, C. (1990). Cognitive and motor performance. In J. E. Birren & K. W. Schaie (Eds.), *Handbook of the psychology of aging* (3rd ed.). New York: Academic Press.

Staats, S. (1974). Internal versus external locus of control for three age groups. *International Journal of Aging and Human Development, 5,* 7–10.

Staines, G. L., & Pleck. J. H. (1983). *The impact of work schedules of the family.* Ann Arbor: University of Michigan.

Sternberg, R. J. (1990). *Wisdom: Its nature, origins, and development.* Cambridge: Cambridge University Press.

Sternberg, R. J., Conway, B. E., Ketron, J. L., & Bernstein, M. (1981). People's conceptions of intelligence. *Journal of Personality and Social Psychology, 41,* 37–55.

Sternberg, S. (1966). High speed scanning in human memory. *Science, 153,* 622–654.

Sternberg, S. (1969). Memory scanning: Mental processes revealed by reaction time experiments. *American Scientist, 57,* 421–457.

Sterns, H. L., Barrett, G. V., & Alexander, R. A. (1985). Accidents and the aging individual. In J. E. Birren & K. W. Schaie (Eds.), *Handbook of the psychology of aging* (2nd ed.). New York: Van Nostrand Reinhold.

Steuer, J., LaRue, A., Blum, J. E., & Jarvik, L. F. (1981). "Critical loss" in the eighth and ninth decades. *Journal of Gerontology, 36*, 211–213.

Stewart, A. L., Greenfield, M. D., Hays, R. D., Wells, K., Rogers, W. H., Berry, S. D., McGlynn, E. A., & Ware, J. E. Sr. (1989). Functional status and well-being of patients with chronic conditions. *Journal of the American Medical Association, 262*, 907–913.

Stoller, E. P. (1983). Parental caregiving by adult children. *Journal of Marriage and the Family, 45*, 851–858.

Stoller, E. P., & Earl, L. L. (1983). Help with activities of everyday life: Sources of support for the noninstitutionalized elderly. *The Gerontologist, 23*, 64–70.

Storandt, M. (1976). Speed and coding effects in relation to age and ability level. *Developmental Psychology, 12*, 177–178.

Storandt, M. (1977). Age, ability level, and method of administering and scoring the WAIS. *Journal of Gerontology, 32*, 175–178.

Stotland, E. (1984). Stress. In R. J. Corsini (Ed.), *Encyclopedia of psychology*. New York: Wiley.

Strehler, B. L. (1978). The mechanisms of aging. *The Body Forum, 3*, 44–45.

Streib, G. F., & Schneider, C. J. (1971). *Retirement in American society: Impact and process.* Ithaca, NY: Cornell University Press.

Stroebe, W., & Stroebe, M. S. (1987). *Bereavement and health.* Cambridge: Cambridge University Press.

Stroebe, W., Stroebe, M. S., Gergen, K. J., & Gergen, M. (1982). The effects of bereavement on mortality: A social psychological analysis. In J. R. Eiser (Ed.), *Social psychology and behavioral medicine*. New York: Wiley.

Stueve, C. A., & Fischer C. (1978, September). *Social networks and older women.* Paper presented at the Workshop on Older Women, Washington, DC.

Stueve, C. A., & Gerson, K. (1977). Personal relations across the life cycle. In C. S. Fischer et al., *Networks and places: Social relations in the urban setting*. New York: Free Press.

Suedfeld, P., & Piedrahita, L. E. (1984). Intimations of mortality: Integrative simplification as a precursor of death. *Journal of Personality and Social Psychology, 47*, 848–852.

Suinn, R. M. (1977). Type A behavior pattern. In. R. B. Williams, Jr., & W. D. Gentry (Eds.), *Behavioral approaches to medical treatment*. Cambridge, MA: Ballinger.

Sullivan, H. S. (1953). *Conceptions of modern psychiatry.* (Original publication: 1947). New York: Norton.

Sullivan, H. S. (1968). *The interpersonal theory of psychiatry.* (Original publication: 1953). New York: Norton.

Suszycki, L. (1981). Intervention with the bereaved. In O. S. Margolis et al. (Eds.), *Acute grief: Counseling the bereaved*. New York: Columbia University Press.

Szafran, J. (1968). Psychophysiological studies of aging in pilots. In G. A. Talland (Ed.), *Human aging and behavior*. New York: Academic Press.

Szilard, L. (1959). On the nature of the aging process. *Proceedings of the National Academy of Science, 45*, 30–45.

Taggart, R. (1973). *The labor market impact of the private retirement system.* Studies in Public Welfare, Paper No. 11, Washington, DC: U.S. Congress, Subcommittee on Fiscal Policy, Joint Economic Committee.

Talland, G. A. (1968). Age and the span of immediate recall. In G. A. Talland (Ed.), *Human aging and behavior.* New York: Academic Press.

Tamir, L. M. (1989). Modern myths about men at midlife: An assessment. In S. Hunter & M. Sundel (Eds.), *Midlife myths: Issues, findings, and practical implications* (pp. 157–180). Newbury Park: Sage Publications.

Tarter, R., Templer, D., & Perley, R. (1974). Death anxiety in suicide attempters. *Psychological Reports, 34,* 895–897.

Taub, H. A. (1976). Method of presentation of meaningful prose to young and old adults. *Experimental Aging Research, 2,* 469–474.

Taub, H. A. (1979). Comprehension and memory of prose materials by young and old adults. *Experimental Aging Research, 5,* 3–13.

Taub, H. A., & Kline, G. E. (1978). Recall of prose as a function of age and input modality. *Journal of Gerontology, 5,* 725–730.

Templer, D. (1970). The construction and validation of a death anxiety scale. *Journal of General Psychology, 82,* 165–177.

Templer, D. (1971). Death anxiety as related to depression and health of retired persons. *Journal of Gerontology, 26,* 521–523.

Templer, D., & Ruff, C. (1971). Death anxiety scale means, standard deviations, and embedding. *Psychological Reports, 29,* 173–174.

Templer, D., Ruff, C., & Franks, C. (1971). Death anxiety: Age, sex, and parental resemblance in diverse populations. *Developmental Psychology, 4,* 108.

Thomae, H. (Ed.). (1976). *Patterns of aging: Contributions to human development (Vol. 3).* Basel–New York: Karger.

Thomae, H. (1980). Personality and adjustment to aging. In J. E. Birren & R. B. Sloane (Eds.), *Handbook of mental health and aging.* Englewood Cliffs, NJ: Prentice-Hall.

Thomas, L. E. (1977). *Motivations for mid-life career change.* Paper presented at the annual meeting of the Gerontological Society, San Francisco.

Thorndike, E. L., Bregman, E. O., Tilton, J. W., & Woodyard, E. (1928). *Adult learning.* New York: Macmillan.

Thurstone, L. L. (1938). Primary mental abilities. *Psychometric Monographs, 1.*

Thurstone, L. L. (1951). Creative talent. *Proceedings of the 1950 invitational conference on testing problems, Educational Testing Service,* 55–69.

Thurstone, L. L., & Thurstone, T. G. (1941). Factorial studies of intelligence. *Psychometric Monographs, 2.*

Tice, R. R., & Setlow, R. B. (1985). DNA repair and replication in aging organisms and cells. In C. E. Finch & E. L. Schneider (Eds.), *Handbook of the biology of aging.* (2nd ed.). New York: Van Nostrand Reinhold.

Till, R. E., & Walsh, D. A. (1980). Encoding and retrieval factors in adult memory for implicational sentences. *Journal of Verbal Learning and Verbal Behavior, 19,* 1–16.

Time. (1985, February 18). New look at the elderly, p. 81.

Time. (1986, March 17). Extra years for extra effort, p. 66.

Time. (1986, November 24). Men have rights too, p. 87–88.

Time. (1991, January 21). America abroad: Mosque vs. palace, p. 43.

Tolor, A., & Reznikoff, M. (1967). Relationship between insight, repression-sensitization, internal-external control, and death anxiety. *Journal of Abnormal Psychology, 72,* 426–430.

Trimmer, E. J. (1980). *Rejuvenation.* New York: A. S. Barnes.

Tripathi, R. C., & Tripathi, B. J. (1983). Lens morphology, aging, and cataracts. *Journal of Gerontology, 38,* 258–270.

Troll, L. E. (1980). Grandparenting. In L. W. Poon (Ed.), *Aging in the 1980s: Psychological issues.* Washington, DC: American Psychological Association.

Troll, L. E., & Bengtson, V. (1979). Generations in the family. In W. Burr, R. Hill, F. I. Nye & I. Reiss (Eds.), *Contemporary theories about the family.* New York: Free Press.

Troll, L. E., Saltz, R., & Dunin-Markiewicz, R. (1976). A seven year follow-up of intelligence test scores for foster grandparents. *Journal of Gerontology, 31,* 583–585.

Troll, L. E., & Smith, J. (1976). Attachment through the life span: Some questions about dyadic bonds among adults. *Human Development, 19,* 156–170.

Tulving, E. (1972). Episodic and semantic memory. In E. Tulving & W. Donaldson (Eds.), *Organization of memory.* New York: Academic Press.

Tulving, E. (1983). *Elements of episodic memory.* New York: Oxford University Press.

Tulving, E. (1985). How many memory systems are there? *American Psychologist, 40,* 385–398.

United States Bureau of the Census. (1976). *Current population reports: Some characteristics of the population.* Washington, DC: U.S. Government Printing Office.

United States Bureau of the Census. (1980). *Social indicators III.* Washington, DC: United States Government Printing Office.

United States Bureau of the Census. (1981). *Statistical abstract of the United States.* Washington, DC: United States Government Printing Office.

United States Bureau of the Census. (1987, September). *Current population reports: State population and household estimates with age, sex, and components of change: 1981 to 1986.* Washington, DC: United States Government Printing Office.

United States Bureau of the Census. (1989). *Statistical abstract of the United States: 1989* (109th ed.). Washington, DC: United States Government Printing Office.

United States Bureau of the Census. (in press). *An aging world.* Washington, DC: United States Government Printing Office.

United States Senate Special Committee on Aging. (1983). *Aging America.* Washington, DC: United States Government Printing Office.

United States Senate Special Committee on Aging. (1985). *America in transition: An aging society* (1984–85 ed.). Washington, DC: United States Government Printing Office.

United States Senate Special Committee on Aging. (1986). *Aging America: Trends and projections* (1985–86 ed.). Washington, DC: United States Government Printing Office.

United States Senate Special Committee on Aging (1987–88). *Aging America: Trends and Projections.* Washington, DC: United States Department of Health and Human Services [LR3377(188)D12198].

Urberg, K. A., & Labouvie-Vief, G. (1976). Conceptualizations of sex roles: A life-span developmental study. *Developmental Psychology, 12,* 15–23.

Vachon, M. L. S. (1981). Type of death as a determinant in acute grief. In O. S. Margolis et al. (Eds.), *Acute grief: Counseling the bereaved.* New York: Columbia University Press.

Vachon, M. L. S., Freedman, K., Formo, A., Rodgers, J., Lyall, W. A. L., & Freeman, S. J. J. (1977). The final illness in cancer: The widow's perspective. *Canadian Medical Association Journal, 177,* 1151–1154.

Vandenbos, G., DeLeon, P., & Pallak, M. (1982). An alternative to traditional medical care for the terminally ill. *American Psychologist, 37,* 1245–1248.

van Geert, P. (1987). The structure of Erikson's model of eight stages: A generative approach. *Human Development, 30,* 236–254.

Vaupel, J. W., & Gowan, A. E. (1986). Passage to Methuselah: Some demographic consequences of continued progress against mortality. *American Journal of Public Health, 76,* 430–433.

Verwoerdt, A., Pfeiffer, E., & Wang, H. S. (1969). Sexual behavior in senescence: Changes in sexual activity and interest of aging men and women. *Journal of Geriatric Psychiatry, 2,* 163–810.

Verzar, F. (1963). The aging of collagen. *Scientific American, 208,* 104–114.

Viney, L. L. (1984–85). Loss of life and loss of bodily integrity: Two different sources of threat for people who are ill. *Omega: Journal of Death and Dying, 15,* 207–222.

Viney, L. L. (1987). A sociophenomenological approach to life-span development complementing Erikson's sociodynamic approach. *Human Development, 30,* 125–136.

Vital and Health Statistics. (1989). *Remarriages and subsequent divorces: United States.* Series 21, No. 45.

Vroom, V. H. (1964). *Work and motivation.* New York: Wiley.

Wachtel, P. L. (1980). Investigation and its discontents: Some constraints on progress in psychological research. *American Psychologist, 35,* 399–408.

Wahl, C. W. (1962). The physician's management of the dying patient. In J. Masserman (Ed.), *Current psychiatric therapies.* New York: Grune & Stratton.

Wahl, C. W. (1969). Should a patient be told the truth? In A. H. Kutscher (Ed.), *But not to lose.* New York: Frederick Fell.

Walford, R. L. (1969). *The immunologic theory of aging.* Baltimore: Williams & Wilkins.

Walford, R. L. (1974). The immunologic theory of aging. *Federal Proceedings, 33,* 2020–2027.

Wallerstein, J. S., & Kelly, J. B. (1974). The effects of parental divorce: The adolescent experience. In J. Anthony & C. Koupernic (Eds.), *The child in his family: Children at psychiatric risk.* New York: Wiley.

Wallerstein, J. S., & Kelly, J. B. (1975). The effects of parental divorce: Experiences of the preschool child. *Journal of the American Academy of Child Psychiatry, 14,* 600–616.

Wallerstein, J. S., & Kelly, J. B. (1976). The effects of parental divorce: Experiences of the child in later latency. *American Journal of Orthopsychiatry, 46,* 256–269.

The Wall Street Journal. (1983, February 21). Older Americans: The aging made gains in the 1970s, outpacing the rest of the population, pp. 1, 20.

The Wall Street Journal. (1983, March 2). Older Americans: In a retirement town, the main business is keeping yourself busy, pp. 1, 17.

The Wall Street Journal. (1983, March 10). Older Americans: Actress and ex-Senator believe in conquering age by staying active, pp. 1, 10.

Walsh, D. A. (1983). Age differences in learning and memory. In D. S. Woodruff & J. E. Birren (Eds.), *Aging: Scientific perspectives and social issues* (2nd ed.), Monterey, CA: Brooks/Cole.

Walsh, D. A., & Baldwin, M. (1977). Age differences in integrated semantic memory. *Developmental Psychology, 13,* 509–514.

Walsh, D. A., Baldwin, M., & Finkle, T. J. (1980). Age differences in integrated semantic memory for abstract sentences. *Experimental Aging Research, 6,* 431–443.

Walsh, D. A., & Prasse, M. J. (1980). Iconic memory and attentional processes in the aged. In L. W. Poon, J. L. Fozard, L. S. Cermak, D. Arenberg & L. W. Thompson (Eds.), *New directions in memory and aging: Proceedings of the George A. Talland Memorial Conference.* Hillsdale, NJ: Erlbaum.

Walsh, D. A., & Thompson, L. W. (1978). Age differences in visual sensory memory. *Journal of Gerontology, 33,* 383–387.

Walster, E., Aronson, V., Abrahams, D., & Rottman, L. (1966). Importance of physical attractiveness in dating behavior. *Journal of Personality and Social Psychology, 4,* 508–516.

Walster, E., & Walster, G. W. (1978). *Love.* Reading, MA: Addison-Wesley.

The Washington Post. (1985, July 18). Health frauds: Quackery thriving among elderly, ill.

Wasow, M. (1977). Sexuality in homes for the aged. *Concern in the Care of Aging, 3(6),* 20–21.

Watkins, J. (1974). A review of short-term memory. *Psychological Bulletin, 81,* 695–711.

Watson, J. D. (1969). *The double helix.* New York: New American Library.

Waugh, N. & Barr, R. (1980). Memory and mental tempo. In L. W. Poon, J. L. Fozard, L. S. Cermak, D. Arenberg & L. W. Thompson (Eds.), *New directions in memory and aging: Proceedings of the George A. Talland Memorial Conference.* Hillsdale, NJ: Erlbaum.

Weale, R. (1985). What is normal aging? Part XI. The eyes of the elderly. *Geriatric Medicine Today, 4(3),* 29–37.

Weber, R. J., Brown, L. T., & Weldon, J. K. (1978). Cognitive maps of environmental knowledge and preference in nursing home patients. *Experimental Aging Research, 3,* 157–174.

Wechsler, D. (1958). *The measurement and appraisal of adult intelligence.* (4th ed.). Baltimore: Williams & Wilkins.

Weg, R. B. (1981). *The aged: Who, where, how well.* Los Angeles: University of Southern California, Davis, School of Gerontology.

Weg, R. B. (1983). Changing physiology of aging: Normal and pathological. In D. S. Woodruff & J. E. Birren (Eds.), *Aging: Scientific perspectives and social issues* (2nd ed.). Monterey, CA: Brooks/Cole.

Weinfeld, F. D. (Ed.). (1981). The national survey of stroke. *Stroke, 12 (Part 2, Suppl. 1).*

Weinstein, B. E., & Ventry, L. M. (1982). Hearing impairment and social isolation in the elderly. *Journal of Speech and Hearing Research, 25,* 593–599.

Weisman, A. D., & Kastenbaum, R. (1968). The psychological autopsy: A study of the terminal phase of life. *Community Mental Health Journal,* Monograph No. 4.

Weksler, M. E. (1981). The senescence of the immune system. *Hospital Practice, 10,* 53–63.

Welch, S., & Broth, A. (1977). The effect of employment on the health of married women and children. *Sex Roles, 3,* 385–397.

Welford, A. T. (1980). Sensory, perceptual, and motor processes in older adults. In J. E. Birren & R. B. Sloane (Eds.), *Handbook of mental health and aging.* Englewood Cliffs, NJ: Prentice-Hall.

Welford, A. T. (1984). Psychomotor performance. In C. Eisdorfer (Ed.), *Annual review of gerontology and geriatrics (Vol. 4).* New York: Springer.

Welkowitz, J., Ewen, R. B., & Cohen, J. (1991). *Introductory statistics for the behavioral sciences* (4th ed.). San Diego: Harcourt Brace Jovanovich.

Wheeler, K. T., & Lett, J. T. (1974). On the possibility that DNA repair is related to age in non-dividing cells. *Proceedings of the National Academy of Science, 71,* 1862–1865.

Whitbourne, S. K. (1976). Test anxiety in elderly and young adults. *International Journal of Aging and Human Development, 7,* 201–210.

Whitbourne, S. K. (1987). Personality development in adulthood and old age: Relationships among identity style, health, and well-being. In K. W. Schaie & C. Eisdorfer (Eds.), *Annual review of gerontology and geriatrics (Vol. 7).* New York: Springer.

White House Conference on Aging (1981). *Chartbook on aging in America.* Washington, DC: United States Government Printing Office.

Wiggins, J. S. (1974). *In defense of traits.* Paper presented at the ninth annual symposium on the use of the MMPI, Los Angeles.

Wilkie, F. L., & Eisdorfer, C. (1977). Sex, verbal ability, and pacing differences in serial learning. *Journal of Gerontology, 32,* 63–67.

Williams, R. H. (1972). *Perspectives in the field of mental health.* Rockville, MD: National Institute of Mental Health.

Williamson, G. M., & Schulz, R. (1990). Relationship orientation, quality of prior relationship, and distress among caregivers of Alzheimer's patients. *Psychology and Aging, 5,* 502–510.

Wilson, C. W. (1975). The distribution of selected sexual attitudes and behaviors among the adult population of the United States. *Journal of Sex Research, 11,* 46–64.

Wilson, D. C., Ajemian, L., & Mount, B. M. (1978). Montreal (1975)—The Royal Victoria Hospital palliative care service. In G. W. Davidson (Ed.), *The hospice: Development and administration.* Washington, DC: Hemisphere Publishing Co.

Wilson, K., & DeShane, M. R. (1982). The legal rights of grandparents: A preliminary discussion. *The Gerontologist, 22,* 67–71.

Wilson, K., & Schulz, R. (1983). Criteria for effective crisis intervention. In M. A. Smyer & M. Gatz (Eds.), *Mental health and aging.* Beverly Hills, CA: Sage Publications.

Witkin, H. A., Dyk, R. B., Faterson, H. F., Goodenough, D. R., & Karp, S. A. (1962). *Psychological differentiation.* New York: Wiley.

Wolinsky, J. (1983). Clues found in isolating Alzheimer's disease. *American Psychological Association Monitor, 14(8),* 26, 28.

Wolk, S. (1976). Situational constraint as a moderator of the locus of control-adjustment relationship. *Journal of Consulting and Clinical Psychology, 44,* 420–427.

Wolk, S., & Kurtz, K. (1975). Positive adjustment and involvement during aging and expectancy for internal control. *Journal of Consulting and Clinical Psychology, 43,* 173–178.

Wood, V., & Robertson, J. F. (1978). Friendship and kinship interaction: Differential effects on the morale of the elderly. *Journal of Marriage and the Family, 40,* 367–375.

Woodruff, D. S., & Birren, J. E. (1972). Age changes and cohort differences in personality. *Developmental Psychology, 6,* 252–259.

Woodruff-Pak, D. S. (1990). Mammalian models of learning, memory, and aging. In J. E. Birren & K. W. Schaie (Eds.), *Handbook of the psychology of aging* (3rd ed.). New York: Academic Press.

Wright, J. D. (1978). Are working women really more satisfied? Evidence from several surveys. *Journal of Marriage and the Family, 40,* 301–313.

Wright, L. (1988). The Type A behavior pattern and coronary artery disease. *American Psychologist, 43,* 2–14.

Wrightsman, L. S., & Deaux, K. (1981). *Social psychology in the 80s* (3rd ed.). Monterey, CA: Brooks/Cole.

Yamamoto, J. (1970). Cultural factors in loneliness, death, and separation. *Medical Times, 98,* 177–183.

Yesavage, J. A., & Sheikh, J. L. (in press). Mnemonics as modified for use by the elderly. In L. W. Poon, D. C. Rubin, & B. A. Wilson (Eds.), *Everyday cognition in adulthood and old age.* New York: Cambridge University Press.

Young, M., Bernard, B., & Wallis, C. (1970). The mortality of widowers. In T. Ford & G. F. DeJong (Eds.), *Social demography.* Englewood Cliffs, NJ: Prentice-Hall.

Yurick, A. G., Spier, B. E., Robb, S. S., Ebert, N. J., & Magnussen, M. H. (1984). *The aged person and the nursing process* (2nd ed.). Norwalk, CT: Appleton-Century-Crofts.

Zaretsky, H., & Halberstam, J. (1968a). Age differences in paired-associate learning. *Journal of Gerontology, 23,* 165–168.

Zaretsky, H., & Halberstam, J. (1968b). Effects of aging, brain damage, and associative strength on paired-associate learning and relearning. *Journal of Genetic Psychology, 112,* 149–163.

Zedlewski, S. R., Barnes, R. O., Burt, M. K., McBride, T. O., & Meyers, J. A. (1989). *The needs of the elderly in the 21st century.* Washington, DC: The Urban Institute.

Zemore, R., & Eames, N. (1979). Psychic and somatic symptoms of depression among young adults, institutionalized aged, and non-institutionalized aged. *Journal of Gerontology, 34,* 716–722.

Zillmer, T. W. (1982). Age impact on employee benefit costs is not a major problem for employees. *Aging and Work, 5,* 49–53.

Zung, W. (1965). A self-rating depression scale. *Archives of General Psychiatry, 12,* 63–70.

Zung, W. (1967). Depression in the normal aged. *Psychosomatics, 8,* 287–292.

Zusne, L. (1976). Age and achievement in psychology: The harmonic means as a model. *American Psychologist, 31,* 805–807.

Zwislocki, J. S. (1960). Theory of temporal auditory summation. *Journal of the Acoustical Society of America, 32,* 1046–1060.

Index